W9-AFE-017

LECTURES ON THE HISTORY

OF THE

JEWISH CHURCH

By ARTHUR PENRHYN STANLEY, D.D.

DEAN OF WESTMINSTER

IN THREE VOLUMES—VOL. III.

THE CAPTIVITY to the CHRISTIAN ERA

NEW EDITION

With two Maps

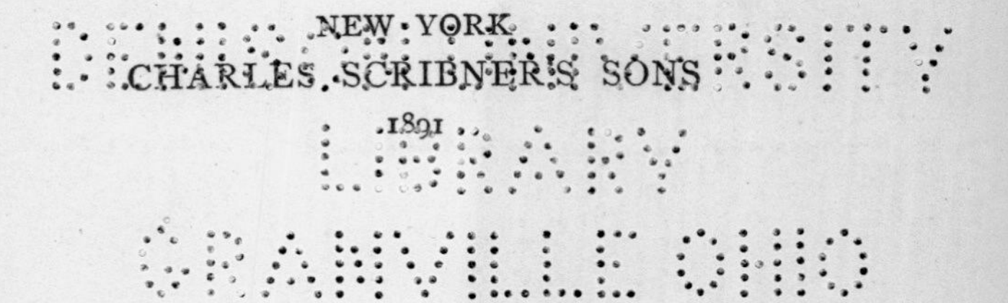

NEW YORK
CHARLES SCRIBNER'S SONS
1891

TO THE BELOVED MEMORY

OF THE INSEPARABLE PARTNER

IN EVERY JOY AND EVERY STRUGGLE

OF TWELVE EVENTFUL YEARS

This Volume

THE SOLICITUDE AND SOLACE OF HER LATEST DAYS

Is Dedicated

WITH THE HUMBLE PRAYER

THAT ITS AIM MAY NOT BE ALTOGETHER UNWORTHY

OF HER SUSTAINING LOVE, HER INSPIRING COURAGE,

AND HER NEVER-FAILING FAITH

IN THE ENLARGEMENT OF THE CHURCH

AND THE TRIUMPH OF ALL TRUTH

CONTENTS.

THE BABYLONIAN CAPTIVITY.

B.C. 587–536.

LECTURE XLI.

THE EXILES.

LECTURE XLII.

THE FALL OF BABYLON.

THE PERSIAN DOMINION.

B.C. 538–333.

LECTURE XLIII.

THE RETURN.

LECTURE XLIV.

EZRA AND NEHEMIAH.

LECTURE XLV.

MALACHI (OR THE CLOSE OF THE PERSIAN PERIOD), B.C. 480-400.

THE GRECIAN PERIOD.

LECTURE XLVI.

SOCRATES (B.C. 468–399).

LECTURE XLVII.

ALEXANDRIA (B.C. 333-150).

LECTURE XLVIII.

JUDAS MACCABÆUS (B.C. 175-163).

THE ROMAN PERIOD.

B.C. 160 to A.D. 70.

LECTURE XLIX.

THE ASMONEAN DYNASTY.

LECTURE L.

HEROD.

APPENDICES.

MAPS.

PREFACE

TO THE ORIGINAL EDITION.

THESE LECTURES, begun at Oxford, and interrupted by the pressure of inevitable engagements in a more laborious sphere, have been resumed during the leisure of an enforced seclusion—under the impulse of an encouragement which overbore all obstacles—in the hope of finding relief from an anxiety which forbade all external occupations. The first volume was dedicated, thirteen years ago, to a dear and most sacred memory, fresh at the time and fresh for ever. This last is bound up with another like memory, if possible, still nearer, still more dear, and no less enduring.

It had been my hope to have comprised in this volume the last stage of the Jewish history from the Captivity to the final destruction of Jerusalem, so as to complete the cycle contemplated in the original plan. Such an arrangement alone would accord with the logical sequence of the narrative and with the due proportions of the subject. To conclude that history without embracing the crowning scenes and characters of its close would be as unjust to the Jewish race itself as it would be derogatory to the consummation which gives to this preparatory period, not, indeed, its only, but unquestionably its chief, attraction. But it appeared to me that the argument allowed, if it did not invite, a division. I have, therefore, broken up the twenty Lectures which, according to the arrangement of the former volumes, would be due to this period, and have confined the present series to the interval from the Exile to the Christian era, leaving, at least for the present, the momentous epoch which involves at once the close of the Jewish Commonwealth and the birth of Christendom. The name of Lectures could properly be applied only to the substance of these pages in the rudimentary form in which they were first conceived, but it has been preserved as most nearly corresponding to the framework in which the whole work has been cast. Their unequal length has been the natural result of the disproportionate amount of materials in the different parts.[1]

I. A few remarks may be permitted in explanation of the method which here, as in the previous volumes, I have endeavoured to follow.

1. As before, so now, but perhaps even to a larger extent, the vast amount of previous historical investigation precludes the necessity, and forbids the desire, of again discussing questions or relating facts which have already been amply treated. The elaborate Jewish researches of Jost, Herzfeld, Grätz, and Salvador, the dry criticism of Kuenen, the brief and lucid narrative of Dean Milman, exempt any later author from the duty of undertaking afresh a labour which they have accomplished once for all, not to be repeated. But on two works relating to this period, very different from each other, a few words may be added.

No English scholar, certainly no English Churchman, can rightly pass through the interval between the Old and New Testament without a tribute to the merit, rare for its age, of Dean Prideaux's 'Connexion of Sacred and Profane History.' It has, no doubt, been in large part superseded by later research and criticism ; its style is heavy, and the management of the subject ungainly. But, for the time when he lived, it shows a singular amount of erudition ; its manly and direct treatment of the controversies that he touches breathes the true spirit of

[1] I have once more to express my obligations to my friend Mr. Grove for his revision of the press.

the sturdy band of Anglican divines to which he belonged ; the selection of so large, and at that time so little explored, a field, and the accomplishment of so laborious a task, as a relief under the stress of severe suffering, indicate both a grasp of mind and an energy of will which theological students of later days may well be stirred to emulate.

Of altogether another order is the volume of Ewald's History which covers this time. To this as to the former volumes it is difficult to over-estimate my obligations.[1] He, since these Lectures were begun, has, after a long and eventful life, been called to his rest. Of all those who have treated of the Jewish history, he alone or almost alone seems to have lived (if the expression may be used) not outside, but inside, the sequence of its events, the rise of its characters, and the formation of its literature. Erroneous conclusions, unreasonable judgments, unwarranted dogmatism, no doubt, may abound ; but these do not interfere with the light which he has thrown, and the fire which he has enkindled, throughout the passages of this dark and intricate labyrinth. By his removal the Church, not only of Germany, but of Europe, has lost one of its chiefest theologians ; and his countrymen will not refuse to a humble fellow-worker in the same paths the privilege of paying this parting testimony of respect to one to whom Christendom owes so deep a debt. It was in the autumn of 1844 that I, with a dear friend, sought him out in an inn at Dresden. We introduced ourselves to him as young Oxford students, and it is impossible to forget the effect produced upon us by finding the keen interest which this secluded scholar, as we had supposed, took in the moral and social condition of our country, the noble enthusiasm with which this dangerous heretic, as he was regarded in England, grasped the small Greek Testament which he had in his hand as we entered, and said : 'In this little book

[1] In the translation begun by Mr. Russell Martineau and continued by Mr. Estlin Carpenter, Ewald's *History* is now accessible to any English reader ; and to this must now be added the like translation of the *Antiquities of Israel*, by Mr. Henry Solly.

'is contained all the wisdom of the world.' We spoke to him of the great English theologian then lately departed ; and of all the tributes paid to the memory of Arnold none is more full of appreciation than that which appeared shortly afterwards in the preface of the second volume of the 'History of the Jewish 'People.' That history has since been unfolded piece by piece ; and assuredly anyone who has watched the progress of his written words can easily understand what was once said of him to me by a German Professor who had attended his spoken lectures, that to listen to him after the harsh and dry instructions of ordinary teachers was like passing from the dust and turmoil of the street into the depth and grandeur of an ancient cathedral.

2. Thoroughly, however, as the ground had been travelled over by these distinguished writers, it seemed to me that there was still occasion, as in the former periods, so here, to draw out the permanent lessons from a story which needs, even more than the familiar narratives which preceded it, to be pressed, as it were, to give forth its peculiar significance.

One main cause of the neglect which has befallen this interval between the Old and New Testament is that, especially after the Macedonian Conquest, the multiplicity of insignificant details and of obscure names has outweighed and overshadowed the events and characters of enduring interest. It is the purpose of the following pages to ease the overloaded narrative of incidents which burden the memory without feeding the mind ; to disentangle the main thread of the story from unmeaning episodes ; to give the most important conclusions without repeating the arguments which have been elaborated in the larger works above mentioned. 'Considering' (if I may use the language of the author of the second book of Maccabees in regard to the work of Jason of Cyrene) 'the infinite number of facts, 'and the difficulty which they find that desire to look into 'the narrations of the story, for the variety of the matter, we 'have been careful that they who will read may have delight, 'and that they who are desirous to commit to memory may 'have ease, and that all into whose hands this book comes 'might have profit. It was not easy, but a matter of labour 'and watching, even as it is no ease unto him that prepareth a 'banquet and seeketh for the benefit of others; yet for the 'pleasuring of many we will undertake gladly this labour, 'leaving to others the exact handling of every particular, 'endeavouring not to stand on every point, or to go over things 'at large, or to be curious in particulars, but to use brevity, and 'avoid elaboration of the work, and to seek fit things for the 'adorning thereof.'[1]

There are some special branches in which I have adopted this reserve with but little scruple. The teaching of the Kabbala[2] requires a study so special as to be inaccessible for one not called to explore it; and its results in connexion with the general moral of the history are too slight to afford reason for occupying space or time with its mysteries. The Samaritan literature,[3] again, is so completely an episode, that it was hardly necessary to do more than notice the few points of direct contact with Judaism.

The traditions of the Talmud might, no doubt, directly or indirectly, be expected to illustrate this period. It might have been hoped that the gifted Hebrew scholar, Emanuel Deutsch, would have been enabled to fulfil the promise of his life by bringing out of his treasure all the things new and old of which he had given us a few specimens in his published essays. This hope had been cut short by his untimely death. But there are two compensations for the loss of a more independent and complete knowledge of this literature. The first is the abundant material furnished by others who have mastered the subject—by Dr. Ginsburg in his numerous articles in Kitto's 'Biblical Cyclopædia,' and in the Prolegomena to his various

[1] 2 Macc. ii. 24-31.

[2] A summary of the Kabbala is given in Munk's *Palestine*, 519-524; and it has also been treated at length by Dr. Ginsburg in a separate work on the subject.

[3] For the Samaritans see Geiger, *Zeitschrift der Morgenl. Gesellschaft*, xx. 527-573; and Jost's *History*, i. 44-90.

works; by Professor Neubauer in his 'Geography of the 'Talmud;' by M. Derenbourg in his 'History of Palestine,' purposely constructed with the view of bringing together all the Talmudical passages which bear on this portion of the history. To these and to like works I have, for the most part, been content to refer, not burdening my pages with citations from the Talmud, unless where I have myself consulted it. But, secondly, the excellent edition of the Mishna by Surenhusius (I venture to call the Dutch scholar by his Latin name) enables any ordinary reader to appreciate the general value of the authoritative Rabbinical teaching of this period. However uncertain must be the date of some of its treatises, those which relate to the Temple, the sacrifices, and the sayings of the great teachers, necessarily contain the traditions of the time preceding the Christian era. But, whilst the historical and antiquarian references are often of profound interest, it must be freely admitted that, on the whole, however striking these purple patches, the wearisomeness and triviality of the great mass of its contents baffle description. And that this impression is shared by Jewish scholars themselves is evident from the trenchant, though covert, irony with which the Mishna is introduced to the English reader by its modern editors.[1] As in the Jewish Church so in the Christian Church, it is well known that vast and groundless pretensions have been put forward, by strange and fantastic speculations, to a divine origin and to special importance. But no historian of the Christian Church would now think it necessary to dwell at length on the fable of the Donation of Constantine, or on the intricate discussions of the Seraphic or Angelic doctors. And no historian of the Jewish Church need be ashamed to pass over the fable of the 'Oral Tradition,' or the casuistry ascribed to the Masters of the Rabbinical Schools, except so far as they are needed to illustrate

[1] English translation of part of the Mishna by De Sola and Raphall. Introduction, p. 14, iv. It must be added that, by the omission in this version of those parts which relate to the Jewish Temple and to the sayings of the Rabbis, the most interesting parts of the Mishna are dropped.

the undoubted narrative or the important issues of the actual history.

3. It is hardly necessary to repeat what has been said in the Prefaces to the two previous volumes, on the advantage and the duty of availing ourselves, as far as possible, of the light of modern criticism in the elucidation of the sacred books. It is true that in so doing we deviate considerably from the method of interpretation pursued in many former ages of the Church. But this is a deviation in which the whole modern world has shared. When Augustine repeatedly insists that the Psalms ascribed in their titles to Korah are descriptions of the Passion, and that the sons of Korah are Christians, because 'Korah' in Hebrew and 'Calvary' in Latin may be translated 'bald 'head,' and because Elisha was derided under that name; when Gregory the Great sees the twelve Apostles, and therefore the clergy, in the seven sons of Job, and the lay worshippers of the Trinity, in his three daughters, it is impossible not to feel that the gulf between these extravagances and the more rational explanations of later times is wider than that which parts any of the modern schools of theology from each other. And it ought to be a matter of congratulation, that in the last volume of the 'Speaker's Commentary,' which may almost be called an authorised exposition, suggestions [1] which a few years ago were regarded from opposing points of view as incompatible with religious faith, are now taken for granted, or treated at least as matters for innocent inquiry.

On some of the questions which arise concerning the authorship of the sacred books of this period it is difficult to pronounce with certainty. It is a temptation to illuminate the darkness of the times succeeding the Captivity by transferring to them, with a distinguished Strasburg scholar, a large [2] part

[1] I may specify the primary reference of various passages in the Book of Daniel to the Maccabæan history (vi. 336-337), and the composite origin of the Book of Zechariah (vi. 904). It was one of the many kindnesses of the late excellent David Morier to have continued in his extreme old age the loan of the valuable Bible annotated by his brother, the late Persian minister.

[2] Reuss's *Commentary*, vol. i. pp. 47-60. It may be as well to add that in the quotation of French or English commentators, when they are available, instead of

of the Psalms. But the grounds for such a transference, even if they were more solid than they appear to be, are so far from established at present that it would be a needless rashness to attempt it. Instructive as it would be to fix the dates of each of the various Psalms, as of each book in the Bible, there are limits beyond which our ignorance forbids us to venture, and within which we must acquiesce in the warning voice which the ancient Rabbi was reported to have heard, when he attempted to re-arrange the Psalter: 'Arouse not the Slum-'berer'—that is, 'Disturb not David.'

But there are other books where it is allowable to tread with a firmer step, where the sleepers may rightly be awakened, and where, when awakened, they have twice the value and the force which they had when they were confounded indiscriminately with their fellow-slumberers. The date of the composition, or of the publication, of the latter portion of the Prophecies of Isaiah—which has been already treated in the second[1] volume of these Lectures—rests on arguments though often assailed yet[2] never shaken; and has, therefore, not been re-argued in the following pages. The same problem with regard to the Book of Daniel, though more complex, demands at least to be regarded as an open question.[3] It must be remembered further that those critics, who are the most determined opponents of the Babylonian date of the Evangelical Prophet and of the Maccabæan date of Daniel, are also upholders of the Pauline origin of the Epistle to the Hebrews, which, by a large majority of scholars in this country, has been totally abandoned. And the same general arguments from mere authority which are used for attributing the second portion of Isaiah to the age of Hezekiah, and the Book of Daniel to the age of Cyrus, might also be pleaded in the analogous cases of the well-

German, I have been guided by the consideration of the convenience of my readers.

[1] See note to Lecture XL.

[2] Of the objections in recent works, the only one that touches the main argument is that drawn from the verbal peculiarities of language, and on this I have purposely abstained from dwelling.

[3] See Lectures XLII., XLVIII.

known Psalms of the Captivity and the Alexandrian Book of Wisdom, which were by similar authority once ascribed respectively to David and Solomon, whose composition of these sacred writings would now be universally deemed to be wholly inadmissible.

II. Turning from the framework of these Lectures to their substance, there are some general reflections which are pressed upon our attention by the peculiarities of this period.

1. It is impossible not to feel that in point of interest the period comprised in the following pages falls below that of the two previous volumes, much below that of the closing years of the history which follow the death of Herod. It is true that the Evangelical Prophet, the Book of Daniel, the two Books of Wisdom are, in some respects, equal, or even superior, to the sacred books of the earlier epochs. But as a general rule we are instinctively conscious of a considerable descent in Ezra, Nehemiah, and Esther, in Haggai and Zechariah, even before we reach the books commonly called Apocryphal. The inferiority of style coincides with the inferiority of instruction in the events and characters, which is the natural result of the narrowing of the course of religious life under the changed circumstances of the Return. Israel after the Exile ceased, or almost ceased, to be a nation, and became only a church; and, becoming only a church, it sank at times to the level of a sect. It is a striking example of that degradation which, by an almost universal law, overtakes Religion when, even whilst attaining a purer form, it loses the vivifying and elevating spirit breathed into it by close contact with the great historic and secular influences which act like fresh air on a contracted atmosphere, and are thus the Divine antiseptics against the spiritual corruption of merely ecclesiastical communities. The one demon may be cast out, but seven other demons take possession of the narrow and vacant house.

There is, however, a point of view from which this period gives an encouragement to a wider and more spiritual side of religious development, such as in the earlier times was lacking. It is the time of 'the Connexion of Sacred and Profane 'History,' not merely in the sense in which the phrase was used by divines of the seventeenth century, as describing the dependence of the Jewish people on foreign powers, but in the larger sense in which it points to the intermingling of the ideas of foreign nations, consciously or unconsciously, with Judaism, and to the epoch at which the great teachers of the Israelite race began to infuse into the main current of the world's religion immortal truths which it has never since lost. It is for this reason that I have thought it right to notice, however superficially, the contemporaneous rise or revival of the three great sages of Persia, China, and India.[1] And although, in these instances, the connexion of the Eastern philosophy and religion with the Jewish history was too dubious and too remote to justify any large digression, it seemed to be necessary, for the sake of preserving the due symmetry of events, to devote a separate lecture[2] to Socrates, as the one Prophet of the Gentile world whose influence on the subsequent course of the spirit of mankind has been most permanent and most incontestable.

There are still, it may be feared, some excellent persons who find causes of alarm and distress in the great Evangelical and Catholic doctrine that Divine Truth is revealed through other than Jewish channels. But in no field has the enlargement of our theological horizon been more apparent than in the contrast which distinguishes the present mode of regarding the founders of the Gentile religions from that which prevailed a century or two centuries ago. No serious writer could now think of applying to Zoroaster the terms 'impostor' and 'crafty 'wretch,' which to Dean Prideaux seemed[3] but the natural and inevitable mode of designating a heathen teacher. Here, as elsewhere, it is a consolation to remember that the value of the

[1] Lecture XLV.
[2] Lecture XLVI. This had in part appeared in the *Quarterly Review* of 1850.
[3] Prideaux, i. 236.

truths which nourish the better part of our nature depends on their own intrinsic divinity, not on the process by which they reach us. The conviction of our moral responsibility cannot be shaken by any theory respecting the origin of our remote ancestors; the authority of the moral sentiments gains rather than loses in strength by the reflection [1] that they are the result of the accumulated experience of the best spirits of the human race; the family bond, though a 'conquest won by culture over 'the rudimentary state of man, and slowly, precariously acquired, 'has yet become a sure, solid, and sacred part of the constitu- 'tion of human [2] nature.' In like manner the great truths of the Unity of God, of the Spirituality of Religion, of the substitution of Prayer for animal and vegetable sacrifice, the sense of a superior moral beauty, or the strong detestation of moral deformity expressed in the ideas of the Angelic and the Diabolical, the inestimable hope of Immortality—all existing in germ during the earlier times, but developed extensively in this epoch—come with a still vaster volume of force when we find that they sprang up gradually, and that they belong not merely to the single channel of the Jewish Church, but have floated down the stream after its confluence with the tributaries of Persian and Grecian philosophy. 'Truth,' it has been well said, 'is the property of no individual, but it is the treasure of 'all men. The nobler the truth or sentiment, the less imports 'the question of authorship.' The larger and deeper the historical basis of our religious conceptions, the less will it be exposed to ruin 'when the rain descends and the floods come 'and the winds blow.

2. This leads us in conclusion to notice one more characteristic of this period. It has been already observed that the original, and indeed the only proper, plan of this volume was to include the great events which are as certainly the climax of the history of the Jewish Church as they are the beginning of

[1] See Grote's *Fragments on Moral Subjects*, pp. 21-26.

[2] See the fine passage in Mathew Arnold's *God and the Bible*, pp. 145-155.

the history of the Christian Church. In former times the Jewish historian passed over the incidents of the Gospel narratives as if they had never occurred; the Jewish pilgrim visited the Mount of Olives with no other remark than that it was the spot on which had been solemnised the sacrifice of the red heifer. And, in like manner, the Christian historian took no heed of the influences of Socrates and Alexander, hardly of the Maccabees or the Rabbis. Yet these influences were unquestionably preludes of the 'one far-off Divine event' towards which the whole of this period was moving, with the motion as of the rapids of Niagara long before they reach the majestic Falls, as surely as the close of the fifteenth century towards the Reformation, or of the eighteenth towards the French Revolution. The artificial isolation of Christianity from its antecedents has now passed away. Not only have serious theologians like Ewald, not only have accomplished scholars like Renan, endeavoured to draw out the thousand threads by which it was connected with the previous history of mankind; but modern writers of Jewish extraction have begun to acknowledge 'that 'to leave out of sight the rise [1] of the Christian Church in con- 'sidering the story of Judaism would be a sin against the spirit 'of history; that Christianity declared itself at its entrance into 'the world to be the fulfilment of the Jewish Law, the coping- 'stone of the Jewish religion.'

There was a thoughtful work written in the earlier years of this century, by one whose genial wisdom I recall with grateful pleasure, entitled 'Propædia Prophetica,' [2] or the 'Prepara- 'tion of Prophecy.' The special arguments therein contained would not now be considered by many as convincing. But, if the word and thought may be so applied, the period between the Captivity and the Christian era might well be called 'Pro- 'pædia Historica,' or the 'Preparation of History.' However much in the study of this part of the Hebrew story we may endeavour to abstract our minds from its closing consummation,

[1] Jost, i. 394.

[2] By Dr. Lyall, formerly Dean of Canterbury.

the thought of that consummation is the main source of the interest of every enlightened student, whether friendly or hostile, in all its several stages. Whether by fact or by prediction, it is the 'Præparatio Evangelica.' Whatever may have been the actual expectations of the Jewish people, however widely the anticipations of an anointed King or Prophet may have wavered or varied, whether fulfilled or disappointed in Cyrus, Zerubbabel, or the Maccabees—there is no question that the brightest light which illuminates this dark period is that reflected from the events which accompany its close. The plain facts of the Asmonean or Herodian history are sufficiently striking, if left to speak for themselves. Christian theology must have sunk to a low ebb, or have been in a very rudimentary state, when Epiphanius[1] thought that to disprove the lineal descent of Herod from David was the best mode of answering those who regarded that wayward and blood-stained Prince as the Messiah, or when Justin, amidst arguments of real weight, insisted on[2] doubtful coincidences of names and words, which, even if acknowledged, are merely superficial. It is one of the advantages of the study of this period that it fixes the mind on the more solid grounds of expectation contained in the history of the time, which, whilst it contains hardly any trace of those artificial combinations, exhibits, even amidst many and perhaps increasing relapses, that onward march of events which is the true prelude of the impending crisis. Just as in the history of Christendom we are sustained by the succession of those larger and more enlightened spirits which even in the darkest ages have never entirely failed, and have been the salt that has saved Christianity from the corruption of its factions and its follies, so in this period of the Jewish Church, amidst the degeneracy and narrowness of Priests and Scribes, of Pharisees and Sadducees, there is a series of broader and loftier souls, beginning with the Evangelical Prophet, reappearing in the Son of Sirach and in Judas Maccabæus, and

[1] *Hær.* i. 20.

[2] *Adv. Tryph.* c. 97, 102, 103, 111.

closing in the Book of Wisdom and the teaching of Hillel and of Philo.[1] These sacred 'Champions of Progress,' though not classed with any of the contemporaneous schools or parties, constantly preserved the ideal of a Spiritual Religion, and, even within the strictest circle of Judaism, kept the door open for the entrance of a wider teaching, and a deeper thinking, and a higher living, than any which had hitherto been recognised as Divine. And the greater the diversity of elements which, outside the pale of Judaism appeared to foreshadow or contribute towards this ideal, so much the more extensive was the horizon which such a character would fill, if ever it should appear.

Yet again, if, as we approach the decisive moment, the scene becomes more crowded with ordinary personages and with vulgar display, more occupied with the struggles of Oriental courts and with the familiar machinery of political controversy and intrigue—if on the soil of Palestine the vague and imperfect though splendid forms of the earlier Patriarchs and Prophets are exchanged for the complete and well-known shapes of Pompey, and Cæsar, and Antony, and Crassus, and Herod, whose very words we possess, whose faces we know, whose coins we have handled—so much the more clear to our view must be the surroundings, so much the more impressive the appearance, of one who shall be born deep amongst the circumstances of the age, yet shall soar high above them all. It is a result of travelling in Palestine that the Gospel history presents itself to the mind in a homely fashion, that seems at times startling and almost profane. A similar effect is produced by stumbling upon that history when following the beaten track of the narrative of Josephus and the tedious disquisitions of the Talmud. But the grandeur of the events becomes not the less but the more remarkable because of the commonplace or degrading atmosphere in which they are enveloped.

[1] To have included Philo's teaching in this survey would have anticipated too much, and it is sufficient to refer to the Essay on the subject in Professor Jowett's *Commentary on S. Paul*, i. 448–514.

It was a saying of Scotus Erigena that whatever is true Philosophy is also true Theology. In like manner on a large scale, whatever is true History teaches true Religion, and every attempt to reproduce the ages which immediately preceded, or which accompanied, the advent of Christianity is a contribution, however humble, to the understanding of Christianity itself.

3. There is still left the yet greater task, in conformity with the plan laid down in these Lectures, of portraying the historical appearance of the Founder and the first teachers of Christianity in the light of their acknowledged, yet often forgotten, connexion with the long series of prophets and heroes of Israel. Much has been attempted in this interesting field within the last few years in England by Dean Milman, and more recently by the author of 'Ecce Homo' and by Dr. Farrar, in France by Renan and Pressensé, in Germany by Neander and Ewald; and it would be audacious and needless to travel once again in detail over their well-worn footsteps. But as in this and the previous volumes of this work an endeavour has been made to discard the temporary, and to insist on the permanent, elements of the earlier Jewish History, so there may be an attempt to gather up from the records of its latest stage, and from the labours to which I have just referred, the like lessons; and these are of more transcendent value and require more urgently to be emphasised, in proportion as the final epoch of the Jewish nation is also its grandest, in proportion as the primal truths of Christianity are more sacred, more spiritual, and, it may be added, often more deeply obscured by the developments of subsequent ages, even than the primal truths of Judaism.

That such a task will be permitted amidst the increasing shadows and the multiplying calls of the years that may remain, it would be presumptuous tc forecast. The manifold shortcomings of the present volume are a sufficient warning not to indulge so precarious and so arduous an expectation. Yet it is a hope which, having its roots in the memory of a past never to be forgotten, may, perchance, carry with it, in some shape, its own fulfilment. It is a hope founded in the conviction that the study of the highest and purest elements of Religion will, though in different forms, repay alike the patient consideration of the speculative inquirer and the reverential search for strength and consolation amidst the sorrows and perplexities of life and of death. We are sure that whatever we have known of good or great can never be wholly taken from our possession. We trust that whatever is or has been the best and greatest is altogether imperishable and Divine.

DEANERY, WESTMINSTER:
May 17, 1876; *Sept.* 7, 1879.

THE JEWISH CHURCH

THE CAPTIVITY to THE CHRISTIAN ERA

THE

BABYLONIAN CAPTIVITY.

B.C. 587–536.

XLI. *THE EXILES.*

XLII. *THE FALL OF BABYLON.*

SPECIAL AUTHORITIES.

I. BIBLICAL AUTHORITIES :—

(1) 2 Kings xxv. 27–30.
(2) Isaiah xiii. ; xiv. 1–23 ; xxi. 1–10 ; xl.–lxvi.
(3) Jeremiah xxix. ; xxxiv. ; xxxix. 11–14 ; l. ; li. ; lii.
(4) Lamentations v.
(5) Ezekiel xxiv.–xlviii.
(6) Psalms xlii. ; xliii. ; xliv. (?) ; lxxiv. (?) ; lxxxix. (?) ; lxxix. (?) ; lxxxviii. (?) ; cii. ; cxxxvii. (*In part*) li. 18, 19 ; xiv. 6 ; liii. 6 ; lxix. 35, 36.
(7) Daniel i.–xii., and (from the LXX.) the History of Susanna in c. i. ; the Song of the Three Children in c. iii. ; and the History of Bel and the Dragon in c. xii. (See Note to Lecture XLII.)
(8) Tobit, Baruch, and the Epistle of Jeremiah. (B.C. 360 ?)

II. JEWISH TRADITIONS :—

Josephus, *Ant.* x. 8-9, 7 ; 10, 11 ; *Chronicon Paschale*, p. 159 (Fabricius ; *Codex Pseudep.*, p. 1124) ; *Seder Olam*, c. 28, 29.

III. B

III. CONTEMPORARY MONUMENTS :—

Inscriptions (given in Rawlinson's *Herodotus*, ii. p. 585; and in *Records of the Past*, i. 131–136; iii. 147–184; v. 111–148).

IV. HEATHEN TRADITIONS :—

(1) Herodotus, B. C. 450; i. 108–130, 200.
(2) Ctesias, B.C. 415; in Diod. Sic. ii. 8.
(3) Xenophon (Cyropædia) B.C. 370.
(4) Megasthenes, B.C. 300; Jos. *Ant.* x. 11, *c. Ap.* i. 20
(5) Berosus, B.C. 260, in Jos. *Ant.* x. 11, *c. Ap.* i. 19
(6) Abydenus (?) Eus. *Præp. Ev.* iv. 41
(7) Strabo, (xvi.) B.C. 60—A.D. 18.

THE BABYLONIAN CAPTIVITY.

LECTURE XLI.

THE EXILES.

WHEN the race of Israel found itself in Chaldæa, it entered once more on the great theatre of the world, which it had quitted on its Exodus out of the valley of the Nile, and from which for a thousand years, with the exception [1] of the reign of Solomon, it had been secluded among the hills of Palestine.

Babylon.

I. Unlike Egypt,[2] which still preserves to us the likeness of the scenes and sights which met the eye of Abraham, Joseph, and Moses, Babylon has more totally disappeared than any other of the great Powers which once ruled the earth.[3] Not a single architectural monument—only one single sculpture—remains of 'the glory of the Chaldees' 'excellency.' Even the natural features are so transformed as to be hardly recognisable. But by a singular compensation its appearance has been recorded more exactly than any of the contemporary capitals with which it might have been compared.

[1] Lecture XXVI. [2] Lecture IV.

[3] For the description of Babylon I refer to the obvious sources of Herodotus and Ctesias (in Diodorus Siculus, ii. 8), Rich's *Memoir on Babylon*, Ainsworth's *Researches in Assyria*, Layard's *Nineveh and Babylon*, Rawlinson's *Ancient Monarchies* and his edition of Herodotus. To these I must add the valuable information I orally received from the late Captain Felix Jones, R.N., employed on the Survey of the Euphrates Valley.

Of Thebes, Memphis, Nineveh, Susa, no eyewitness has left us a plan or picture. But Babylon was seen and described, not indeed in its full splendour, but still in its entirety, by the most inquisitive traveller of antiquity within one century from the time when the Israelites were within its walls, and his accounts are corrected or confirmed by visitors who saw it yet again fifty years later, when the huge skeleton, though gradually falling to pieces, was distinctly visible.

Of all the seats of Empire—of all the cities that the pride or power of man has built on the surface of the globe—Babylon was the greatest. Its greatness, as it was originated, so in large measure it was secured, by its natural position. Its founders took advantage of the huge spur of tertiary rock which projects itself from the long inclined plane of the Syrian desert into the alluvial basin of Mesopotamia, thus furnishing a dry and solid platform on which a flourishing city might rest, whilst it was defended on the south by the vast morass or lake, if not estuary, extending in that remote period from the Persian Gulf. On this vantage-ground it stood, exactly crossing the line of traffic between the Mediterranean coasts and the Iranian mountains; just also on that point where the Euphrates, sinking into a deeper bed, changes from a wide expanse into a manageable river, not broader than the Thames of our own metropolis; where, also, out of the deep rich alluvial clay[1] it was easy to dig the bricks which from its earliest date supplied the material for its immense buildings, cemented by the bitumen[2] which from that same early date came floating down the river from the springs in its upper course. Babylon was the most majestic of that class of cities which belong almost exclusively to the primeval history of mankind; 'the cities,' as they are called by Hegel,[3] 'of the 'river plains'; which have risen on the level banks of the mighty streams of Egypt, Mesopotamia, India, and China, and thus stand in the most striking contrast to the towns which

Its situation.

[1] Layard, *Nineveh and Babylon*, 526, 529.

[2] Gen. xi. 3. *Chemar*: the word translated 'slime' in the A. V.; 'bitumen' by the Vulgate. See Layard, *Nineveh and Babylon*, p. 202-208; Herod. i. 179

[3] *Philosophy of History*, p. 93.

belong to the second stage of human civilisation, clustering each on its Acropolis or its Seven Hills, and thus contracted and concentrated by the necessities of their local position as obviously as those older capitals possessed from their situation an illimitable power of expansion. As of that second class one of the most striking examples was Jerusalem on its mountain fastness, with the hills standing round it, as if with a Divine shelter, and fenced off by its deep ravines as by a natural fosse,[1] so of that earlier class the most remarkable was the city to which the new comers suddenly found themselves transplanted. Far as the horizon itself, extended the circuit of the vast capital of the then known world. If the imperceptible circumference of our modern capitals has exceeded the limits of Babylon, yet none in ancient times or modern can be compared with its definite enclosure, which was on the lowest computation forty, on the highest sixty miles round. Like Nineveh or Ecbatana, it was, but on a still larger scale, a country or empire enclosed in a city. Forests, parks, gardens were intermingled with the houses so as to present rather the appearance of the suburbs of a great metropolis than the metropolis itself. Yet still the regularity and order of a city were preserved. The streets, according to a fashion rare in Europe, whether ancient or modern, but common in ancient Asia[2]—and adopted by the Greek and Roman conquerors when they penetrated into Asia, perhaps in imitation of Babylon—were straight, and at right angles to each other. The houses, unlike those of most ancient cities, except at Tyre, and afterwards in Rome, were three or four storeys high. But the prodigious scale of the place appeared chiefly in the enormous size, unparalleled before or since, of its public buildings, and rendered more conspicuous by the flatness of the country from which

Its grandeur.

Public buildings.

[1] See *Sinai and Palestine*, c. ii.

[2] It has also been followed in the United States, and it is curious to read the remarks of Dean Prideaux on the Babylonian aspect of one of the earliest of the great American cities founded just at the time that his work was composed. 'Much according to 'this model William Penn, the Quaker, 'laid out the ground for his city of Phila-'delphia. . . . Yet fifty-six of such cities 'might stand in the walls that encompassed 'Babylon.'—*Prideaux*, i. 105, 106.

they rose. Even in their decay, 'their colossal piles, domi-'neering over the monotonous plain, produce an effect of 'grandeur and magnificence which cannot be imagined in any 'other situation.'[1]

The walls by which this Imperial city, or, as it might be called, this Civic Empire, rising out of a deep and wide moat, was screened and protected from the wandering tribes of the Desert, as the Celestial Empire by the Great Wall of China, as the extremities of the Roman Empire by the wall of Trajan in Dacia, or of Severus in Northumberland, were not, like those famous bulwarks, mere mounds or ramparts, but lines as of towering hills, which must have met the distant gaze at the close of every vista, like the Alban range at Rome. They appeared, at least to Herodotus, who saw them whilst in their unbroken magnificence, not less than 300 feet high;[2] and along their summit ran a vast terrace which admitted of the turning of chariots with four horses, and which may therefore well have been more than eighty feet broad.[3]

The walls.

If to the inhabitants of Jerusalem, who were accustomed to the precipitous descent of the walls overhanging the valley of the Kedron, the mere height of the Babylonian enclosure may not have seemed so startling as to us, yet to the size of the other buildings the puny dimensions whether of the Palace or Temple of Solomon bore no comparison. The Great Palace of the Kings was itself a city within the city—seven miles round; and its gardens, expressly built to convey to a Median princess[4] some reminiscence of her native mountains, rose one above another, to a height of more than seventy feet, on which stood forest trees of vast diameter side by side with flowering shrubs. On the walls of the Palace the Israelites might see painted[5] those vast hunting-scenes which

The palace.

[1] Ainsworth, 126. The Birs-Nimrud, in its ruins, seemed to an English merch nt who saw it in 1583, 'as high as the stone-'work of the steeple' of the old St. Paul's. (Rich, xxxi.)

[2] This is nearly the height of the Victoria Tower of Westminster Palace—340 feet high.

[3] *i.e.* the breadth of Victoria Street, Westminster.

[4] Rawlinson's *Ancient Monarchies*, iii 345, 502.

[5] Diod. Sic. ii. 8.

were still traceable two centuries later—of which one characteristic fragment remains in sculpture, a lion trampling on a man—which would recall to them the description in their own early annals of 'Nimrod the mighty hunter.'[1]

But the most prodigious and unique of all was the Temple of Bel—which may well have seemed to them the completion of that proud tower 'whose top was to reach to 'heaven.' It was the central point of all; it gave its name to the whole place—Bab-el or Bab-bel,[2] 'the gate 'of God or Bel,' which by the quaint humour of primitive times had been turned to the Hebrew word 'Babel,' or 'confu-'sion.'[3]

The temple.

It was the most remarkable of all those artificial mountains, or beacons, which, towering over the plains of Mesopotamia,[4] 'guide the traveller's eye like giant pillars.' It rose like the Great Pyramid, square upon square; and was believed to have reached the height of 600 feet.[5] Its base was a square of 200 yards. No other edifice consecrated to worship, not Carnac in Egyptian Thebes, nor Byzantine St. Sophia, nor Gothic Clugny, nor St. Peter's of Rome, have reached the grandeur of this primeval sanctuary, casting its shadow[6] far and wide, over city and plain. Thither, as to the most sacred and impregnable fortress, were believed to have been transported the huge brazen laver, the precious brazen pillars,[7] and all the lesser vessels of the Temple of Jerusalem, together doubtless with all the other like sacred spoils which Babylonian conquest had swept from Egypt, Tyre, Damascus, or Nineveh.[8] And when from the silver shrine at the summit of this building, the whole mass of mingled verdure and habitation for miles and miles was overlooked, what was wanting in grace or proportion must

[1] Gen. x. 9.

[2] If, as is most probable, the Temple is represented by the ruins called Mujellibè, it still is called Babil by the Arabs. It was perhaps partly confused by Herodotus with the Temple of Borsippa (Birs-Nimrud).—Rawlinson's *Herodotus*, vol. i. 321.

[3] Gen. xi. 9.

[4] Ainsworth, 157.

[5] Strabo, xvi. p. 738. Perhaps the winding and not the perpendicular height. If the perpendicular height, it was higher than Strasburg Cathedral. See Rawlinson's *Ancient Monarchies*, iii. 343; Grote, *Greece*, iii. 392.

[6] Milman, *Hist. of Jews*, i. 417.

[7] Dan. i. 2; 2 Chr. xxxvi. 7; Jos. *Ant.* x. 11, § 1. See Lectures XLII., XLIII.

[8] Rawlinson, iii. 343.

have been compensated by the extraordinary richness of colour. Some faint conception of this may be given by the view of Moscow from the Kremlin over the blue, green, and gilded domes and towers springing from the gardens which fill up the vacant intervals of that most Oriental of European capitals. But neither that view nor any other can give a notion of the vastness of the variegated landscape of Babylon as seen from any of its elevated points.

From the earliest times of the city, as we have seen, the two materials of its architecture were the bricks baked from the plains on which it stood, and the plaster[1] fetched from the bitumen springs of Hit. But these homely materials were made to yield effects as bright and varied as porcelain or metal. The several stages of the Temple itself were black, orange, crimson, gold,[2] deep yellow, brilliant blue, and silver. The white or pale brown of the houses, wherever the natural colour of the bricks was left, must have been strikingly contrasted with the rainbow hues with which most of them were painted, according to the fancy[3] of their owners, whilst all the intervening spaces were filled with the variety of gigantic palms[4] in the gardens, or the thick jungles or luxuriant groves by the silvery lines of the canals, or in the early spring the carpet of brilliant flowers that covered the illimitable plain without the walls, or the sea of waving corn, both within and without, which burst from the teeming soil with a produce so plentiful that the Grecian traveller dared not risk his credit by stating its enormous magnitude.[5]

When from the outward show we descend to the inner life of the place, Babylon may well indeed to the secluded Israelite have seemed to be that of which to all subsequent ages it has been taken as the type—'the World' itself. No doubt there was in Jerusalem and Samaria, especially since the days of Solomon, a little hierarchy and aristocracy and court, with its factions, feasts, and fashions. But nowhere

The society.

[1] Rawlinson, iii. 385.

[2] *Ibid.* iii. 382–385. Layard, *Nineveh and Babylon*, p. 517.

[3] Rawlinson, iii. 342.

[4] Layard, *Nineveh and Babylon*, p. 485.

[5] See Herod. i. 193, with Rawlinson's notes. Compare Grote, iii. 395.

else in Asia, hardly even in Egypt, could have been seen the magnificent cavalry careering through the streets, the chariots and four, 'chariots like whirlwinds,' 'horses swifter than eagles,' —'horses, and chariots, and horsemen, and companies,' with 'spears' and 'burnished helmets.'[1] Nowhere else could have been imagined the long muster-roll, as of a peerage, that passes in long procession before the eye of the Israelite captive—'the 'satraps, captains, pachas, the chief judges, treasurers, judges, 'counsellors,[2] and all the rulers of the provinces.' Their splendid costumes of scarlet—their parti-coloured[3] sashes— 'all of them princes to look to;' their elaborate armour— 'buckler, and shield, and helmet'—their breastplates,[4] their bows and quivers, and battleaxes—marked out to every eye the power and grandeur of the army. Nowhere was science or art so visibly exalted, as in 'the magicians, and 'the astrologers, and the sorcerers, and the wise 'Chaldæans,'[5] who were expected to unravel all the secrets of nature, and who in point of fact from those wide level plains, 'where the entire celestial hemisphere is continually visible to 'every eye, and where the clear transparent atmosphere shows 'night after night the heavens gemmed with countless stars 'of undimmed brilliancy,'[6] had laid the first foundations of astronomy, mingled as it was with the speculations, then deemed pregnant with yet deeper significance, of astrology. Far in advance of the philosophy, as yet unborn, of Greece, in advance even of the ancient philosophy of Egypt,[7] the Chaldæans long represented to both those nations the highest flights of human intellect—even as the majestic Temples, which served to them at once as college and observatory, towered above the buildings of the then known world. Twice over in the Biblical history—once on the heights of Zophim, once beside the cradle of Bethlehem—do the stargazers of Chaldæa[8]

Its science.

[1] Ezek. xxvi. 7; Jer. iv. 13, 29; vi. 23; xlvi. 4; l. 37. (Rawlinson's *Ancient Monarchies*, iii. 439.)

[2] Dan. iii. 2, 3, 27 (Heb.).

[3] Ezek. xxiii. 14, 15; *ib.* 24.

[4] Jer. li. 3; Ezek. xxvi. 9.

[5] Dan. ii. 2; iv. 6, 7.

[6] Rawlinson, iii. 415.

[7] Grote's *Hist. of Greece*, iii. 392.

[8] Num. xxii. 5, xxiv. 17; Matt. ii. 1. See an ingenious though fanciful book by Dr. Francis Upham, *Who were the Wise Men?*

lay claim to be at once the precursors of Divine Revelation, and the representatives of superhuman science.

Its music.

Returning to the ordinary life of the place, its gay scenes of luxury and pomp were stamped on the memory of the Israelites by the constant clash and concert,[1] again and again resounding, of the musical instruments in which the Babylonians delighted, and of which the mingled Greek and Asiatic names are faintly indicated by the British catalogue of 'cornet, flute, harp, sackbut, psaltery, dulcimer, 'and all kinds of music.'[2] Nor could they forget how, like the Athenian exiles in later days at Syracuse, their artistical masters besought them to take their own harps and sing one of the songs of their distant mountain city;[3] though, unlike those prisoners, who gladly recited to their kindred enemies the tragedies of their own Euripides, they could not bring themselves to waste on that foreign land the melody which belonged only to their Divine Master. Yet one more feature peculiar to Chaldæa, both natural and social, is recalled by the scene of that touching dialogue between the captors and the captives. The trees on which their harps were hung were unlike any that they knew in their own country. They called them by the name that seemed nearest to the willows of their own watercourses. But they were in fact the branching poplars[4] mingled with the tamarisks, which still cluster beside the streams of Mesopotamia, and of which one solitary and venerable specimen[5] long survived on the ruins of Babylon, and in the gentle waving of its green boughs sent forth a melancholy, rustling sound, such as in after times chimed in

[1] For the Babylonian love of music see Rawlinson, iii. 451. [2] Dan. iii. 5, 7, 15.

[3] Psalm lxxxvii. 1, 2.

[4] The weeping willow to which from this passage Linnæus gave the name of *Salix Babylonica* is not found in Babylonia. 'The weeping willow is indigenous in 'China and Japan, cultivated in Europe, 'but is neither indigenous nor cultivated 'in Babylonia.'—(Koch's *Dendrologie*, ii. 507.) It may be either the tamarisk (*attlè*) or the poplar (*Populus Euphratica*), to which the Arabs still give the name of *ereb* the word used in this Psalm.

[5] It is by tradition the single tree preserved from the destruction of Babylon in order, in long subsequent ages, to offer to Ali, the Prophet's son-in-law, a place to tie up his horse after the Battle of Hillah (Rich, 67; Layard, 507). What tree on earth has a more poetic story than this? I grieve to see since writing this that in these latest days the depredations of travellers and pilgrims have reduced this venerable relic to a mere trunk (*Assyrian Discoveries*, by Mr. George Smith, p. 56).

with the universal desolation of the spot, such as in the ears of the Israelites might have seemed to echo their own mournful thoughts. The 'waters' by which they wept were 'the *rivers* 'of Babylon 'The river'—that word was of unknown or almost unknown sound to those who had seen only the scanty torrent beds of Judæa, or the narrow rapids of the Jordan.

Its rivers.

The 'river' in the mouth of an Israelite meant almost always the gigantic Euphrates [1]—'the fourth 'river' of the primeval garden of the earth—the boundary of waters,[2] from beyond which their forefathers had come. And now, after parting from it for many centuries, they once more found themselves on its banks—not one river only, but literally, as the Psalmist calls it, 'rivers;' for by the wonderful system of irrigation which was the life of the whole region it was diverted into separate canals, each of which was itself 'a river,' the source and support of the gardens and palaces which clustered along the water's edge. The country far and near was intersected with these branches of the mighty stream. One of them was so vast as to bear then the name, which it bears even to this day, of the Egyptian Nile.[3]

On the banks of the main channel of the 'river' all the streets[4] abutted, all the gates opened; and immediately on leaving the city it opened into that vast lake or estuary which made the surrounding tract itself 'the desert[5] of the sea'—the great sea,[6] tossed by the four winds of heaven, and teeming with the monster shapes of earth—the sea on which floated innumerable ships or boats, as the junks at Canton, or the gondolas at Venice, or even as the vast shipping at our own renowned seaports. 'Of the great waters,' such is the monumental inscription[7] of Nebuchadnezzar—'like the waters of 'the ocean, I made use abundantly.' 'Their depths were like 'the depths of the vast ocean.' The inland city was thus

[1] *Sinai and Palestine*, Appendix, § 34.

[2] See Lecture I. p. 8.

[3] The word *Ior*, in Dan. xii. 5, is elsewhere only used for the Nile. *Sinai and Palestine*, Appendix, § 35. There is a canal to this day called 'the Nile' (*Bahr-el-Nil*) between the Euphrates and the Tigris. This is a retention of local colour in the Book of Daniel which I owe to Captain Felix Jones, and which has escaped even the vigilant research of Dr. Pusey.

[4] Rawlinson, iii. 342.

[5] Isa. xxi. 1.

[6] Dan. vii. 2, 3.

[7] Rawlinson's *Herod.*, vol. iii. p. 586.

converted into a 'city of merchants'—the magnificent empire into 'a land of traffic.' 'The cry,' the stir, the gaiety of the Chaldæans was not in the streets or gardens of Babylon, but 'in their ships.'[1] Down the Euphrates came floating from the bitumen pits of Hit the cement with which its foundations were covered,[2] and from Kurdistan and Armenia huge blocks of basalt, from Phœnicia gems and wine, perhaps its tin from Cornwall; up its course came from Arabia and from India the dogs for their sports, the costly wood for their stately walking-staves, the frankincense for their worship.[3] When in far later days the name of Babylon was transferred to the West to indicate the Imperial city which had taken its place in the eyes of the Jewish exiles of that time, the recollection of the traffic of the Euphrates had lived on with so fresh a memory that this characteristic feature of the Mesopotamian city was transplanted to its Italian substitute, Rome. Nothing could be less applicable to the inland capital on the banks of the narrow Tiber; but so deeply had this imagery of the ancient Babylon become a part of the idea of secular grandeur that it was transferred without a shock to that new representative of the world. 'The merchandise of gold, and silver, and precious 'stones, and of pearls, and fine linen, and purple, and silk, and 'scarlet, and all wood of incense, and all manner of vessels of 'ivory, and all manner of vessels of most precious wood, and 'of brass, and of iron, and marble, and cinnamon, and odours, 'and ointments, and frankincense, and wine, and oil, and fine 'flour, and wheat, and beasts, and sheep, and horses, and 'chariots, and slaves, and souls of men; the shipmasters, and 'all the company in ships, and sailors, and as many as trade by 'sea, and the craftsmen, and the merchants who were the great 'men of the earth.'[4]

Nebuchadnezzar.

And over this vast world of power, splendour, science, art, and commerce, presided a genius worthy of it (so at least the Israelite tradition represented him)—'the 'Head of Gold,'—'whose brightness was excellent'—the Tree

[1] Isa. xliii. 14 (Heb.).
[2] Rawlinson, *Monarchies*, iii. 441.
[3] Layard, *Nin. and Bab.* i. 526.
[4] Rev. xviii. 11, 12, 13, 17, 23.

whose height reached to heaven, and the sight thereof 'to the 'end of all the earth'—'whose leaves were fair, and the fruit 'thereof much, and in it meat for all—under which the beasts 'of the field dwelt, and upon whose branches the fowls of the 'air had their habitation.'[1] He whose reign reached over one-half of the whole period of the Empire[2]—he who was the last conqueror amongst the primeval monarchies, as Nimrod had been the first—the Lord of the then known historical world from Greece to India—was the favourite of Nebo, who when he looked on his vast constructions[3] might truly say, 'Is not this 'Great Babylon that I have built for the house of my king-'dom, by the might of my power, and for the honour of my 'majesty?'[4]

Hardly any other name than Nebuchadnezzar's is found 'on the bricks[5] of Babylon.' Palace and Temple were both rebuilt by him; and not only in Babylon but throughout the country. The representations of him in the Book of Daniel may belong to a later epoch; but they agree in their general outline with the few fragments preserved to us of ancient annals or inscriptions; and they have a peculiar interest of their own, from the fact that the combination which they exhibit of savage power with bursts of devotion and tenderness is not found elsewhere amongst the Hebrew portraitures of any Gentile potentate. It is loftier and more generous than their conception of the Egyptian Ph raoh, the Assyrian Sennacherib, or the Greek Antiochus; it is wilder and fiercer than the adumbrations of the Persian Cyrus or the Roman Cæsar.

His decrees as recorded in the Hebrew Scriptures may breathe a more didactic spirit than they actually bore; but they are not unlike in tone to those which are preserved on the monuments. And the story of his insanity, even if the momentary light thrown upon it by the alleged[6] interpretation of the inscriptions be withdrawn, may remain as the Hebrew version

[1] Dan. iv. 20, 21, 38.
[2] Rawlinson, iii. 489. Dr. Pusey, p. 119.
[3] Nebo-kudurri-ussuf, *i.e.* 'May Nebo 'protect the crown.'
[4] Dan. iv. 30. Comp. the Inscription in *Records of the Past*, v. 119-135.
[5] Rawlinson, *Monarchies*, iii. 498.
[6] The interpretation of the *negative* clauses of the Inscription, as given in Rawlinson's *Herodotus*, vol. ii. p. 586.

of the sickness described by Berosus and the sudden disappearance described by Abydenus,[1] and also as the profound Biblical expression of 'the Vanity of Human Wishes'[2]—the punishment of the 'vaulting ambition that overleaps itself'—the eclipse and the return of reason, which when witnessed even in modern times in the highest places of the State have moved the heart of a whole nation to sympathy or to thanksgiving. He was to the Israelite captives, not merely a gigantic tyrant, but with something like 'the prophetic soul of the wide world, 'dreaming on things to come'[3]—himself the devoted worshipper of his own[4] Merodach, yet bowing before the King of Heaven, 'whose works are truth, and whose ways judgment.'[5]

The Captivity.

II. Into 'this golden city,' underneath this magnificent oppressor, the little band of Israelites were transported for the period which is known by the name of the Babylonian Captivity. It might at first sight seem that it was a period of which the records are few, and of which the results were scanty. It lasted for little more than a single generation.[6] But it sowed the seeds of a change deeper than any that had occurred since the destruction of the sanctuary at Shiloh, almost than any that had occurred since the Exodus.

The number of exiles was comparatively small. A large part of the lower classes were left in Palestine, and those who were transported consisted chiefly of the princes, nobles, and priests, with the addition of artisans in wood and iron. But still it was the kernel[7]—the flower—what the older prophets would have called the 'remnant,' the sufficient remnant of the nation.

We have already spoken of the other fragments of the Captivity—the colony of the Ten Tribes in the remote provinces

[1] Jos. *c. Ap.* i. 20; Eus. *Præp. Ev.* ix. 41.

[2] The possibility of such a malady as that described in Dan. iv. 33-36 is established with interesting illustrations in Dr. Pusey's *Daniel the Prophet*, p. 426-433.

[3] Dan. ii. 31, iv. 5; and see Abydenus, in Eus. *Præp. Ev.* ix. 41.

[4] Rawlinson, *Monarchies*, iii. 459.

[5] Dan. iv. 37.

[6] The 70 years foretold by Jeremiah must be considered as a round number, expressing that before two generations had passed the deliverance would come. If literally computed, they must be reckoned from B.C. 606 to 536. But the real Captivity was only from 587 to 536, *i.e.* 47 years.

[7] For this whole question of the numbers see Kuenen, *History of the Religion of Israel*, vol. ii., Note C.

of the Assyrian Empire;[1] the first beginnings[2] of the colony in Egypt, ultimately destined to attain such significance.

The two remaining groups of exiles from the kingdom of Judah, those under Jehoiachin, and those under Zedekiah, must have soon blended together; and containing as they did within themselves all the various elements of society, they enable us, partly through the writings and partly through the actions of the little community, to form an idea, fragmentary, indeed, but still sufficient, of the effects of the Captivity. As before we saw the main results[3] of 'Israel in Egypt,' so now we enter on the characteristics of Israel in Babylon.

With the fall of Jerusalem the public life of the people had disappeared. The Prophets could no longer stand in the Temple courts or on the cliffs of Carmel to warn by word of mouth or parabolical gesture. 'The law 'was no more. The Prophets[4] found no vision from the 'Eternal.'

Literary character.

There is one common feature, however, which runs through all the writings of this period, which served as a compensation for the loss of the living faces and living words of the ancient seers. Now began the practice of committing to writing, of compiling, of epistolary correspondence, which (with two or three great exceptions) continued during the five coming centuries of Jewish History. 'Never before[5] had literature pos'sessed so profound a significance for Israel, or rendered such 'convenient service as at this juncture.'

The aged Jeremiah still lived on in Egypt,[6] far away from the mass of his people. But already his prophecies had begun to take the form of a book; already he had thrown his warnings and meditations into the form of a letter to the exiles of the first stage of the Captivity, which was the first example of religious instruction so conveyed, which was followed up, we know not when, by the apocryphal letter bearing his name, and which ultimately issued in the Apostolic Epistles of the New Testament. The same tendency is seen

Jeremiah.

[1] See Lecture XXXIV.
[2] Lecture XL., XLVII.
[3] Lecture IV.
[4] Lam. ii. 9; Ezek. vii. 26.
[5] Ewald, v. 10.
[6] See Lecture XL.

in the rigidly artificial and elaborate framework [1] in which even the passionate elegy of the Lamentations is composed, in contrast with the free rhythm of the earlier songs of the Davidic age. Already the Prophecies of Ezekiel [2] had been arranged in the permanent chronological form which they have since worn. 'Baruch the scribe' had inaugurated this new era, the first of his class, by transcribing and arranging the works of Jeremiah; had already, according to Jewish tradition, read to the exiles in Babylon itself, to the captive king, and princes, and nobles, and elders, and 'all the people from 'the highest to the lowest,' of those that dwelt by one of the branches of the Euphrates,[3] the book of his warnings and consolations.

Ezekiel.
Baruch.

Are we to conjecture that something of this famous scribe [4] may be traced in the Prophet who poured forth during this period of expectation the noblest of all the prophetic strains of Israel—noblest and freest in spirit, but in form following that regular flow and continuous unity which in his age, as has been said, superseded the disjointed and successive utterances of the older seers? [5] Or is it possible that in the author of that strain of which the burden is the suffering and the exaltation of the Servant of the Lord we have that mysterious prophet registered in ancient catalogues as Abdadonai,[6] 'the Servant of the Lord,' himself the personification of the subject of his book? Whether Baruch or Abdadonai—whether in Chaldæa, Palestine, or Egypt—whether another Isaiah, in more than the power and spirit of the old Isaiah—or whether, as some would prefer to think, that older Isaiah, transported by a magical influence into a generation not his own—the Great Unnamed, the Evangelical Prophet, is our chief guide through this dark period of transition, illuminating

The Second Isaiah.

[1] Each part is arranged alphabetically.

[2] See Lecture XL.

[3] '*Sud*,' an Arabic name for Euphrates. Baruch i. 4.

[4] Bunsen's *God in History* (i. 131). Hitzig (*Geschichte*, 264) conjectures the High Priest Joshua.

[5] For the whole question of the position of the second Isaiah, see Lecture XL. Compare Ewald's *Prophets*, ii. 404–487, Matthew Arnold, *The Great Prophecy of Israel's Restoration*, Cheyne's *Book of Isaiah*.

[6] Clem. Alex. (*Strom.* i. 21). (See Note to Lecture XX.)

it with flashes of light, not the less bright because we know not whence they come. In his glorious roll of consolations, warnings, aspirations, we have, it is not too much to say, the very highest flight of Hebrew prophecy. Nothing finer had been heard even from the lips of the son of Amos. No other strain is so constantly taken[1] up again in the last and greatest days of Hebrew teaching. For the splendour of its imagery and the nerve of its poetry, nothing, even in those last days of Evangelist or Apostle, exceeds or equals it.

Yet once more, in the enforced leisure of captivity and exile, like many a one in later days—Thucydides, Raleigh, Clarendon—now in the agony of the dispersion, in the natural fear lest the relics of their ancient literature should be lost through the confusion of the time, began those laborious compilations[2] of the Annals of the past which issued at last in 'the 'Canon of the Old Testament,' of which perhaps several might be traced to this epoch, but of which it will be sufficient to specify the most undoubted instance—the Book of the Kings. It is touching to observe from its abrupt conclusion how this nameless student continued his work to the precise moment[3] when he was delighted to leave his readers in the midst of his sorrows with that one gleam which was shed over the darkness of their nation by the kindly treatment of the last royal descendant of David in the Court of Babylon.

The Book of Kings.

There were also the company of minstrels and musicians, male and female,[4] who kept up the traditions of the music of David and Asaph. Their resort, as we have seen, was by the long canals, where they still wandered with their native harps;[5] and though they refused to gratify the demands of their conquerors, they poured forth, we cannot doubt, some of those plaintive strains which can be placed at no date so suitable as this, or else worked up into accord with

The minstrels.

[1] There are 21 quotations in the New Testament from Isaiah xl.-lxvi., against 13 from the earlier chapters.

[2] Ewald, v. 18.

[3] 2 Kings xxv. 27-30.

[4] Ezra ii. 65

[5] Ps. cxxxvii. 1, 2.

the circumstances of their time some of those which had been handed down from earlier and happier days.

The social condition of the Exiles.

From the writers we turn to the actors in the scenes. The Greek word by which the Captivity is called—μετοικεσία,[1] *migration* or *transportation*—aptly expresses the milder aspect of the condition of the great mass of the exiles. Just as the Greeks, transported in like manner by Darius Hystaspis into the heart of Asia, remained long afterwards peaceable settlers under the Persian rule, so at the time and for centuries afterwards did many of the Jewish exiles establish themselves in Chaldæa. Babylon from this time forth became, even after the return, even after the powerful settlement of the Jews at Alexandria, the chief centre of Jewish population and learning. There was an academy established, according to tradition, at Neharda during the exile, which, it may be, fostered the studies of the sacred writers already mentioned, and which certainly became the germ of the learning of Ezra and his companions, and caused all Israel through its manifold dispersions to look to Babylon as the capital of their scattered race, and as possessing the love of the law.[2] Such an habitual acquiescence in their expatriation coincided with the strains of marked encouragement which came from the Prophets of the Captivity. 'Build ye houses, and dwell in 'them,' said Jeremiah to the first detachment of exiles. 'Plant 'gardens and eat the fruit of them: take wives and beget sons 'and daughters: take wives for your sons, and give your daugh-'ters to husbands, that ye may be increased there and not 'diminished. And seek the peace of the city, and pray unto 'the Lord for it, for in the[3] peace thereof ye shall have 'peace.' 'Pray for the life of Nebuchadnezzar, king of Baby-'lon, and for the life of Balthasar his son, that their days 'may be upon earth as the days of Heaven,' was the advice ascribed to Baruch, 'and he will give us strength and lighten 'our eyes, and we shall live under the shadow of Nabuchado-'nosor, king of Babylon, and under the shadow of Balthasar his

[1] Also ἀποικία.

[2] Deutsch's *Remains*, 342. Lightfoot on 1 Cor. xiv. Comp Jos. *Ant.* xv. 2, 2; xvii. 2, 1-3.

[3] Jer. xxix. 5, 6, 7.

'son, and we shall serve them many days, and find favour 'in their sight.'[1]

Such is the picture handed down or imagined from the earlier Assyrian captivity of Tobit and his family—himself the purveyor of Shalmaneser, living at ease with his wife and son, with their camels and their dog, its first apparition as a domestic friend in sacred history—the hospitable communications with his friends at Ecabatana, with his countrymen throughout[2] Assyria.

Tobit.

Such at Babylon or in its neighbourhood were the homes of the nobles of Israel, who became possessed of property, with slaves, camels, horses, asses, even with the luxury of hired musicians.[3] The political and social framework of their former existence struck root in the new soil. Even the shadow of royalty[4] lingered. It appears, indeed, that Zedekiah, the King, as well as his predecessor Jehoiachin and the High Priest, Josedek, whose father had perished at Riblah, were at first rigorously confined, and Zedekiah remained in prison blind and loaded with brazen fetters till his death, which occurred soon after his arrival. But he was then[5] buried in royal state by Nebuchadnezzar with the funeral fires and spices, and with the funeral lamentations—even to the very words, 'Ah! Lord'—which were used at the interments of the Kings of Judah; and Josedek, the High Priest, was then set at liberty.

The Royal Family.

A singular fate awaited the last lineal heir of the house of David, Jehoiachin or Jeconiah. He, after seven and thirty years of imprisonment, was released by the generosity of Evil-merodach, the son of Nebuchadnezzar, who, according to another legend, in disgrace himself, had encountered Jehoaichin in the same prison,[6] and who disapproved his father's harshness. The beard of the captive king,[7] which, contrary to the Jewish practice, had been allowed to grow through all those mournful years, was shaved; his dress was

Jehoiachin.

[1] Baruch i. 11.
[2] Tobit i. 13; ix. 2; x. 4.
[3] Isa. lxvi. 20; Ezra ii. 65-67.
[4] Ezek. viii. 1; xiv. 1; xx. 1.
[5] Jer. xxxiv. 5; Jos. *Ant.* x. 8, 7.
[6] Jerome, Comm. on Isa. xiv. 19.
[7] Jer lii. 32 (LXX.).

changed; a throne was given him above the thrones of the other subject or captive kings; he ate in the royal presence, and was maintained at the public cost till the day of his death. In the later traditions of his countrymen this story of the comparative ease of the last representative of David was yet further [1] enlarged with the tale how he sat with his fellow-exiles on the banks of the Euphrates and listened to Baruch,[2] who himself had meanwhile been transported hither from Egypt [3]—or how that he married a beautiful countrywoman of the name of Susanna,[4] or 'the lily,' the daughter of one bearing the honoured name of Hilkiah—that he lived in affluence,[5] holding a little court of his own, with judges from the elders as in the ancient times, to which his countrymen resorted; with one of the Babylonian 'parks' or 'paradises' adjoining to his house; surrounded by walls and gates; and adorned with fountains, ilexes, and lentisks.[6] It was believed that on this spot, at a short distance from Babylon, at the 'Cunaxa' of the defeat of Cyrus the younger, he had established a synagogue which was long known. And, although from some of the accounts it might seem as if he had been literally the only heir of David's lineage, yet it would seem from others that there was a princely personage born or adopted into his house, Salathiel, whose son had become so Babylonian as to have borne a Chaldæan name for both his titles—Zerubbabel and Sheshbazzar.[7] So, too, there was the Benjamite family which traced its descent from an exile who had accompanied Jehoiachin, and of which the two most illustrious members both bore foreign names, Mordecai and Esther.[8]

Such, also, was the tale which narrates how, in the Court of Babylon, there were four children of surpassing beauty, placed,[9]

[1] Africanus (Routh, *Rel. Sac.* ii. 113).
[2] Baruch i. 3. [3] Jos. *Ant.* x. 9, 7
[4] History of Susanna, 1, 2, 4, 5, 6.
[5] This was the beginning of the office of 'the Prince of the Captivity,' *Resh Golah*, in Greek *Æchmalotarcha*; as there was at Alexandria the corresponding chief called Alabarch and at Antioch Ethnarch, and afterwards in the different settlements Patriarch. Prideaux, ii. 249; i. 120.
[6] Hist. of Susanna, 4, 7, 15, 54, 58. That this whole story is a later fiction, with whatever ground in earlier traditions, appears at once from the Greek play on the words (see note after Lecture XLII). But the remains of 'la chaste Susanne de Babylon' are still shown in the Cathedral of Toulouse.
[7] See Lecture XLII.
[8] See Lecture XLV.
[9] Jos. *Ant.* x. 10, 1.

according to the cruel custom of the East, in the harem under the charge of the Master of the Eunuchs—who filled high places amongst the priestly or the learned class, and exchanged their Hebrew names for Chaldæan[1] appellations, one becoming Belteshazzar (Bilat-sarra-utsur, 'may Beltis,' the female Bel, 'defend the king!'), another 'the Servant of Nebo' (Abed-nego); the two others, Shadrach and Meshach, of which the meaning has not been ascertained. They were allowed to take part in the government of Chaldæa, and were to all actual appearance officers of the great Imperial Court. Their very dress is described as Assyrian or Babylonian, not Palestinian—turbans, trowsers, and mantles.[2]

The Four Children.

There is no improbability in the favour shown to these Jewish foreigners, first, or, at any rate, first since Joseph, of that long succession of Israelites who, by the singular gifts of their race, have at various intervals, from that time down to the present day, mounted to the highest places of Oriental or European States. But, towering high above the rest, the Jewish patriots of nearly four centuries later looked back to one venerable figure, whose life[3] was supposed to cover the whole period of the exile, and to fill its whole horizon. His career is wrapped in mystery and contradiction—not a prophet, yet something greater—historical, yet unquestionably enveloped in a cloud of legend. Whilst the Chaldæan names of the three younger youths have almost superseded their Hebrew designations, the Hebrew name of the elder, Daniel—'the Divine Judge'—has stood its ground against the high-sounding title of Belteshazzar. It may seem to have corresponded with those gifts which have made his name famous, whether in the earlier or in the later version of his story. That which Ezekiel had heard was as of one from[4] whose transcendent wisdom no secret could be hid—who was

Daniel.

[1] See a full discussion of these names in the Speaker's *Commentary on Daniel*, p. 243-246.

[2] Dan. iii. 21; Herod. i. 195, with Rawlinson's notes.

[3] According to the Jewish tradition he was born at Upper Bethhoron: a spare, dry, tall figure, with a beautiful expression. (Fabricius, 1124.)

[4] Ezek. xiv. 14; xxviii. 3.

on a level with the great oracles of antiquity. That which first brings him into notice in the opening pages of the Greek and Latin Book of Daniel is the wisdom [1] with which, by his judgment of the profligate elders, he 'was had in great reputation 'among the people.' He is, to all outward appearance, an Eastern sage rather than a Hebrew Prophet. Well did the traditions of his countrymen represent him as the architect of Ecbatana or even of Susa, as buried in state—not, like the other saints of the Captivity, in a solitary sepulchre, but in the stately tower which he himself had built, in the tombs of the kings of Persia.[2] Well did the mediæval legends make him the arch-wizard and interpreter of dreams.[3] Rightly did the Carthusian artist at Dijon represent him amongst his exquisite figures of the Prophets in the garb, posture, and physiognomy of an Oriental Magnate. Fitly did Bishop Ken,[4] when he wished to portray an ideal courtier before the Stuart Kings, take 'the man' greatly beloved: 'Not of the sacerdotal, 'but royal line; not only a courtier, but a favourite; not only 'a courtier and a favourite, but a minister;'—'one that kept 'his station in the greatest of revolutions,' 'reconciling policy 'and religion, business and devotion, magnanimity and humility, authority and affability, conversation and retirement, 'interest and integrity, Heaven and the Court, the favour of 'God and the favour of the king.'

III. Such was the general condition of the Israelite exiles. It is marked by several clear peculiarities.

1. The first characteristic of the time is one which seems inconsistent with the quiet settlement just described.

It is the poignant grief as of personal calamity that broods over its literature.

The Hebrew word for 'the Captivity,' unlike the Greek word, expresses a bitter sense of bereavement: '*Guloth*'—'stripped bare.'[5] They were stripped bare of their country

[1] It is the story of Susannah, doubtless, which gives occasion to the exclamation in the *Merchant of Venice* which has made his name proverbial in English: 'A Daniel 'come to judgment.'

[2] Jos. *Ant.* x. 11, 7.

[3] Fabricius, *Codex Pseudep.* 1134-1136.

[4] Ken, *Prose Works*, 144, 169, 171.

[5] The same word as in *Golan*, *Gaulanitis*.

and of their sanctuary; almost, it would seem, of their God. The Psalms of the time answer to the groans of Ezekiel, the Lamentations of Jeremiah, as deep to deep. It will be hard to find another sorrow that has vented itself in so loud, so plaintive, so long-protracted a wail. We hear the dirge over the perpetual desolation[1] which envelopes the ruins of Jerusalem. We catch the 'Last Sigh' of the exiles as they are carried away beyond the ridge of Hermon.[2] We see the groups of fugitive stragglers in the desert, cut off by the sword of robbers, or attacked by the beasts of prey, or perishing of disease in cavern[3] or solitary fortress. We see them in the places of their final settlement, often lodged in dungeons with[4] insufficient food, loaded with contumely; their faces spat upon; their hair torn off; their backs torn with the lash. We see them in that anguish, so difficult for Western nations to conceive, but still made intelligible by the horror of a Brahmin suddenly confronted with objects polluting to his caste, or a Mussulman inadvertently touching swine's flesh; when they were brought into an enforced contact with the unaccustomed food or cookery of the Gentile nations, which was as repugnant as the most loathsome filth or refuse of common life,[5] and preferred the most insipid nourishment rather than incur the possible defilement of a sumptuous feast. We hear the songs which went up from their harps, whenever the foreigner was not present, blending tender reminiscences of their lost country with fierce imprecations on those cruel kinsmen who had joined in her downfall, with fond anticipations that their wrongs would at last be avenged.[6] We catch the passionate cry which went up 'out[7] of the 'depths,' in which the soul of the people threw itself on the Divine forgiveness, and waited for deliverance with that eager longing which filled the sentinels on the Temple wall who were wont of old time to watch and watch again for the

Their desolation.

The Psalms of the Captivity.

[1] Isa. xliii. 28; xlix. 16–19; li. 17–19; lii. 9; lviii. 12; lxii. 6 (Ewald, v. 6).
[2] Psalm xlii. 6; see Lecture XL.
[3] Ezek. xxxiii. 27 (Ewald, v. 6).
[4] Isa. xli. 14; xlii. 22; xlvii. 6; l. 6; li. 13–21; liii. Jer. l. 7–17. Psalm cxxix. 3; cxxiii. 4; cxxiv. 7 (Ewald, v. 7).
[5] Ezek. iv. 12–15 (*ib.* 6). Dan. i. 5–16.
[6] Psalm cxxxvii. Jeremiah, l. 2.
[7] Psalm cxxx.

first rays of the eastern dawn. No other known period [1] is so likely to have produced that 'prayer of the afflicted when he is 'overwhelmed and poureth forth his complaint' before the Divine Comforter, when the nation, or at least its most oppressed citizens, could compare themselves only to the slowly-dying brand on the deserted hearth, or to the pelican standing by the desert pool, pensively leaning its bill against its breast, or to the moping owl haunting some desolate ruin, or to the solitary thrush,[2] pouring forth its melancholy note on the housetop, apart from its fellows, or to the ever-lengthening shadow of the evening, or to the blade of grass withered by the scorching sun. There [3] were the insults of the oppressors, there were the bitter tears which dropped into their daily beverage, the ashes which mingled with their daily bread; there was the tenacious remembrance which clung to the very stones and dust of their native city; there was the hope that, even before that generation was past, her restoration would be accomplished, but, if not, there remained the one consolation that, even if their own eyes failed to see the day, it would be brought about in the eternity of that Wisdom which remained whilst all outward things were changed as the fashion of a vesture.[4] And, again, there are more ancient songs, sometimes of scornful derision, sometimes of penitence, sometimes of bitter recrimination, which would seem to have been seized by the captives of Babylon and applied to their own condition, and incorporated into it, by adding the burden never [5] absent from their thoughts. 'Build Thou the walls of Jerusalem.' 'Oh, that salvation would come out of Zion! when God 'bringeth back the captivity of his people, Jacob shall rejoice, 'and Israel shall be glad.' 'God will save Zion, and will build 'the cities of Judah: that they may dwell there, and have it in 'possession.'

It is this feeling which renders the history of the Exile or Captivity capable of such wide application. It is, if one may

[1] Psalm cii. 3, 4, 6, 7–11.

[2] See 'Sparrow' in *Dictionary of the Bible*, p. 1315.

[3] Psalm cii. 8. This is the only verse which seems more applicable to the Maccabæan age.

[4] Psalm cii. 8, 14, 24–28.

[5] Psalms li. 18, 19: xiv. and liii. 6; lxix. 35, 36.

so say, the expression of the Divine condescension to all those feelings of loneliness, of desolation, of craving after sympathy, which are the peculiar and perpetual lot of some, but to which all are liable from time to time. The Psalms which express, the Prophecies which console, the history which records, these sorrows of the exiled Israelites are the portions of the Hebrew Bible which, if only as the echo of our own thoughts, have always sounded gratefully to the weary heart. When the English residents in Lucknow were reduced to the last extremity of want and of despair during their long siege, the one word of comfort which broke in upon their misery was a page containing a fragment of the consolations with which the Evangelical Prophet strove to cheer the captives of Babylon.[1] Want of friendly companionship, the bitter pain of eating the bread of strangers, the separation from familiar and well-known objects, here are woven into the very heart of the Sacred Books. 'Prosperity,' says Lord Bacon, 'is the blessing of the Old 'Testament, and adversity is the promise of the New.' 'Yet,' as the wise man adds, 'even in the Old Testament you shall 'hear as many hearse-like airs as carols.' It is now that this sacredness of adversity first clearly appears. The tragic fates of Jeremiah and Ezekiel in its opening scene were living examples of the truth that virtue could be revered and honoured in the depths of national disaster and personal sorrow no less than from the height of victory and of splendour.

The Man of Sorrows.

The figure under which, in the most striking prophecy of this period, the Anointed, the Chosen of the Eternal, appears is of a Servant or Slave deeply afflicted,[2] smitten of God, a man of sorrows and acquainted with grief. The Messiah of glory had long been looked for, but now began to fade away. It is from this epoch that the Jewish people could first distinctly conceive an Ideal of humiliation and suffering. Judæa seated, not beneath her native palm, but beneath the Euphratean willow or poplar, is the first exemplification of that sad vision which reached its highest consummation in those scenes of

[1] Isa. li. 11–14. See the story in Kaye's *History of the Indian Mutiny*, iii. 483.

[2] Isa. liii. 3, 4, 5.

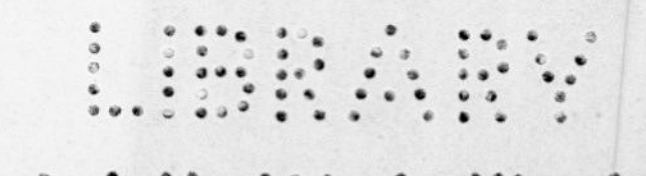

sacred suffering, that 'Divine depth of sorrow' when the first Evangelist saw its accomplishment in the tender sympathy with the various forms of sickness[1] and infirmity on the hills of Galilee; when Philip pointed out to the Ethiopian Chamberlain[2] its resemblance to the majestic silence and the untimely death which had lately been enacted at Jerusalem; when[3] Peter comforted the slaves of the hard Roman taskmasters by reminding them of Him whose flesh was torn by stripes as cruel as those to which they were daily exposed.

The more vividly that delineation of the afflicted Servant resembles the Prophet or Prophets of the Captivity, the Israel within an Israel in that sorrowful time, the more clearly will it be made manifest that the application of it in the ultimate stage of the story of Israel to the Prophet of Prophets—suffering with and for his people,—is no arbitrary fancy, but the fulfilment of the same moral law, which, as Butler has well pointed out, pervades the whole nature and history of man.[4] 'The soft 'answer which restores good humour in a casual conversation; 'the forbearance with which the statesman meets the ignorances 'and prejudices, the censures and the slanders, of those to 'whom he only sues for leave to do them good; are but in-'stances of an universal law of man's constitution, discoverable 'in all human relationships, and which enacts that men can, 'and do, endure the evil doings of their brethren, in such sort 'that, through that endurance on the part of the innocent, the 'guilty are freed from the power of their ill deeds. There is 'hardly anyone but has known some household in which, year 'after year, selfishness and worldliness, and want of family 'affection, have been apparent enough; and yet, instead of the 'moral shipwreck which might have been expected, and the

[1] Matt. viii. 17. [2] Acts viii. 32, 33.

[3] 1 Pet. ii. 24.

[4] 'Men by their follies run themselves 'into extreme distress, which would be 'fatal to them, were it not for the inter-'position and assistance of others. God 'commands by the law of Nature that we 'afford them this assistance in many cases 'where we cannot do it without very great 'pains, and labour, and suffering to our-'selves.' (*Analogy*, c. v.) This is the modern equivalent of the Hebrew expression, 'It pleased the Eternal to bruise 'him: he was wounded for our transgres-'sion.' In this sense the historical meaning of Isa. liii. 1-10 is the best explanation of its application to the sufferings of Christ. Compare Col. i. 15.

'final moral ruin of the various members, the original bond of 'union has held together: there has plainly been some counter-'acting, redeeming power at work. And when we look to see 'what is that redeeming power, ever at work for those who 'know and care nothing about it, we always find that there is 'some member of that family—oftenest the wife or mother—'who is silently bearing all things, believing all things, hoping 'all things, for them, but for her or himself expecting little or 'nothing in this world, but the rest of the grave. Such a one 'is really bearing the sins of that household: it is no forensic 'phrase transferred by way of illustration from the practice of 'the law courts; but a fact, a vital formation, actually taking 'place, here, under our very eyes. He who has seen and 'understood this fact, in any one of its common, daily, shapes, 'needs no commentary'[1] on the realisation of the Man of Sorrows, alike in the suffering Prophet or People of the Captivity, and in the Divine Sufferer on Calvary.

2. In one visible and incontestable form[2] the purification of the national character by calamity appeared at once. Jerusalem was lost. The Holy Place where their fathers worshipped was burnt with fire. The holy cities throughout the Holy Land were a wilderness. All their pleasant or regal things were laid waste.[3] The venerable summits of their thousand hills, the green circles of their consecrated groves, the hallowed clifts of the rocks, the smooth stones of the brooks,[4] on which they poured their libations, were no longer theirs. In unexpected ways this bereavement worked back upon their national life. It broke the fascination of the idolatry of Canaan. It has been disputed of late whether the Semitic race has or has not an exclusive instinct of monotheism. It would appear from the Israelite history that at least in Palestine there was a direct tendency to the contrary. Only by a constant and energetic struggle could the Jewish people be kept from giving way to the natural seductions of the kindred nations—it might almost be said, of the outward

The rejection of Polytheism.

[1] Sir E. Strachey's *Hebrew Politics*, 344.

[2] See Hitzig, *Geschichte des Volkes Israel*, 261.

[3] Isa. lxiv. 10, 11, 12.

[4] *Ibid.* lvii. 5, 6.

scenes, the hill-tops, the green trees, among which they dwelt. But 'the nests were now pulled down and the rooks had flown 'away.' It was not till the connexion with their native soil was snapped rudely asunder by exile that the belief in One God, as if freed from the dangerous associations of that soil, rose at once into the first place. The nation, as it were, went into retreat, and performed penance for its long errors and sins. Before this time there had been but one fast-day in the Jewish ritual, that of 'the great day of atonement.' But henceforth there were added four new periods of humiliation, all connected with this epoch, and all carrying on, even to this day, the renewal of their contrition and their sorrow, for the beginning and end of the siege, for the burning of the Temple, and for the murder of the last Judæan prince.[1] From this time forward the national bias was changed. They leaped over the whole intervening period of the mixed glories of David and Solomon, and found the ideal of their religion in their first[2] father Abraham. It was like the impulse with which the Christian world in the sixteenth century sprang back over the whole of the Middle Ages to the Primitive or the Apostolical times. It was the Puritanism of the Jewish Church. Their iconoclastic fervour became the channel of their future fanaticism, as their purer monotheism became the seed-plot of Christianity. It seemed as though the identification of Polytheism with the odious thought of the Babylonian exile and oppression had destroyed its spell; even as the fires of Smithfield disenchanted the English people of the charm of the Roman Church and turned them into zealous adherents of the Reformation. The Babylonian worship was in form very different from that of the Grecian mythology. But it was the recoil against its extravagances which braced the mind of the Jewish nation to resist the seductions of the Macedonian conquerors, three centuries later, and accordingly the sentiments of the two periods run into each

[1] Zech. vii. 5; viii. 19. 2 Kings xxv. 8-25. Jer. xl. l.; lii. 4, 12 (Ewald, v. 22). See Lectures XL. and XLIII.

[2] Isa. li. 2; xli. 8. Zech i. 2-5; vii. 7-14. Isa. xlviii. 18, 19; xlii. 23, 25; lxiii. 10. Ezra ix. 6, 7, 13, 15. Neh. i. 6; ix. 7-37; xiii. 18, 26. Mal. iii. 7 (Ewald, v. 22).

other. The scenes which belong to the period of the Captivity are made the framework of the patriotic exhortations of the War of Independence. The literature of those exhortations throws itself back without effort into the sufferings of the exiles. It is from the writings, contemporary or subsequent, of this period that there has come down the bitter scorn, the uncompromising defiance, which have served as the examples of every like protest, of the Maccabees, of the early Christians, of the Waldenses, of the Huguenots, of the Puritans. There is nothing in the earlier sacred writings, if we except the fierce taunts of Elijah, to equal the sarcastic invectives levelled against the folly and futility of idol-worship, such as breathe through the stories or strains of the Captivity. Nowhere is there a bolder invocation of reason and conscience against the external authority and form of religion than in the solemn yet disdainful appeal made by the Evangelical Prophet to the common sense of the artificers [1] of a sacred image—detailing the whole process of its manufacture, and closing with the indignant question: 'Is there not a lie in my right hand?' Many are the modern ecclesiastical idols of what Bacon calls 'the Market place' and 'the Den'—of words, and of ceremonies—which would be dissolved by passing through the crucible of the like searching analysis into their origin and composition. In the later books which treat of the same epoch the same attack is sustained almost with the fierceness of the sixteenth century against the priestcraft which makes its sordid gains out of the pious impostures, and against the impotency of the impostures themselves. In the apocryphal Epistle of Jeremiah [2] we have the complete picture of the religious processions through the streets of Babylon, images plated with gold and silver, clothed in purple, with gilt crowns on their heads; followed and preceded by crowds of worshippers. We see them, too, in their temples, with sword and battle-axe in their hands,[3] covered with the dust stirred up by the feet of pilgrims, blackened with the smoke of incense or candle or with the rust which gathers over ancient gold; we see the bats, the swallows, and the cats that

[1] Isa. xliv. 9–20. [2] Baruch vi. 4, 12, 72. [3] *Ib.* 15, 20, 23, 24.

creep about the corners of the temple ; we hear the affected lamentations of the Priests, with their rent clothes,[1] shaven beards and loud screams, and the feasts placed before them, the doors locked against intruders.[2] We are invited to look at the petty pilferings of the establishment by the sacred attendants. And then, in the yet later book of the Greek Daniel, we are shown the whole machinery of fraud which was at work in those sumptuous chapels at the summit and base of the Temple of Bel, which Herodotus saw, himself not without suspicion of foul intrigue—the enormous feasts on the vast golden tables—the seventy Priests with their families—the secret door by which they carried out their plots.[3] These stories have the very ring of the early Christian or the early Protestant iconoclasts, at once in the grotesqueness and the energy of their tone. But there was even in these dark reminiscences of Babylon the nobler feeling that it is not merely by negation that the false can be driven out, but by the fullest assertion of the true. Here again we have the sentiment of the time expressed both in a later, and in a contemporaneous form. Legendary and late though it be, a gifted teacher of our time has loved again and again to call attention to the Song[4] of the Three Children, the hymn called 'Benedicite,' as the very crown and flower of the Old Testament, as containing the fullest protest against idolatry, and for the simplicity of the true religion. If so intended, it is indeed a fruitful and elevating thought that this supreme denial of the Gods of Babylonia, the Gods of sun, and stars, and moon, and earth, and sea, was expressed, not by a mere contradiction, but by a positive invocation of all that is beautiful and holy and great in nature and man to join in the perpetual benediction, praise, and exaltation of the supreme source of all beauty, strength, and power. And in the Evangelical Prophet, close upon this time, it is yet more vividly set forth, in a bold and striking metaphor, how in such dread extremities, whether of man or of nations, the primitive and

[1] Baruch vi. 31, 32, and 33.

[2] *Ib.* 28, 29.

[3] Bel and the Dragon, 3, 10, 13, 14, 15. Compare Herodotus, i. 181, 182, 183. As in the Hebrew, so in the Greek, Daniel, the local allusions are mostly correct.

[4] Kingsley's *Good News of God*, p. 23. *Westminster Abbey Sermons*, p. xiii.

fundamental truths of religion reassert their power. The Eternal Supreme, as it were, takes His place by an irresistible movement.[1] 'Too long in the turmoil of the world's great 'race had He held silence and restrained Himself—too long 'permitted His name to be despised and rejected among the 'nations of the earth. Now He neither would nor could hold 'His peace any longer: with the thunder of His voice He could 'make the earth tremble from end to end, and step into the 'battle as the only true and eternal hero, to re-establish, even 'though by the profoundest perturbation that could no longer 'be avoided, and by the conflict of all the gravest forces, the 'eternal right that had been overthrown.' "I am[2] He; before 'Me was no God formed, neither shall there be after Me. I 'will work, and who shall hinder it?"' 'Hast[3] thou not 'known? hast thou not heard, that the everlasting God, the 'Eternal, the Creator of the ends of the earth, fainteth not, 'neither is weary? there is no searching of His understanding. 'He giveth power to the faint, and to them that have no might 'he increaseth strength. Even the youths shall faint, and the 'young warriors shall utterly fall. But they that wait on the 'Eternal shall renew their strength; they shall mount up with 'wings as eagles; they shall walk and not be weary; they shall 'run and not faint.' The ancient truths are able to bear all and more than all the burden which the new age can lay upon them.

Independence of Conscience.

3. With this conviction naturally sprang up that strong sense of individual conscience and responsibility which Ezekiel[4] had so profoundly expressed. 'The soul that 'sinneth, it shall die. The soul that doeth right-'eously, it shall live.' Nowhere in the whole of the Hebrew records (with the exception, perhaps, of the narrative of Elijah) is this perception of the grandeur of solitary virtue brought out so strongly as in the three stories of the Book of Daniel, which have enshrined this sentiment of the Captivity, and which in the early ages of the Christian Church were

[1] Ewald, v. 53.
[2] Isa. xliii. 10-13.
[3] Isa. xl. 28-31 (Heb.).
[4] Ezekiel xviii. 4, 9. See Lecture XL.

the three scenes which most visibly encouraged the early martyrs.

Susanna.

The first was the story of the young Jewish wife who, firm in the faith of an Almighty Judge, stood unmoved in the dreadful choice between death and dishonour. 'I 'am straitened on every side; for if I do this thing, 'it is death to me; and if I do it not, I cannot escape your 'hands. It is better for me to fall into your hands, and not 'do it, than to sin in the sight of the Lord. . . . O Everlasting 'God, that knowest the secrets and knowest all things before 'they be . . . . behold I must die.'[1] So in the Catacombs stands the innocent lamb of the Church between the two foxes ready to devour her.

The Three Children.

The second was the story of the three youths, who, as in the later legend of Abraham and Nimrod, were to be thrown into the burning fiery furnace,[2] destined to be the instrument of terror to sufferers for conscience sake during so many ages. This, also in the Catacombs, and also in the immemorial usages of the Eastern Church, is the scene again and again repeated, of the three boys in all the peculiarity of their Eastern costumes of Phrygian caps and Persian trowsers. Theirs were the words which the father[3] of the Wesleys is reported to have used in reply to the unlawful order of James II.: 'O Nebuchadnezzar, we are not careful to 'answer thee in this matter. Be it known unto thee, O King, 'that we will not serve thy gods, nor worship the golden image 'which thou hast set up.' This is the story which came with such a preternatural force from the lips of Fletcher[4] of Madeley to the poor peasant woman, trembling in fear of her ungodly home, and which by the poet of the 'Christian

[1] Susannah, 22, 23, 42. In the Catacombs the story is identified by the name *Susanna* over the lamb, and *Seniores* over the foxes.

[2] The death by fire is Chaldæan, as indicated in Jer. xxix. 22. The legend of Abraham's escape from the furnace of Nimrod is by some supposed to be a result of the mistranslation of 'Ur (*i.e.* light or 'fire) of the Chaldees.' But it is a widespread Eastern tradition, localised on the mound opposite to the Birs-Nimrud, celebrated in the Syrian Church on January 25, and incorporated into the Koran, xxi. 52-75. (See Lane's *Selections*, p. 148.)

[3] Dan. iii. 16, 18. Macaulay's *Hist. of Eng.* ii. 355.

[4] Benson's *Life of Fletcher*, ch. ix. § 8.

'Year' has been so beautifully worked up into the needs of common life.

> When Persecution's torrent blaze
> Wraps the unshrinking Martyr's head;
> When fade all earthly flowers and bays,
> When summer friends are gone and fled,
> Is he alone in that dark hour
> Who owns the Lord of love and power?

The story of the Den of Lions[1] is told in three different versions, the one in Hebrew, most generally known, which places the incident under 'Darius the Mede;' the second, in Greek, which places it under Cyrus, in connexion with the intrigues of the Priests of Bel; the third in John[2] of Malala, who places it also under Cyrus, from Daniel's refusal to answer the question whether he shall succeed against Crœsus. It is the second of these which the early Christians of the Catacombs adopted when they painted the youth standing upright in prayer naked between the lions, and rescued by the flight of Habakkuk the Prophet from Palestine to Babylon, a grotesque addition to the Hebrew record, redeemed by the fine answer of the captive: 'Thou hast 'remembered me, O God, neither hast thou forsaken them 'that seek thee and love thee.'[3]

Daniel.

But, as in the story of the Three Children, so in that of the Den of Lions, the element which has lived on with immortal vigour is that which tells how, when Daniel[4] knew 'that the 'writing was signed, he kneeled upon his knees three times a 'day, and prayed and gave thanks before his God, as he did 'aforetime.' How often have these words confirmed the solitary protest not only in the Flavian Amphitheatre, but in the more ordinary, yet not more easy, task of maintaining the rights of conscience against arbitrary power or invidious insult!

[1] Dan. vi. Here again the local colour is faithfully preserved. The herds of lions which prowl round the ruins of Babylon might almost seem to make them its natural inhabitants, like the bears of Berne (Layard's *Nineveh and Babylon*, p. 567). The one sculpture that remains is of a lion trampling on a man.

[2] Fabricius, *Codex Pseudep.* 1129.

[3] Bel and the Dragon, 33-39.

[4] Dan. vi. 10. See Arnold's Sermons, vol. iii. 265.

How many an independent patriot or unpopular reformer has been nerved by them to resist the unreasonable commands of King or Priest! How many a little boy at school has been strengthened by them for the effort when he has knelt down by his bedside for the first time to say his prayers in the presence of indifferent or scoffing companions! If these stories were first written to sustain the Maccabean Jews, yet their impressive force is greatly strengthened by the scenes of Babylonian state in which they are embedded. The more[1] overpowering the grandeur of Babylon, the more absorbing the impulses of the outer world, so much the more striking, so much the more needed, is the proof that the freedom of the human will, the sacredness of truth and duty, are loftier and nobler than all. The problem of the necessity of living in the midst of earthly influences and yet of escaping from their evil is difficult with an exceeding difficulty, and has been portrayed with wonderful power in one of the most profound and penetrating[2] of modern poems. Yet it is not without solution. Shadrach, Meshach, and Abednego in the court of Nebuchadnezzar, Daniel in the court of Darius, are the likenesses of 'the 'small transfigured band whom the world cannot tame;' who, by faith in the Unseen, have in every age 'stopped the mouths 'of lions and quenched the violence of fire.'[3] This was the example to those on whom, in all ages, in spirit if not in letter, 'the fire had no power, nor was an hair of their head singed, 'neither were their coats changed, nor the smell of fire passed 'upon them;' but it was 'as it were a moist[4] whistling wind,' and 'the form of the fourth, who walked with them in the 'midst of the fire, was like a Son[5] of God.'

Further, it is not without significance that the same isolation which nourished this independence in regard to

[1] The colossal size of the golden image in Dan. iii. 1 (whatever may be meant by it) is quite in accordance with the golden statue, 40 feet high, described by Diodorus, ii. 9—probably of gilded wood. The plain of Dura may be (as in the LXX.) 'a plain 'within the walls;' see Speaker's *Commentary on Daniel*, p. 271.

[2] Clough's *Dipsychus*.

[3] Heb. xi. 33, 34.

[4] Song of the Three Children, verse 27. The 'astonishment' of Nebuchadnezzar is in the LXX. made to follow on his hearing the hymn.

[5] Dan. iii. 25. (Heb., and Jerome *ad loc.*)

outward secular observances nourished an independence no less remarkable in regard to outward religious observances.

Spirituality of Religion.

The Israelite mind was now weaned, to use the expression of one of the nearly contemporary Psalms,[1] not only from Pagan, but from Jewish objects of external worship. Whatever may have been the form of the revival of the Levitical code on the return to Palestine, however minute the regulations afterwards engrafted upon it, it would seem as if the vast reaction of spiritual religion which it finally provoked had been anticipated in these earlier days in which the exiles were for the time raised to a higher sense of unseen things than ever before. The absence of any ritual or local form threw them back on their own hearts and consciences, to hold communion with Him who had thus declared to them by the overthrow of His earthly sanctuary that 'the 'Heaven only was His throne and the earth His footstool:' 'Where is the house that ye build unto me?'[2] 'There was 'at this time neither Prince or Prophet, or leader, or burnt-'offering or sacrifice, or oblation, or incense, or place to 'sacrifice . . . . Nevertheless, in a contrite heart and an 'humble spirit' they hoped 'to be accepted.'[3] From the very nature of the case the sacrificial system ceased. 'Thou 'hast not brought me the lambkins of thy burnt-offerings, 'neither hast thou honoured me with thy sacrifices. I have 'not caused thee to serve with an offering, nor wearied thee 'with incense.'[4]

Man's necessity is God's opportunity; the loss of earthly ceremonial is the occasion for heavenward aspirations. And hence it is that from the Captivity dates, not indeed the first use, but the continued and frequent use of prayer 'as a potent 'instrument for sustaining the nobler part of man,' as the chief access to the Invisible Divinity. Prayer now literally took the

Importance of Prayer.

place of their morning and evening '*sacrifice*,' their morning and evening[5] '*incense*;' now for the first time we hear of men 'kneeling upon their knees three times a

[1] Psalm cxxxi. 2. [2] Isa. lxvi. 1, 2. [4] Isa. xliii. 23.

[3] Song of the Three Children, verses 14, 15.

[5] Dan. ix. 3, 19. Psalm cxli. 2 is possibly earlier.

'day'[1] praying and making supplication before God. Now for the first time assemblies for prayer and lamentation and praise, as afterwards in houses and synagogues, were gathered by the water-side—'by the rivers of Babylon,'[2]—'by the river Ulai,'[3] —'by the river of Hiddekel,'[4] by the river of the Mesopotamian 'Nile,'[5] to supply the place of the brazen laver of the Temple Courts. Now more distinctly than before do we hear of faithful worshippers in fixed forms of prayer 'setting their 'faces unto the Lord their God, to seek by prayer and suppli-'cation that He would hear and do, hearken and forgive for 'His own sake.' 'The long prayers which henceforth appear 'in the sacred books are only the reflection of the earnestness, 'power, and constancy with which this most simple and 'wonderful instrument for strengthening the spirit laid hold on 'every branch of life.'[6]

That which befell the Jewish people in their Babylonian exile has befallen them again in their European exile. When the eternal principles of spiritual worship are represented by the greatest master of modern fiction in the person of the Hebrew Maid of the twelfth century they are but the echo of what her ancestors might have sung on the banks of the Euphrates. When Spinoza, the excommunicated Jew of Amsterdam, insisted on those principles in the treatises which have been the fountains of modern philosophy and theology, he was but following in the footsteps of the Evangelical Prophet. The overthrow of the Temple was needed yet a second time to start the soul alike of the Jewish and of the Christian Church afresh on its upward course.

Importance of Almsgiving.

And not prayer only, but the homely acts of beneficence and kindness rose now for the first time to the full dignity of religious ordinances. Almsgiving steps into the place of ceremonial purification, and kindliness mounts into the rank of conformity to the requirements of the law. These, also, four centuries later were hardened into mechanical observances. But in the times which are represented

[1] Dan. vi. 10. [2] Psalm cxxxvii. 1. [3] Dan. viii. 24. [4] *Ibid.* x. 4.
[5] *Ibid.* xii. 5, 6, 7. [6] *Ibid.* ix. 3, 19. Ewald, v. 23, 24.

by the book of Tobit such moral virtues are the natural and commendable substitutions for mere external forms. The advice of Tobit[1] to Tobias, the 'good' father to the 'good' son, is the counterpart of that which a Jewish[2] teacher of later days, addressing 'the twelve tribes scattered abroad,' described as the pure and undefiled 'ritual' of the true faith.

And in the more direct warnings of the Evangelical Prophet we find the protest rising against the superstitions which already began to cling to the new and simpler religious observances, as before to the more complex. The whole external system of religion he criticises with a withering analysis. He declares generally the true sanctuary of the Invisible to be the human heart; he shows that every item of the sacrificial worship may drift into a meaning exactly the reverse of that which the offerer imagines. It is possible for the consecrated ox to become as odious as a human victim, the unblemished sheep as profane as the unclean dog, the prescribed meat-offering as abominable as the blood of swine, the incense no better than that which is offered to idols.[3] But he also has warned the coming generations that the practice of devotion which this new era had inaugurated in commemoration of the recent calamities was itself liable to pass into the same hollowness and perversion as the system which it had begun to supersede. With a shout,[4] with the call as of a trumpet like to that with which in olden days solemn assemblies were convened, the Prophet warns the worshippers against heedlessly frequenting them. The black sackcloth, the couch of ashes, the pendulous movement of the head to and fro, after the mechanical fashion of Eastern devotees, corresponding to the upturned eyes and folded hands and demure demeanour of the West, were to him objects of a mockery hardly less keen than he directs against the heathen idols. The fast of the true religion consisted, according to his doctrine, in the moral duties of giving freedom to the slave,

[1] Tobit iv. 3–20.

[2] James i. 1–27. 'The pure and undefiled "ritual" of religion is to visit the 'fatherless and widows in their affliction, 'and to keep himself unspotted from the 'world.'

[3] Isa. lxvi. 1–3.

[4] *Ibid.* lviii. 1–12.

provision to the hungry, shelter to the homeless, and hospitality to kindred.

4. There was yet one final result of the Captivity in which its outward and inward lessons were both combined. The contact of the exiles with the conquering race, their separation from their own country, the higher spiritual view of the Divine nature thus revealed, united in opening to them more widely the larger horizon of which before they had enjoyed but imperfect glimpses, and strengthened the conviction that the religion which they professed was not and could not be confined to one nation only. The son of the stranger was no longer to say that the Eternal had utterly separated him from His people: even the Priesthood was no longer to be confined to a Jewish tribe.[1] The truth was gradually dawning that the Unseen Divinity whom all the nations of the earth worshipped was, strange as it seemed to them, strange as it seems to many even now, essentially the same.

The widening of view.

Even in detail the impress of Babylon was stamped on the future of their race. Their vernacular tongue henceforth ceased to be Hebrew, and became instead the Aramaic or Chaldæan of the country of their exile.[2] The Aramaic dialect penetrated even into their sacred books. The Aramaic calendar, beginning with the autumn, with new names for the months, superseded the Hebrew calendar, which had begun with the spring.[3] The lower arts of astrology and exorcism in all probability passed from Chaldæa into the Jewish usages, assuming at some critical periods of their history a strange predominance and a long persistency.[4] The imagery of Ezekiel and Daniel is taken direct from the gigantic figures, monster-headed, and with vast wings, that we see sculptured on the walls of Nineveh and Persepolis. But the effect on the general expansion of their mental ideas was yet more visible. Scattered as they were amongst foreign nations, they derived from this

[1] Isa. lvi. 3; lxvi. 21 (Ewald, v. 26).

[2] See the elaborate passage in Deutsch's 'Essay on the Targums' (*Remains*, 324).

[3] Kalisch's Commentary, ii. 269.

[4] Comp. Juvenal, *Sat.* iii. 13; vi. 541–546; Acts xix. 13, 19; Matt. xii. 27; Layard's *Nineveh and Babylon*, p. 510–513.

intercourse sympathies and consolations which, humanly speaking, would have been impossible had they always been shut up within the narrow limits of Palestine. The fall of these ancient empires strikes a pang[1] of deep pity through the hearts of the Prophets, who in the previous generation would only have rejoiced in the judgment overtaking them. In this sense the visions of the Book of Daniel are not unsuitably placed in this new unfolding of the world's destinies. Part of that book, as we have seen, attaches itself to the events of the Captivity; part of it, as we shall see, to the events of the Maccabæan age; but the purpose of the whole is the expression of the universal plan of human history. It is not only the first germ of the apocalyptic literature, which expanded through the Sibylline oracles, and the Book of Enoch, into the kindred writings, canonical or apocryphal, of the Christian era, but it is the first attempt, rude and simple, but most impressive, at a Philosophy of History—the first forerunner of Herder and Lessing and Hegel. However we date or interpret the details of the four Empires, each with its guardian spirit, we see in them the first perception of the continuous succession of ages—the recognition of the truth that the nations of the earth are not merely to be regarded in relation to the Jewish people, as by the older Prophets, but to be watched for their own sakes—the appreciation of the instructive fact that the story of humanity is that of a regular development of epochs, one growing out of another, cause leading to effect, race following race, and empire following empire,[2] on a majestic plan, in which the Divine Economy is as deeply concerned as in the fate of the Chosen People.

The Philosophy of History in Daniel;

Although many of the details of these visions point to a far later date for their combination as exhibited in the Book of Daniel, there is a singular congruity in fixing the scene of their

[1] See Lecture XL.

[2] Comp. Jos. *Ant.* x. 11, 7. This general view of Daniel's vision of the four empires remains the same whether, with Ewald and Bunsen, we make it to be the Assyrian, Babylonian, Median, and Persian; or, with Dr. Westcott, the Babylonian, Median, Persian, and Greek; or, with Dr. Pusey, the Babylonian, Persian, Greek, and Roman; or, with Mr. Desprez and Dr. Williams, the Babylonian, Persian, Macedonian, and Græco-Syrian.

first appearance at this particular crisis. In no other point of view could a seer so well be placed for the survey of the various Powers which were to succeed the Babylonian Empire on the stage of Asiatic history. But apart from these doubtful though magnificent visions, there remains the unquestioned elevation of the whole political horizon of the Jews as seen in the Evangelical Prophet, of whose writings it has been well said that they possess, 'not only a religious and 'poetical, but an historical interest of the highest order, for 'they mark the very point where the Jewish history is caught 'in the current of the wars and policy of a rising imperial power, 'is carried into the great open stream of the world's history, 'never again to be separated from it.'[1]

In the Second Isaiah.

In his delineations of the future glory of the restored Jerusalem the prospect opens on both sides. On the remote outskirts of the East the Prophet sees the troops of the endless caravans; the waving necks, the laden humps of the camels and the dromedaries bearing the gold and frankincense, the fleets, as it were, of the desert; the crowded flocks of Oriental sheep, with their sweeping tails, and the rams and goats with their stately horns, following their Arabian or Nabathean shepherds. All these were images familiar to those who dwelt amongst the immemorial usages of Asiatic life. But the Prophet turns suddenly round in the opposite direction, and sees from the Western horizon another procession moving, like clouds of birds through the air, the broken promontories of the Mediterranean dimly emerging like a vast archipelago—'the islands,' as they appear to the inhabitants of the old continent of Asia; he watches them loosed from their moorings in the Ægean or Tyrrhenian waters, and standing ready for the Divine command; he sees the white wings of the sails of the Tyrian ships advancing from the distant Tarshish of Carthage and of Spain, and heading the argosies that are to bring in the treasures from the unexplored regions which only those hardy adventurers could reach.[2]

Contact of East and West.

[1] Matthew Arnold, *The Great Prophecy of Israel's Restoration*, p. xiv.
[2] Isa. lx. 4-9.

Thus is for the first time unfolded the strange and striking contact between the East and the West, which, even after the lapse of more than two thousand years, has never ceased to impress the imagination of mankind; which inspired the Father of History with the motive idea of his great work; which has given its peculiar and unique interest to the One Religion of after times, that, springing from the East, was developed to its full proportions only by travelling Westward. It is thus the Religion of the One Master who belongs to both —'Jesus Christ,'—as He has been called by a gifted son of the far Oriental World—'the inheritance of Europe and of 'Asia.'[1]

The sense that this prospect was beginning to open was quickened and deepened by the imminence of the great event which shall be described in the next Lecture.

[1] Keshub Chunder Sen's *Essays*.

LECTURE XLII.

THE FALL OF BABYLON.

THE moment of the Jewish history which we have now reached coincides with one of the most strongly-marked epochs in the history of the world. As far as the course of human progress is concerned there have been three vast periods, of which two have already passed away. They may be called, in general terms, Primæval History, Classical History, and Modern History. Each of these periods has its beginning, middle, and end—its ancient and modern stage—but the whole of each is marked by its own general characteristics. In the Primæval History we must include all that series of events which begins with the first dawn of civilisation in Egypt and Mesopotamia. It is a period of which the Semitic races (taking that word in its most extended sense) were the predominant elements of power and genius—the Assyrians at Nineveh, the Phœnicians in Tyre and Sidon and their distant colonies, the Israelites in Palestine, the Egyptians, though with infusion of other races, in the valley of the Nile, the Chaldæans, though with a like heterogeneous infusion, on the banks of the Euphrates. Of these nations, with the single exception of the Israelites, we have, properly speaking, no history. Their manners and customs, their religion, the succession of their sovereigns, are known to us. But we have no continuous series of events; although the knowledge of them is fuller, through the investigations of the last fifty years, than in former times, yet it is still shadowy, fragmentary, mythical. They are like the figures seen in the dreams of Sardanapalus, as depicted by the modern poet;

The End of Primæval History.

Beginning of Classical History.

here a mighty hunter or conqueror like Nimrod or Sesostris or Sennacherib, there a fierce and voluptuous queen like Semiramis—

> All along
> Of various aspects, but of one expression.[1]

The time was now arrived when this giant age was to come to an end. It is the epoch in the Eastern World when we begin to discern the lineaments and traits of the first teachers of further[2] Asia, whose careers are distinctly known to us, and whose influence still lives down to our own time. In the Western World it is the date, almost to a year, when Grecian literature begins to throw its light far and wide on everything that it touches. Even in Egypt, Amasis is the first King of whose personal character we have any knowledge as distinct from the public acts,[3] or the length of the reigns, of the other Pharaohs. In the same generation, even in the very same year, we meet the accession of two great potentates in Greece and in the Grecian colonies of Asia Minor—Pisistratus at Athens, Crœsus at Sardis. The same date brings us into the midst of the first authentic characters of Roman history in the reign of the Tarquins.[3] From this time forward the classical world of Greece and Italy occupies the whole horizon of our thoughts, till its own days are numbered by the fall of Rome and the invasion of the German tribes, which was to usher in the period of Modern History in Europe. With a like catastrophe did the earlier epoch come to its conclusion, but in the continent which had been its chief seat—in Asia.

B.C. 566. Amasis. B.C. 560. Accession of Cyrus, Pisistratus, and Crœsus. B.C. 572. Tarquinius Superbus.

And it is exactly this momentous juncture of secular history, this critical pause between the middle and the final epoch of Jewish history, at which we are now arrived. The fall of Jerusalem coincides with the fall, or the beginning of the fall, of those ancient monarchies and nations which had occupied the attention of civilised man down to this time. We have already

[1] Byron's *Sardanapalus*, act iv. scene 1. [2] See Lecture XLV.
[3] Kenrick's *Egypt*, ii. 429.

seen how the chorus of the Jewish Prophets at the close of the monarchy prepared the way for the final overthrow of the oldest historic world, much as the Christian Fathers heralded the overthrow of the Græco-Roman world. We have seen how [1] Ezekiel sat over against the grave of the nations, into which tribe after tribe, kingdom after kingdom, even the stately ship of Tyre, the cedar of Assyria, the venerable Egypt, went plunging down to the dark abyss where 'the bloody corpses' of the past,

> yet but green in earth,
> Lay festering in their shrouds.

But now the oldest, the grandest of all was about to descend into the same sepulchral vault which had received all its predecessors and rivals.

The ap-proach of the Fall of Babylon.

The event when it came to the Israelite captives could have been no surprise. It had been long foreseen by those who sang by the water-side.[2] They were told how, even before the Captivity, on occasion of a visit of homage which the Jewish King Zedekiah paid to Nebuchadnezzar in the early part of his reign, Jeremiah had recorded his detailed prediction of the overthrow of Babylon in a scroll, which he confided to Seraiah, brother of Baruch, himself a high [3] officer in the Judæan Court. Not till he reached the quays of the Euphrates was Seraiah to open and read the fatal record, with the warning that 'Babylon shall sink, and shall not rise again 'from the face of the evils that shall come upon her.'[4] Deep in its bed the mighty river was believed to have kept its secret as a pledge of the approaching doom. What that doom was the events now began to disclose.

It will be our object to indicate the impression left by it on the Israelite spectators, the only spectators who, by means of these thrilling utterances, remain, as it were, the living witnesses of the whole transaction; confirmed on the whole by the

[1] Ezek. xxiv.-xxxii. See Lecture XL.

[2] Psalm cxxxvii. 3.

[3] Jer. li. 59. A. V. 'a quiet prince'—probably the 'officer of the king's bed-'chamber,' and therefore indispensable on the journey.

[4] Jer. li. 61-64; xxix. 10.

broken and scattered notices preserved in later Chaldæan annals, or gathered together by the Greeks who penetrated during the next century into Central Asia.

It might have been thought difficult to imagine from what quarter the destroyer should come. The chief rivals of Babylon were gone. The dominions that had with it played their part on the battlefield of the nations had passed away, and the Empire of Nebuchadnezzar was left, as it seemed, in solitary and unassailable majesty. 'I have made completely strong the 'defences of Babylon,' said Nebuchadnezzar in his great inscription; 'may it last ever!'[1]

The Persian Invasion, B.C. 539.

Not so. The prescient eye of the Hebrew Prophets was clearly fixed on that point of the horizon whence the storm would issue. There was a mightier wall even than the walls of Babylon, with gates which could not be opened and shut at the command of Princes, that runs across the centre of the whole Ancient World; the backbone alike of Europe and Asia. It begins in the far East with the Himalayas; it attaches itself to the range of the diverging lines of the Zagros and Elburz ranges; it unites them in the Imaus, the Caucasus, and the Taurus; it reappears after a slight interruption in the range of Hæmus; it melts into the Carpathian and Styrian mountains; it rises again in the Alps; it reaches its western buttress in the Pyrenees.

On the southern side, on the sunny slopes of this gigantic barrier grew up the civilised nations of antiquity, the ancient monumental religions and polities of India, Mesopotamia, and Egypt, as afterwards, further west, the delicate yet powerful commonwealths of Asia Minor, Greece, and Italy. On the northern or darker side, behind this mighty screen, were restrained and nurtured the fierce tribes which have from time to time descended to scourge or regenerate the civilisation of the South. Such in later days have been the Gauls, the Goths, the Vandals, the Huns, the Tartars; such, more nearly within the view of the age of which we are now speaking, the [2] Scythians;

[1] Standard Inscription, in Rawlinson's Herodotus, vol. ii. 586.
[2] See Lectures XXXIX. and XL.

and such was now, although in a somewhat milder form, the enemy to whom, as Tacitus in the days of Trajan already fixed his gaze with mingled fear and admiration on the tribes of Germany, so the Israelite Prophets looked for the development of the new crisis of the world. Already the Psalmist had seen that neither in the East nor West nor South, but in the North, was the seat of future change.[1] Already Ezekiel had been startled by the vision[2] of the wild nomads pouring over the hills that had hitherto parted them from their destined prey. And now Jeremiah, and it may be some older prophet, heard yet more distinctly the gathering of war—an assembly of great nations against Babylon from the north country, with the resistless weapons[3] for which all those races were famous.

And now, yet more nearly, prophetic voices pointed not only to the north, but to the eastern quarter of the north. Already on 'the bare hill-top' a banner was raised and the call was gone forth; there was a rushing sound as of multitudes[4] in the distant mountain valleys; the shriek of alarm went up from the plains; the faces of the terrified dwellers in Mesopotamia were lit up with a lurid glow of fear.

It was the mighty race occupying the table-land between the two mountain-ranges of Zagros and Elburz, of which we have just spoken—the Median and Persian tribes now first rising into importance. That nation whose special education was to ride on horses, to shoot with the bow, and to speak the truth,[5] was now in full march against no less a prey than Babylon itself.

Their bright 'arrows[6] were the arrows of a mighty[7] expert 'man; the archers, the nation of archers, with their bows 'all bent,' were gathering to camp against the city. They hold their bows and lances, they bend their bows and shoot and spare[8] no arrows. They are there with their splendid

[1] Psalm lxxv. 6. [2] See Lecture XL.

[3] Jer. l. 9.

[4] Isa. xiii. 2, 3; *ib.* 4, 5. The question of the date of Isa. xiii. 1—xiv. 23, and xxi. 1–10 stands on different grounds from that of the date of Isa. xl.-lxvi., and Ewald and Gesenius agree in regarding them as predictive and not merely descriptive of the fall of Babylon. Still, they probably belong to the same general period of the Captivity, though incorporated in the earlier part of the Book of Isaiah.

[5] Herodotus, i. 136. [6] Jer. l. 9; li. 11.

[7] *Ibid.* l. 14, 42. [8] *Ibid.* l. 42.

cavalry riding on horses in battle array; they shout with their deafening war-cry.[1]

The force and energy with which their descent is described agrees with their significance in the history of the Eastern empires. 'With the appearance of the Persians,' says a brilliant French writer, 'the movement of history begins and humanity 'throws itself into that restless march of progress which hence-'forth is never to cease. A vague instinct pushes them forward 'to the conquest of all around them. They throw themselves 'headlong on the Semitic races. They are not contented with 'Asia. The East under them seems to migrate towards the 'West. They do not halt even at the Hellespont, nor till they 'have reached the shores of Salamis.'[2]

And not merely the nation, and the hour, but the very man was now in sight who should accomplish this great work.

Cyrus.

The fated hero had arisen, in the same eventful year of which we have already spoken, the year 560, twenty years after the beginning of the Jewish exile—Cyrus, or Koresh, or Khosroo, the King of the Persians. Already the Grecian colonies had felt his heavy hand: already Media had been absorbed into his dominion. On him the expectation of the nations was fixed. Would he be, like the other chiefs and princes of the age, a mere transient conqueror, or would he indeed be the Deliverer who should inaugurate the fall of the old and the rise of the new world? 'I have called the righteous 'man from the East, the ravenous bird,' the eagle[3] of Persia, which long blazed on its standards. With no uncertain sound the greatest prophetic voice of the time marked him out as the one Anointed Prince,[4] the expected Messiah alike of the Chosen People and of all the surrounding nations. 'Thus[5] 'saith the Eternal to Cyrus, whom I have anointed, whose 'right hand I have holden, to subdue nations before him. 'Cyrus is my shepherd and shall perform all my pleasure.'

[1] Jer. li. 14; l. 15.

[2] A striking passage, though with some exaggeration, from Quinet, *Génie des Religions*, pp. 301, 302.

[3] Isa. xli. 2; xlvi. 11. Comp. Æsch. *Pers.* 205-210; Xen. *Cyrop.* vii. 1.

[4] See Lecture XL.

[5] Isa. xliv. 8; xlv. 1. Comp. Dan x. 25.

The era of Persian glory which he ushered in, the empire which he founded, for that brief time, embraced all that there was of civilisation from the Himalayas to the Ægean sea. 'For 'one brilliant moment the Persian, like the Greek afterwards, 'and the Roman at a still later time, was the central man of 'the world.'[1]

There was, indeed, everything which conspired to fit the new conqueror for this critical place in the history of the world and of the Church. To us, looking at the crisis from a distance that enables us to see the whole extent of the new era which he was to open, this poetic and historic fitness is full of deep significance. We are entering on an epoch when the Semitic race is to make way for the Aryan or Indo-Germanic nations, which, through Greece and Rome, are henceforth to sway the destiny of mankind. With these nations Cyrus, first of Asiatic potentates, is to enter into close relations—with Greece henceforth the fortunes of Persia will be inseparably bound up.

Nay, yet more, of all the great nations of Central Asia, Persia alone is of the same stock as Greece and Rome and Germany. It was a true insight into the innermost heart of this vast movement which enabled the Prophet, as we have seen, to discern in it not merely the blessing of his own people, but the union of the distant isles of the Western sea with the religion hitherto confined to the uplands of Asia. It was a moment of meeting between the race of Japheth and the race of Shem, those meetings that have been truly said to be the turning-points of human history.

The representative of the Aryan races.

Yet again, Cyrus, first of the ancient conquerors, appears in other than a merely despotic and destructive aspect. It can hardly be without foundation that both in Greek and Hebrew literature he is represented as the type of a just and gentle prince. In the Cyropædia of Xenophon, however mingled with fiction, he appears, as no other barbaric sovereign that figured in Grecian story, humane, philosophic, religious. In the Jewish Prophet and Chronicler he is a Liberator and Benefactor

[1] The 'Wise Men,' by Dr. Upham, p. 115.

of Israel such as had never crossed their path. First of the great Asiatic kings, we can track him through the varying adventures of youth and age, from his cradle to his grave, and stand (as who could stand unmoved?) before the simple yet stately tomb of snow-white marble which still remains at Pasargadæ, and once contained the golden coffin of 'Cyrus the King, 'the Achæmenian.'[1]

But, yet more, he belongs to the only nation in the contemporary world which, in any sense at all approaching to the Israelite, acknowledge the unity of the Godhead. The religion of the Persians was, of all the Gentile forms of faith, the most simple and the most spiritual. Their abhorrence of idols was pushed almost to fanaticism. 'They have 'no images of the gods, no temples, no altars, and consider the 'use of them a sign of folly.' This was Herodotus' account of the Persians of his own day, and it is fully borne out by what we know of their religion[2] and of their history. When Cyrus broke in upon Babylon, as when his son Cambyses broke in upon Egypt, as when Xerxes broke in upon Greece, it might almost have seemed as if the knell of Polytheism had been sounded throughout the world.

The great Monotheist.

Who or what was the Prince that reigned[3] over Babylon in this the supreme hour of her fate, or how long her defence was maintained against the invading army, we can only discern with difficulty amongst the conflicting accounts. The only king in whom, after Nebuchadnezzar, the Hebrew and the Chaldæan[4] annals clearly agree is Evil-Merodach, the liberator of Jehoiachin. Then come, in rapid succession in the Chaldæan annals, Neriglissar,[5] Laborosoarchod, and Nabu-nahid.[6] In Herodotus the interval is filled by the one name of Labynetus,[7] in the Book of Daniel[8] by the one name of Belshazzar, which, there alone preserved in written

Belshazzar.

[1] Rawlinson, iv. 294.

[2] Herod. i. 131; see Rawlinson's Herodotus, vol. i., Essay 5.

[3] See the long discussion in Keil; and the Speaker's *Commentary* on Dan. v. 1.

[4] Berosus, in Joseph. *c. Ap.* i. 20.

[5] Probably Nergal Sharezer, Jer. xxxix. 3, 13.

[6] This name appears on the monuments —probably 'Nebo blesses,' see Speaker's *Commentary*, p. 306.

[7] Rawlinson, i. 191, iii. 515, and notes on Herodotus (vol. i. 525).

[8] Dan. v. 1.

records, has recently received from the monuments a confirmation from the probability that it is the same as [1] Bil-shar-uzar, the son and colleague of Nabu-nahid. But 'amongst all the 'later reminiscences of the conquest of Babylon [2] one never-to-'be forgotten feature always rises above the rest, namely, the 'amazing rapidity with which the victory was gained, and the 'manner in which the whole Chaldæan supremacy was shattered 'by it as at a single blow. The capture of Babylon in a single 'night, while the Babylonians were celebrating in 'careless ease a luxurious feast, is the fixed kernel of 'the tradition in all its forms; and the outline of it in the Book 'of Daniel stands out all the more boldly from the dark back-'ground, and casts a fiery glow upon the whole narrative.' [3]

B.C. 538.

That faint 'outline' has taken a place in the solemn imagery of the world that no doubtfulness of details can ever efface or alter. 'There was the sound of revelry by 'night' in the streets of Babylon at some high festival of Nebo or Merodach. Regardless of the dread extremity of their country and of the invading army round their walls, the whole population, through street and garden, through square and temple, were given up to the proverbial splendour and intoxication of the Babylonian feasts; music, perfumes, gold and silver plate, nothing was wanting. In the midst and chief of this was the feast of the King, whom the Hebrew tradition called 'Belshazzar, the son of Nebuchadnezzar.' On this fatal night he comes out from the usual seclusion of the Eastern [4] kings, and sits in the same hall with thousands of his nobles at a scene the likeness of which, even in our modern days, can be imagined by those who have seen the state banquets of the most Oriental of European potentates on the shores of the Neva or the Mosqua. Before them is the choice wine with which, from far countries, the Babylonian tables were laden. From the Temple of Bel, where they have been treasured up since the conqueror had carried them from Jerusa-

The last night of Babylon.

[1] Probably 'Bel protects the king.' See Speaker's *Commentary*, p. 308.

[2] Ewald, v. 50, 51.

[3] *Ibid.* v. 51. Compare the Greek accounts in Herod. i. 190; Xenophon. *Cyrop.* vii. 5 and 15.

[4] Athenæus, *Deipnos.* iv. 10.

lem, are brought the vessels of gold and silver, the bowls and caldrons, and the spoons, the knives, the cups, which had been regarded by the Jewish nation as the very palladium of the State—alike the thirty chargers and thirty vases of gold which had been made for the Temple of Solomon, and had continued there till the captivity of Jehoiachin, and the thousand chargers and four hundred basins of silver by which Zedekiah had supplied their place, and which were carried away in the final [1] deportation.

Into them the wine is poured and drunk by the King, with his nobles, and with the women of his harem, who, according to the shameless custom [2] of the Babylonians, are present at the banquet. Round about are placed the images of the gods of wood and stone, of iron and brass, plated with gold and silver.[3]

'In that same hour came forth the fingers of a man's hand 'and wrote over against' the great candlestick which lighted up the pale stucco on the wall of the Palace, to which [4] the banqueting hall was attached, 'and the King saw the part of 'the hand which wrote.' Then follows the panic of the assembled spectators as they find themselves in the presence of an enigma which they cannot decipher. 'I know,' said a great French scholar and philosopher in the Imperial Library of Paris in the winter of 1870, 'I know that I am turning over the leaf of a 'fresh page in history, but what is on the page I cannot read.' Such is the perplexity described when the wisdom of all the world-renowned learning of Babylon was summoned to interpret the writing, with the offer of the purple robe and golden chain of royal favour, and the next place in the kingdom after the two royal persons of the State.[5] Then appears the venerable personage always regarded in Eastern Monarchies with especial reverence, the Queen Mother—the 'Sultana Validé.'

[1] Baruch, i. 8; Ezra i. 8, 9. See Lecture XL. 475.

[2] Curtius v. 1; Herod. i. 499.

[3] Isa. xxx. 22; xliv. 13; Baruch vi. 4; Jer. x 3-5.

[4] Esther i. 5. But see Layard's *Nineveh and Babylon*, 651.

[5] Perhaps meaning Belshazzar and Nabunadius (Speaker's *Commentary*, p. 308). But, as Nabunadius is not recognised in Daniel, the Queen Mother seems more probable.

In this instance the respect would be enhanced if she may be identified with Nitocris,[1] the daughter of Nebuchadnezzar, herself the architect of some of the great outworks of the city.

Once more, in her mouth, the all-transcending wisdom and judgment of Daniel is set forth, reviving and recalling from long seclusion, as after the manner of the East, the antique sage[2] or statesman of the former generation to rebuke the folly of the younger. And then, like Elijah before Ahab, like Tiresias before Creon in the Grecian drama, is brought the hoary seer, with his accumulated weight of years and honours to warn the terror-stricken King, and to read the decree of fate which no one else could interpret. Where the astrologer and the diviner had failed, true science had discovered the truth.[3] Again and again have those mystic words been repeated, and will be repeated to the end of time; yet never with more significance than on the occasion whence they are derived. They were, as befitted the city which claimed to be the mother of letters, not in mere signs or hieroglyphics, but in distinct Hebrew characters; and through their brief and broken utterance there ran a double, treble significance. *Mene*[4] the first word, twice recorded, carried with it the judgment[5] that the days of the kingdom were *numbered* and *ended*; *Tekel* pronounced the doom that it was *weighed* and found *light*; *Peres*,[6] the third, that it was *divided* and given to the *Persians* (*Pharsin*)—almost the[7] first appearance in history of that famous name which now, for the first time, stepped into the place of 'Elam,' and has never since been lost.

[1] Herodotus, i. 185.

[2] Comp. 1 Kings xii. 6; compare also the story of the Constantinopolitan Council of State told in *Essays on Church and State*, p. 195.

[3] Comp. Isa. xix. 3 (Ewald).

[4] In LXX. and Josephus *Mene* is only once.

[5] The variation between the various versions suggests the probability that there was something anterior to all of them. (1) In Dan. v. 25, *Mene* occurs twice; in Dan. v. 26, once. (2) In Dan. v. 25, it is *And to the Persians*, as though something had dropped out. In Dan. v. 28 it is *Peres*, 'divided.' Mr. Aldis Wright suggests that the original inscription ran perpendicularly, and was 'Meni, Tekel, *Medi u* '*Pharsin*;' and that *Medi* was, by reading it horizontally, mistaken for a reduplication of *Meni*.

[6] The same word for 'division,' as appears in *Pharisee*.

[7] The substitution of *Phars* for *Elam* in the Book of Daniel, which it has in common with all books after the Captivity, and with none (unless we except Ezek. xxvii. 10, xxxviii. 5) during or before, is one of the indications of its later date.

'In that same night was Belshazzar the King slain'—so briefly and terribly is the narrative cut short in the Book of Daniel. But from the contemporary authorities, or those of the next century, we are able to fill up some of the details as they were anticipated or seen at the time. It may be that, as according to Berosus,[1] the end was not without a struggle; and that one or other of the kings who ruled over Babylon was killed in a hard-won fight without the walls. But the larger part of the accounts are steady to the suddenness and completeness of the shock, and all combine in assigning an important part to the great river, which, as it had been the pride of Babylon, now proved its destruction. The stratagems by which the water was diverted, first in the Gyndes and then in the Euphrates, are given partly by Herodotus and partly by Xenophon. It is their effect alone which need here be described. 'A way was made in the sea'[2]—that sea-like lake—and a path in the 'mighty waters.' 'Chariot and horse, army 'and power' are, as in the battle of the Milvian bridge, lost in the dark stream to rise up no more, extinguished like a torch[3] plunged in the waters. The hundred gates, all of bronze, along the vast circuit of the walls,[4] the folding-doors, the two-leaved gates,[5] which so carefully guarded the approaches of the Euphrates, opened as by magic for the conqueror; 'her waves 'roared like great waters, the thunder of their voice was 'uttered.' The inhabitants were caught in the midst of their orgies. The Hebrew seer trembled as he saw the revellers unconscious of their[6] impending doom, like the Persian seer for his own countrymen before the battle of Platæa—ἐχθίστη ὀδύνη. But it was too late. 'Her princes, and her wise men, 'and her captains, and her rulers, and her mighty men were 'cast into a perpetual sleep' from which they never woke.[7] They succumbed without a struggle, they forbore to fight. They remained in the fastnesses of their towering houses; their might failed; they became as women, they were hewn

The capture of Babylon.

[1] Jos. *Ant.* x. 11, § 2.
[2] Isa. xliii. 16.
[3] *Ibid.* xliii. 17.
[4] Herod. i. 129.
[5] Isa. xlv. 1, 2.
[6] *Ibid.* xxi. 4. Herod. ix. 17.
[7] Jer. li. 39, 57.

down like the flocks of lambs, of sheep, of goats, in the shambles or at the altar.[1] To and fro, in the panic of that night, the messengers encountered each other[2] with the news that the city was taken at one end, before the other end knew.[3] The bars were broken, the passages were stopped, the tall houses were in flames, the fountains were dried up by the heat of the conflagration.[4] The conquerors, chiefly the fierce mountaineers from the Median mountains, dashed through the terrified city like wild beasts. They seemed to scent out blood for its own sake; they cared not for the splendid metals that lay in the Babylonian treasure-houses; they hunted down the fugitives as if they were chasing deer or catching runaway sheep.[5] With their huge bows[6] they cut in pieces the young men whom they encountered; they literally fulfilled the savage wish of the Israelite captives, by seizing the infant children and hurling them against the ground, till they were torn limb from limb in the terrible havoc.[7] A celestial sword flashes a first, a second, a third, a fourth, and yet again a fifth time, at each successive blow sweeping away the chiefs of the State, the idle boasters, the chariots, the treasures, the waters.[8] The Hammer of the Nations struck again and again and again, as on the resounding anvil, and with repeated blows beat down the shepherd as he drove his flock through the wide pasture of the cultivated spaces, the husbandman as he tilled the rich fields within the walls with his yoke of oxen—no less than the lordly prince. The houses were shattered; the walls with their broad walks on their tops, the gateways mounting up like towers, were in flames.[9]

And yet more significant even than the fall of the monarchy and the ruin of the city was (at least in the expectation of the Jewish captives) the overthrow of the old religion of the Chaldæan world by the zeal of the Persian monotheists. The huge golden statue of Bel, the Sun-God—from which Babylon itself, 'the gate of Bel,' derived its name—on the summit of his

[1] Jer. li. 30. [2] *Ibid.* li. 31, 32. [3] See Herod. i. 191; iii. 158; Arist. *Pol.* iii. 1, 12. [4] Jer. li. 32, 36. [5] Isa. xiii. 17, 18. [6] *Ibid.* [7] Psalm cxxxvii. 8, 9; Isa. xiii. 16, 18. [8] Jer. l. 35. [9] *Ibid.* li. 58.

lofty temple; Nebo, the Thoth, the Hermes, the God of the Chaldæan learning, to whom at least three of the Babylonian kings were consecrated by name, in his sanctuary at Borsippa, of which the ruins still remain; Merodach, the tutelary god of the city, the favourite deity[1] of Nebuchadnezzar, 'the Eldest, 'the most ancient' of the divinities—trembled, as the Israelites believed, from head to foot, as the great Iconoclast approached. 'Bel bowed down and Nebo stooped, Merodach is broken in 'pieces.'[2] The High Priest might stand out long against the conquerors, and defend the venerated images at the cost of his life;[3] they could not resist the destroyer's shock; their vast size did but increase the horror, it may be said the grotesqueness, of their fall; the beasts of burden on which the broken fragments would have to be piled groaned under the expectation of the weight; the waggons which bore them away creaked under the prospect of the unwieldy freight.[4] With the fall of these greater divinities, the lesser fell also. In the more cynical form of the later traditions the frauds of the selfish Priesthood were exposed; the monster shapes of the old worship were burst asunder by the sagacity of the Jewish captive and the special favour of the Persian king.[5] But in the ancient contemporary witnesses there is no such littleness mixed with the proud exultation, which tells only how in the same general ruin all the sculptured figures came clattering down and were broken to fragments.[6]

And where was the King? The Chaldæan records describe how the Prince who had taken refuge at Borsippa was carried off captive to the mountains of Caramania. But the Jewish

[1] Rawlinson, iii. 459.

[2] Isa. xlvi. 1. Jer. l. 1, 2.

[3] Herod. i. 183.

[4] Isa xlvi. 1, 2. According to the account of the Priests whom Herodotus saw, the chief statue of Bel remained till it was destroyed by Xerxes, i. 183.

[5] Bel and the Dragon, 27.

[6] It is disappointing to find that the actual facts hardly correspond to this magnificent foreboding. The cylinder discovered in 1879 amongst the ruins of Babylon, containing Cyrus' own account of the capture of the city, puts quite another face on the event. Instead of the destroyer of Merodach and Bel and Nebo, Cyrus describes himself as their devoted servant (*Royal Asiatic Society*, January, 1880), and in point of fact the temple of Bel remained till the time of Alexander, and the statue of Bel, with it, was destroyed by Xerxes (Herodotus, i. 183). Either the prophetic anticipations were pitched too high, or the official decree was couched in the style of the Chaldæan hierarchy.

records [1] know of nothing but the king who 'in that same 'night' was slain.

> Belshazzar's grave is made,
> His kingdom passed away.
> He, in the balance weigh'd,
> Is light and worthless clay;
> The shroud, his robe of state;
> His canopy the stone.
> The Mede [2] is at his gate,
> The Persian on his throne!

That same vivid description which in the Book of Daniel tells how 'his countenance was changed, and his thoughts 'troubled him, and the joints of his loins were loosed, and his 'knees smote one against another' [3]—finds an echo or a forecast in the Book of Jeremiah [4]—'the King of Babylon hath heard 'the report, and his hands waxed feeble, and anguish took hold 'of him, and pangs as of a woman in travail.' But there was yet a loftier strain in which (it may be, first spoken [5] of the fall of Sennacherib) the captive Israelites were enjoined in the days that they should find 'rest from their sorrow and their fear and 'their hard bondage' to take up this ancient song against the king of Babylon and say: 'How hath the oppressor ceased, and 'ceased the Golden City!' They should figure to themselves the world of shades, where, as in the tombs of Egyptian Thebes, the kings of the nations are resting on their thrones each in his glory. They should imagine those dark regions stirred through all their depths at the approach of the new comer. It is not the feeble Belshazzar or the unknown Nabonadius that is thus conceived as alarming those phantoms of the mighty dead. It must be, if not Nebuchadnezzar, at least Nebuchadnezzar's spirit enshrined in his descendant, who, as 'the Last of the 'Babylonians,' seems to bear with him all the magnificence of

[1] Isa. xxi. 9. Dr. Pusey's application of Habakkuk ii. 4–20 to the fall of Babylon, as Ewald's of Isa. xxiv.–xxvii., must be regarded as uncertain.

[2] For the vexed question of 'Darius the 'Mede,' see Speaker's *Commentary*, p. 309–314.

[3] Dan. v. 6.

[4] Jer. l. 43.

[5] Isa. xiv. 4. For the probability of this 'proverb' having been first applied to Sennacherib, see Lecture XXXVIII. vol. ii. 413.

his empire. Down, down that deep descent has come his splendour, and his music with him, as in Ezekiel's vision the heroes enter the lower world with their swords of state, as in the Egyptian tombs the dead kings are surrounded with the harping and the feasting of the Palaces they have left.[1] It is the Morning[2] Star of the early dawn of the Eastern nations that has fallen from his place in the sky. It is the giant who, like those of old, would be climbing up above the clouds, above the stars, above the assembly of Heaven, on the highest heights of the mountains of the sacred North.[3] It is the oppressor who made the earth to tremble, who shook kingdoms, desolated the world, and destroyed its cities, and opened not the house of his prisoners. This was he, on whom as the shadows of the departed looked, they saw that he was become weak as one of them—this was he (and here the reference to Belshazzar becomes more apposite) who was laid in no royal sepulchre, but cast aside like a withered branch, buried under the heaps of the bleeding corpses.[4]

Ruin of the city.

And the city itself,[5] which to the Hebrew exiles appeared, like their own beloved Jerusalem, in the form of a stately Queen—the Daughter, the Incarnation, as it were, of the place itself—the Virgin, the Impregnable, Fortress,—she, too, crouches on the dust with the meanest of her slaves: in the penal labour of grinding in the mill with the lowliest of Eastern women. She has to bare her limbs, as she passes through her own streams; she is to sit silent and pass into darkness; she shall no more be called the Lady of the Kingdoms. The pride of power, the pride of science, alike are levelled; neither her astrologers nor her merchants can save her; she is become a threshing-floor—the winnowing fan shall sweep over her.

It was a crash of which the thunder resounded far and

[1] Isa. xiv. 4–11.

[2] *Ibid.* xiv. 12, 13. This, which from the Vulgate is the origin of the name of *Lucifer*, was by Tertullian and Gregory the Great applied to Satan, and from their mistake have arisen the modern Byronic title of the Evil Spirit and the modern Miltonic doctrine of the fall of the Angels.

[3] Mount Meru of India—Olympus of Greece—Elburz in Persia. See Gesenius on Isaiah ii. 316–326.

[4] Isa. xiv. 16–19.

[5] *Ibid.* xlvii. 1–5.

near. 'At the noise of the taking of Babylon the earth was 'moved as by an earthquake, and the cry was heard among the 'nations'—'a sound of a cry came from Babylon, and great 'destruction from the land of the Chaldæans.'[1] In every varying tone of exultation and awe the shout of triumph was raised. 'How is the Hammer of the whole earth rent asunder 'and broken!' 'How is Babylon become a desolation among 'the nations!' 'How is Sheshach taken! How is the praise of 'the whole earth surprised! How is Babylon become an 'astonishment among the nations!' So nearer and closer at hand the dirge went up. And yet more impressive, though with a more distant echo, was the cry of the Prophet, who, whether in the anticipations of an earlier age[2] or on the outpost of some remote fortress, waited for 'the burden of the 'desert of the sea'—the desert that surrounded the sea-like river which spread around the great city. From afar he hears the rushing of a mighty storm, like the whirlwind, the simoom of the wilderness. Then comes the war-cry of Media and Persia, which in a moment hushed, in the deep stillness of thankful expectation, the sighs of the oppressed subjects of Chaldæa. His heart thrills with the mingled delight and horror of the siege; he sympathises alternately with shuddering over the fierce onslaught of the conquerors, and with the anguish of the besieged city. At last across the desert he sees first the long array of the northern army, the lengthening columns of the prancing horse, and the fierce Persian ass, and the swift dromedary; he wearies with watching and waiting through the long nights, like the watchman in the Æschylean Tragedy, like a hungry lion snuffing the prey from afar; and at last the messengers draw nearer, and he sees distinctly the human figures approaching, and they announce: 'Babylon is fallen, is 'fallen; and all the graven images of her gods He hath broken 'upon the ground.'[3]

Babylon is fallen.—So, from mouth to mouth, the tidings flew through every Israelite community. Nor did it die then.

[1] Jer. li. 54.
[2] Isa. xxi. 1–10. Both Ewald and Gesenius regard this as previous to the capture.
[3] Isa. xxi. 4–10.

Six centuries after, when the only other empire and city which in its grandeur and significance can be compared to the ancient capital of the primæval world seemed to be drawing near to a doom no less terrible, the same word still lived in the mouth of another Jewish exile, who, on the rock of Patmos, heard and repeated again with the same thrill of exultation : 'Babylon the 'Great [1] is fallen, is fallen.'

We take breath for a moment to ask what there was of transitory and what there was of permanent instruction in this catastrophe and in these utterances of the Jewish Prophets concerning it. As the author of the Apocalypse expected that, even within his own generation, 'quickly, even so quickly,' the City on the Seven Hills would be swept away with all its abominations, and would become the habitation of demons, and the haunt of every foul spirit, and the haunt of 'every 'unclean and hateful bird,' so and yet more strongly did the Prophets of the Captivity expect and express, in the imagery which the Seer of Patmos has but repeated, that the capture of Babylon would end in its immediate and total destruction.

'It shall be no more inhabited for ever : neither shall it be 'dwelt in from generation to generation . . . . No man shall 'abide there, neither shall any man dwell therein.' [2] 'Babylon, 'the glory of kingdoms, the beauty of the Chaldees' excellency, 'shall be as when God overthrew Sodom and Gomorrah. It 'shall never be inhabited, neither shall it be dwelt in from 'generation to generation ; neither shall the Arabian pitch 'his tent there ; neither shall the shepherds pitch their folds 'there.' [3]

No such desolation in the literal sense followed on the Persian conquest. For two centuries more Babylon remained to be a flourishing city, the third in the Empire ; shorn, indeed, of its splendour, its walls reduced in height, its gates [4] removed, but still the wonder of the world, when it was seen by Grecian travellers in the next century, or when, yet later, it was on the verge of reinstatement in its metropolitan grandeur by Alexander. Then came the fatal blow struck by the erection of the Greek

[1] Rev. xviii. 2. [2] Jer. l. 39, 40. [3] Isa. xiii. 19, 20. [4] Herod. iii. 159.

city Seleucia on the Tigris; and from that time the ancient capital withered away, till, in the first century of the Christian era, it was but partially inhabited, though still retaining within its precincts a remnant of the Jewish settlers. In the fourth century it became in great measure a hunting park for the Persian Kings, but its irrigation still kept up the fertile and populous character of the district. It was not till[1] the Middle Ages, when a Jewish traveller (Benjamin of Tudela) once more visited the ruins, that it was seen in the state in which it has been ever since—a wide desert tract, interrupted only by the huge masses of indestructible brick, its canals broken, its rich vegetation gone; the habitation of the lions, the jackals, the antelopes of the surrounding desert. In detail of time and place, the predicted destruction did not literally come to pass. It was neither so early, nor so complete in all its parts, as might have been inferred, and as has been sometimes represented. But it is remarkable that, alone of the many pictures of ruin which the Prophets foreshadowed for the enemies of their country, this has, after a delay of sixteen centuries, and now for a period of seven centuries, been almost literally[2] accomplished. Damascus and Tyre, though menaced with a desolation no less complete, have never ceased to be inhabited towns, more or less frequented. Petra is again the resort of yearly visitors. It is true that even Babylon has never ceased to be inhabited. Hillah, a town with a population of five thousand souls, is within its walls, and the Arabs still wander through it. But in its general aspect the modern traveller can add nothing to the forebodings of the Hebrew Prophets. The marshes,[3] as of a sea, spread round it—'the pools for bitterns' take the place of its well-ordered canals. 'The wild beasts of 'the desert lie there; their houses are full of doleful creatures; 'ostriches dwell there; and the demons[4] that haunt the wilder-

[1] See the authorities collected in St. Croix, or Rich's Memoir.

[2] Rich, Preface, p. xlvi. So Cyril of Alexandria (Layard's *Nineveh and Babylon*, 534, 565).

[3] *Ibid.*

[4] Isa. xiii. 21, 22. It is a curious instance of the persistency of an ancient fancy that the creatures (rendered by the LXX. δαιμόνια, and by our version very properly 'satyrs') still, according to the Arab tradition, haunt the shores of the Euphrates—figures with human heads and hairy thighs and legs (Rich, 76).

'ness dance there, and the wild-cats scream in their desolate 'houses, and jackals in their pleasant palaces.'

It is a yet more signal instance of insight into the true nature of the catastrophe that, though this outward manifestation of its extreme consequences was so persistently delayed, its moral and essential character was caught from the first. Not more completely than the physical Babylon has perished by the insensible operation of natural laws, did the Imperial Babylon, the type and impersonation of the antique world, expire on the night that Belshazzar fell. In a solemn figure, indeed, she lived again in the City of the Seven Hills, as the nearest likeness which later history has seen. She lives again, in a more remote and partial sense, in the great capitals of modern civilisation. But, in all that was peculiar to herself, the Queen of the East was dead and buried. 'Babylon[1] as a 'sovereign empire was put down for ever by the Persian Con-'quest. Its influence as an active element in determining the 'fate of other nations was stopped at once. Moral and intel-'lectual results in Asia have been only or chiefly effected 'through the action of physical power. "Græcia capta ferum '"victorem cepit," is one of the peculiarities of the history of 'Europe. Babylonian science, or art, or religion became 'powerless over the world when the sceptre of Babylonian 'dominion was broken. The genius of Babylon had received 'a deadly wound—he drooped for a while and died.'

The ruin of the Empire.

But this is not the permanent or only thought left on the mind of the Jewish captives by the fall of the Old World. We know not whether already in their days there had sprung up the legend which to the pilgrim whom modern curiosity attracts to the wreck of Babylon contrasts so forcibly the vitality of that which is immortal in human history and the mutability of that which is mortal. Face to face on the plain stand two huge fragments of ruin,[2] in one of which the Arab wanderers see the Palace of Nimrod, and in the other the furnace into which Abraham was cast for denying his divinity. In like manner it was the Hebrew belief

The kingdom of Heaven.

[1] Arnold's *Sermons on Prophecy*, p. 40. [2] Layard's *Nineveh and Babylon.*

that in the last days of the Babylonian Empire the marvellous sage who had seen and interpreted those vast vicissitudes foretold, with unwavering confidence, that out of them all the God of Heaven would set up a kingdom which should never be destroyed, but which should stand for ever [1]—a dominion of the Ancient of Days, which is an 'everlasting dominion, a 'dominion which shall not pass away, and his kingdom that 'which shall not be destroyed.' [2] And to him it was said: 'Go thou thy way till the end be; for thou shalt rest and 'stand in thy lot at the end of the days.' [3] The aged Daniel was, according to the Biblical conception, the eternal and mysterious Israelite whose experience seemed to have covered the whole course of that eventful age—the Apocalyptic seer, who would revive again in the nation's utmost need, 'tarrying 'till the Lord come.'

It was the first announcement of a 'kingdom of Heaven,' that is of a power not temporal, with the rule of kings or priests, but spiritual, with the rule of mind and conscience—'cut out of 'the mountain without hands.'

And in the same tone, but still more certainly speaking the spirit of that time, was the voice which came from the Evangelical Prophet, to whom, as has been well said, the nation of Israel was an Eternal People,[4] in a far higher sense than that in which either Babylon or Rome was an Eternal City, because it contained within itself the seed of the spiritual life of mankind. That voice said 'Cry,' and he said 'What shall I cry?' 'All flesh [5] is grass, and all the goodliness thereof as the flower 'of the field; the grass withereth, the flower fadeth.' Thus far he partook in the sentiment which, in later times, has seen in the decadence of empires and churches the symptoms of the approaching dissolution of the world. But in the same moment his spirit 'disdains and survives' this despondency, and he looks forward to a remote future, in which the moral and Divine

[1] Dan. ii. 44.

[2] *Ibid.* vii. 14. These are the words which, written over the portico of the church of Damascus, once a temple, now a mosque, still significantly survive

[3] *Ibid.* xii. 13.

[4] Ewald, v. 47.

[5] Isa. xl. 6-8.

elements of the course of human affairs shall outlive all temporary shocks, and adds, with an emphasis which is the keynote of his whole prophecy, 'But the word of our God shall stand 'for ever.'

NOTE ON THE DATE OF THE BOOK OF DANIEL.

In discussing the date of any book we must carefully separate the time of the events and characters portrayed in it, whether historical or fictitious, from the time when the book itself was produced. The events of the Thirty Years' War remain unquestionably part of the history of the seventeenth century, though they have been described and coloured by the genius and the passion of Schiller, who lived more than a hundred years afterwards. The characters and state of society represented in 'Ivanhoe' belong to the twelfth century, though they are seen through the medium of the art and sentiment of the nineteenth. It is necessary to bear in mind this obvious distinction, because, in treating of the Biblical writings, it is often forgotten. The fixed idea of the ancient Jewish and Christian theologians was that every book was written, if not at the actual time of all the events related in it, at least at the time and by the pen of the chief person to whose deeds it refers—the Books of Moses by Moses, of Joshua by Joshua, of Samuel by Samuel, of Job by Job, of Esther by Mordecai. And, on the other hand, it has often been maintained by critics that it is sufficient to destroy the value or the contemporaneousness of traditions if it can be proved that they first appeared in their present form a century or two centuries later than the times which they describe. It is to be lamented that a double-edged weapon of this kind, which has long ago been laid aside in secular criticism, should still be used on either side in sacred literature. Of this the controversy respecting the Book of Daniel is a memorable example. It has been urged, both by those who arrogate to themselves the title of the defenders, and by some of those who are accounted assailants, of the book, that its whole interest would disappear if it were proved to have been composed in its present form by any one except Daniel.

There is much which still remains doubtful respecting this mysterious book. But it may be granted on all sides that, as it is now received in its larger form in the Greek and Latin versions of the Hebrew, or even in the shorter form which it bears in the Hebrew, there are traditions of unequal value, some of them unquestionably of the period of the Captivity, some of a later date, some, as Ewald and Bunsen supposed, reaching to an earlier age even than the Babylonian Empire.

This is now so generally acknowledged that it need not be argued at length. Even Lengerke, who maintained (*Das Buch Daniel*, p. xcv.) that it is entirely poetical, admits that there must have been an historical character to whom the Prophet Ezekiel refers; and many of his objections to the accuracy of the Chaldæan colouring have been answered.

But the date of the composition of the book as a whole is still much contested. It is well known that after the final reception (at whatever period) of the Book of Daniel into the Canon, the theory of its later date was advanced by Porphyry, in the third century of the Christian era, chiefly on the ground that it contains a description of historical events down to a certain period, after which its exact delineations suddenly cease. From that time till the seventeenth century the question was not stirred. The assumption prevailed everywhere, as with regard to the Books of Moses, Joshua, Samuel, that the book was written by the person whose name it bore. When the objections of Porphyry have since been from time to time started afresh, the reply has often been that they are merely Porphyry's old objections reappearing. On this rejoinder it was once remarked by a venerable scholar and divine of our day: 'They 'have always reappeared because they have never been answered.' This is substantially true, and it may be well briefly to enumerate the general grounds on which rests the concurrence of critics so authoritative and so various as Bentley, Arnold, Milman, in England, as Gesenius, Ewald, Bleek, De Wette, Kuenen, Reuss, on the Continent.

The linguistic arguments, drawn from the nature of the Hebrew or Chaldee words used, we may put aside as too minute and too doubtful to be insisted on; as also the arguments drawn from the improbabilities of the story, because they lead into too large a field of speculative argument, and also because, for the most part, they do not, properly speaking (as has been before said), affect the date of the composition of the narrative.

We may confine ourselves to those which appear on either side to have any decisive weight.

I. The arguments for the late composition of the book (*i.e.* B.C. 168–164) are partly external and partly internal.

1. The external arguments are as follows:

External Arguments.

(*a.*) It is not arranged in the Hebrew Canon with the 'Prophets,' but with the miscellaneous 'Hagiographa'[1] (the Psalms, Proverbs, Job, Ruth, Ecclesiastes, Canticles, Ezra, Nehemiah, and Chronicles), *i.e.* the part avowedly of later date and lesser authority, and constantly receiving fresh additions. See Lectures XLVII., XLVIII.

(*b.*) Daniel is not mentioned by Ezra, Nehemiah, Zechariah, Haggai, nor in the catalogue of worthies by the Son of Sirach (Ecclus. xlix. 8, 9, 10), which is the more remarkable from his mention of all the other Prophets, even including the twelve lesser Prophets. The only counterpoise to the argument from this omission is that in Ecclus. xlix. 13 Ezra is left out.

(*c.*) The Greek translation of the book is involved in obscurity. In the place of that of the LXX. was substituted, for some unknown reason ('hoc cur 'acciderit nescio,' says Jerome), a translation by Theodotion; and both are inextricably mixed up with Greek additions, which, though part of the Canon of the Eastern and of the Latin Churches, have been rejected by the Protestant Churches, and one of which (the History of Susannah) is apparently of Greek origin, as may be inferred from the play on two Greek words (Susanna 55, 59).

2. The internal arguments are as follows:

Internal Arguments.

(*a.*) The use of Greek words κιθάρα and σαμβύκη, συμφωνία and ψαλτήριον, in the Hebrew of iii. 5, 7, 10. In the case of κιθάρα the argument is strengthened by the fact that in Ezek. xxvi. 13, and Psalm cxxxvi. 2 (unquestionably of the epoch of the Captivity) the word for 'harp' is still *kinnur*.

(*b.*) The difficulty of reconciling much of the story as it

[1] This exclusion of Daniel from the 'Prophets' by the Jews was a matter of bitter complaint with Theodoret, pp. 1056, 1057.

now stands with Ezekiel's mention of Daniel as on a level with Noah and Job, and as an oracle of wisdom (xiv. 14, xxviii. 3), when, according to Dan. i. 1, he must have been a mere youth.

(*c.*) The matter-of-fact descriptions of the leagues and conflicts between the Græco-Syrian and Græco-Egyptian Kings, and of the reign of Antiochus IV., in Dan. xi. 1-45; which, if written 300 years before that time, would be without parallel or likeness in Hebrew prophecy. These descriptions are minute, with the minuteness of a contemporary chronicler, and many of their details lack any particle of moral and spiritual interest such as might account for so signal a violation (if so be) of the style of Biblical prophecy. This, accordingly, is the chief argument for fixing the date of the book at the time when these conflicts occurred—an argument which, in the case of any other book (as, for example, the 'Sibylline Oracles' or the Book of Enoch), would be conclusive.

II. On the side of the earlier date (*i.e.* B.C. 570–536) the external arguments are as follow:

(*a.*) The assertion of Josephus (*Ant.* xi. 8) that Jaddua showed to Alexander the predictions of his conquests in the Book of Daniel. But the doubt which rests over the story generally, and the acknowledged incorrectness of some of its details (see Dr. Westcott in Dictionary of the Bible ['Alexander'], and Lecture XLVII.) deprive this allusion of serious weight; and it is difficult not to suspect something of an apologetic tone in Joseph. *Ant.* x. 11, 7—'Methinks the historian doth protest too 'much.'

(*b.*) The allusion to the furnace and the lions' den in the dying speech of Mattathias, A.D. 167 (1 Macc. ii. 59, 60). But this (granting the exact accuracy of the report of the speech of Mattathias), in a book written as late as B.C. 107—therefore certainly after the publication of the book of Daniel on any hypothesis—does not testify to more than the previous existence of the traditions of these events, of which there need be no question.

PALESTINE AFTER THE RETURN

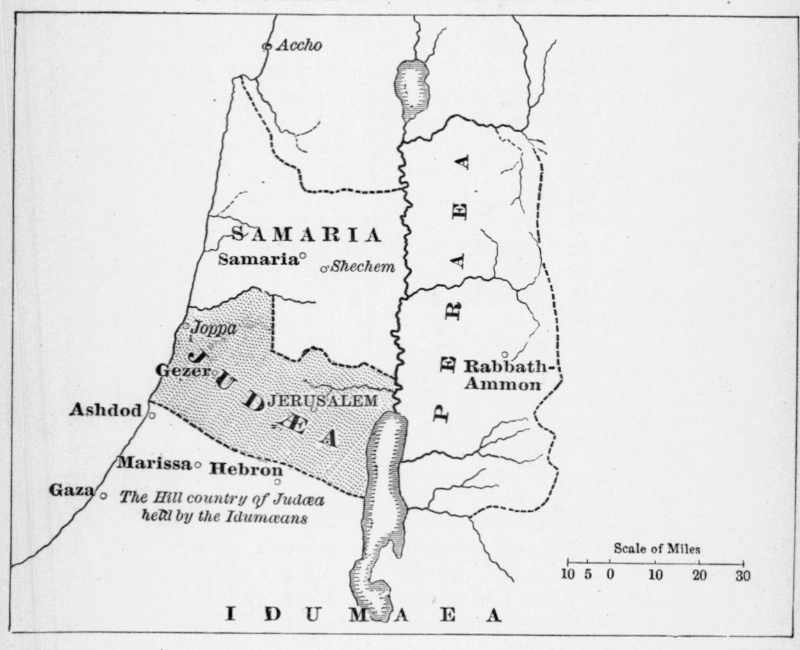

(*c*.) The reference in the Received Text of two of the Gospels to the book of 'Daniel the Prophet.' But the force of this reference is weakened by its omission [1] in the best MSS. of Mark xiii. 14, and in all the MSS. of Luke xxi. 24. And, under any circumstances, it would only prove, what is not doubted, that at the time of the Christian era the book had been received into the Canon—in Palestine, without the Greek additions; at Alexandria, with them.

The internal arguments in favour of the earlier date rest on the exactness of the references to Chaldæan usages, and of coincidence with the monumental inscriptions; and examples are given of the possibility of Greek words straying into the East before the time of Alexander. These arguments are carefully given in Dr. Pusey's Lectures on 'Daniel the Prophet' (Lecture VII.), and yet more elaborately in Mr. Fuller's notes on Daniel in the 'Speaker's Commentary.' Of the coincidences with the Babylonian monuments, the most striking is the name of Bil-shar-uzur, the probable equivalent to Belshazzar, which, before the recent discovery of this word at Babylon, was not known except from Daniel. On the other hand, Darius the Mede is still an unsolved enigma. But if we accept (with most of the critics who have advocated the later date) the existence of Babylonian traditions or even documents incorporated in the book, this exactness of allusion, whilst it adds to the interest of the work, and removes an argument sometimes used for its Maccabæan origin, does not prove its early composition, any more than the use of unquestionably ancient traditions and narratives precludes the unquestionably Macedonian date (see Lecture XLVII.) of the Books of Chronicles.

The result is, therefore, that the arguments incline largely to the side of the later date; and this result is strengthened by the consideration (1) that though something may be said to attenuate the force of each argument singly, yet each derives additional weight from the collective weight of all; and (2) that the objections raised to some of them evade almost or altogether the most conclusive, no parallel instance having been adduced from the Hebrew Scriptures to the details of the eleventh chapter, nor any explanation of such an exception from the general style of Biblical Prophecy.

[1] In Dean Alford's edition of the Greek Testament, the name of Daniel is said to be omitted in the Philoxenian version of Matt. xxiv. 15; but this is an error.

Accordingly, the course followed in these Lectures has been, on the one hand, to give the incidents relating to the Captivity, whether in the Greek or Hebrew or Chaldee parts of Daniel, in connexion with the scenes to which they refer, indicating that the authority on which they rest is inferior to that of the unquestionably contemporary prophets and historians; and, on the other hand, to reserve those parts which handle the Macedonian history to the period to which they belong, and in which, probably, they were written.[1]

[1] See the arguments put in a clear form and brief compass in *Notes on the Defence of the Book of Daniel*, by a Clergyman.

THE PERSIAN DOMINION.

CYRUS, B.C. 560.
Fall of Babylon, B.C. 538.
The Return, B.C. 536.
CAMBYSES, B.C. 529.
DARIUS I., B.C. 522.
Completion of the Temple, B.C. 516.
XERXES, B.C. 485.
Story of Esther, B.C. 480—490?
ARTAXERXES, B.C. 465.
Coming of Ezra, B.C. 459.
Coming of Nehemiah, B.C. 415.
Secession of Manasseh, B.C. 419.
Malachi, B.C. 400?

LECTURE XLIII.

THE RETURN.

SPECIAL AUTHORITIES.

(1) Isaiah xl.-lxvi.
(2) Ezra i.-vi.
(3) Psalms cvii.-cl., cxxxiv.
(4) Haggai.
(5) Zechariah i.-viii.

TRADITIONS.

1 Esdras ii.-vii.
Jos. *Ant.* xi. 1 4.
Seder Olam, p. 107, 108 (with comments of Derenbourg, *Histoire de la Palestine*, pp. 19, 20, 21.)

THE PERSIAN DOMINION.

LECTURE XLIII.

THE RETURN.

THE Return from the Captivity opens the final era of the history of the Jewish Church and Nation. That any nation should have survived such a dislocation and dissolution of all local and social bonds is almost without example. But as in the case of the Greek race centuries of foreign dominion have been unable to eradicate the memory of their distant glory, so the transplantation of the Israelites to another country was unable to efface the religious [1] aspiration which was the bond of their national coherence. The [2] other Semitic tribes, Moab, Ammon, Edom, felt that with the loss of their home they would lose all. Israel alone survived the shock.

The Restoration was an event which, unlikely and remote as it might have seemed, was deemed almost a certainty in the expectations of the exiles. Jeremiah and Ezekiel never lost their confidence that within two generations from the beginning of the Captivity their countrymen would return. The patriotic sentiment, which had existed as it were unconsciously before, found its first definite expression at this period. The keen sense as of personal anguish at the overthrow of Jerusalem

[1] See Milman, *History of the Jews*, i. 404, 405.

[2] Jer. xlviii. 11. See the interesting remarks upon the passage by Mr. Grove in the *Dictionary of the Bible*, ii. 397, 398.

poured forth in the Lamentations—the touching[1] cry, 'If I 'forget thee, O Jerusalem, may my right hand forget herself' —the clinging[2] to the remembrance of the very dust and stones of Jerusalem—the face in prayer directed towards Jerusalem, the earnest supplication[3] for the Holy Nation and the Holy City, kept alive the flame which from this time never died till it was extinguished under the ruins of their country in the final overthrow by Titus. And when the day at last arrived which was to see their expectations fulfilled, the burst of joy was such as has no parallel in the sacred volume; it is indeed the Revival, the Second Birth, the Second Exodus of the nation. There was now 'a new song,' of which the burden was that the Eternal[4] again reigned over the earth, and that the gigantic idolatries which surrounded them had received a deadly[5] shock: that[6] the waters of oppression had rolled back in which they had been struggling like drowning men; that the snare[7] was broken in which they had been entangled like a caged bird. It was like a dream,[8] too good to be true. The gaiety, the laughter of their poetry, resounded far and wide. The surrounding nations could not but confess what great things had been done for them.[9] It was like the sudden rush of the waters into the dry torrent-beds of the south of Palestine, or of the yet extremer south, of which they may have heard, in far Ethiopia.[10] It was like the reaper bearing on his shoulder the golden sheaves in summer which he had sown amongst the tears of winter. So full were their hearts, that all nature was called to join in their thankfulness. The[11] vast rivers of their new Mesopotamian home, and the waves of the Indian Ocean, are to take part in the chorus, and clap their foaming crests like living hands. The mountains of their own native land are invited to express their joy; each tree[12] in the forests that clothed the hills, or that

The joy of the Return.

The Psalms.

[1] Psalm cxxxvii. 5 (Heb.).
[2] *Ibid.* cii. 14.
[3] Dan. vi. 10; ix. 16-19.
[4] *Ibid.* xcvi. 1, 4, 5; xcvii. 1; xcix. 1.
[5] *Ibid.* xcvii. 7; xcix. 8.
[6] *Ibid.* cxxiv. 4.
[7] *Ibid.* cxxiv. 7.
[8] *Ibid.* cxxvi. 1.
[9] *Ibid.* cxxvi. 2.
[10] *Ibid.* cxxvi. 4. Comp. Sir S. Baker's description of the flooding of the dry bed of the Atbara.
[11] *Ibid.* xcviii. 7, 8.
[12] *Ibid.* xcvi 12.

cast their shade over the field, is to have a tongue for the occasion.

In accordance with these strains of the Psalmists there was the Prophetic announcement of the beginning of the new epoch in words which, whilst they vibrate with a force beyond their own time, derive their original strength from the circumstances of their first utterance, and which gave to their unknown author, who thus 'comforted[1] 'them that mourned in Sion,' the name of 'the Prophet of 'glad tidings.' 'Comfort[2] ye, comfort ye my people, saith 'your God. Speak unto Jerusalem that her warfare is accom-'plished, that her iniquity is pardoned, for she hath received 'at God's hand the double for all her woe.' 'A voice cries, 'Through the wilderness prepare the way of the Eternal, make 'smooth in the desert a highway for our God. Every valley 'shall be exalted, every mountain and hill shall be made low, 'and the crooked shall be made straight, and the rough places 'plain, and the glory of the Eternal shall be revealed, and all 'flesh shall see it together, for the mouth of the Eternal hath 'spoken it.'

The Evangelical Prophet.

That opening strain of the Prophet, so full of the great Evangelical truth—Evangelical in its literal sense and true to the depths of human nature—that nations and individuals alike can leave their past behind them, and start afresh in the race of duty; so impressive from its peculiar historical significance as the keynote of the new period of Asiatic and European[3] history; so striking in the imagery with which it figures that Divine progress—demanding for its approach and preparation the reduction of pride, the exaltation of humility, the simplification of the tortuous, the softening of the angular and harsh—was heard in part once again when long afterwards in the wild[4] thickets of the Jordan a voice was raised

[1] Ecclesiasticus xlviii. 24.

[2] Isa. xl. 1. (Heb.)

[3] See Lectures XL., XLII.

[4] Matt. iii. 3; Mark i. 3. In this application of Isaiah xl. 3, the words 'in the 'wilderness' have been separated from their proper context; and also the word which properly describes the Mesopotamian desert has been transferred to the wild country of the Jordan. The grand prelude of this new prophecy has suffered a singular eclipse. Its words escaped citation in the New Testament. In later times the whole passage has been entirely

inaugurating another new epoch, and preparing the way for another vaster revolution in nations and in churches. But nevertheless the whole expression of the exhortation breathes the atmosphere of the moment[1] when it was first delivered. The sense of the expected deliverance at last come—the heart of an oppressed people again breathing freely—the long prospect of the journey yet before them, through the trackless desert—are all irradiated with the hope that no wilderness would be too arid, no hills too high, no ravine[2] too deep for the Divine Providence to surmount.

Another utterance of the same Prophet is still more directly fitted to the emergency of his own time, though still more sacredly associated with the mighty future. 'The 'Spirit of the Lord God rests upon me, because the Eternal 'hath anointed me to preach good tidings unto the suffering, 'He hath sent me to bind up the broken-hearted, to proclaim 'liberty to the captives, and the opening of the prison to them 'that are bound; to proclaim the acceptable year of the 'Eternal.'

It was five centuries onwards that in the synagogue of a hitherto unknown Jewish village the scroll which contained the writings which by that time were all comprised under the one name of the Prophet Isaiah was handed to a young Teacher,[3] who unfolded the roll and found the place where it was thus written. He closed the book at the point where the special application to the Israelite exiles began. He fixed the attention of His audience only on these larger words which enabled Him to say to all those whose eyes were fastened on His gracious countenance, 'This day is this 'Scripture fulfilled in your ears.'

B.C. 536.

But the original fulfilment of the consolation was that

omitted in the public services of the Latin Church, and only used on incidental occasions in the Greek Church. In the Sunday services of the Church of England this splendid chapter was almost pointedly excluded till the revision of the English Calendar of Lessons in 1872. It is to its selection as the opening of Handel's Messiah' that it owes its proper position before Christendom. See Lecture XL.

[1] In Jos. *Ant.* xi. 1 these prophecies under the name of Isaiah are substituted for those of Jeremiah given in the earlier account of Ezra i. 1.

[2] The word for 'valley' in Isa xl. 4, is 'ravine.'

[3] Luke iv. 16-21.

contemplated by the Prophet who saw before him the exiles depart in their holiday attire for their homeward journey; destined to strike root again like the sturdy ilex of their native country, and carry on the righteous work for which alone home and freedom are worth possessing. His mission was 'to comfort all that mourn, to appoint unto them that 'mourn in Zion, to give them beauty for ashes, the oil of 'joy for mourning, the garment of praise for the spirit of 'heaviness, that they might be called the terebinths of 'righteousness, the planting of the Eternal, that He might 'be glorified.'

Such is the ideal of the Return: nor is it unworthy of the mighty issues which ultimately hung on that event. Although the actual event seems small and homely, yet that very homeliness indicates one of the main characteristics of the epoch on which we have entered. Unlike the first Exodus, this second Exodus was effected not by any sudden effort of the nation itself, nor by any interposition of signs and wonders, but by the complex order of Providence, in which the Prophet thus bids his people see an intervention no less Divine than that which had released them from Egypt. 'Wheel within [1] wheel' was the intricate machinery which Ezekiel had seen in his visions on the Chebar; but not the less was a spirit as of a living creature within the wheels. The document that inaugurates the new [2] era is not the word of Jewish lawgiver or prophet or priest, but the decree of a heathen king. 'Now 'in the first year of Cyrus king of Persia, that the word of 'Jehovah by Jeremiah might be fulfilled, Jehovah stirred up 'the spirit of Cyrus king of Persia, that he made a proclama-'tion throughout all his kingdom and put in writing.'

Connected with the natural order of events.

Decree of Cyrus.

It is difficult not to suppose that the language of the decree is coloured by the Hebrew medium through which it passes, but in tone and spirit it resembles those which have been

[1] Ezek. i. 20.

[2] The emphatic solemnity of the decree is confirmed by its repetition no less than three times, in Ezra i. 1-4; 2 Chron. xxxvi. 22, 23; 1 Esdras ii. 3-7.

found inscribed on the Persian monuments ; and, if Ormuzd be substituted for Jehovah, and 'the Creator[1] of the earth, 'the heavens, and mankind,' for the single form of 'the 'Creator of earth,' there is nothing impossible in the thought that we have the very words of the decree itself. But at any rate it stands as the guiding cause of the liberation, and stamps itself as the turning-point of the whole subsequent history. Before this time the people of Israel had been an independent nation ; from this moment it is merged in the fortunes of the great Gentile Empires. There are three successive periods through which it has to pass, and each will derive its outward form and pressure from an external power. Of these the first is the Persian. Cyrus, Darius, Xerxes, and Artaxerxes were henceforth for two hundred years to exercise the influence which in earlier times had been exercised by the Princes and Kings of Israel. The year henceforward is dated from the accession of the Persian Kings as afterwards of the Rulers of Antioch and of Rome.

We shall hereafter trace some direct effects of this connexion on the religious condition of the people. It is enough for the present to remark that the community which returned under these circumstances was no longer a sovereign people, a nation in the full sense of that word. Thenceforth it had to eke out the inestimable element of independent nationality by its connexion with the powerful monarchies with which it was brought into contact. But this very change was transfigured in the language of the great contemporary Prophet into the vision which has never since died out of the hopes of mankind. He foresaw that the wide course of human history, the mighty powers of the earth, instead of standing, as hitherto, apart from the course of religion and progress, would combine with that hitherto isolated movement. 'Arise,[2] shine, for thy light is 'come, and the glory of the Eternal is risen upon thee. The 'nations shall come to thy light, and kings to the brightness of 'thy rising. Thou shalt suck the milk of the nations, and shalt

[1] Ewald v. 48. The Persian form is slightly varied in Isa. xlii. 5 ; xliv. 24.

[2] Isa. lx. 1, 3, 16

'suck the breast of kings.' Kings [1] shall be thy nursing fathers 'and queens thy nursing mothers.' 'The nations shall see thy 'righteousness and all kings thy [2] glory.'

Doubtless the real fell far short of the ideal, as in the actual Return, so in the actual Cyrus.[3] But the fact which enkindled those hopes, and those hopes themselves, have lent a framework to the noblest aspirations of humanity: they are the same as Plato expressed in the well-known saying, that the world would not be happy till either philosophers became kings, or kings became philosophers—the same as the last seer of the Jewish race expressed in the cry. 'The [4] kingdoms of this world 'are become the kingdoms of the Lord and of his Anointed.'

The partial character of the Return.

It is evident that the return was not that of the whole of the exiles. Those who had been transplanted from the north of Palestine in the Assyrian captivity never returned at all, or only in small numbers. Those who had been transported to Babylon and became settlers, as we have seen, in those rich plains and in that splendid city, were many of them contented to remain—some holding high places in the Persian court, though still keeping up communication with their brethren in Palestine, some permanently becoming the members of that great Babylonian colony of Jews which caused [5] Mesopotamia to become as it were a second Holy Land, and round which were planted the tombs, real or supposed, of the three great Jewish saints of this epoch, Ezekiel, Daniel, and one who is yet to come, Ezra.

The caravan.

Still, there were some both of the highest and the lowest of the settlement who listened to the call alike of their inspiring Prophet and of their beneficent Ruler; and we can discern the chief elements [6] which constituted the seed of the rising community. The whole caravan consisted of 42,000; besides this were 7,337 slaves, 200 of whom were minstrels, male and female. We recognise at once some con-

[1] Isa. xlix. 23.
[2] *Ibid.* lxii. 2.
[3] See Ewald v. 29.
[4] Revelation xi. 15.
[5] See Lectures XXXIV., XLI.
[6] For the inferior elements mixed up in the return see the tradition of the Targums in Deutsch on the Targums (*Remains*, p. 321), 'foundlings, proselytes, and 'illegitimate children.' 'The flour,' it was said, 'remained at Babylon, the chaff 'came to Palestine.'

spicuous and familiar names. Twelve[1] chiefs, as if in reminiscence of the twelve tribes, were marked out as the leaders. Amongst these was the acknowledged head of the community, the grandson, real or adopted, of the beloved and lamented Jehoiachin, last direct heir of the House of David and Josiah —the son of Shealtiel or Salathiel, who bore the trace of his Babylonian birthplace in his two Chaldæan names, Zerubbabel 'the Babel-born,' or Sheshbazzar, or Sarabazzar,[2] and who, by his official titles, was marked out as the representative amongst them of the Persian king, 'the[3] Tirshatha,' or 'the Pasha,' that old Assyrian word which has never since died out amongst the governments of the East. Next to him was Jeshua or Joshua, the son of Josedek, the High Priest who had been carried into exile with Zedekiah, and shared his imprisonment. Next to them in rank and elder in years was Seraiah the priest, son of Hilkiah.[4] But of the ancient four-and-twenty sacerdotal courses, four only joined in the procession; it may be from the havoc of the priestly caste in the desperate struggle at the time of the capture of the Temple; it may be from the attachment of the others to their Babylonian homes. Still the number of priests (4,000) was large in proportion to the people, yet larger in proportion to the Levites, who numbered only 74 besides the 128 singers of the family of Asaph, and the 139[5] descendants of those stalwart gatekeepers, the sacerdotal soldiery or police, that had guarded the whole circuit of the Temple walls, and were believed to have rendered the state such important service on the day that Jehoiada[6] planned the overthrow of Athaliah.[7] Along with them were the 392 representatives of the ancient Canaanite bondmen, whose ancestral names indicated their foreign origin, the Nethinim,[8] or 'consecrated 'giftsmen' bound over to the honoured work of the Temple service—or 'the children of Solomon's slaves'—that is,

[1] Ezra ii. 2; Neh. vii. 7; Ewald v. 86.
[2] Ezra i. 8, 11; v. 14, 16.
[3] *Ibid.* ii. 63; Nehem. vii. 65, 70; Haggai i. 1 and 14; ii. 2, 21; Ezra vi. 7. (See Gesenius *in voce.*)
[4] Compare Neh. xi. 11 with Ezra ii. 2.
[5] Ezra ii. 41-42; Neh. vii. 43-45; 1 Chron. ix. 17-21.
[6] According to 2 Chron. xxiii. 2, 4, 5.
[7] See Lecture XXXV.
[8] See 'Nethinim' in *Dict. of Bible.*

doubtless, of those Phœnician artists whom the great king had employed in the construction of his splendid works.

So the names stood in a register[1] which a century afterwards was found by an inquiring antiquary in the Archives of Jerusalem, and its accuracy was tested by the additional record that there was a rigid scrutiny on the departure from Babylon to exclude from this favoured community those who could not prove their descent. Such was a body of unknown applicants from the villages in the jungles or salt marshes near the Persian Gulf.[2] Such was another band, claiming to be of priestly origin, and justifying their pretensions, but in vain, by appealing to an ancestor who had married a daughter and taken the name of the renowned old Gileadite chief Barzillai.[3]

In the front or centre of this caravan, borne probably by the Nethinim—in place of the Ark that had formed the rallying point of the earlier wanderings—were the carefully collected vessels of the Temple, the Palladium to which the hopes of the nation had been attached, which had been the badges of contention between Jeremiah and his opponents before the Captivity; which had been carried off in triumph by Nebuchadnezzar and lodged in the most magnificent of all receptacles, the Temple of Bel; which had adorned the banquet of Belshazzar; and which now, by special permission of Cyrus,[4] were taken out of the Babylonian treasury, according, as one tradition said, to a special vow made by the King in his earlier days.[5] There they were borne aloft. Each article of plate was carefully named in lists three times recorded, the thousand cups of original gold, the thousand cups of silver, which marked the double stage of the Captivity, with all the lesser vessels, even the nine and twenty knives,[6] amounting in all, as was carefully noted, to 5,499.

It was like the procession of the Vestal Virgins, with the sacred fire in their hands, in their passage between Rome and

[1] Neh. vii. 6-73; Ezra ii. 1-70; 1 Esdras v. 1-46; comp. 1 Chron. ix. 1-34.

[2] Ezra ii. 59.

[3] *Ibid.* ii. 59-61; Neh. vii. 61, 62; and the confused text of 1 Esdras v. 36-38.

[4] Ezra i. 7; vi. 5; 2 Chron. xxxvi. 10; Jer. xxvii. 16-22; xxviii. 2, 3; Dan. v. See Lectures XL., XLI., XLII.

[5] 1 Esdras v. 44.

[6] Ezra i. 9.

Veii; like Æneas with his household gods from Troy. Homely as they were, grates, knives, spoons, basins, recalling alike the glory of the time of Solomon in their original gold, the decline of the last days of Jerusalem in the silver substitutes of Zedekiah, they were the links which seemed to weave a continuous chain across the gulf which parted the old and the new era of Israelite history.

Forth from the gates of Babylon they rode on camels, mules, asses, and (now for the first time in their history) on horses, to the sound of joyous music—a band of horsemen [1] playing on flutes and tabrets, accompanied by their own two hundred minstrel slaves, and one hundred and twenty-eight singers of the temple,[2] responding to the Prophet's voice, as they quitted the shade of the gigantic walls and found themselves in the open plains beyond. 'Go [3] ye out of Babylon. 'Flee from the Chaldæans, with a voice of singing declare ye, 'tell this, utter it even to the end of the earth; say ye, The 'Eternal hath redeemed His servant Jacob.'

The prospect of crossing that vast desert, which intervened between Chaldæa and Palestine, was one which had filled the minds of the exiles with all manner of terrors. It seemed like a second wandering in the desert of Sinai. It was a journey of nearly four [4] months at the slow rate at which such caravans then travelled. Unlike the wilderness of Sinai, it was diversified by no towering mountains, no delicious palm groves, no gushing springs. From the moment they left the banks of the Euphrates till they reached the northern extremity of Syria, they were on a hard gravel plain, with no solace except the occasional wells [5] and walled stations; or, if their passage was in the spring, the natural herbage and flowers which clothed the arid soil. Ferocious hordes of Bedouin [6] robbers then, as now, swept the whole tract.

This dreary prospect preoccupied with overwhelming prominence the Evangelical Prophet. But he would not hear of

[1] 1 Esdras v. 1–8 transfers to Darius what belongs to Cyrus.

[2] Ezra ii. 41–65.

[3] Isa. xlviii. 20, 21.

[4] Ezra vii. 8, 9. The journey now takes ordinarily about two months.

[5] Layard, *Nineveh and Babylon*, 535.

[6] Ezra viii. 31.

fear. It was in his visions not a perilous enterprise but a march of triumph: 'Therefore the redeemed of the Eternal shall 'return, and come with singing unto Zion, and everlasting joy 'shall be upon their heads; they shall obtain gladness and joy 'and sorrow and mourning shall flee away.' As before some Royal potentate, there would go before them an invisible Protector, who should remove the hard stones from the bare feet of those that ran beside the camels, and cast them up in piles on either side to mark the broad track seen for long miles across the desert. It should be as if Moses were again at their head, and the wonders of the Red[1] Sea and Sinai re-enacted. The heat of the scorching sun shall be softened; they shall be led to every spring and pool of water;[2] if water is not there, their invisible Guide shall, as of old, bring it out of the cloven rock. Even the wild animals of the desert,[3] the ostrich and the jackal, shall be startled at its unexpected[4] rush. Even the isles of palms which cheered the ancient Israelites in Arabia shall not be sufficient. Cedar as well as acacia, olive and myrtle, pine and cypress, all that is most unlike to the vegetation of the desert shall spring up along these fountains.

It is a curious instance of the prosaic temper which has led many modern commentators to expect a literal fulfilment of the poetic expressions of the Hebrew Prophets, that the Jewish rabbis of later times suppose all these wonders to have actually occurred, and were surprised to find no mention of them in the narrative of the contemporary[5] chronicler. But the spirit of these high-wrought strains is the same as that expressed in the simpler language yet similar faith of the songs of the 'ascents,' some of which we can hardly doubt to have been chanted by the minstrels of the caravan during their long ascending journey up the weary slope which reached from the level plains of Babylon to their own rocky fortress of Judæa. They lifted up their eyes to the distant mountains of Syria, and when they thought of the long interval yet to traverse they asked whence

[1] Isa. li. 10; lxiii. 11.
[2] *Ibid.* xli. 18; xlviii. 20, 21; xliv. 3; xlix. 10.
[3] *Ibid.* xliii. 20.
[4] *Ibid.* xli. 18, 19.
[5] Kimchi, quoted by Gesenius on Isa. xlviii. 20–21.

was to come their help? Their answer was, that they looked to the eternal, unsleeping watchfulness of the Guardian of Israel, who should guard them by night and day, stand as their shade on their southern side against the noonday sun, and at last guard their entrance into Palestine, as He had guarded their Exodus from Babylon.[1]

The high, snowclad ridge of Hermon would be the first object that at the distance of four or five days' journey would rise on the uniform horizon of the exiles. We know not whether they would enter Syria at the nearer point of Damascus or at the further point (but, as it would appear, the usual route at that time) of Hamath or Riblah.[2]

Even then there would still be a long journey of hill and vale to traverse before they reached their home. But, already (so we gather from the shouts of joy with which the Prophet anticipated this happy moment), the dead city would be roused up from her slumber of seventy years. The sleeping potion of the Divine wrath has been drunk to the dregs—she is to shake off the dust[3] of the ruins amongst which she has lain—she is to break the chain which fastened her neck down to the ground. She is to listen for the joyful signal of the messengers[4] stationed on the eastern hills, who will descry the exiles from afar and hand on the good tidings from hill to hill, like beacon flames, till at last it reaches the height of Olivet, or of Ramah; where Zion herself stands on tiptoe to catch the news, and, like the maidens of old who welcomed the returning heroes, proclaim to the cities of Judah, each on their crested hills around her, that the Divine Presence is at hand; that the little flock has been guided through the wilderness safely; even the weary laggards are cared for, even the lambs are folded in the shepherd's bosom, even the failing ewes are gently helped onwards.[5]

[1] Psalm cxx.—cxxxiv., especially Psalm cxxi. 1-8.

[2] 2 Kings xxv. 6, 20, 21; xxiii. 33. The route which I have described appears both from the ancient and modern practice to have been the one that must have been taken. 'The only traveller that is known 'to have taken the direct track in ancient 'times was Nebuchadnezzar, who, on 'hearing of his father's death, struck 'straight across the desert from Palestine 'to Babylon.' Berosus, in Jos. *Ant.* x. 11, 1 (Upham, p. 31).

[3] Isa. lii. 1, 2, 7, 8.

[4] For the custom of these telegraphic beacon fires see Jer. vi. 1; Raphall's *History of the Jews*, ii. 70.

[5] Isa. xl. 9-11.

It is not difficult to figure to ourselves the general aspect of Palestine on the Return. Monarchy, priesthood, art, and commerce had departed, but a large population had been left, partly of the aboriginal tribes, partly of the humbler classes of Israel, to till the ground. There was the Persian governor, perhaps more than one, who controlled the whole.[1] The central portion was occupied, as we have seen, by mixed settlers from the East, who combined with the original[2] habitants to compose the people, alternately called, from their twofold origin, Cutheans or Samaritans. The Scythians still remained in possession of the Canaanite stronghold of Bethshan—the centre, at that time, of the borderland between Israel and the heathen nations, already forming itself under the Monarchy, but now becoming more and more defined, and gradually taking itself the name, which was at last in fame to eclipse that of any other division of Palestine—Galilee of the Gentiles, or Galilee, 'the Heathen-march,' or 'the March.'[3]

Appearance of Palestine.

In the Transjordanic territory, although the country of Moab and Ammon had been frightfully devastated[4] by the Chaldæan invasion, the inhabitants had been allowed to remain in their homes, and their chiefs[5] occupied independent and powerful positions.

The western coast was occupied by the old enemies of Israel, the Philistines, now reasserting their independence, and in their chief city, Ashdod, still speaking their own language[6]—still worshipping their ancient sea-god Dagon.

The south was overrun by the vindictive and ungenerous race of Edom, which even claimed[7] the whole country as its own, with the capital of Akrabbim.

There only remained, therefore, for the new comers the small, central strip of the country round Jerusalem occupied by the tribes of Judah and Benjamin. From these two tribes the larger part of the exiles were descendants, and to this, their ancient home, they returned. Henceforth the name of Judah

[1] Ezra iv. 11, v. 3.
[2] See Lecture XXXIV.
[3] Ewald, v. 98.
[4] Jer. xxvii. 3, 6; xxviii. 14; xlviii. 11.
[5] Neh. ii. 10; iv. 7. Josephus, *Ant.* xiii. 8, 1.
[6] Neh. iv. 7; xiii. 24; 1 Macc. x. 84.
[7] Ewald, v. 81. 1 Macc. iv. 29; v. 3.

took the predominant place in the national titles. As the primitive name of 'Hebrew' had given way to the historical name of Israel, so that of Israel now gave way to the name of *Judæan*, or *Jew*, so full of praise and pride, of reproach and scorn. 'It was born,' as their later historian [1] truly observes, 'on the day when they came 'out from Babylon,' and their history thenceforth is the history not of Israel but of Judaism.

The name of 'Judæan' or 'Jew.'

We trace the settlers of those rocky fastnesses, returning, each like a bird to its nest, after the migration of winter. Each hill-fort, so well known in the wars of Saul and David, in the approaches of Sennacherib,[2] once more leaps into view; Gibeon, and Ramah, and Geba, and the pass of Michmash, and the slope of Anathoth, and the long descent of Bethel and Ai, and the waving palms of Jericho, and the crested height of Bethlehem, and the ancient stronghold of Kirjath-jearim,[3] all received back their 'men,' their 'children,' after their long separation. Some gradually crept further south through the now Idumæan territory to the villages round Hebron, to which the old Canaanite possessors once more had given its ancient name of 'Kirjath-arba.'[4] Some stole along the plains of the south coast down to the half-Bedouin settlements of Beersheba and Molada on the frontier of the desert. The bands of singers established themselves in the neighbourhood of Jerusalem, at Geba, or at Gilgal, in the Jordan valley.

But these all, as it were, clustered round Jerusalem, which now for the first time in history assumes the name never since lost, and which in the East still remains its only title, 'The Holy [5] City,' and, if the country at large also takes for the first time in the mouths of the returning exiles the name which has clung to it with hardly less tenacity, 'The 'Holy [6] Land,' it is as the seat and throne of the consecrated capital, which, though fallen from its antique splendour, reigned supreme, as never before, over the affections and the reverence

Jerusalem.

[1] Jos. *Ant.* xi. 5, 7.
[2] Neh. vii. 25-30.
[3] Ezra ii. 23, 25, 28, 34.
[4] Neh. xi. 25 (see Mr. Grove on *Kirjath Arba* in *Dict. of Bible*).
[5] Isa. xlviii. 2; lii. 1; lvi. 7; lxiv. 10. *El Khods* in Arabic.
[6] Zech. ii. 12 (Ewald, v. 60).

of the people. When Herodotus in the next century passed by it he knew it only by this name, 'The Holy Place,' *Kadesh*, Grecised[1] into *Kadytis*. When, three centuries later, Strabo saw it again, though the name of Jerusalem had been recognized, it was transformed into *Hierosolyma*,[2] the Holy Place of Salem or Solomon,[3] and he felt that it properly expressed the awe and veneration[4] with which he regarded it, as though it had been one of the oracular seats of his own religion.

All the other shrines and capitals of Israel, with the single exception of that on Mount Gerizim, had been swept away. The sanctity of Bethel and Shiloh, the regal dignity of Samaria and Jezreel, had now disappeared for ever. Jerusalem remained the undisputed queen of the whole country in an unprecedented sense. Even those very tribes which before had been her rivals, acknowledged in her misfortunes the supremacy which they had denied to her in her prosperity. Pilgrims from Shechem, Shiloh, and Samaria, immediately after the Babylonian Captivity began, came, with every outward sign of[5] mourning, to wail and weep (like the Jews of our own day) over the still smoking ruins.

It was natural, therefore, that the exiles constantly nourished the hope of the rebuilding of Jerusalem, which they had never forgotten in their brightest or their darkest days on the banks of the Euphrates;[6] that the highest reward to which any of them could look forward would be that they should build the old waste[7] places, raise up the foundations of many generations, be called the repairer of the ruins, the restorer of paths to dwell in. It was natural that along the broken walls of the city of David there should have been, as the Return drew nearer, devout Israelites seen standing like sentinels, repeating their constant watchwords, which consisted of an incessant cry day and night, giving the Divine Protector no rest until He establish and make Jerusalem a praise upon the earth.[8] It was natural

[1] Herod. iii. 5. It may possibly be Gaza; but Jerusalem is the most probable.

[2] Philo calls it *Hieropolis*.

[3] Eus. *Præp. Ev.* ix. 34.

[4] Strabo, xvi. 10, 37.

[5] Jer. xli. 5-8 (Ewald, v. 97); see Lecture XL.

[6] Psalm cxxxvii. 1, 5; see Lecture XLI.

[7] Isa. lviii. 12; lxi. 4.

[8] *Ibid.* lxii. 6, 7.

that the name which had begun to attach to her during her desertion, as though she were the impersonation of Solitude and Desolation, should give place to the joyful names[1] of the Bride and the Favourite returning to her married home with all the gaiety and hopefulness of an Eastern wedding. It was natural that Ezekiel by the banks of the Chebar should so concentrate his thoughts on the City and Temple of Jerusalem that their dimensions grew in his visions to such a colossal size as to absorb the whole of Palestine by their physical structure, no less than they did actually by their moral significance.

Accordingly, the one object which filled the thoughts of the returning exiles, the one object, as it was believed by them, for which the Return had been permitted by the Persian king, was 'the building of an house of the Lord God of Israel 'at Jerusalem which is in Judah.'

The consecration of the new altar.

There was a moment, it might have been supposed, when the idea of a more spiritual worship, like that of the Persians, would dispense altogether with outward buildings. 'The heaven is my throne, the earth is my footstool: where 'is the house that ye build unto me? and where is the place 'of my rest?'[2] But this doctrine of the Evangelical Prophet was not yet capable of being put into practice; perhaps in its literal sense never will be. Ezekiel's ideal was, as we have seen, rather the restoration of the Temple on a gigantic scale. It was the chief, the one mission of Zerubbabel, and in a few weeks or months after his arrival the first step was taken towards the erection of the second Temple of Jerusalem, the Temple which was destined to meet the requirements of the national worship, till it gave way to the third Temple of the half-heathen Herod. That first step was precisely on the traces of the older Temple. As the altar which David erected long preceded the completion of the splendid structure of Solomon, so before any attempt was made to erect the walls, or even to lay the foundations of the Temple of the coming era, there was erected on the platform formerly occupied[3] by the threshing-floor of Araunah, then for five centuries by the stately

[1] Isa. lxii. 4, 5; liv. 1–7. Beulah and Hephzibah. [2] Isa. lxvi. 1. [3] Ezra. iii. 3.

altar of David and his son Solomon, the central hearth of the future Temple ; but, as if to vindicate for itself an intrinsic majesty despite of its mean surroundings, it was in its dimensions double the size even of its vast predecessor. The day fixed for the occasion of its consecration was well suited to do it honour. It was the opening of the great autumnal Feast of the Jewish year—the Feast of Tabernacles—the same festival as that chosen by Solomon for the dedication of his Temple, and by Jeroboam for the dedication of the rival sanctuary at Bethel.[1] It was the first day of the seventh month, which, according to the Babylonian, now adopted as the Jewish, calendar, henceforth took the Chaldæan name of Tisri, 'the opening' month, the 'January,' and thus became the first [2] of the year.

B.C. 536, October.

The settlers from all parts of the country, as well as the aboriginal inhabitants, gathered for the occasion and witnessed the solemnity from the open space in front of the eastern gate of the Temple.[3]

That day accordingly was fitly the birthday of the new city. Henceforth there were once more seen ascending to the sky the columns of smoke, morning and evening, from the daily sacrifices—the sign at once of human habitation and of religious worship in the long-deserted capital. Now that the central point was secured, the impulse to the work went on. The contributions which the exiles themselves had made—the offerings, as it would appear, from some of the surrounding tribes, under the influence of the Persian Government, added to the resources. The artisan population [4] which had been left in Palestine were eagerly pressed forward to the work; the cedars of Lebanon were again, under Royal command, hewn down and brought, on receiving payment in kind, by Phœnician vessels to Joppa. The High Priest, with the various members of the sacerdotal caste, superintended the work. At last, in the seventh month of the second year from

B.C. 535.

[1] See Lecture XXVII.

[2] September (see Kalisch's *Commentary*, ii. 269). Ewald (*Ant.* 343, 344) supposes that the Mesopotamian reckoning had never quite died out in Palestine.

[3] 1 Esdras v. 47.

[4] Ezra iii. 3–8.

their return—that is, within a year from the erection of the altar—the foundation of the new Temple was laid. So important seemed to be the step thus gained that the day was celebrated with the first display of the old pomp on which they had yet ventured. The priests, in the rich dresses that Zerubbabel out of his princely munificence had furnished, blew once more their silver trumpets; the sons of Asaph once more clashed their brazen cymbals. Many of the Psalms which fill the Psalter with joyous strains were doubtless sung or composed on this occasion.[1] One strain especially rang above all—that which runs through the 106th, 107th, 118th, and the 136th Psalm: 'O give thanks unto the 'Eternal; for He is good, and His mercy endureth for ever.' Through all the national vicissitudes of weal and woe it was felt that the Divine goodness had remained firm. If, in spite of some appearances to the contrary,[2] the 118th Psalm was originally appropriated to this occasion, it is easy to see with what force the two choral companies must have replied, in strophe and antistrophe: 'Open to me the gates of righteousness,' 'This is the gate through which the righteous shall enter;' or must have welcomed the foundation stone which, after all difficulty and opposition, had at last been raised on the angle of the rocky platform; or have uttered the formula which afterwards[3] became proverbial for all such popular celebrations: 'Hosanna! Save us'—'Blessed be whosoever 'cometh in the name of the Eternal,'—or the culminating cry with which the sturdy sacrificers were called to drag the struggling victim and bind him fast to the horns of the newly-consecrated altar.[4]

Foundation of the second Temple.

Loud and long were these Jewish *Te Deums* re-echoed by the shouts of the multitude. It was not, indeed, a day of unmingled joy, for amongst the crowd there stood some aged men, who had lived through the great catastrophe of the Captivity; who, in their youth, had seen the magnificent

[1] Ezra iii. 10–13.

[2] Ps. cxviii. 8–12 would refer more naturally to a battle; verses 18, 19 might imply that the walls were finished.

[3] Matt. xxi. 9 (Reuss on Psalm cxviii. 26).

[4] Ps. cxviii. 27.

structure of Solomon standing in its unbroken stateliness; and when they compared with that vanished splendour these scanty beginnings they could not refrain from bursting forth into a loud wail of sorrow at the sad contrast. The two strains of feeling from the older and younger generation mingled together in a rivalry of emotion, but the evil omen of the lamentation was drowned in the cry of exultation: and those who stood on the outskirts of the solemnity caught only the impression of the mighty shout that rang afar off—far off, as it seemed, even to the valleys of Samaria.[1]

That mixed expression, however overborne for the moment, well coincided with the actual condition of the Jewish community. It is one of the instructive and pathetic characteristics of this period that we have come down from the great days of the primitive triumph of grand ideas, or the exploits of single heroes, to the complex, pedestrian, motley struggles (if one may so speak) of modern life.

The country[2] was unsettled—robber hordes roved through it—the harvest and the vintage were uncertain. And, yet further, now began the first renewal of that jealousy between the north and south of Palestine, which for a time had been subdued in the common sense of misfortune; and the feud between Jew and Samaritan, which, under various forms, continued till the close of this period—a jealousy which, if it represents the more tenacious grasp of a purer faith, indicates also the more exclusive and sectarian spirit now shrinking closer and closer into itself.

The opposition of the Samaritans

It is the story again and again repeated in modern times: first, the natural desire of an estranged population—heretical and schismatical as they might be—to partake in a glorious national work; then the rude refusal to admit their co-operation; then the fierce recrimination of the excluded party and the determination to frustrate the good work in which they cannot share. The Protestants of the sixteenth, the Puritans of the seventeenth century may see their demands in the innocent, laudable request of the

[1] Ezra iii. 12, 13 (Ewald, v. 102).

[2] Zech. viii. 10.

northern settlers: 'Let us build with you, for we seek your 'God as ye do.' The stiff retort of the Church, whether in Italy or England, may fortify itself by the response of the 'chief 'of the fathers of Israel:' 'Ye have nothing to do with us 'to build an house unto our God; but we ourselves together 'will build unto the God of Israel.' Each alike appeals for historic precedent and sanction to the Imperial Government which gave them their position—the one to 'Esar-haddon, 'king of Assyria,' the other to 'Cyrus, king of Persia,' Constantine or Charlemagne, Elizabeth or Cromwell. Each alike continues its appeal before that power, forecasting, even to the letter, the litigations by which Greek, Latin, and Armenian invoke the aid of the Sublime Porte in their disputes over the Holy Places on the very same soil. Each alike, and all their successors, deserve the rebuke which had been anticipated by the Great Prophet of the Captivity, when in his ideal glorification of Jerusalem he described that its walls should be built, not by its own children, but by the sons of strangers, and that its gates should not be rigidly closed, but should be open continually, and be shut neither day nor night.[1]

In these miserable accusations and counter-accusations carried on before the Princes who successively mounted the throne of Persia—the fierce Cambyses, the usurping Smerdis—twelve precious years were wasted.[2] At last the revolution, which raised the son of Hystaspes to power, gave a new opening to the oppressed and bewildered community at Jerusalem. He, the second Founder of the Persian kingdom, was, as it were, a second Cyrus to them. And it is just at this moment that the scanty information afforded by the nameless Chronicler[3] is suddenly illuminated by the appearance of the two Prophets who had taken, though in shreds and tatters, the mantle of prophecy which had fallen upon them from Jeremiah, Ezekiel, and the Great Unknown.

Cambyses, B.C. 529. Darius Hystaspis, B.C. 522–485.

They stand side by side. One is far advanced in years, apparently belonging to that older generation which had wept

[1] Isa. lx. 10 11. Comp. xlix. 20; lxiii. 16; lxvi. 20, 21.

[2] Ezra iv. 6–23.

[3] *Ibid.* v. 1, 4. 'We,' but not Ezra himself.

over the contrast between the first and second Temple—Haggai—who bore a name which no Prophet had ever assumed before, but which henceforth seems to have become familiar—the 'Messenger, or Angel, of the 'Eternal.'[1] The other must have been quite young, being the grandson of one of the returning exiles. Zechariah belonged to the priestly tribe, and is thus remarkable as an example of the union of the two functions, which, being long so widely separated in ancient times, had in the last days of the Monarchy gradually become blended together.

Haggai and Zechariah.

Unlike the uncertainty which attaches to the dates of the older Prophecies, we can trace the year, the month, the very day on which the utterances of these two seers were delivered. It was in the second year of the new Persian king, and on the first[2] day of the sixth month, and again on the one-and-twentieth day of the seventh month, that Haggai appeared before the chiefs of the nation, in the Temple court; in the[3] eighth month Zechariah joined him; in[4] the ninth month, on the four-and-twentieth day, Haggai delivered his two farewell messages, and then once more[5] followed Zechariah, first in the eleventh month, and again,[6] after a longer interval, in the ninth month of the fourth year of the same reign.

B.C. 521. September, October.

B.C. 521, November.

B.C. 520, January. B.C. 519, November.

It is characteristic of the true prophetic spirit that, whilst the Chronicler and the Prophets are equally bent on the accomplishment of the same end—the rebuilding of the Temple—the only obstacle that the Chronicler sees is the opposition of external adversaries; the chief obstacle that the Prophets indicate is the moral failure of their own fellow-citizens.

In each of the two Prophets the hope and the lesson is the same, but it comes in a different form. To the aged Haggai the recollection of the ancient[7] Temple is always present, but he is convinced that, even if the present tranquillity of the world must needs be broken[8] up, even if

Haggai.

[1] Haggai i. 13. Compare Malachi iii. 1. (Lecture XLV.)
[2] Haggai i. 1, 15; ii. 1.
[3] Zech. i. 1.
[4] Haggai ii. 10.
[5] Zech. i. 7.
[6] *Ibid.* vii. 1.
[7] Haggai i. 2, 9.
[8] *Ibid.* ii. 6, 7, 22.

some violent convulsion should once again shake all nations, yet abundant treasures[1] would flow into the Temple. If its own children should neglect it, the heathen whom they despised would come to the rescue.

He fiercely rebukes, not the captiousness of the Samaritans, but the apathy of his countrymen. There were those who, taking advantage of the long delay, counted with a curious casuistry the number of years that the Captivity[2] ought to last; and, finding that two were still wanting to complete the mystic seventy, sheltered themselves behind this prophecy to indulge their own indifference and luxury. 'The time is not 'come,' they said, 'the time for the Temple to be built.' 'The time not come for this!' exclaimed the indignant Prophet. 'Is it time for you to dwell[3] in your panelled 'houses, and the Temple to lie waste?' There were those, too, who had been tenaciously holding back their contributions, and hoarding up the produce of their newly-acquired[4] fields. With telling effect he pointed to the drought that had withered up corn, and vine, and olive, and fig, on hill and in valley, and broken the energy both of man and beast. There were those who, whilst carefully stinting the greater work of the Temple, prided themselves on the offerings which they brought to the freshly-consecrated[5] altar, the only finished part of the sanctuary. He warned them that such niggardly selfishness vitiated the offering which they brought;

High Heaven disdains the lore
Of nicely-calculated less or more.

In all these admonitions a profound meaning is wrapped up. It may be that there is but little of the poetic fire of the First or Second Isaiah. But there is a ponderous and simple dignity in the emphatic reiteration addressed alike to every class of the community—prince, priest, and people. *Be strong*,

[1] Haggai ii. 7. The word rendered 'desire of all nations' is properly the 'treasures of all nations,' and the idea is in accordance with the context of the whole passage (as in Matt. xxii. 10 and Romans xi. 14) that what the Jews would not do, the heathen would do.

[2] Haggai ii. 3 (see Dr. Pusey and Dr. Henderson).

[3] *Ibid.* i. 2, 3, 4.

[4] *Ibid.* i. 9, 10, 11; ii. 15, 17.

[5] *Ibid.* ii. 10-13.

be strong, be strong.[1] 'Cleave, stick fast, to the work you have 'to do.' Or, again, *Consider your ways, consider, consider, consider.*[2] It is the Hebrew phrase for the endeavour, characteristic of the gifted seers of all times, to compel their hearers to turn the inside of their hearts outwards to their own view, to take the masks from off their consciences, to 'see life steadily, 'and to see it whole.'

Far more explicit and florid was the utterance of the younger prophet[3] who came to Haggai's assistance.

Zechariah.

Zechariah's ideal of the restored Jerusalem was not of the returning glory of the old time, but of a fresh and prosperous community—peaceful old age carried to its utmost verge, and leaning in venerable security on its staff; the boys and girls, in childlike mirth, playing in the streets; the unfinished walls not a cause for despondency, but a pledge that they were not needed in a city of which the sufficient defence was the wall of Divine Flame, and of which the population was to outgrow all such narrow bounds.

And, as might be expected from one whose prime had been spent under Persian rule, his visions were all tinged with Persian imagery. He saw in his dreams 'the seven lamps,' or 'the 'seven eyes'—as of the seven Princes who had admission to the throne of Darius—glancing from the Divine presence through the world. He saw the earth, as it now presented itself to the enlarged vision of those who had listened to the Wise Men of Chaldæa, its four corners growing into the four horns that toss and gore the lesser powers of the world; the celestial messengers[4] riding on horses, red or dappled, hurrying through the myrtle-groves that then clothed the base of Olivet, or from the four quarters of the heavens, driving in chariots, each with its coloured horses, to and fro, across the Persian empire, as in the vast[5] machinery of the posts for which it was celebrated, and bringing back the tidings of war and peace.

[1] Haggai ii. 4.
[2] *Ibid.* i. 5, 7; ii. 15, 18. (See Dr. Pusey.)
[3] In speaking of Zechariah, it must be remembered that it is only the first part (i. viii.) which is here dealt with. The latter part (ix.-xiii.) has no bearing on this period, and, in all probability, belongs to an earlier prophet. (See Lecture XXXVII.)
[4] Zech. i. 8-11; iv 10; vi. 1-8.
[5] Herod. viii. 98. Esther iii. 13, 15.

But he, too, poured forth his invectives against the moral[1] depravity which annulled the value of the ceremonial worship; he, too, held out the prospect of harvest and vintage, but only as the fitting reward of a nobler and less grovelling spirit; he, too, urged the duty—so homely, so obvious, yet so rarely accepted—that every man and every nation should do the one work set before them at the special time of their existence.

The two leaders on whom these expectations were concentrated, were now, as throughout the period of the return, the Prince Zerubbabel and the High Priest Joshua. The Prince occupies the chief place in the eye of the older Prophet, the Priest in the eye of the younger Prophet, who was himself of priestly descent.[2] They, naturally, were the chief objects of the machinations of the Samaritan adversaries, and it would seem that an accusation had been lodged against them in the Persian Court. Regardless of this they were pressed by their prophetical advisers to proceed in their work; and were encouraged by every good omen that the prophetic lore of the period could produce.

Joshua the High Priest.

The splendid[3] attire of the High Priest, studded with jewels, had been detained at Babylon, or, at least, could not be worn without the special permission of the King; and until the accusations had been cleared away this became still more impossible.[4] But the day was coming, as it was seen in Zechariah's dream, when the adversary would be baffled, the cause won, and the soiled and worn clothing[5] of the suffering exile be replaced by the old magnificence of Aaron or of Zadok. He, with the Prince Zerubbabel, were to be together[6] like two olive-trees on each side of the golden candlestick. For these were destined the crowns which, by a happy coincidence, were at this moment brought[7] as offerings from the wealthy exiles of Babylon.

But Zerubbabel was still the principal figure. According to a later tradition[8] he himself was at this crisis in the court of

[1] Zech. i. 4; vii. 9, 10, 11; viii. 12.
[2] See Kuenen, ii. 214. But this is modified by Ewald's view.
[3] *Ibid.* iii. 1-5.
[4] 1 Esdras iv. 54; Ewald, v. 85.
[5] For the importance of the High Priest's clothes see Lectures XXXVI XLIX.
[6] Zech. iv. 1-5 (so Ewald).
[7] *Ibid.* vi. 9-14 (Ewald).
[8] 1 Esdras v. 13.

Darius, and labouring for his country's good. Of this the contemporary history knows nothing. But, whether in Persia or in Palestine, he was still the hope and stay of all. 'Seed of 'promise sown at Babylon' (as his name implied), he was the branch, the green sprout, that should shoot forth again from the withered stem of Jesse.[1] The expectation of a royal succession of anointed kings did not cease till Zerubbabel passed away. But his memory was invested with a nobler than any regal dignity. He was the layer of the foundation-stone. 'The hands[2] of Zerubbabel laid the 'foundation of this house, and his hands shall finish it.' The foundation-stone which had been laid amidst such small beginnings was the pledge of all that was to follow. On it were fixed the seven eyes of Providence. The day of its dedication was the day of 'small things' that carried with it the hope of the great future. He stands forth in history as an example of the sure success of a lofty purpose, secured by the reverse of the Fabian policy—not by prudently waiting for results, but by boldly acting at the moment. He and characters like his are truly the signet rings[3] by which the Eternal purposes are sealed. By no external power, but by the internal strength of a determined will, as by the breath[4] of the wind of heaven that sweeps all before it, was every obstacle to be surmounted. 'Who art thou?' said the loyal and courageous Prophet, confronting the Hill Difficulty that rose before him like Mount Olivet. 'Who art thou, O great[5] mountain? before Zerub-'babel thou shalt become a level plain.' It was the same doctrine as that which, in a simpler but sublimer form, and with a far more extended fame, has been placed in the mouth of Zerubbabel himself in a later tradition, which represents him, in the Court of the Persian King at this very juncture, in answer to the challenge to name the strongest of all things, as having replied in words which in their Latin version[6] have become proverbial: 'Great is the Truth and stronger than all

Zerubbabel.

[1] Zech. iii. 8.
[2] *Ibid.* iv. 9, 10.
[3] Haggai ii. 23.
[4] *Ibid.* i. 14.
[5] Zech. iv. 7.
[6] 1 Esdras iv. 33-41, 'Magna est veritas 'et prævalet'—altered in the proverb into the yet stronger phrase, 'prævalebit.'

'things . . . wine is wicked, the king is wicked, women are 'wicked . . . but the Truth endures and is always strong . . . 'With her there is no accepting of persons or rewards . . . she 'is the strength, kingdom, power, and majesty of all ages. 'Blessed be the God of Truth.' That is a truly Messianic hope—into that secret the 'seven eyes' may well have looked. It is the doctrine especially suited to every age, in which, like that of the Return, intrinsic conviction is the mainstay of human advancement.

The long-expected day at last arrived. The royal decree cleared away all obstacles. 'The mountain had become a 'plain.' In the sixth year of Darius, on the third day of the month Adar, the Temple was finished.[1]

Completion of the Temple, B. C. 516, March.

Of this edifice, the result of such long and bitter anxieties, we know almost nothing. If the measurements indicated in the decree of Cyrus were acted upon,[2] the space which it covered and the height to which it rose were larger than the corresponding dimensions of its predecessor. It must have been in the absence of metal and carving that it was deemed so inferior to the First Temple. The Holy of Holies was empty. The ark,[3] the cherubs, the tables of stone, the vase of manna, the rod of Aaron were gone. The golden shields had vanished. Even the High Priest, though he had recovered his official dress, had not been able to resume the breastplate with the oracular[4] stones. Still, there was not lacking a certain splendour and solidity befitting the sanctuary of a people once so great, and of a religion so self-contained. The High Priest and his family were well lodged, with guest chambers and store chambers on a large scale for the Temple furniture.[5] The doors of the Temple were of gold. In three particulars the general arrangements differed from those of the ancient sanctuary. With the

[1] Ezra vi. 15.

[2] *Ibid.* vi. 3. Perhaps these are specified as the limits not to be exceeded (Professor Rawlinson in Speaker's *Commentary* on Ezra).

[3] The ark was supposed either to have been buried by Jeremiah on Mount Sinai (2 Macc. ii. 5) or to have been carried up into Heaven (Rev. xi. 19), there to await the coming of the Messiah. See Ewald on Rev. ii. 17.

[4] Ezra ii. 63; Neh. vii. 65. See Prideaux, i. 148, for 'the five lost things.'

[5] Ezra x. 6; Neh. xiii. 5.

rigid jealousy which rendered this period hostile to all which approached the Canaanite worship, there were no more to be seen in the courts those beautiful clusters of palm,[1] and olive, and cedar, which had furnished some of the most striking imagery of the poetry of the Monarchy, but which had also lent a shelter to the idolatrous rites that at times penetrated the sacred enclosure. 'No tree,' 'no [2] grove,' we are told, 'was to 'be seen within the precincts.' Another feature characteristic of the period was the fortress-tower built at the north-western corner of the sanctuary, which, serving in the first instance as a residence of the Persian governor, became in later days the Tower of Antonia, from which, in like manner, the Roman garrison controlled the proud [3] population of Jerusalem. Like to this was the sign of subjection to the Persian power preserved in the Eastern gate of the Temple, called the Gate of Susa, from its containing [4] a representation of the Palace of the Persian capital. Thirdly, the court of the worshippers was [5] divided for the first time into two compartments, of which the outer enclosure was known as the court of the Gentiles or Heathens. It is difficult to say to which of the two countercurrents of the time this arrangement was due. It may have been that now, for the first time, the offerings from the Persian kings and the surrounding tribes required more distinctly than before a locality where they could be received, and that the enlarged ideas of the Prophets of the Captivity were thus represented in outward form; or it may have been that, with the exchange of the free spirit of earlier times for the rigid narrowness of a more sectarian age, there was a new barrier erected.[6]

The consecration of the new Temple was not delayed, like that of Solomon, to meet the great autumnal festival of the Jewish year. It was enough that it should coincide with the

[1] See Lecture XXVII.

[2] Hecatæus of Abdera (Jos. *c. Ap.*) i. 22. See De Saulcy, *Art Judaïque*, p. 357. Also, 'The Temple' in *Dict. of the Bible*.

[3] Neh. ii. 8; vii. 2. Is is called Bireh (Greek *Baris*), which is elsewhere the word used for Shushan, as if the Persian capital in miniature were thus represented at Jerusalem.

[4] Middoth, iii. 43 (Surenhusius, v. 326).

[5] 1 Macc. ix. 54.

[6] Ezra vi. 19, 22, 17.

earlier, yet hardly less solemn, feast which fell in the spring—the Passover.[1] There was a general sacrifice of 100 oxen, 200 rams, 400 lambs; but the victims which attracted most attention were twelve venerable goats, chosen to represent the twelve tribes, as an indication that the whole nation, though only represented in Judah and Benjamin, still claimed the sanctuary as their own.[2]

Festive character of the occasion.

It was a season of universal festivity. A few months before its close a deputation [3] from Bethel had come to inquire whether the four [4] days of fasting and mourning established during the Captivity were still to be observed; and the answer of the Prophet was an indignant repudiation of these religious mockeries of sentiments which were not felt. Even during the exile they had been but hollow observances—now they were still more unreal.[5] In the later years of Judaism these four melancholy commemorations of the sorrows and sins of Judah have been revived; but then, and in that freshness of returning happiness, the Prophet had the boldness to reverse their meaning—to make them feasts of joy and gladness—holy days, of which the only celebration should be the love of truth and peace.

In accordance with this natural burst of joy after so hard-won a struggle are the Psalms, some of which, by natural inference, some by universal consent, belong to this period. Those which either before or now were composed for the Passover could never have been sung with such zest as on this, the first great Paschal festival after the re-establishment of their worship. They might well be reminded of the time when Israel came out of Egypt and the house of Jacob from [6] a strange land; and the call to trust in the Shield and Helper of their country would well be addressed to the whole nation, to the priestly tribe, and to those awe-stricken spectators who stood as it were outside 'and feared the God of Judah.'

[1] Ezra vi. 17.
[2] Zech. vii. 2, 3, 5; (Heb.) viii. 19.
[3] See Lecture XL.
[4] It was the same moral as that which forbade the new garment to be patched to the old, or the new wine to be poured into the old vessels, Matt. ix. 15, *Similia similibus conjungantur*.
[5] Ps. cxiv.-cxv. in LXX. one Psalm.
[6] Ps. cxlvi.—Ps. cl. (LXX.).

But those which (at least as far back as the time of the Greek translation) bore the names of the two Prophets of this period were the jubilant songs, of which the first words have been preserved in their Hebrew form through all Christian Psalmody: 'Hallelujah,'[1] 'Praise the Eternal.' Other hymns may have been added to that sacred book as years rolled on; but none were thought so fit to close the Psalter, with a climax of delight, as the four exuberant Psalms which sum up the joy of the Return. There, more than even in any other portion of the mirthful Psalter, we hear the clash of cymbal, and twang of harp, and blast of trumpet, and see the gay dances round the Temple courts, and join in the invitation to all orders of society, to all nations of the earth, to all created things, to share in the happiness of the happy human heart. Centuries afterwards, when a scrupulous Pontiff hesitated whether he should accord the use of the Sacred Scriptures in their own tongue to the nations on the banks of the Danube, he was converted, in defiance of the rule of his own Church, by the comprehensive and catholic words with which Haggai and Zechariah wound up their appeal to all nature on that day—'Let every thing 'that hath breath praise the Eternal.'[1] It has been well said that, 'whereas much good poetry is profoundly melancholy, 'the life of the generality of men is such that in literature they 'require joy. Such joy is breathed so freely and with such a 'genuine burst through the period of the Restoration of Israel 'that we cannot read either its Prophets or its Psalmists with-'out catching its glow. The power of animation and consola-'tion in such thoughts, which, beginning by giving us a hold 'on a single great work, like that of the Evangelical Prophet, 'end with giving us a hold on the history of the human spirit, 'and the course, drift, and scope of the career of our race as a 'whole, cannot be over-estimated.'[2]

[1] Psalm cl. 6. See Lectures on the Eastern Church (Lecture IX.).
[2] Matthew Arnold, *The Great Prophecy of the Restoration*, p. 33.

LECTURE XLIV.

EZRA AND NEHEMIAH.

AUTHORITIES.

CONTEMPORARY HISTORY.

Ezra vii.–x.; Nehemiah i.–xiii. (called in the Vulgate the First and Second Books of Esdras).

TRADITIONS.

1. Josephus, *Ant.* xi. 5.
2. Fabricius, *Codex Pseudepigr.*, pp. 1145—1164
3. 1 Esdras (see previous note).
4. 2 Esdras (see previous note).
5. 2 Macc. i. 18–36; ii. 13.
6. Koran, c. ii. 261 (see Lane's *Selections*, pp. 102, 143).
7. Talmudical traditions in Derenbourg's *Histoire de la Palestine*, c. i., ii.

NOTE ON THE BOOKS OF EZRA AND NEHEMIAH.

It is convenient, without entering on the detailed analysis of these two books, to indicate the main features of their composition open to the view of all readers.

1. In the original Hebrew Canon they form, not two books, but one.
2. In this one book is discoverable the agglomeration of four distinct elements; which is instructive as an undoubted instance of the composite structure shared by other books of the Old and New Testaments, where it is not so distinctly traceable.
3. These component parts are as follows:—

   a The portions written by the Chronicler—the same as the compiler of the Books of Chronicles (comp. Ezra i. 1, 2, 2 Chron. xxxvi. 22, 23)—Ezra i., iii.–vi.; Neh. xii. 1–26.

   b Ezra's own narrative, Ezra vii.–x.

   c Nehemiah's own narrative, Neh. i.–vii. 5; viii.–xi. 2; xii. 27–xiii. 31.

   d Archives; Ezra ii.; Neh. vii. 6–73; xi. 3–36.

In the divisions *a*, *b*, and *c*, it may be questioned whether Ezra vii. 1–26; x. 1–44; Nehemiah viii. 1–xi. 2; vii. 27–xiii. 3 (in which Ezra and Nehemiah are described in the third person) belong to another narrative interwoven by the Chronicler who compiled the whole book.

Of the two Apocryphal Books, that which in the English version is called 'the First Book of Esdras,' and in the Vulgate the Third, is a compilation of the history of Ezra with additions regarding Zerubbabel. Being in Greek, it must be after the time of Alexander; being used by Josephus as of equal authority with the canonical books, it must be before the Christian era. Beyond these two landmarks there is nothing to fix the date.

That which in the English version is the Second Book of Esdras, otherwise called the Fourth, but more properly the 'Apocalypse of Ezra,' is not received into the Vulgate. It exists only in the Latin version of the lost Greek, and its date is probably in the beginning of the second century of our era.

LECTURE XLIV.

EZRA AND NEHEMIAH.

SEVENTY YEARS of total silence roll over the history from the completion of the building of the Temple till the next event in Palestine of which there is any certain record. During that time Zerubbabel had passed from the scene—according to the Jewish tradition had even returned to his native Babylon [1] to die. His descendants lingered on,[2] but without authority—and in his place no native Prince had either arisen by his own influence, or been appointed by the Persian Government, to the first place in the new settlement. The line of the High Priesthood was continued from Joshua the son of Jozedek; and now, for the first time since the death of Eli, did the chief authority of the nation pass into the hands of the caste of Aaron, though still under the general control of the Persian governor, native or not, who lived in the fortress overlooking the Temple.[3] The colonists settled down into their usual habits. They lived on easy terms with their neighbours, some of the chief families intermarrying with them. Eliashib, the High Priest, who lived in large apartments within the Temple precincts, was doubly connected with the two native Princes, who, at Samaria and in the Transjordanic Ammon, represented the Persian Government.[4] The tide of commerce again began to flow through the streets of Jerusalem. Asses heavily laden with sheaves of corn and clusters of fruit might be seen passing into the city, even on the sacred day of rest. Tyrian sailors also were there, selling their fish, and other

B.C. 516—459.

The new colony.

[1] Seder Olam (Ewald, v. 118); Derenbourg, 20, 21.

[2] 1 Chron. iii. 17-20; Luke iii. 23-32; Ewald, v. 119, 120.

[3] Neh. v. 15.

[4] *Ibid.* xiii. 4.

articles of Phœnician trade. Goldsmiths'[1] and moneychangers' and spicedealers' stalls were established in the bazaars.

The poorer classes had, many of them, sunk into a state of serfage to the richer nobles, in whom the luxurious and insolent practices of the old aristocracy, denounced by the earlier Prophets, began to reappear. Jerusalem itself was thinly inhabited, and seemed to have stopped short in the career which, under the first settlers, had been opening before it.[2] If we could trust the conjecture of Ewald that the eighty-ninth Psalm expresses the hope of a Davidic king in the person of Zerubbabel and his children, and the extinction of that hope in the troubles of the time, we should have a momentary vision of the shadows which closed round the reviving city.[3] It is certain that, whether from the original weakness of the rising settlement, or from some fresh inroad of the surrounding tribes, of which we have no distinct notice, the walls of Jerusalem were still unfinished; huge gaps left in them where the gates had been burnt and not repaired; the sides of its rocky hills cumbered with their ruins; the Temple, though completed, still with its furniture scanty and its ornaments inadequate. As before, in the time of Zechariah, when the arrival of three wealthy Babylonian Jews filled the little colony with delight, so now its hopes were fixed on their countrymen in those distant settlements. The centre of the revived nation was in its own ancient capital; but its resources, its civilisation, were in the Court of Persia.[4] There were two of these voluntary exiles who have left an authentic record of the passionate love for their unseen country, which, amidst much that is disappointing in their career and narrow in their horizon, compared with the great Prophets of the Monarchy or of the earlier period of the Captivity, yet stamps every step of their course with a pathetic interest, the more moving because its expression is so incontestably genuine.

The first was Ezra. He was of the priestly tribe, but his chief characteristic—which already had gained him a fame in

[1] Neh. xiii. 15-17; iii. 8, 31.
[2] *Ibid.* v. 6-10; vii. 4; xi. 2.
[3] Ps. lxxxix. 20, 35, 39.
[4] Yearly gifts came across the desert (Philo, *Leg. ad Caium* 1013).

the far-off East—was that he was the most conspicuous of that order of men which now first came into prominence, and was destined afterwards to play so fatal a part in the religious history of Judaism—the Scribes. The Scribes, or Sôpherim, had in some form long existed. They had originally been the registrars or clerks by whom the people or the army were numbered.[1] They then rose into higher importance as royal secretaries. Then, as the Prophetic writings took a more literary form, and the calamities of the falling Monarchy and the subsequent exile stimulated the nation to collect and register the fragments of the past, they took a conspicuous place by the side of the Prophets. Such an one in the earlier generation had been Baruch, the friend of Jeremiah. Such an one now was Ezra in the Jewish schools[2] of Chaldæan learning, fostered by the atmosphere of the sacred scientific caste which had its seat in Borsippa or in the Temple of Bel, and in which afterwards sprang up the Chaldee Paraphrase and the Babylonian Talmud. Ezra had devoted himself to the study of 'The Law,' in whatever form it was then known, and was seized with a burning desire to enforce its provisions amongst his own countrymen. To him Artaxerxes of the Long Arms[3]—the mild Sovereign who now ruled the Persian Empire—entrusted the double charge of providing for the due execution of the national code and for the proper adornment of the national sanctuary.

Ezra B.C. 459.

It was almost a second return that Ezra thus organised. There was the same terror of the dangers of the long journey, the same shrinking back of the sacerdotal caste. 'There was not one of the sons of Levi.' But the cheering confidence, which on the first return had been inspired by Ezekiel and the Evangelical Prophet, was on this return supplied by Ezra himself. He clings to the unseen Support by the same expressive figure that had been first specially indicated by Ezekiel, 'The Hand of God.'[4] 'I was

Journey of Ezra. B.C. 459.

[1] See 'Scribes' in *Dict. of the Bible.*

[2] Ezra vii. 10, 12.

[3] Artaxerxes Makrocheir in Greek, Ardishir Dirozdust in Persian. Malcolm's *Persia*, i. 67.

[4] Ezek. xxxvii. 1; Ezra vii. 6, 9; viii. 22, 31. Comp. 1 Kings xviii. 46.

'strengthened,' said the solitary exile to himself, 'as the Hand 'of my God was upon me.' 'The good Hand of our God was 'upon us.' 'The Hand of God is upon all them for good that 'seek Him.' 'The Hand of our God was upon us.' It is as if he felt the returning touch of those Invisible Fingers at every stage of the journey. On the twelfth day they halted on their road at 'the river of Ahava;' in all probability [1] the well-known spot where caravans make their plunge into the desert, where, from the bitumen springs of 'His' or 'Hit,' the Euphrates bends northwards. There, with a noble magnanimity, throwing himself on the Divine protection, he declined the escort which had accompanied the former expedition, and braved the terrors of the wandering Arabs alone. It was in the flowery spring when they crossed the desert, and they reached Jerusalem in the midsummer heats.

It is characteristic of the predominant idea in Ezra's mind throughout this period that, after a brief summary of the reception of the gifts and offerings to the Temple, his whole energies pass immediately into the other and chief purpose for which he had come. He was a Scribe first and a Priest afterwards. The Temple was an object of his veneration. But it was nothing compared to 'The Law.' And the vehemence of his attachment to it is the more strongly brought out by the comparatively trivial, and in some respects questionable, occasion that called it forth. It was the controversy which, from this time forward, was to agitate in various forms the Jewish community till its religious life was broken asunder—its relation to the Heathen population around. It may be that at that time the larger, nobler, more humane views which belonged to the earlier and also to the later portion of the Jewish history were impossible. There had not been the faintest murmur audible when the ancestors of David once and again married into a Moabite family, nor when David [2] took amongst his wives a daughter of Geshur; nor is there a more exuberant Psalm [3] than that which celebrates the union of an

The mixed marriages.

[1] See 'Ahava' in *Dictionary of the Bible* But it is much contested in Ewald, v. 136

[2] Ruth i. 4; iv. 13; 2 Sam. iii. 3.

[3] Psalm xlv. 12, 16.

Israelite King with an Egyptian or Tyrian Princess. Even if the patriarchal alliance of Abraham with the Egyptian Hagar or the Arabian Keturah, or the marriage of Moses with the Midianite or the Ethiopian, provoked a passing censure, it was instantly and strongly repelled by the loftier tone of the sacred narrative. Nor is there in the New Testament a passage more redolent of acknowledged wisdom and charity than that in which the Rabbi of Tarsus [1] tolerates the union of the heathen husband and the believing wife. Nor are there more critical incidents in Christian history than those which record the consequences which flowed from the union of Clovis with Clotilda, or of Ethelbert with Bertha. But it was the peculiarity of the age through which the religion of Israel was now passing that to the more keenly-strung susceptibilities of the nation every approach to the external world was felt as a shock and pollution. The large freedom of Isaiah, whether the First or Second, was gone; the charity of Paul, and of a Greater than Paul, had not arisen. The energy of Deborah and of Elijah remained; but for the present generation it was destined to fight, not against a cruel oppressor or an immoral worship, but against the sanctities of domestic union with their neighbour tribes—dangerous, possibly, in their consequences, but innocent in themselves. We are called upon to bestow an admiration, genuine, but limited, on a zeal which reminds us of Dunstan and Hildebrand rather than of the Primitive or the Reforming Church.

It is Ezra himself who places before us the scene with a vividness which shows us that, if the spirit of the ancient days is altered, their style still retains its inimitable vigour; and, though he did not compose [2] the narrative till many years afterwards, the consciousness of the importance of the event burnished the recollection of it with the freshness as of yesterday.

The festival was already closed, in which the new vessels had been fully reserved and weighed, the twelve oxen and twelve goats for the twelve tribes with the attendant flocks of

[1] 1 Cor. vii. 14.

[2] Ezra viii. 1; ix. 1.

sheep been slaughtered, the commissions to the Persian governors delivered, and Ezra[1] was established as the chief judge over the whole community. This was on the fourth day of the fifth month; the sixth, the seventh, the eighth month rolled away, and nothing had occurred to ruffle the tranquil tenor of the restoration of the Temple arrangements.

August.

But on the sixteenth day of the ninth month came a sudden storm. The copies of the Law which Ezra had brought from Chaldæa must have become in the interval known to the settlement in Palestine, and those copies, whatever their date, must have contained the prohibitions of mixed marriages which, it would seem, had been wholly unknown or ignored down to that time, and overruled by the practice of centuries. Suddenly the chiefs of the community appeared before Ezra as he stood in the Temple court and confessed that such usages had penetrated into every class of their society. In the stricter practices of his Babylonian countrymen he had seen nothing like it. The shock was in proportion to the surprise: he tore his outer cloak from top to bottom; he tore his inner garment no less; he plucked off the long tresses of his sacerdotal locks, the long flakes of his sacerdotal beard, and thus, with dishevelled head and half-clothed limbs, he sank on the ground, crouched like one thunderstruck, through the whole of that day. Round him were drawn those whom sympathy for the same cause filled with a like sentiment, and he and they sate silent till the sunset called for the evening sacrifice, and the Temple courts began once more to be crowded with promiscuous worshippers. Then Ezra arose from his sitting posture, and all tattered and torn as were his priestly garments, he fell on his bended knees (that attitude of devotion so unusual in Eastern countries) and stretched forth his open hands, with the gesture common to the whole ancient world (now lost everywhere except amongst the Mussulmans), and poured forth his agonised prayer to the God whose law had thus been offended.[2] As he

December.

[1] Ezra vii. 25. The quasi-independent jurisdiction of the Patriarchate of Constantinople under the Sublime Porte well illustrates this position, as well as that of the later High Priests.

[2] Ezra ix. 3–5.

prayed his emotion increased, and with his articulate words were mingled his passionate tears; and by the time that he had concluded, a sympathetic thrill had run through the whole community.[1]

Crowds came streaming into the Temple court and gathered round him and they too joined their cries and tears with his. Full-grown men and women were there, and youths; and under the excitement of the moment, led by one whose name was deemed worthy of special praise as having given the first signal, Shechaniah, the son of Elam, they placed themselves under Ezra's orders: 'Arise, for this matter belongeth unto thee; we 'will also be with thee; be of good courage and do it.' At once the prostrate, weeping mourner sprang to his feet, and exacted the oath from all present, that they would assist his efforts; and, having done this, he disappeared, and withdrew into the chamber of the High Priest's son, in one of the upper storeys of the Temple, and there remained in complete abstinence, even from bread and water, for the three days which were to elapse before a solemn assembly could be convened to ascertain the national sentiment.

It is interesting at this point to indicate the form of the Jewish constitution, so far as it can be dimly discerned at this period. The Persian[2] satrap who ruled over the whole country west of the Euphrates was the supreme authority. Under him were the various governors or Pashas[3] in the chief Syrian towns. The Persian garrison was in the central fortress of Samaria.[4] But within their general jurisdiction the Jewish community possessed an organisation of its own. The princely dignity of the Anointed House of David had died with Zerubbabel. The High Priesthood, perhaps from the unworthy character of its occupants, lapsed, during almost the whole period of the Persian dominion, into political and social insignificance. The ordinary government was in the hands of 'the Elders' or 'Chiefs,'[5] who were themselves subordinate or co-ordinate to 'the Inspectors'[6] of the various

The constitution.

[1] Ezra x. 1–6. [2] *Ibid.* v. 1–13. [3] *Ibid.* vi. 7; viii. 36; Nehemiah ii. 10, 19. [4] Neh. iv. 2. See Herzfeld, i. 378–387. [5] Ezra x. 8, 14. [6] Neh. xi. 9, 14, 16.

districts; two offices which had existed in germ[1] at the time of the Return—even entering in an idealised form into the visions of the Evangelical Prophet—two offices whose names as rendered into Greek, 'presbyter' and 'bishop'—under circumstances how different, and with a fate how little foreseen!—passed into the Christian Church, to be the material of controversies which would have lost half their bitterness and half their meaning had the homely origin of the titles when they first appeared been recognised.

But it would seem that there was still on great emergencies the power or the necessity of a 'provocatio ad populum'—an appeal to the whole people. Accordingly, the scene which followed is a striking instance, on the one hand, of the deference paid to such a spontaneous and deliberate act of the popular voice; on the other hand, of the powerful impression which the community received from the character and demeanour of a single individual. The summons convoked, as one man, all the outlying inhabitants of the hills of Judah and Benjamin. They congregated in the open square in front of the Temple gate.[2] And here again we stumble on the first distinct notice of that popular element which, deriving, in later times, its Grecian name from the Athenian assemblies, passed into the early Christian community under the title of *Ecclesia*,[3] and thus became the germ of that idea of the 'Church' in which the voice of the people or laity had supreme control over the teachers and rulers of the society—an idea preserved in the first century in its integrity, retained in some occasional instances down to the eleventh century, then almost entirely superseded by the mediæval schemes of ecclesiastical polity, until it reappeared, although in modified and disjointed forms, in the sixteenth and following centuries.

The assembly or Ecclesia.

December.

It was now the twentieth day of the ninth month, in the depth of the Syrian winter; the cold rain fell in

[1] Isa. lx. 17. In English translated 'exactors,' in Greek ἐπισκόπους, and as such applied by Clement of Rome (i. 42) to 'Bishops'—altering, however, ἀρχόντας into διακόνους, to suit the purpose of his argument. For the whole question of the constitution at this time see Herzfeld, i. 253-260.

[2] Ezra x. 9 (Heb.). Comp. Jos. *B. J.* ii. 17, 2.

[3] Ezra x. 9-14.

torrents; and the people, trembling under the remonstrance of their consecrated chief, and shivering in the raw, ungenial weather, confirmed the appointment of a commission of inquiry, which should investigate every case of unlawful marriage, and compel the husbands to part with their wives and even with their children. By the beginning of the new year the list was drawn up, including four of the priestly family, and about fifty more. 'All of these had [1] taken strange 'wives, and some of them had wives by whom they had children.' With these dry words Ezra winds up the narrative of the signal victory which he had attained over the natural affections of the whole community; a victory doubtless which had its share in keeping alive the spirit of exclusive patriotism and of uncompromising zeal that was to play at times so brilliant and at times so dark a part in the coming period of Jewish history, but which, in its total absence of human tenderness, presents a dismal contrast to that pathetic passage of the primitive records of their race which tells us how when their first father drove out the foreign handmaid with her son into the desert, it 'was 'very grievous in his sight,' and 'he rose up early in the morning 'and took bread, and a waterskin, putting it on her shoulder 'and the child;' and how 'God heard the voice of the lad, and 'the angel of God called to Hagar out of heaven.' [2]

B.C. 459.

It can hardly be doubted that this acknowledged supremacy of Ezra's personal force was felt to the extremities of the nation, and awakened a new sense of energy wherever it extended; but it is fourteen years before we again catch a glimpse of its penetrating influence, and here we have the rare fortune of another character and career described by the man himself.

In the season when the Court of Persia was at its winter residence of Susa a young Jew was in attendance on the king as cupbearer. According to the later tradition, it appeared that, as he was walking outside the capital, he saw a band [3] of wayworn travellers entering the city and heard them speaking to each other in his own Hebrew tongue.

Nehemiah, B.C. 445.

[1] Ezra x. 44.
[2] Genesis xxi. 11, 14, 17.
[3] Jos. *Ant.* xi. 5, 6.

On finding that they were from Judæa, he asked them for tidings of his city and his people. They told him of the overthrow of the walls, of the aggressions of the surrounding nations, and of the frequent murders in the roads round Jerusalem. He burst into tears at the sad tidings, and broke forth into the lamentation familiar from the Psalms: 'How 'long, O Lord, wilt Thou endure Thy people to suffer?' As he approached the gate a messenger came to announce that the king was already at table. He hurried in as he was, without washing from his face the signs of his grief. This arrested the attention of Artaxerxes, and led to the permission to return to his native country, and with power to rectify the disorders which had so distressed him. So, with the constant tendency of later times to embellish even the simplest narrative, was conceived in after years the opening scene of Nehemiah's life. His own account is not less[1] vivid, though perhaps less dramatic. It was not a band of strangers but his own brother who had been engaged in a pilgrimage, which of itself indicates the patriotic sentiment of the family. It was not the passionate burst of a momentary sorrow, but a deep and brooding anguish, which had its root in the thought[2] that his forefathers lay buried in the city thus desolated and oppressed, as though he and the ancestors who lay in those dishonoured tombs were themselves responsible for these calamities. It was not a few hours, but four long months during which he stood aloof from the royal presence, and so lost the usual cheerfulness of his demeanour as to provoke the King's kindly question, and his pathetic answer:[3] 'Then the King said unto me, For what dost thou 'make request? So I prayed to the God of heaven. And I 'said unto the King, If it please the King, and if thy "slave" 'have found favour in thy sight, that thou wouldest send me 'unto Judah, unto the city of my fathers' sepulchres, that I 'may build it.'

The importance of the place of cupbearer, according to

[1] Neh. i. 1, 2, 3. [2] *Ibid.* ii. 3, 5. [3] *Ibid.* ii. 4, 5.

the minute etiquette described by Xenophon,[1] gave such means of access to the king and queen, that they at once yielded to his request, and he set off, with escort and authority, to accomplish the desire so near his heart. It has been conjectured that the recent humiliation[2] of the Persian Empire by the Athenian victory in Cyprus may have rendered it part of the Persian policy to fortify a post so important as Jerusalem, in the vicinity of the Mediterranean and on the way to Egypt. At any rate, the one idea in Nehemiah's mind is the restoration of the broken circuit of the once impregnable walls of the Holy City.[3] The change to this conviction from the confidence of Zechariah in the unfortified security of Jerusalem is as remarkable as was the change under[4] the Monarchy from the confidence of Isaiah to the despair of Jeremiah. It was now felt that what the walls of Babylon on a gigantic scale had been to the Chaldæan Empire, that the walls of Jerusalem were to the little Jewish settlement. In those days, rather one may say in those countries, of disorder, a city without locked gates and lofty walls was no city at all.[5] The arrival of Nehemiah at Jerusalem with his 'firman,' his royal guard, and his retinue of slaves, was regarded as a great event both on the spot, and by the 'watchful jealousy' of the surrounding tribes. He lived, we must suppose, in the fortress or palace of the Governors overlooking the Temple area, and then, with a splendid magnanimity unusual in Eastern potentates, he declined the official salary, and the ordinary official exactions, and kept open house for a hundred and fifty[6] guests from year to year, with a profusion of choice dishes, on the delicacy of which even the munificent governor seems to dwell in his recollections with a complacent relish. But this

B.C. 445. The Rebuilding of the Walls.

[1] Xenophon, *Cyrop.* i. 3, 4; Ewald, v. 148.

[2] B.C. 449. In Milman's *Hist. of the Jews*, i. 435, this by inadvertence has been confused with the battle of Cnidus, B.C. 394.

[3] It is difficult to decide to what occasion to refer the desolation of the walls. It might seem natural to suppose that they had not been rebuilt at the first return. But the language of Nehemiah (i. 2, 3) implies something more recent. Ewald conjectures the distresses which clouded the last years of Zerubbabel from the action of the hostile party in Syria.

[4] See Lecture XL.

[5] Neh. iv. 2, 6, 12.

[6] *Ibid.* v. 14-18.

and every other step which Nehemiah took was subordinated to the one design which possessed his mind. It was the third day after his arrival that he resolved, without indicating the purpose of his mission to any human being, to explore for himself the extent of the ruin which was to be repaired. It was in the darkness of the night that he, on his mule or ass, accompanied by a few followers on foot, descended into the ravine [1] of Hinnom, and threaded his way in and out amongst the gigantic masses of ruin and rubbish through that memorable circuit, familiar now to every traveller like the track of his native village. Each point that Nehemiah reaches is recorded by him as with the thrill inspired by the sight of objects long expected, and afterwards long remembered,—the Spring of the Dragon (was [2] it that already the legend had sprung up which describes the intermittent flow of the Siloam water, as produced by the opening and closing of the dragon's mouth?); the gate outside of which lay the piles of the sweepings and offscourings of the streets; the masses of fallen masonry, extending as it would seem all along the western and northern side; the blackened gaps left where the gates had been destroyed by fire; till at last by the royal reservoir the accumulations became so impassable that the animal on which he rode refused to proceed. Then he turned, in the dead of night, along the deep shade of the Kedron watercourse,[3] looking up at the eastern wall, less ruinous than the rest, and so back once more by the gate that opened on the ravine of Hinnom. And now having possessed himself with the full idea of the desolation, he revealed to his countrymen the whole of his plan, and portioned out the work amongst them. It was like the rebuilding of the wall of Athens after the invasion of Xerxes—like the building of the walls of Edinburgh after the battle of Flodden. Every class of society, every district in the country, took part in it. Of each the indefatigable Governor recorded the name. He told for after

The exploration of the ruins.

[1] Neh. ii. 13 (Heb.).

[2] Robinson, *B. R.* i. 507.

[3] Neh. ii. 15 (Heb.). For the whole ride see Robinson, *B. R.* i. 473. But the difficulty of identifying the names makes any detailed topographical explanation provokingly insecure.

times how, when the priests had finished their portion, they at once consecrated it, without waiting for the dedication of the whole.[1] He recorded for the indignation of posterity how the proud nobles of Tekoah[2] refused to work with the humbler artisans. He arranged how this or that quarter should be restored by those whose houses were close by; so that each inhabitant might look on that portion of the wall as his own. He called out the corporations[3] of apothecaries, goldsmiths, and merchants, to complete what individuals could not undertake. He noted the various landmarks of the ancient city, now long since perished and their sites unknown, but full of interest to him (and to all later times) as relics and standing monuments of the old capital of David. The tower[4] of Hananeel, the fragment of 'broad wall,' the royal garden by which the last king had escaped,[5] the stairs, the steps (it may be those still existing), hewn out of the rock—the barracks where David's 'heroes' had been quartered, the royal tombs, the ancient armoury, the traces of the palace and prison, the huge tower of Ophel—all these stand out distinctly in Nehemiah's survey like spectres of the past, most of them to be seen and heard of no more again for ever. It was a severe toil. The mere removal of the rubbish and broken fragments was almost too hard[6] a task for those who had to carry it off. The hostile neighbours, who were determined to prevent this new capital from rising amongst them, used alternate threats and artifices.[7] But Nehemiah was proof against all. High above Priest or Levite, on an equality with the other resident governors of Syria, he was the successor of Zerubbabel—the Tirshatha or Pasha of the Persian Court. To the enemies without he had but one answer, repeated once, twice, thrice, four times, in the same words of stern determination:[8] 'I am 'doing a great work, so that I cannot come down; why should 'the work cease, whilst I leave it and come down to you?' To the traitors and false prophets within, who advised him to

[1] Neh. iii. 1.
[2] *Ibid.* iii. 5.
[3] *Ibid.* iii. 8, 31, 32.
[4] *Ibid.* iii. 1, 15, 16, 19, 25, 27.
[5] See Lecture XL.
[6] Neh. iv. 2, 10.
[7] Ewald places Psalm lxxxiii. at this period (v. 155).
[8] Neh. vi. 3.

take refuge in the Temple from expected assassination, he replied—with a rebuke alike to the fears of cowardice and the hopes of superstition: 'Should such a man as I flee? and 'who is there, that, being as I am, would go into the Temple 'to save his life?[1] I will not go in.' And with this same magnanimous spirit in the more critical moments of danger he animated all his countrymen: 'Be not ye afraid of them: 'remember the Lord which is great and terrible, and fight for 'your brethren, your sons, and your daughters, your wives,[2] 'and your houses.'

There was one body of men on whom he could thoroughly depend—the slaves who had accompanied him from Susa. Half of these[3] worked at the building, half stood behind them, guarding the shields, bows, and breast-plates to be seized at a moment's notice. The loyal members of the nobility were stationed close by, so as to take the immediate command. Every builder, too, had his sword fastened to his sash. By the side of Nehemiah himself stood a trumpeter, at whose blast they were all to rally round him, wherever they might be. And thus they laboured incessantly from the first dawn[4] of day till in the evening sky, when the sun had set, the darkness which rendered the stars visible compelled them to desist. And when night fell, there was a guard kept by some, whilst those who had been at work all day took off their clothes and slept. Only of Nehemiah, with his slaves and the escort which had followed him from Persia, it is proudly recorded that not one took off even the least article of his dress.[5] So he emphatically repeats, as if the remembrance of those long unresting vigils had been engraven on his memory, down to the slightest particular.

Such was the nobler side of that gallant undertaking in which were fulfilled the passionate longings of the exiles, throughout their whole stay in Babylon, 'that the walls of 'Jerusalem should be built.'[6]

[1] Neh. vi. 11. Compare Becket's words. 'I will not turn the Cathedral into a castle.'

[2] *Ibid.* iv. 14 It is curious that his appeal is throughout *pro focis*, and not *pro aris*.

[3] *Ibid.* iv. 16–23.

[4] *Ibid.* iv. 21 (Heb.).

[5] With the exception indicated in the last words of iv. 23. (See Ewald, v. 156.)

[6] See Lecture XLI.

Even when the walls were completed the danger was not entirely over: the empty spaces of the town had[1] still to be filled from the nearest villages; the gates were still to be closed till the sun was[2] fully risen; guards were still to be kept. But Jerusalem was now once more a strong fortress. When the great military historian and archæologist of the Jewish nation looked at the defences of the city in his own time, he could truly say that 'though Nehemiah 'lived to a good old age, and performed many other noble acts, 'yet the eternal monument of himself which he left behind him 'was the circuit of the walls of Jerusalem.'[3] The day[4] on which this was accomplished was celebrated by a dedication, as if of a sanctuary, in which two[5] vast processions passed round the walls, halting at one or other of those venerable landmarks which signalised the various stages of their labour; whose shadows had been their daily and nightly companions for such weary months of watching and working. The Levites came up from their country districts, with their full array of the musical instruments which still bore the name[6] of their royal inventor; the minstrels, too, were[7] summoned from their retreats on the hills of Judah and in the deep valley of the Jordan. They all met in the Temple Court. The blast of the priestly trumpets sounded on one side, the songs of the minstrels were loud in proportion on the other. It is specially mentioned that even the women and children joined in the general acclamation, and 'the joy of Jerusalem was heard even afar off.' Perhaps the circumstance that leaves even yet a deeper impression than this tumultuous triumph is the meeting which on this day, and this day alone, Nehemiah records in his own person, of the two men who in spirit were so closely united--he himself as heading one procession, and 'Ezra the scribe' as heading the other.[8]

The dedication of the walls.

Ezra, it would seem, had taken no part in the fortification

[1] Neh. vii. 4; xi. 1, 2.
[2] *Ibid.* vii. 3.
[3] Jos. *Ant.* xi. 5, 8.
[4] Neh. vi. 15. The length of time which the rebuilding occupied is somewhat doubtful. See Ewald, v. 157.
[5] Neh. xii. 27-43
[6] *Ibid.* xii. 36.
[7] *Ibid.* xii. 28, 29. See Lecture XLIII.
[8] *Ibid.* xii. 36, 40.

of the walls. But there is one tradition [1] that connects him with the internal arrangements of the city. He was believed for the first time to have carried out the rule, afterwards so rigidly observed, of extramural interment. All the bones already buried within the city he cleared out, leaving only two exceptions, the tomb of the Kings and the tomb of the Prophetess Huldah.[2]

Once before, however, if we may trust the Chronicler of this period, Ezra and Nehemiah had been brought together—on the occasion of the Festival of the Tabernacles, so dear to the Jewish [3] nation, interwoven with the recollections of the dedication alike of the first and of the second Temple. Then as before when the startling conflict between their present condition and the regulations of the ancient law was brought before them, they broke out into passionate tears.

B.C. 455.

But this was not to be allowed.[4] The darker side of religion had not yet settled down upon the nation. The

Festival of Tabernacles.

joyous tone of David, and of Isaiah, which Haggai and Zechariah had continued, was not to be abandoned even in the austere days of the two severe Reformers.[5] Nehemiah the Tirshatha, and Ezra the Scribe—the Ruler first, and the Pastor afterwards—joined in checking this unseasonable burst of penitence. With those stern and stout hearts a flood [6] of tears was the sign, not of reviving strength, but of misplaced weakness. Feasting, not fasting, was the mark of the manly, exuberant energy which the national crisis required. 'This day 'is holy. Mourn not, nor weep. Go your way; eat the fat, 'and drink the sweet, and send portions unto them for whom 'nothing is prepared . . . neither be ye sorry, for the joy of 'the Eternal is your strength.' 'Hold your peace;' none of these fruitless lamentations: 'for the day is holy: neither be 'ye grieved.'

[1] Derenbourg, *Palestine*, p. 26. See Lecture XL.

[2] See Lecture XL.

[3] Neh. viii. 9–18. See Lecture XLIII.

[4] *Ibid.* viii. 9–12. See this admirably described by Ewald, v. 146.

[5] Neh. viii. 9.

[6] A like expression has been pointed out to me in the Homeric contrast between the Greeks and Trojans in this respect, *Iliad*, vii. 303.

Such was the Revival of Jerusalem; and even in details it was found to be borne out by the ancient law. That great festival of the Vintage which had been intended to commemorate the halt in the Exodus made within the borders of Egypt—the Dionysia,[1] the Saturnalia, the Christmas, if we may so say, of the Jewish Church—had during centuries fallen into almost entire neglect. They had to go back even to the days of Joshua to find a time when it had been rightly observed.[2] From the gardens of Mount Olivet, they cut down branches from the olives, the palms, and pines, and myrtles [3] that then clothed its sides, and on the flat roofs, and open grounds, and Temple courts, and squares before the city gates wove green arbours, with the childlike festivity which probably from that day to this has never ceased out of the Jewish world in that autumnal season. One there was who partook five centuries later in this feast, and whose heart's desire was that the joyous feelings represented by it might be perpetuated, though His followers have too often repelled or ignored them.[4]

From this point the two great restorers of Jerusalem who hitherto had moved in spheres apart—the aged scribe, absorbed in the study of the ancient law; the young layman, half warrior, half statesman, absorbed in the fortification of the city—were drawn closer and closer together, and henceforth, whether in legend or history, they became indistinguishably blended. The narrative of Nehemiah himself does not again mention Ezra; but it is devoted to deeds which, whether for good or evil, might almost equally belong to both. It is not the last time that the architect or the engineer has been the best colleague of the reformer or theologian. Vauban saw more truly, felt more keenly the true needs of France than Fénelon or Bossuet.[5] So Nehemiah rebuked the nobles for their oppressions and usurious exactions;[6] he summoned the Levites and the singers [7] to their appointed duties; he closed [8] the gates against the merchants who came with their laden

Reforms of Nehemiah.

[1] See Lecture XLVIII.
[2] Neh. viii. 17.
[3] *Ibid.* viii. 16.
[4] John vii. 2, 37.
[5] *Memoirs of St. Simon*, c. xviii.
[6] Neh. v. 1–16.
[7] *Ibid.* xiii. 10–12.
[8] *Ibid.* xiii. 15–22.

asses on the Sabbath day. He was the originator of the treaty or compact by which the whole nation bound itself[1] over to these observances. It was on a day of solemn abstinence (which, instead of preceding, as in later, and, perhaps, in earlier, times, followed[2] the Feast of Tabernacles) that this close and concentration of all their efforts was accomplished. Two at least of the pledges were fulfilled—the Levitical ritual was firmly established; the Sabbatical rest, both of the day and of the year,[3] struck deep root. And two lesser institutions also sprang from this time. One was the contribution of wood to the Temple. So vast was the consumption of timber for the furnaces in which the sacrificial flesh was roasted, or burnt, and so laborious was the process of hewing down the distant forest trees and bringing them into Jerusalem, that it was made a special article[4] of the national covenant, and the 14th of the month Ab (August) was observed as the Festival of the Wood-Carriers. It was the security that the sacred fire—which, according to the later legend, Nehemiah had lighted by preternatural means[5]—should always have a supply of fuel to preserve it from the slightest chance of extinction. Another was the rate levied on every Jew for the support of the Temple in the form of the third of a shekel, represented in the Greek coinage by two drachmas, and afterwards remaining as the sign[6] of Jewish citizenship.

Nehemiah's collision with the surrounding tribes still continued. They had contested inch by inch his great enterprise of making Jerusalem a fortified capital. There were three more obstructive than the rest, probably the three native princes established by the Persian satrap over the three surrounding districts of Transjordanic, Southern, and Northern Palestine. Tobiah was the resident at Ammon, and it would seem that, like the Hospodars in the Danubian Principalities, he had reached that post by having been a slave in the Imperial court,

[1] Neh. x. 29–34. [2] *Ibid.* ix. 1.

[3] 1 Macc. vi. 49, 53; Jos. *Ant.* xi. 8, 5; xiii. 8, 1; xiv. 10, 6; xv. 1. 2.

[4] Neh. x. 34: xiii. 31; Jos. *B. J.* ii. 17, 6; Ewald, 5, 166. [5] 2 Macc. i. 18.

[6] Neh. x. 32; Jos. *Ant.* xviii. 9, 1; Matt. xvii. 24–27. Kuenen (iii. 7) conjectures that the text of Ex. xxx. 11–16 was altered to half a shekel when it was found necessary to increase the payment.

and this antecedent Nehemiah does not allow us to forget. '*The slave*,[1] the Ammonite,' is the sarcastic expression by which Nehemiah more than once insists on designating him. Tobiah prided himself on his knowledge of the internal state of Jerusalem. He it was who, when his colleagues expressed alarm at the rebuilding of the walls, took upon himself to treat the whole matter as a jest: 'For if a jackal were to crawl up, 'he could knock them down.' He it was who had constant intrigues with the disaffected party within the walls, menacing Nehemiah by means of the puny representatives of the ancient prophets who still were to be found there, corresponding with the nobles, with whom he was doubly connected by his own marriage with the daughter of Shechaniah, and by his son's marriage with the daughter of Meshullam.[2] Even after the completion of the walls he still kept on his friendly relations with the chief priest Eliashib, and established himself in one of the great store-chambers of the Temple, until Nehemiah on his return from Susa indignantly drove him out with all his furniture.

Gashmu

The Arabian prince, who had apparently established himself in the Edomite territory, was Gashmu[3] or Geshem, founder probably of the Nabathæan dynasty, but living only in Nehemiah's memory as the idle chatterer who brought false charges against him as endeavouring to establish an independent sovereignty at Jerusalem.

and Sanballat.

But the most powerful of this triumvirate was Sanballat, whose official position at Samaria gave him special influence with the Persian garrison[4] which was quartered there. It is doubtful whether he was a native of Beth-horon, which would agree with his establishment on the western side of the Jordan, or of the Moabite Horonaim, which would agree with his close adhesion to the Ammonite Tobiah. There was a peculiar[5] vein of irritating taunt, for which those two tribes

[1] Neh. ii. 10–19. See Ewald, v. 153.

[2] *Ibid.* iv. 3; vi. 12, 14, 17, 18; xiii. 4, 7.

[3] *Ibid.* vi. 6. See a striking address of Robert Collyer (of Chicago), 'The Life 'that now is,' p. 137, on 'Gashmu,' probably the only sermon ever preached on this wild Arab, and full of quaint wisdom.

[4] Ezra iv. 23; Neh. iv. 2.

[5] Zeph. ii. 8; Neh. iv. 4; vi. 13. The same word is used. See Mr. Grove's in-

had an odious reputation, and which characterises all the communications of both those chiefs. Sanballat also, like Tobiah, was allied with the High Priest's family. There was a youth of that house, Manasseh, who had taken for his wife Sanballat's daughter, Nicaso.[1] Like Helen of Sparta, like La Cava of Spain, like Eva of Ireland, her name was preserved in Jewish tradition as the source of the long evils which flowed from that disastrous union. It was this that was the most conspicuous instance of those foreign marriages that had plunged Ezra into the silent abstraction of sorrow, and had roused the more fiery soul of Nehemiah to burning frenzy. He entered into personal conflict with them ; he struck them, he seized them by the hair and tore it from their heads. He chased away Manasseh with a fierce imprecation 'because he had defiled the priesthood and 'the court of the priesthood and of the Levites.' With this burst of wrath, blended with the proud thanksgiving that, after all, he had done something for the purification of the sacerdotal tribe, something too (there is a grotesque familiarity in the thought) for his settlement of the troublesome question of the firewood, Nehemiah closes his indignant record.

There is a pathetic cry, again and again repeated throughout this rare autobiographical sketch, hardly found elsewhere in the Hebrew records, which shows the current of his thoughts, as though at every turn he feared that those self-denying, self-forgetting labours might pass away, and that his countrymen of the future might be as ungrateful as his countrymen of the present. 'Think upon me, my God,[2] for good, according to 'all that I have done for this people.' 'Remember me, O my 'God, concerning this, and wipe not out my good deeds that I 'have done for the House of my God, and for the offices 'thereof.' 'Remember me, O my God, concerning this also, 'and spare me according to the greatness of thy mercy.' 'Re- 'member me, O my God, for good.'

That prayer for posthumous fame in great measure was

structive article on 'Moab' in the *Dict. of the Bible*, ii. p. 398.

[1] Neh. xiii. 28 ; Josephus (*Ant.* xi 7, 2), who, however, transfers the whole story to a later time. Ewald, v. 213, 214.

[2] Neh. v. 19 ; vi. 14 ; xiii. 14–31.

fulfilled in regard to both Reformers, but more remarkably in the case of Ezra than of Nehemiah. They were both glorified in the traditions of their country. At first Nehemiah, as might be expected from his more commanding position, takes the first place. It is he, and not Ezra, 'whose renown was great,' and who is the one hero of this epoch, in the catalogue of worthies[1] drawn up by the son of Sirach. It is Nehemiah, and not Zerubbabel, who in the next[2] age was believed to have rebuilt the Temple, reconsecrated the altar and found in the deep[3] pit, where it had been hidden, the sacred fire. It is Nehemiah, and not Ezra, who figures in the recollections of the same time as the collector of the sacred books.[4] But then, as sometimes happens in the reversal of popular verdicts, by which the obscure of one generation is advanced to the forefront of another, Ezra came out into a prominence which placed him on the highest pinnacle beside the heroes of the older time. He and not Nehemiah gave his name to the sacred book which records their acts. He was placed on a level with the first and the greatest of the Prophets, Moses and Elijah. He was identified with the last of the Prophets, Malachi. He was supposed to have[5] been contemporary with the Captivity, to have despaired of the restoration, and then after a hundred years risen again, with his dead ass, to witness the marvellous change. This is the only record of him in the Koran—a legend with the same moral as that of the awaking of the Seven Sleepers of Ephesus, but with the additional point that he came to life again after all those years for a special purpose. It is this sentiment which, in a hardly less transparent fiction, supposes that Ezra by a divine inspiration of memory reproduced the whole of the Scriptures of the Old Testament which had been burnt by the Chaldæans. This was the fixed belief of Irenæus, Tertullian,

Traditions of Nehemiah;

of Ezra.

[1] Ecclus. xlix. 11–13.

[2] 2 Macc. i. 22.

[3] Since the tenth century the well of 'En-rogel' or of 'Job,' at the confluence of the Hinnom and Kedron valleys, has, from this legend, been called 'the well of 'Nehemiah' (Robinson's *Researches*, i. 490).

[4] 2 Macc. ii. 13.

[5] 2 Esdras iii. 1, 29; D'Herbelot, *Bibliothèque*, iv. 539–543 (Ozair Ben Scherahia).

Clement of Alexandria, and Augustine,[1] based probably on the legend in the Second Book of Esdras, which tells how Ezra as he sate under an oak heard a voice from a bush over against him, warning him that 'the world had lost his youth, and the 'times begun to wax old,' and that for the weakness of these latter days he was to retire into the field for forty days with five men, 'ready to write swiftly;'—how he then received a full cup, full as it were 'of water, but the colour of it was like fire [2] '. . . and when he had drunk of it, his heart uttered under-'standing, and wisdom grew in his breast, for his spirit 'strengthened his memory . . . and his mouth was opened 'and shut no more, and for forty days and nights he dictated 'without stopping till 204 [3] books were written down.' [4]

This story thus first appearing at the close of the second century of the Christian era, and diluted by later divines into the more refined representation that Ezra was the collector or editor of the sacred books of the Old Testament Scriptures, has no historical basis. Neither of its wilder nor of its tamer form is there the slightest vestige in the authentic words of himself or of Nehemiah, nor yet in the later Chronicler, nor yet in the Son of Sirach, nor in the Books of Maccabees, nor in Josephus, nor yet in the first Apocryphal Book of Esdras, nor yet in the writings of the New Testament, where his name is never mentioned. Equally fabulous is the Jewish persuasion that he invented the Masoretic interpretations, and received the oral tradition of Mosaic doctrine, which from him was alleged to have been handed on to his successors.[5] The absolute silence of the contemporary or even following documents excludes all these suppositions.

Yet behind all this cloud of fables it is not difficult in the authentic documents of the time to discover the nucleus of fact round which it has gathered, or to render its due to the great

[1] See the quotations at length in the Bishop of Natal's work on the Moabite Stone, p. 314.

[2] This is varied in the traditions of the Eastern Church, which, applying to Ezra the story of Nehemiah in 2 Macc. i. 13, represent him as having acquired the gift of inspiration by swallowing three mouthfuls of the dust where the sacred fire was hid (D'Herbelot, iv. 643).

[3] This is the true reading, and leaves 24 for the Canonical Books.

[4] 2 Esdras xiv. 1–10, 23–44.

[5] Ewald v. 169.

historic name which represents, if not, as in the legends of his people, the 'Son of God,' at least the Founder of a new order of events and institutions, some of which continued to the close of the Jewish history, some of which continue still.

Ezra and Nehemiah (for in some respects they are inseparable) are the very impersonations of that quality which Goethe described as the characteristic by which their race has maintained its place before the Judgment seat of God and of history—the impenetrable toughness and persistency which constitute their real strength as the Reformers of their people.

As Reformers.

Reformers in the noblest sense of that word they were not. There is not, as in the first or second Isaiah, as in Jeremiah or Ezekiel, a far-reaching grasp of the future, or a penetration into the eternal principles of the human heart. They moved within a narrow, rigid sphere. They aimed at limited objects. They were the parents of the various divisions which henceforth divided Palestine into parties and sects. They were—by the same paradox according to which it is truly said that the Royalist Prelates of the English Restoration originated Nonconformity—the parents of the Samaritan secession.[1] They inaugurated in their covenants and their curses that fierce exclusiveness which in the later years burned with a 'zeal not 'according to knowledge' in the hearts of those wild assassins who bound themselves together with a curse not to eat bread or drink water till they had slain the greatest of their countrymen [2]—of those zealots who fought in a frenzy of desperate tenacity with each other and with their foes in defence of the walls which Nehemiah had raised. But within that narrow sphere Ezra and Nehemiah were the models of good Reformers. They set before themselves special tasks to accomplish and special evils to remedy, and in the doing of this they allowed no secondary or subsidiary object to turn them aside.[3] They asked of their countrymen [4] to undertake no burdens, no sacrifices, which they did not themselves share. They filled the people with a new enthusiasm because none could doubt that

[1] For the details of the Samaritan sect, see Lecture XXXIV. and Jost. i. 44.

[2] Acts xxiii. 21.

[3] Neh. vi. 3.

[4] Neh. v. 10.

they felt it themselves. The scene of Ezra sitting awestruck on the ground at the thought of his country's sins, the sound of the trumpet rallying all the various workmen and warriors at the wall to Nehemiah's side, inspire us still with their own inspiration. When we read of the passion, almost the violence, of Nehemiah in cleansing the Temple and clearing its chambers, we see the spark, although the sulphureous spark, of that same Divine flame, of which, when One came who found the house of prayer turned into a cavern of robbers, it was said 'the zeal 'of Thine House hath even consumed me.'[1]

As antiquaries.

They were again the first distinct and incontestable examples of that antiquarian, scholastic, critical treatment of the ancient history and literature of the country which succeeds and is inferior to the periods of original genius and inspiration, but is itself an indispensable element of instruction. Something of the kind we have indicated[2] in the efforts of Baruch the scribe when he gathered together the scattered leaves of Jeremiah's prophecies, or of the earlier compiler, who during the exile collected in the Books of Kings the floating fragments of the earlier history and poetry of his race. But now we actually see the process before our eyes.

Nehemiah, when he came to Jerusalem, not contented with the rough work of building and fighting, dived[3] into the archives of the former generations and thence dug out and carefully preserved the Register of the names, properties, and pedigrees of those who had returned in the original exile. Some other antiquary or topographer must in other days have done the like for that which we have called elsewhere the Domesday Book of Canaan in the Book of Joshua. But in Nehemiah we first meet with an unquestionable person whose name we can connect with that science whose title owed no small part of its early fame to the Jewish history which was so designated—Josephus's 'Archæology.' It is Nehemiah's keen sympathy with those antique days which made him so diligent an explorer of the ruined walls and gates and towers and well-worn stairs, and of the legal ancestral documents of the city of his fathers'

[1] John ii. 17. [2] Lectures XL. and XLI. [3] Neh. vii. 5-73; xi. 3-36.

sepulchres. And not only so, but (if we may trust the first tradition on the subject which can be traced, and which contains the one particle of probable truth in the legends concerning the origin of the Jewish canon) it was Nehemiah[1] who first undertook in the self-same spirit implied in the authentic notices just cited to form a Library of the books of the past times: namely, of 'the Books of the Kings, and Prophets, 'those which bore the name of David, and the Royal Letters 'concerning sacred offerings.' This earliest tradition respecting the agglomeration of the sacred Hebrew literature certainly indicates that it was in Nehemiah's time that the various documents of the past history of his race were united in one collection. Then, probably, was the time when the Unknown Prophet of the Captivity was attached to the roll of the elder Isaiah, and the earlier Zechariah affixed to the prophecies of his later namesake;[2] when the Books of Jasher and of the 'Wars of the Lord' finally perished, and were superseded by the existing Books of 'Samuel' and 'of the Kings.' It is evident from the terms of the description that 'Nehemiah's Library' was not coextensive with any existing canon. It was not a formation of divine oracles so much as a repository of whatever materials from whatever source might be useful for the future history of his people. It was not the complete canon of the 'Old Testament' which was then formed, for some even of the earlier Books, such as Ezekiel, had not yet fully established their right; and many books or parts of books now contained in it were still absent. The various treatises of 'Ezra,' Malachi, the Chronicles, Esther, the Maccabean Psalms, the Maccabean Histories, perhaps Ecclesiastes, probably Daniel, were still to come. Nor was it based on the modern idea of a strictly sacred volume; for one of its chief component parts consisted of the official letters of the Persian kings, which have never had a place in the ecclesiastical roll of the consecrated Scriptures. It was the natural, the laudable attempt to rescue from oblivion such portions of the Hebrew literature as, with perpetually increasing

As collectors of the sacred books.

[1] 2 Macc. ii. 13.

[2] Kuenen, iii. 12.

additions, might illustrate and enforce[1] the one central book of the Pentateuch, round which they were gathered. The 'Prophets' were still outside, occupying a position analogous to that filled in the early Christian Canon by the Deutero-canonical writings of the Old Testament, and the 'doubtful' writings of the New Testament.[2] These, in common with all 'the other books' which followed them, formed a class by themselves, known as 'the Books,'[3] 'the Bible' (to adopt the modern word), outside 'the Holy Book' or 'Holy Bible,' which was the Law itself.

And this brings us to the point at which Nehemiah the Governor recedes from view to make way for Ezra the Scribe, who in the later traditions, alike of Jew, Arab, and early Christian, entirely takes his place.

As interpreters of the sacred book.

There is an almost contemporary[4] representation of Ezra which at once places before us his true historical position in this aspect. It was on the occasion of that great celebration of the Feast of the Tabernacles which has been before mentioned. The whole people were assembled—not the men only, but the women issuing from their Eastern seclusion; not the old only, but all whose dawning intelligence[5] enabled them to understand at all, were gathered on one of the usual gathering-places outside the city walls. On the summit of the slope of the hill (as the *Bema* rose on the highest tier of the Athenian Pnyx) was raised a huge wooden tower on which stood Ezra with a band of disciples round him. There, on that September morning, just as the sun was rising above Mount Olivet, he unrolled before the eyes of the expectant multitude the huge scroll of the Law, which he had doubtless brought with him from Chaldæa. At that moment the whole multitude rose from the crouching postures in which they were seated, after the manner of the East, over the whole

[1] ἐπισυνήγαγεν. 2 Macc. ii. 13.

[2] So the oldest Talmudic statements ('Mishna Megilla' iv., 'Jerusalem Megilla' 73, Sepher Israel iii., Sopherim iii.). These references, and the conclusions therefrom, I owe to Dr. Ginsburg. Comp. Dan. ix. 2.

[3] See Lecture XLVIII.

[4] It is not in Nehemiah's own records, but in that by which the Chronicler has filled up the interstices in Neh. viii. 8, ix. 38.

[5] Neh. viii. 3.

of the open platform. They stood on their feet, and he at the same instant blessed 'the Eternal, the great God.' Thousands of hands were lifted up from the crowd, in the attitude of prayer, with the loud reverberated cry of *Amen*: and again hands and heads sank down and the whole people lay prostrate on the rocky ground. It was then the early dawn. From that hour the assembly remained in fixed attention till the midday heat dispersed them. The instruction was carried on partly by reading the sacred book, partly by explaining it. Sometimes it was Ezra himself who poured forth a long passionate summary of their history, sometimes it was the Levites who addressed the people in prayer.[1]

We feel that in this scene a new element of religion has entered on the stage. The Temple has retired for the moment into the background. There is something which stirs the national sentiment yet more deeply, and which is the object of still more profound veneration. It is 'the Law.' However we explain the gradual growth of the Pentateuch, however we account for the ignorance of its contents, for the inattention to its precepts, this is the first distinct introduction of the Mosaic law as the rule of the Jewish community. That lofty platform on which Ezra stood might be fitly called 'the Seat of Moses.'[2] It is from this time that the Jewish nation became one of those whom Mohammed calls 'the people of a book.' It was but one book amongst the many which Nehemiah had collected, but it was the kernel round which the others grew with an ever-multiplying increase. The Bible, and the reading of the Bible as an instrument of instruction, may be said to have been begun on the sunrise of that day when Ezra unrolled the parchment scroll of the Law. It was a new thought that the Divine Will could be communicated by a dead literature as well as by a living voice. In the impassioned welcome with which this thought was received lay the germs of all the good and evil which were afterwards to be developed out of it; on the one side, the possibility of appeal in each successive age to the primitive, undying document that should rectify the fluctuations

[1] Neh. ix. 3, 4, 5 (LXX.).

[2] Matt. xxiii. 2.

of false tradition and fleeting opinion ; on the other hand, the temptation to pay to the letters of the sacred book a worship as idolatrous and as profoundly opposed to its spirit as once had been the veneration paid to the sacred trees or the sacred stones of the consecrated groves or hills.

But we have said that the book which was thus reverenced was not coextensive even with the Hebrew Scriptures as they are now received. It contained no single song of David, no single proverb of Solomon, no single prophecy of Isaiah or Jeremiah. It was '*the Law*.' When Manasseh, in his passion for his Samaritan wife, fled from the fury of Nehemiah to the height of Gerizim, he carried with him, either actually or in remembrance, not all the floating records which the fierce Governor of Jerusalem in his calmer moods was gathering here and there like the Reliques which Percy or Scott collected from the holes and corners of English minstrelsy, or Livy from the halls of Roman nobles. It was the five books of Moses only, with that of Joshua appended, which the fugitive priest had heard from Ezra, or Ezra's companions, and which alone at the moment of his departure commanded the attention of the community from which he parted.[1] We trace the exact point which the popular veneration had reached by the point at which it was broken off in the Samaritan secession.

The Law.

It is not without importance to notice the ascendency of this one particular aspect of the ancient Jewish literature over every other, and to observe that the religion of this age was summed up, not in a creed or a hymn, but in the Law—whether on its brighter or its darker side. On its brighter side we see it as it is represented in the 119th Psalm,[2] belonging,

[1] In like manner the retention of the ancient Hebrew characters by the Samaritans confirms the Talmudic tradition that the introduction of the Chaldaic characters dates from the time of Ezra. The Hebrew characters still continued to be used on coins, like Latin, as the official language of Europe after it had been discontinued in literature. The use of the Chaldæan characters for the sacred books was probably originated by the desire to have an additional mark of distinction from the Samaritans, as the English pronunciation of Latin is said to have been suggested or confirmed by the wish to make an additional test to detect the Roman conspiracies against the Protestant Sovereigns. See Derenbourg, p. 446.

[2] See Ewald, v. 173.

in all probability, to this epoch. In every possible form the change is rung on the synonyms for this great idea. Every verse expresses it :—*Law*, *Testimony*, *Commandments*, *Statutes.* The Psalmist never lets us forget for a moment what is the object of his devotion. It is the Biblical expression of the unchanging Law of Right, through which, as it has been said by one of later times,

Even the stars are kept from wrong,
And the most ancient heavens through thee are fresh and strong.

It is the vindication of the grandeur of that side of human goodness which both the religious and the cynical world have often condemned as commonplace morality, but which the author of this Jewish Ode to Duty regards as the highest flight both of piety and of philosophy. 'The 119th Psalm,' says a writer of our time, 'that meditation which with sweet 'monotony strikes ever the golden string deep buried in the 'human heart, a string implying by its strange susceptibilities 'the reality of a music not of this world, yet harmonising all 'worlds in one ! There is no poetry, there is little rhythm, 'there is no intellectual insight, there is no comprehensive 'philosophy, in the gentle life that yearns and pleads through 'those undying words. But there is not one verse which does 'not tell of a man to whom the Infinite Power was a living 'Presence and a constant inspiration.'[1] Such is the form under which the Law presented itself to a religious mind in that age of the Jewish Church, and which well agrees both with the passionate devotion of Ezra to its service, and the attachment to it, with a mingling of tears and laughter, which made it the main lever of his revival of his people. It is strange to reflect that this grand idea had become so perverted and narrowed as time rolled on, that in the close of the Jewish Commonwealth 'the Law,' instead of being regarded by the highest spirit of the age as the main support of goodness, was at least at times regarded by him as its worst and deadliest enemy.[2] But the aspect of the Law as presented by the

[1] *Mystery of Matter*, by the Rev. J. Allanson Picton, p. 280.

[2] Rom. iii. 20, 28 ; iv. 15 ; vii. 5 ; viii. 2, 3 ; Gal. ii. 16, iii. 2, 10, iv. 5, 9, 10 ; v.

Psalmist is the more persuasive and more enduring. He saw, and the course of ages has made us see even more clearly, that all other things come to an end, but that the commandment of God is bounded by no narrow compass.[1]

And this leads us to the attitude in which Ezra himself stood towards the Pentateuch. He was a Jewish Priest; he was a Persian judge. But the name by which he is emphatically called, throwing all else into the shade, is 'the Scribe.' We have already indicated the earlier beginnings of the office. But in Ezra it received an importance[2] altogether unprecedented. In him the title came to mean 'the man of the Book.' Those long readings and expositions of the Law called into existence two classes of men; the one inferior, the Interpreters or Targumists, or (which is another form of the same word), Dragomans; the other the Scribes, who took their places beside the Elders and the Priests, at times as the most powerful institution of the community. The Interpreters or Dragomans resulted from the necessity of rendering the archaic Hebrew into the popular Aramaic. They were regarded for the most part as mere hirelings—empty, bombastic characters, without the slightest authority, ragged, half-clothed mendicants, who could be silenced in a moment by their superiors in the assembly,[3] compelled to speak orally lest their words should by chance be mistaken for those of the Scripture. The Scribes or 'Lawyers,' that is, the learned in the Pentateuch, were far different. Here, again, as in the case of 'the Law,' we find ourselves confronted with an element which contains at once the noblest and the basest aspects of the Jewish, and we must add, of the Christian religion. It is evident that in the Scribes rather than in any of the other functionaries of the Jewish Church is the nearest original of the clergy of later times. In the ancient Prophet, going to and fro, sometimes naked, sometimes wrapt in his hairy cloak, chanting his wild melodies, or dramatising his own

The Scribes.

18; 1 Cor. xv. 56; See, however, Rom. vii. 12; 1 Tim. i. 8.
Ps. cxix. 96 (Perowne).

[2] Derenbourg, 25.

[3] Deutsch's *Remains*, pp. 325, 326.

message, always strange and exceptional—in the ancient Priest, deriving his sanctity from his clothes, with his strong arms imbrued, like a butcher's, in the blood of a cow or a sheep, no one would recognise the religious[1] ministers of any civilised country for the last eighteen centuries. But in the Scribe, poring over the sacred volume, or reading and enforcing it from his lofty platform, or explaining it to the small knots of 'those that had understanding,' and gathered round him for instruction, there is an unmistakable likeness to the religious teachers of all the various forms which have arisen out of the Judaism of Ezra and Nehemiah. The Rabbi in the schools of Safed and Tiberias, expounding or preaching, from whatever tribe he may have sprung—the Cadi founding his verdicts on the Koran—the Imam delivering his Friday Sermon from the Midbar or instructing his little circle of hearers on the floor of the mosques—the Christian clergy through all their different branches—Doctors, Pastors, Evangelists, Catechists, Readers, Revivalists, studying, preaching, converting, persuading—all these in these their most spiritual functions, have their root not in Aaron's altar, nor even in Samuel's choral school, but in Ezra's pulpit.

The finer elements of this widely-ramifying institution thus inaugurated appear at its outset. It was the permanent triumph of the moral over the purely mechanical functions of worship. The prophets had effected this to a certain extent; but their appearance was so fitful—their gifts so irregular—that they were always, so to speak, outside the system, rather than a part of it—Preaching Friars, Nonconformists, or, at the most, Occasional Conformists on the grandest scale. But from the time of Ezra the Scribes never ceased. The intention of their office, as first realised in him and his companions, was the earnest endeavour to reproduce, to study, to translate, to represent in the language of his own time, the oracles of sacred antiquity; to ascertain the meaning of dark words, to give life to dead forms, to enforce forgotten duties; to stimulate the apathy of the present by invoking the

[1] See Lecture XXXVI.

loftier spirit of the past. Such was the ideal of the 'Minister 'of Religion' henceforth; and when the Highest teacher described it in His own words He found none better than to take the office of Ezra, and say: 'Every Scribe which 'is instructed[1] unto the Kingdom of Heaven is like unto an 'householder which bringeth forth out of his treasure things 'new and old.'

And when in the sixteenth century of the Christian Church the intellectual and spiritual element of Religion was once again brought to the front, with the appeal to its original documents —the English Martyr at the stake could find no fitter words to express the permanent triumph of his cause than those which in the Apocryphal Book of Esdras are spoken in reference to the ideal Scribe, the ideal Reformer of Israel: 'I shall light a 'candle of understanding in thine heart, which shall not be 'put out.'[2]

But to this great office there was and is a darker side. There was, indeed, nothing of itself Priestly in the functions of the Scribe; the idea of their office was as distinct, almost as alien, from the mechanical, bullock-slaying, fumigating ministrations of the Priesthood as had been the office of the Prophets. But, unlike the Prophets, this distinction was in their case often more of form than of spirit. Ezra, though a Scribe first and foremost, was yet a Priest; and his chief associates, until the arrival of the Governor, Nehemiah, were Levites. The Scribes and the Priests hung together; and at some of the most critical moments of their history the interests, the passions, and the prejudices of the two were fatally indissoluble. And in like manner, although from the more spiritual nature of the religion in a less degree, the Pastors of the Christian Church have again and again been tempted to formalise and materialise their spiritual functions by associating them once more with the name and the substance of the ancient Jewish[3] or Pagan Priesthood.

[1] Matt. xiii. 52.

[2] 2 Esdras xiv. 25. Compare Froude's *History of England*, vi. 387.

[3] See Professor Lightfoot on the Philippians, 243-266.

And yet further the peculiar ministrations of the Scribes became more and more divorced from that homely yet elevated aspect imparted to his office by Ezra. There was, as we have seen, the fable which ascribed to him the formation of a body of Scribes called the Great Synagogue,[1] by which the Canon of Scripture was arranged, the first Liturgy of the Jewish Church composed, and of which the succession continued till its last survivor died two centuries afterwards. Some such circle doubtless may have grown up round the first great Scribe—a circle of 'men of understanding' such as Johanan and Eliashib, who are described [2] by that name as having accompanied him from Babylon—though of the existence or the doings of any such regular body no vestige appears in any single historical or authentic work before the Christian era. But there is one traditional saying ascribed to the Great Synagogue which must surely have come down from an early stage in the history of the Scribes, and which well illustrates the disease, to which, as to a parasitical plant, the order itself, and all the branches into which it has grown, has been subject. It resembles in form the famous mediæval motto for the guidance of conventual ambition, although it is more serious in spirit: 'Be circumspect in judg-'ing—make many disciples—make a hedge round the law.'[3] Nothing could be less like the impetuosity, the simplicity, or the openness of Ezra than any of these three precepts. But the one which in each succeeding generation predominated more and more was the last: 'Make a hedge about the Law.' To build up elaborate explanations, thorny obstructions, subtle evasions, enormous developments, was the labour of the later Jewish Scribes, till the Pentateuch was buried beneath the Mishna, and the Mishna beneath the Gemara. To make hedges round the Koran has been, though not perhaps in equally disproportioned manner, the aim of the schools of

[1] All that can be said on this subject is well summed up by Derenbourg, c. 3, and by Ginsburg in Kitto's *Cyclopædia* ('Great 'Synagogue'), where it is conjectured that the 120 members were made up out of the list in Nehemiah. Comp. Herzfeld, iii. 380–387.

[2] 'Mebinim.' Ezra viii. 16.

[3] Derenbourg, 34. The mediæval saying is, 'Parere superiori, legere breviarium 'taliter qualiter, et sinere res vadere ut 'vadunt.'

El-Azar and Cordova, and of the successive Fetvahs of the Sheykhs-el-Islam. To erect hedges round the Gospel has been the effort, happily not continuous or uniform, but of large and dominant sections of the Scribes of Christianity, until the words of its Founder have well-nigh disappeared, behind the successive intrenchments, and fences, and outposts, and counter-works, of Councils, and Synods, and Popes, and anti-Popes, and Sums of Theology and of Saving Doctrine, of Confessions of Faith and Schemes of Salvation ; and the world has again and again sighed for one who would once more speak with the authority of self-evidencing Truth, and 'not[1] as the Scribes.' A distinguished Jewish Rabbi of this century, in a striking and pathetic passage on this crisis in the history of his nation, contrasts the prospect of the course which Ezekiel and Isaiah had indicated with that which was inaugurated by Ezra, and sums up his reflections with the remark that : 'Had the spirit been preserved 'instead of the letter, the substance instead of the form, then 'Judaism might have been spared the necessity of Christianity.'[2] But we in like manner may say that, had the Scribes of the Christian Church retained more of the genius of the Hebrew Prophets, Christianity in its turn would have been spared what has too often been a return to Judaism, and it was in the perception of the superiority of the Prophet to the Scribe that its original force and unique excellence have consisted.

One further germ of spiritual life may, probably, be traced to the epoch of Ezra. If in the long unmarked period which follows, the worship of the Synagogue silently sprang up such as we shall see it at the latest stage of their history,[3] it must have originated in the independent, personal, universal study of the Law, irrespective of Temple or Priest, which Ezra had inaugurated. The great innovation of Prayer[4] as a substitute for Sacrifice thus took root in Jewish worship ; the eighteen prayers which are still recited in Jewish synagogues,[5] and of which some at least are, both by ancient tradition and modern criticism, ascribed to Ezra and his companions, are the

The Synagogues.

[1] Matt. vii. 29.
[2] Herzfeld, ii. 32-36.
[3] See Lecture L.
[4] See Lecture XLI.
[5] See Kuenen, *Religion of Israel*, iii. 19.

first example of an articulate Liturgy. On the one hand, the personal devotion of the Psalms now found its place as the expression of the whole community; and, on the other hand, the conviction which the Prophets entertained of the perpetual existence of the nation, prepared the way for the conviction of the endless life of the single human being. 'In a word, 'Judaism was now on the road towards the adoption of the hope 'of personal immortality.'[1]

NOTE.

Of the 'Eighteen Benedictions' (p. 134), as they are called, the 1st, 2nd, and 3rd, the 17th, and 18th and 19th (Prideaux, i. 419-422) are believed to date from Ezra. They are as follows:—

1. Blessed be Thou, O Lord, our God, the God of our fathers, the God of Abraham, the God of Isaac, the God of Jacob, the great God, powerful and tremendous, the high God, bountifully dispensing benefits, the Creator and Possessor of the Universe, who rememberest the good deeds of our fathers, and in Thy love sendest a Redeemer to those who are descended from them, for Thy name's sake, O King, our Helper, our Saviour, and our Shield. Blessed art Thou, O Lord, who art the Shield of Abraham.

2. Thou, O Lord, art powerful for ever. Thou raisest the dead to life, and art mighty to save; Thou sendest down the dew, stillest the winds, and makest the rain to come down upon the earth, and sustainest with Thy beneficence all that live therein; and of Thine abundant mercy makest the dead again to live. Thou helpest up those that fall; Thou curest the sick; Thou loosest them that are bound, and makest good Thy Word of Truth to those that sleep in the dust.

Who is to be compared to Thee, O Thou Lord of might? and who is like unto Thee, O our King, who killest and makest alive, and makest salvation to spring up as the herb out of the field? Thou art faithful to make the dead to rise again to life. Blessed art Thou, O Lord, who raisest the dead again to life.

3. Thou art holy, and Thy name is holy, and Thy Saints do

[1] Kuenen, iii. 30.

praise Thee every day. For a great King and an holy art Thou, O God. Blessed art Thou, O Lord God most holy.

17. Be Thou well pleased, O Lord our God, with Thy people Israel, and have regard unto their prayers. Restore Thy worship to the inner part of Thy house, and make haste with favour and love to accept of the burnt sacrifices of Israel and their prayers; and let the worship of Israel Thy people be continually well pleasing unto Thee. Blessed art Thou, O Lord, who restorest thy Divine presence to Zion.

18. We will give thanks unto Thee with praise. For Thou art the Lord our God, the God of our fathers for ever and ever. Thou art our Rock, and the Rock of our life, the Shield of our salvation. To all generations will we give thanks unto Thee and declare Thy praise; because of our life, which is always in Thy hands; and because of our souls, which are ever depending upon Thee; and because of Thy signs, which are every day with us; and because of Thy wonders, and marvellous loving-kindnesses, which are, morning and evening and night, continually before us. Thou art good, for thy mercies are not consumed; Thou art merciful, for Thy loving-kindnesses fail not. For ever we hope in Thee; and for all these mercies be Thy name, O King, blessed, and exalted, and lifted up on high for ever and ever; and let all that live give thanks unto Thee. And let them in truth and sincerity praise Thy name, O God of our salvation and our help. Blessed art Thou, O Lord, whose name is good, and whom it is fitting always to give thanks unto.

19. Give peace, beneficence, and benediction, grace, benignity, and mercy unto us, and to Israel Thy people. Bless us, O our Father, even all of us together as one man. With the light of Thy countenance hast Thou given unto us, O Lord our God, the law of life, and love, and benignity, and righteousness, and blessing, and mercy, and life, and peace. And let it seem good in Thine eyes to bless Thy people Israel with Thy peace at all times and in every moment. Blessed art Thou, O Lord, who blessest Thy people Israel with peace. Amen.

XLV.

MALACHI.

(OR THE CLOSE OF THE PERSIAN PERIOD.)

B.C. 480—400.

AUTHORITIES.

Malachi.
Esther (Hebrew and Greek).
Josephus, *Ant.* xi. 6, 7.

MALACHI.

LECTURE XLV.

MALACHI.

'THE age[1] of Ezra—the last pure glow of the long days of the 'Old Testament seers—produced one more prophetic work, the 'brief composition of Malachi. With its clear insight 'into the real wants of the time, its stern reproof even 'of the priests themselves, and its bold exposition of the eternal 'truths and the certainty of a last judgment, this book closes 'the series of prophetic writings in a manner not unworthy of 'such lofty predecessors. And, indeed, it is no less important 'than consistent in itself that even the setting sun of the Old 'Testament days should still be reflected in a true prophet, and 'that the fair days of Ezra and Nehemiah should in him be 'glorified more nobly still.'

The last of the Prophets.

Malachi was the last of the Prophets. The prophets and prophetesses that had appeared since the time of Haggai and Zechariah[2] were but of a weak and inferior kind. He alone represents the genuine spirit of the ancient oracular[3] order—as far at least as concerns the purely Hebrew history—till the final and transcendent burst of Evangelical and Apostolical prophecy, when a new era was opened on the world. The approximate time of the work can be fixed by its allusions to the surrounding circumstances, which are still of the same kind as those which form the scene of the operations of Ezra and Nehemiah. To

[1] Ewald v. 176. [2] Neh. vi. 7, 12, 14. [3] Macc. iv. 46; ix. 27; xiv. 41; Dan. iii. 38 (LXX.); Psalm lxxiv. 9; Ecclus. xxxvi. 15.

them he must have stood in the same relation as Isaiah to Hezekiah, or Haggai to Zerubbabel ; and, although there is no probability in the tradition which identifies him with Ezra, it is true that he represents the prophetic aspect of the epoch of which the two great Reformers were the scholastic and secular representatives.

There is the same close union as then between[1] the office of Priest and Scribe. There is the same demoralisation[2] of the Priesthood as then in the questionable associations of the house of the High Priest Eliashib—the Eli of those later days—the gross and audacious[3] plundering of Hophni and Phineas repeated on the paltry scale of meaner and more niggardly pilfering. There are, as in Ezra's time, the faithless husbands, deserting for some foreign alliance their Jewish wives, who bathe the altar with their tears.[4] There are the wealthy[5] nobles, as in the days of Nehemiah, who grind down the poor by their exactions. Against all these the Prophet raises up his voice in the true spirit of Amos or of Joel. There is also the passionate denunciation of Edom,[6] which runs like a red thread through all the prophetic strains of this epoch, from Jeremiah and Ezekiel and the Second Isaiah, through Obadiah and the Babylonian Psalmist, down to this last and fiercest expression, which goes so far as to enhance the Divine love for Jacob by contrasting it with the Divine hatred for Esau. But there are three ideas peculiar, if not in substance yet in form, to Malachi —significantly marking the point from which, as it were, he looks over the silent waste of years that is to follow him, unbroken by any distinct prophetic utterance, yet still responding in various faint echoes to the voice of this last of the long succession of seers that had never ceased since the days of Samuel.

I. We speak first of the chief idea which is inwrought into the very structure of his work and of his being. The expectation of an Anointed King of the House of David has ceased. Since the death of Zerubbabel, neither in Ezra, nor Nehemiah, nor Malachi, nor in any contemporary

The Messenger.

[1] Mal. ii. 7. [2] *Ibid.* i. 6–12 ; ii. 8, 9. [3] See Lecture XVIII.
[4] Mal. ii. 10–14. [5] *Ibid.* iii. 5. [6] *Ibid.* i. 2, 3. See Lecture XL.

books, is there any trace of such a hope. It is another form in which the vision of the future shaped itself, and which was peculiarly characteristic of the time. The prominent figure is now that of the Messenger, the *avant courier*—to use the Greek word, 'the Angel,' to use the Hebrew word, the *Malachi*—of the Eternal. Such a figure had, doubtless, been used before. In the Patriarchal age, and at times in the Monarchy, there had been heavenly Messengers who brought the Divine Word to the listening nation. Once by the Great Prophet of the Captivity Israel himself is termed the Angel or the Messenger.[1] In Haggai[2] after the return that idea had been still further localised. He was himself 'the Angel of the Eternal.' In Zechariah the same expression (was it the aged Haggai of whom he[3] spoke, or the unseen Presence which Haggai represented?) describes the mysterious guide that led him through the myrtle groves and through the court of the High Priest's trial. But now the word pervades the whole prophetic Book. The very name of the Prophet is taken from it; whether he bore the title of Malachi as indicating the idea with which the age was full, or whether it was transferred to a Prophet without a name[4] (as, possibly, the title of Abdadonai, 'the servant of the Lord,' may have been given to the Great Unnamed of the Captivity[5]), from the subject of his prophecy. The ideal Priest whom Malachi describes is in like manner the Messenger of the Lord of Hosts.[6] The eventful consummation to which he looks is the arrival, not of the Warrior-king or the Invisible Majesty of Heaven, but of the Messenger who should enforce[7] the treaty which had been made of old time between God and His people, which had of late been renewed by Nehemiah. This was to be the moment of the unexpected[8] sifting and dividing of the essential from the unessential, the worthless from the valuable. It was to be like the furnace in which the precious metals were cleansed; it was to be like the tank in which the fullers beat and washed out the clothes of the inhabitants of Jerusalem; it

[1] Isa. xlii. 19.
[2] Haggai i. 13.
[3] Zech. i. 11, 12; iii. 1; iv. 1.
[4] Mal. i. 1. This is well argued in Reuss on the Prophets, ii. 379-381.
[5] See Clem. Alex. *Strom.* i. 2. (Lecture XLI.)
[6] Mal. ii. 7.
[7] *Ibid.* iii. 1.
[8] *Ibid.* iii. 2, 3.

was to be like the glorious yet terrible uprising of the Eastern sun[1] which should wither to the very roots the insolence and the injustice of mankind; but, as its rays extended, like the wings of the Egyptian Sun-god, should by its healing and invigorating influences call forth the good from their obscurity, prancing and bounding like the young cattle in the burst of spring, and treading down under their feet the dust and ashes to which the same bright sun had burnt up the tangled thicket of iniquitous dealing. Yet for this day of mingled splendour and gloom, a Prelude, a Preparation was needed; and, in forecasting the forms which it would take, two colossal figures rose out of the past. One was Moses,[2] to whom on Horeb had been given the Law, which now through Ezra had been revived, expounded, and brought within their reach. The Pentateuch was to live in their remembrance. The memory of their past history, the fulfilment of those ruling principles of 'conduct which 'are three-fourths of human life,' was their guide for the perilous future. And for the enforcement of these there was needed yet another spirit of the mighty dead. It was the great[3] representative of the whole Prophetic order, now, as it were, by the last of his race, evoked from the invisible world. Already there had sprung up round the mysterious figure of Elijah that belief which reached its highest pitch in the Mussulman world, where he is 'the Immortal one,' who in the greenness of perpetual youth is always appearing to set right the wrong—and which in the Jewish nation has expected him to revive in each new crisis[4] of their fate, and to solve all the riddles of their destiny. But for Malachi the chief mission of the returning Elijah was to be that of the Forerunner of the final crisis: who should arrest[5] in their diverging courses the hearts both of the older and the younger generation, and who should enable (if we thus far venture to unfold the thought which is not expressed in the Prophecy, but lies deep in the

[1] Mal. iv. 2, 3 (Heb.). See Lecture IV.
[2] *Ibid.* iv. 5. [3] *Ibid.* iv. 5.
[4] See Lecture XXX.
[5] Mal. iii. 6. It is the figure implied in the word 'turn' which is perpetuated in the Latin phrase *conversion*, and in the Greek μετάνοια. The idea is of a wrench of the mind in another than its ordinary direction.

history of that, as of all like ages) the fathers to recognise the new needs and the new powers of the children, and the children to recognise the value of the institutions and traditions which they inherit from the fathers.

Such an insistance on the necessity of patient preparation—on the importance of working out the old and homely truths of justice and truthfulness, as the best means of meeting the coming conflict—received its full point and meaning when such a rough Precursor, such an Angel[1] of moral reformation, did arise and recall, even in outward garb and form, the ancient Tishbite who had last been seen in the same valley of the Jordan. But the principle of the necessity of a Messenger or Angel in the place or in the anticipation of that which is still to come—of the opening of the way by the Great for the Greatest—of the announcement of pure morality, which commends itself to the many, leading towards the spiritual religion which commends itself chiefly to the few—this is the main idea of Malachi's teaching, which shall now be expanded and explained by the corresponding events and ideas of his time.

Awe of the Divine Name.

I. It branches into two parts. The sense of the need of this intermediary dispensation, if it is not directly connected, at any rate coincides, with the awe which shrinks from familiar contact with the Divine Name and Presence, with the reverence which fears, the irreverence which despises, the mention of the Supreme Unseen Cause. In the book which probably approaches most nearly to the time of Malachi the change is complete. In[2] the Book of Ecclesiastes there is no name but Elohim—'God'—and the whole book is penetrated with a reserve and self-control expressed in words which have a significant import when within sound of the multitude of theological phrases and devotional iteration by which, both in East and West, the religious world often has sought to approach its Maker: 'God is in Heaven and thou

[1] Mark i. 2. So completely in the Eastern Church—probably from the constant use of the word ἀγγελος both for angel and messenger—have the two deas been combined, that John the Baptist, in reference to this passage, is, in the traditionary Greek pictures (as at Mount Athos), represented as a winged angel.

[2] For the date of Ecclesiastes see Ginsburg's *Koheleth*, 244-255.

'upon earth, therefore let thy words be few.'[1] And it is summed up in the brief conclusion of the whole matter, after contemplating the many proverbs, the words of the wise, the endless making of many books, which had already begun to characterise the nation : 'Fear God and keep His command-'ments, for this is the whole duty of man.' We have seen how in earlier times the name first of 'Jehovah,'[2] and then of 'Jehovah Sabaoth,' became the national name of the Divine Ruler of Israel. We have now arrived at the moment when this great title is to disappear. In the parallel passages of duplicate poetry or duplicate history the simpler 'Elohim' began to take the place of the more[3] sacred 'Jehovah.'

Adoption of *Adonai* for *Jehovah*.

In accordance with these isolated indications was the general practice, of which we cannot ascertain the exact beginning, by which the special name of the God of Israel was now withdrawn, and, as far as the Hebrew race was concerned, for ever withdrawn, from the speech and even the writings of the nation. Already[4] at the time of the Samaritan secession in the days of Nehemiah the change began to operate. In their usages, instead of the word 'Jehovah'[5] was substituted 'Shemeh,' 'the Name;' but they still had retained the word unaltered in their own copies of the Law. But the Jews of Jerusalem in the place of the ancient name substituted, first by pronunciation, and then by changing the points of the vowels, throughout the sacred writings, the word 'Adonai,' 'Lord or Master'[6]—the same word that appears for the Phœnician deity whom the Syrian maidens mourned on Lebanon ; by the time that the Greek translators of the Hebrew Scriptures undertook their task they found that this conventional phrase had become completely established, and therefore,

[1] Eccles. v. 2.

[2] Lectures V. and XXIII.

[3] Compare, for this gradual introduction of 'Elohim' ('God') in the later books for 'Jehovah' ('The Lord') in the earlier, 2 Sam. v. 24, 25 ; 1 Chron. iv. 15, 16 ; 2 Sam. vi. 5, 9, 11 ; 1 Chron. xiv. 10, 15, 16 ; 2 Sam. xxiv. 10, 17 ; 1 Chron. xxi. 7, 8 ; Psalm xiv. 2, 4, 7, liii. 2, 5, 7. I owe these references and the inference from them to Dr. Ginsburg.

[4] See Lecture XLIV.

[5] The name *Jehovah* in the Moabite Stone shows that it must have been in use down to the eighth century B.C. (Dr Ginsburg).

[6] Thus Plutarch (*Quest. Conv.* v. 612) regards *Adonis* as the name of the God of the Jews, and makes it one of the reasons for identifying him with Bacchus.

whenever the word *Jehovah* occurs in the Hebrew, misrendered it, Κύριος, 'Master;' and the Latin translators, following the Greek, misrendered it again, with their eyes open, *Dominus*; and the Protestant versions,[1] with a few rare exceptions, misrendered it yet again, 'Lord.' And thus it came to pass that the most expressive title of the Eternal and Self-existent, which in the time of Moses and Samuel, of Elijah and Isaiah,[2] it would have been deemed a sin to keep silent, it became in these later ages a sin to pronounce. On the m sconstruction which had been thus dictated by superfluous reverence were engrafted all manner of fancies and exaggerations. Arguments, solid in themselves, even in the New Testament were based on this manifestly erroneous version The most extravagant superstitions were attached to this rejection of the sacred phrase as confidently as in earlier times they would have been attached to its assertion. The Greek translators even went the length of altering or retaining the alteration of a text in Leviticus, which condemns to death any one who blasphemed the name of Jehovah, into the condemnation of anyone who pronounces it.[3] The name itself lingered only in the mouth of the High Priest, who uttered it only on the ten occasions which required it, on the day of Atonement; and after the time of Simon the Just even this was in a whisper.[4] If anyone else gained possession of it, it was a talisman by which, if he was bold enough to utter its mysterious sound, miracles could be worked, and magical arts exercised. 'The Ineffable Name,' the 'Tetragram-'maton,' became a charm analogous to those secret, sacred names on which the heathen writers had already prided themselves.

These were the strange results of a sentiment in its origin springing from that natural, we may almost say, philosophical caution, which shrinks abashed before the inscrutable mystery of the Great Cause of all. When in our later days any have been scandalised by the reserve of sceptical inquirers, or by

[1] The French Protestant versions and Bunsen's *Bibelwerk* render it 'the 'Eternal;' the Protestant translation into Spanish renders it 'Jehovah.'

[2] Nicolas, *Doctrines religeuses des Juifs*, 165, 166,

[3] Ewald, v. 198, 199. Nicolas, 166-170

[4] Edersheim's *Temple*, p. 270.

the adoption of other forms and phrases, than those in common use, for the Supreme Goodness and Wisdom in whose power we live and move and have our being, they may be comforted by the reflection that such reticence or such deviations have a precedent in that silent revolution which affected the whole theology of the Jewish Church from the period of the book of Malachi downwards, and which has left its mark on almost every translation of the Bible throughout the world.

> If, then, this earthly mind
> Speechless remain or speechless e'en depart,
> Nor seek to see—(for what of earthly kind
> Can see Thee as Thou art?)
> If well assur'd 'tis but profanely bold
> In thought's abstractest forms to seem to see,
> It dares not dare the dread communion hold
> In ways unworthy Thee,
> O, not unowned, Thou shalt unnam'd forgive.[1]

2. In itself this awe expressed the well-known difficulty of defining the Immeasurable, or of exploring the primal origin of existence. Some of the forms of belief to which it gave rise will appear more clearly as we proceed. But at the mcment of which we are now speaking it took the shape, or fostered the growth, of a doctrine which, though never altogether absent from the Jewish mind, now leaped into unusual prominence. It has been already[2] indicated in the book of Malachi; the necessity, the craving for 'messengers,' intermediate spirits, earthly or celestial, to break, as it were, the chasm between the Infinite and the finite. 'Who may abide the day of His 'coming?' The same tendency which in our nineteenth century clothes itself in the phraseology of 'Nature,' 'the Reign of Law, 'the forces of Nature,' caused the Oriental mind of the fourth century before our era to adopt the nomenclature of a hierarchy of unknown ministering spirits, who as 'Messengers' or 'watchers' guarded the fortunes of nations and individuals and directed the movements of the universe.

In the Greek version of the earlier books this belief appears

[1] Clough's *Poems*, ii. 87.

[2] Mal. iii. 1.

in the constant substitution of 'Angels' in passages where the original Hebrew contained only the name of God. In the Psalms immediately following the Return,[1] they stand at the head of the works of Creation. Already, in the visions[2] of Ezekiel and Zechariah, their innermost circle was dimly arranged in the mystic number of seven. In the Book of Daniel, whether Babylonian or Syrian, we find, for the first time, two names assigned—Michael[3] the champion of Israel, with the challenge 'Who is like God?' to reappear as the guardian of the High Places of Christendom and as the Protector of the kingdom of France; Gabriel,[4] 'the hero of God,' the harbinger of the Divine purposes. In the Book of Tobit a third is added—Raphael,[5] the 'sociable spirit' of healing, the 'Divine Healer.' The others are not yet named. But the fourth, Uriel, 'the 'Light of God,' the regent of the sun, follows next. And then, with doubtful splendour, we faintly hear of Phaniel, Raguel, and Zarakiel, or else of Zaphkiel, Zadkiel, and Gamaliel, or else of Salathiel, Jehudial, and Berachiah, or else of Jeremial, Sariel and Azael.[6] The contradictory and wavering nomenclature reminds us how uncertain is the ground on which we tread. And when we inquire yet further for the traces of those doctrines which have left so deep an impress on the theology and poetry of Christendom, the creation and the fall[7] of the Angels, or yet again for the warrant of those splendid winged forms[8] with which Guido and Fra Angelico have made us familiar in the realm of Art, and which have sunk deep into the common parlance of Europe, it must be confessed that not even in these

[1] Psa m cxlviii. 2.

[2] Ezek. viii. 11; Zech. iv. 2, 10; Tobit xii. 15; Rev iii. 1; iv. 5, 6; viii. 2.

[3] Dan. xii 1; x. 13, 21; Jude 9; Rev. xii. 7.

[4] Dan. viii. 1 x. 21; Luke i. 11, 19, 26, 35.

[5] Tobit iii. 17; xii. 15; Enoch xl. 8. When God would cure any sick person He sends the Archangel Raphael to accomplish the cure. (Jerome on Dan. viii.)

[6] See the references in the exhaustive note of Dr. Ginsburg on Eccles. v. 5, and also in Kalisch's *Commentary* (vol. ii. 290). Compare Nicolas' *Doctrines religieuses des Juifs*, 220.

[7] The only passages which would appear to indicate this doctrine are 2 Peter ii. 4, and Jude 6, and these manifestly refer only to Gen. vi. 4.

[8] The six-winged seraphs of Isa. vi. 2 and the double-winged cherubs of 1 Kings vi. 24 are not 'messengers' or 'angels' at all. The expression in Dan. ix. 21, 'flying 'swiftly,' should be either 'coming swiftly' or 'greatly fatigued.' The first indication of the wings of 'angels' is in Rev. xiv. 6.

later books, still less in the earlier visions of the prophets of Israel, is there the least foundation. Still, the general and pervasive belief in the intervention of these unearthly 'messengers,' combining with the earthly but not less Divine 'Messenger' of the prophecy of Malachi, dates from this epoch. There is a lofty truth, however overgrown with fantastic legend, in the vision of a long vista of celestial beauty, power, and goodness through which the soul looks upwards to the Throne of the Unseen ; and this truth has become, from the age of Malachi, firmly enshrined in the poetic side of Hebrew and Christian no less than of Persian and Arabian theology. Out of the slight and often coarse materials that the Books of the Captivity and of the Return provide, have been evolved, not only the prodigious extravagances[1] of the Talmud, but also the noblest strains of Spenser and of Milton, the image, never since to depart from mankind, of 'the angelic' character as distinct even from 'the saintly' or 'the virtuous'—the conviction that there is a fulfilment of the Divine Will more perfectly carried out in the ideal heaven than on the actual earth.

The contrast between the real and ideal.

II. The second doctrine which pervades the Book of Malachi is one which, though never absent altogether from the Prophetic mind, is brought out here with a point which cannot be evaded. It is the contrast—so vital to any true conception of religion in every age, but so frequently forgotten—between the real and the ideal in religious institutions. By the side of the selfish and untruthful hierarchy, who were the main causes of the unbelief which prevailed around them, there rose the vision of perfect truthfulness and fairness,[2] the unswerving fear of the Eternal name, as conceived in the original idea of the Priesthood. And, again, within the innermost pale of the Church, behind the cynical questionings of some and the superficial devotions of others, the Prophet saw the almost invisible[3] circle of those whose reverence for the Eternal remained unshaken, who kept the sacred treasure of truth intact ; of whom the names are for the

[1] See Kalisch's *Commentary*, ii. 305-317.

[2] Mal. ii. 5, 6.

[3] Matt. iv. 16, 17.

most part unknown in the long, vacant history of four centuries that follow, but who may be traced in a true Divine succession which runs through this obscure period, and of which the links from time to time appear—Simon the Just, Jesus the son of Sirach, Judas Maccabæus, the martyred Onias, the high-minded Mariamne, the large-minded Hillel, Zachariah and Elizabeth, Simeon and Anna, Joseph and Mary. To recover these lost jewels, to disentangle the dross of society from the ore of gold and silver which lies in the worst rubbish of superstition and moral degradation, is the hope of the Prophet amidst the despairing sense of failure and dejection, which, if less clamorous than the Lamentations of Jeremiah, or the invectives of Isaiah, implies a deeper conviction of the weight of evil against which the cause of uprightness has to contend.

In harmony with this inquiring, perhaps melancholy, vein of thought is the mournful tone of the contemporary book of Ecclesiastes,[1] whose story we have already drawn out in describing its portraiture of Solomon, but whose lessons derive a profounder significance if taken as expressing the same dark view of the world as breathes through the almost equally misanthropic cries of Malachi.[2] The Asiatic world seemed to be sick of crime and folly. The weary soul tossed to and fro in the effort to distract and sustain its upward tendencies. In the midst of this perplexity it is not surprising that for the first time we begin to trace a keener sense of an obstinate, inveterate principle of evil—the consciousness of a more determined obstruction against good than the Hebrew Scriptures had yet exhibited. Faintly, very faintly, in the Book of Job,[3] and in the vision of Micaiah the son of Imlah, there was disclosed in the Courts of Heaven a spirit rendering its account with the other ministers of the Divine Will, yet with something of a malicious pleasure in the mischief produced by the calamities which it caused. Perhaps, in the vision of Zechariah, the same spirit, as had appeared in the opening of the poem of Job, returns as the 'adversary' of the innocent.[4] Certainly, in

Doctrine of the Evil Spirit.

[1] See Lecture XXVIII.
[2] Eccles. i. 13-15; iii. 16; iv. 1; vi. 2.
[3] Job i. 6; 1 Kings xxii. 21.
[4] Zech. iii. 1.

the Book of Chronicles, it appears in the place which the earlier Prophetic books assigned to the Eternal [1] himself, as tempting David to number Israel. Certainly, in the Book of Tobit, a demon plays the malignant part which in the Greek or the Teutonic world is assigned to the evil deities or wicked fairies of their mythology.[2] In the Book of Wisdom—whatever be its date—is the first [3] mention of the 'envy of the Devil' in connexion with the entrance of death into the world. In the Maccabæan history the obnoxious fort which overhung the temple is [4] described, almost in modern phrase, as a living creature, 'a wicked fiend or devil.' Such are the fragmentary notices of an incipient personification, out of which has gradually sprung up the doctrine of a hierarchy of evil spirits, corresponding to the hosts of Angels—which has in its turn passed through every shape and form from the Talmud to the Fathers, from the grotesque Satyr of the Middle Ages to the splendour of the ruined Archangel of Milton's 'Paradise Lost,' the scoffing cynicism of Goethe's Mephistopheles, and the ill-nature of the 'Little Master' of La Motte Fouqué. That peculiar sense of the depth and subtlety of the evil principle which manifested itself in the various figures of a malignant power—now single, now multiplied, now shadowy, now distinct, now ridiculous, and now sublime—had its root in the dark and solemn view of the perplexities in the moral government of the world, of which the first germs are seen in Malachi and Ecclesiastes. This Hebrew conception of the evil, the devilish, element in man and in nature is twofold. It is either of the 'accusing' spirit, that seizes on the dark and the trivial side of even the greatest and the best—or else of the 'hostile' obstruction that stands in the way of progress and of goodness. Round these two central ideas, of which the one has prevailed in the [5] Hellenic and Latin, the other in the Semitic [6] and Teutonic forms of speech, have congregated all the various doctrines, legends, truths, and fictions which have so long played a part in the theology and

[1] Comp. 2 Sam. xxiv. 1, and 1 Chron. xxi. 1.
[2] Tobit iii. 8.
[3] Wisdom ii. 23.
[4] 1 Macc. i. 36.
[5] The Accuser—Slanderer—'Diabolus'—'Devil.'
[6] The Enemy—'Satan'—'Fiend.'

the poetry alike of Judaism, Islam, and Christendom. The antagonism which had prevailed in the earlier[1] books of the Old Testament between Jehovah and the gods of the heathen world disappeared as the idea of the Divine Nature became more elevated and more comprehensive, and in its place came the antagonism between God as the Supreme Good, and evil as His only true enemy and rival—an antagonism, which, however much it may have been at times degraded and exaggerated, yet is in itself the legitimate product of that nobler idea of Deity. A profound detestation of moral evil, the abhorrence of those more malignant forms of it to which the language of Christian Europe has given the name of 'diabolical' or 'devilish,' or 'fiendish,' is the dark shadow which precedes or accompanies the bright admiration of virtue, is the indispensable condition of the intense worship of the Divine Goodness.

Universality of God.

III. This leads us to a third doctrine of the Prophet Malachi, which serves as a starting-point for the questions which this particular epoch suggests for our consideration. It is the assertion—not new in itself, as we have already pointed out, but new from the force and precision with which the truth is driven home—of the absolute equality, in the Divine judgment, of all genuine and sincere worship throughout the world. In rejecting the half-hearted and niggardly offerings of the Jewish Church, the prophet reminds his readers not only that their sacrifices are not needed by Him whom they seek to propitiate by them, but that from the furthest East, where the sun rises above the earth, to the remotest western horizon, where he sinks beneath it, the Eternal name, under whatever form, is great; that among the innumerable races outside the Jewish pale—not only in Jerusalem, but in every place over that wide circumference—the cloud of incense that goes up from altars, of whatever temple, is, if faithfully rendered, a pure, unpolluted offering to that Divine Presence, known or unknown, throughout all the nations of mankind.[2] It is a truth which met with a partial exemplification, as we shall see, in connexion with the great religious

[1] Ewald, v. 184.

[2] Mal. i. 11.

systems which, in the vacant space on which we are now entering, pressed upon the Jewish creed and ritual. It is a truth which was raised to the first order of religious doctrine by Him who declared that 'many should[1] come from East and 'West, and sit down in the kingdom,' and by the disciples, who repeated it after Him almost in the words of Malachi, though without a figure, that: 'In every nation he that feareth[2] Him 'and worketh righteousness is accepted of Him;' and that 'not 'the hearers of the law, but the doers of the law, who have not[3] 'the law, shall be justified.' It is a truth which, after a long period of neglect, and even of bitter condemnation, has become in our days the basis of the great science of comparative theology, and has slowly re-entered the circle of practical and religious thought.

In the entire vacancy which occupies the annals of the Jewish nation after the times of Nehemiah there is one single incident recorded which exactly coincides with the contrast which Malachi draws between the degenerate Priesthood of his own day and the purer elements of the Gentile world.

Story of Bagoses.

In that corrupt family of Eliashib, which occupied the High Priesthood, there was one deed at this time, darker than any that had preceded it—'more dreadful,' says the historian—who reports it in terms which seem almost the echo of Malachi's indignant language—'than any which 'had been known among the nations, civilised or uncivilised, 'outside the Jewish pale.' His two sons both aimed at their father's office, which then, as often before and afterwards, was in the gift of the foreign Governor residing at Jerusalem. John was in possession. But Bagoses, the Governor, favoured Joshua.[4] The two brothers met in the Temple, and the elder, stung by jealousy, murdered the younger on the floor of the sanctuary. The Governor, filled with just anger, descended from his fortress-tower, like Lysias in later days, and burst into the Temple. The sacerdotal guardians endeavoured to

[1] Matt. viii. 11. [2] Acts x. 34, 35. [3] Rom. ii. 13, 14.
[4] Jos. *Ant.* xi. 7, § 1. For the possible connexion of this event with Malachi ii. 5-8, see Hitzig, *Geschichte*, 304.

resist the sacrilegious intruder, as he advanced reproaching them with the crime. But he thrust them aside and penetrated, it would seem, into the sacred edifice itself, where the corpse lay stretched upon the Temple pavement. 'What,' he exclaimed, 'am I not cleaner than the dead carcase of him 'whom ye have murdered?' The words of Bagoses lived in the recollection of those who heard them. They expressed the universal but unwelcome truth, 'Is not a good Persian better 'than a bad Jew?'—or, to turn it into the form of the indignant question of a great modern theologian, 'Who would 'not meet the judgment of the Divine Redeemer loaded with 'the errors of Nestorius rather than with the crimes of 'Cyril?'[1]

Relations to the Gentile world.

IV. It is in the light of this principle, clearly foreshadowed by the Evangelical Prophet of the Captivity, that we may proceed to ask the question, which naturally forces itself upon us, before we leave this period of the Jewish history: What traces were left upon it by the circumstances of the new sphere which had opened upon them through the connexion of Israel with the Persian Empire? We have seen what elements in the development of the national religion were due to their stay in Babylon. We have now to ask what elements, if any, were added by the other forces brought into contact with them in the Eastern or Western world.

The Persian Empire.

1. The first influence to be considered in the retrospect of this period is the general effect of the Persian Monarchy on the manners and the imagination of the Jewish race. If, with all the alienation of exiles, almost of rebels, there had yet been an attraction for them in the magnificent power of the Babylonian Empire, there could not have been less in the forms, hardly less august, and far more friendly, that surrounded the successors of their benefactor Cyrus. We have seen how closely they clung to that protection; how intimate their relations with the Persian Governor, who resided almost within the Temple precincts; how complete[2] his

[1] Milman's *Hist. of Latin Christianity*, i. 145.

[2] Neh. xiii. 4-9: Jos. *Ant.* xi. 7.

control over their most sacred functionaries; how the letters and decrees of its kings were placed almost on the level of their sacred books. From the exceptionally kindly relations between the Court of Susa and the Jewish colony at this time it has come to pass that even to this day the King of Persia is the only existing[1] Potentate of the world whose name appeals to the common sentiment as a Biblical personage.

There is one writing of this period in which these relations are especially brought out. Even more than the Book of Job is Idumæan, and the Book of Daniel Babylonian, is the Book of Esther Persian. It is the one example in the sacred volume of a story of which the whole scenery and imagery breathes the atmosphere of an Oriental Court as completely and almost as exclusively as the 'Arabian Nights.' We are in the Palace at Susa.[2] We are in that splendid hall of Darius, of which no vestige now remains, but which can be completely represented to our sight by the still existing ruins of the contemporary hall at Persepolis, that edifice of which it has been said that no interior of any building, ancient or modern, not Egyptian Karnac, not Cologne Cathedral, could rival it in space and beauty. The only feature found at Persepolis which was wanting at Susa was the splendid staircase—'noblest example of a flight of stairs to be found in any 'part of the world.'[3] All else was in Shushan 'the Palace 'fortress'—the colossal bulls at the entrance; the vast pillars, sixty feet high, along its nave; the pavement of coloured marbles, as the author of the Book of Esther repeats, as if recalling colour after colour that had feasted his eyes—'red, and blue, and white, and black'—and the curtains[4] hanging from pillar to pillar, 'white and green

The Book of Esther;

Its local interest.

[1] This was beyond doubt one main reason of the extraordinary interest manifested by the lower classes of England in the visit of the Shah of Persia in 1874. I may, perhaps, be permitted to refer to a sermon preached on that occasion in Westminster Abbey on the 'Persian King.'

[2] 'Shushan the Palace' is the form in Esther i. 2, Dan. viii. 1, as if it was the official name of the royal residence. The word (Bireh) is elsewhere only used for the Persian Governor's residence at Jerusalem—as (like the Prætorium in the Roman camps and provinces) each such residence was regarded as Susa in miniature.

[3] See Fergusson on 'Susa' in the *Dict. of the Bible.* Rawlinson's *Ancient Monarchies*, iv. 269-287.

[4] Esther i. 6.

'and purple,' fastened with cords of 'white and purple.' There it was that, overlooking, from the terraced heights on which the hall was built, the plains of the Ulai, Ahasuerus, whose name was Grecised into Xerxes, gave, in the third year of his reign, a half-year's festival. There, in the gardens[1] within the palace, on the slope of the palatial hill, was the banquet, like those given by the Emperor of China, to the whole population of the Province. Round the Great King,[2] as he sat on his golden throne, with the fans waving over his head, which still linger in the ceremonial of the chief ecclesiastic of the Latin Church, were the seven Princes of Persia and Media who saw the King's face 'when others saw it not,' and the first in the kingdom—the sacred number 'seven' which pervaded the whole Court. There took place the succession of violent scenes, so thoroughly characteristic of Oriental despotism, but to which the Hebrew historian was so familiarised that they appear to fill him rather with admiration than astonishment and horror, the order for the Queen to unveil herself before the assembled Court, contrary to the immemorial[3] usage of Persia, and therefore the sure sign of the King's omnipotence—the rage of the King at her refusal, her instantaneous divorce, the universal decree founded on this single case, the strange procession of maidens for the selection of the new Queen. Of like kind are all the incidents which follow—the long conversations in the harem; the jealousy between the two foreign courtiers;[4] 'the King's gate'—the large square[5] tower, still in part remaining, where the Jewish

[1] This seems to be implied in Esther i. 5.

[2] That Ahasuerus is Xerxes, and that the third and seventh years of his reign (Esther i. 3, ii.) thus coincide respectively with his departure on his great expedition to Greece and his return from it is now generally agreed. It is curious to observe that the halo thrown round Ahasuerus by the Book of Esther, whilst it blinded modern readers to the violence in which he resembled Xerxes, caused commentators to be reluctant in admitting his identification with a Prince whose memory our sympathy with the Greek historians had so disparaged.

[3] In the annual Persian representation of the tragedy of the Sons of Ali an English Ambassador is brought in as begging their lives; and to mark his nationality a boy dressed up as an unveiled woman accompanies him as an ambassadress.

[4] Anyone declining to stand as the Grand Vizier passes is almost beaten to death (Morier.)

[5] Fergusson on 'Susa.' The entrance where the Grand Vizier and others sit awaiting the King's pleasure is still called in Persia Derekhonef-Shah, 'The King's 'Gate' (Morier).

favourite sat, as in his place of honour, like the Gate of Justice in the Alhambra, or the Sublime Porte at Stamboul—and the reckless violence of the royal command to enjoin the massacre of the whole Jewish race. Then come the various scenes of the catastrophe, every one of which is full of the local genius of the Empire, as we know it alike through the accounts of the earliest Grecian travellers and the latest English investigators. The same chronicles in which, as Xerxes[1] sat on the rocky brow 'that looks o'er sea-born Salamis,' he had ordered to be[2] recorded the valiant acts of any who did the State good service are brought before him at Shushan to soothe his sleepless nights. We are made to feel the inaccessibility of the King to any but the seven Councillors, the awe with which his presence was surrounded, which required all persons introduced to fall on their faces before him, and on pain of death to cover their hands in the folds of their sleeves,[3] the executioners standing round with[4] their axes, instantly to behead any rash intruder. It is this that makes the turning-point of Esther's danger, from which she is only spared by the mark of royal absolution in the extension of the golden sceptre (as in modern[5] times by touching the skirt of the King's robe); it is this which brings about the sudden extinction of Haman's whole family, falling, as Oriental households still fall, in the ruin of their[6] head. We are led to understand the fantastic consequences of the investment of the king with the attribute of personal infallibility,[7] making it impossible for him even to offer to repeal any of his own decrees, which, immediately on their utterance, pass into the sacred recesses of the laws of Medes and Persians that no power can alter. Hence results the difficulty in the way of revoking the atrocious decree against the Jewish settlers, and therefore the necessity (as in the well-known modern parallel of the Roman pontiffs) of minimising its effect by issuing orders in theory acknowledging,

[1] Esther vi. 1, 2; Herod. viii. 90.
[2] Such was the Shah Nahmeh of Firdousi.
[3] Rawlinson, iv. 180.
[4] Joseph. *Ant.* xi. 6, 3.
[5] Morier.
[6] Esther vii. 8. A dark shawl is still thrown over the face of a condemned person (Morier).
[7] Dan. vi. 15; Esther viii. 11; Herod. ix. 109. See Rawlinson, iv. 181.

in practice contradicting it. And, finally, we come across the world-renowned institution of the Persian posts, established by Darius throughout the Empire, the relays of horses [1] along the plains, mules on the mountain districts, camels and dromedaries on the arid table-lands; [2] the couriers succeeding each other with a rapidity that could only be compared to the flight of birds. This it was which enabled the victims of the intended massacre to receive the royal permission for their own self-defence to the last extremity against the executioners of the King's own orders.

Even the names which most closely connect the story with the history of Israel are not Hebrew, but Chaldæan or Persian. Mordecai is 'the worshipper of Merodach, the War-God of 'Babylon.' [3] 'Esther' is 'the star [4] of the planet Venus.' The *Purim*,[5] from which the Festival of Deliverance took its name, is the Persian word for 'lot,' and has even been supposed to be the name for an ancient Persian solemnity.

There is a singular antiquarian value attaching to this the most vivid picture that we possess of the inner life of the Persian seraglio. But beneath this external show there is a genuine strain of national and human interest, which secured for the little narrative, worldly as it might seem to be, a welcome into the sacred books of the Jews, and drew round it, like the writings of Daniel and Ezra, a fringe of amplifications and additions by which the theological susceptibilities of later times sought to correct its supposed deficiencies.

Its religious interest.

The treatment of the book has much varied in the Jewish and the Christian Churches.

The immediate claim of the story to a place in the Holy

[1] Esther viii. 10; Herod. viii. 98. Xen. *Cyrop.* viii. 6, 17, 18.

[2] Esther viii. 10 (Morier).

[3] See Gesenius *ad voc.*

[4] *Ibid.*, quoting the Targum on Esther ii. 7. It is the Persian word *sitara*; in Sanscrit *tara*; in Zend *stara*; in Western languages *aster, stira, star. Hadassah* (her Hebrew name) is either '*myrtle*' or else a Hebraized form of the Persian *Atossa*.

[5] *Pur*, the Persian word for *division*, reappearing in the other Aryan languages as *pars, part*. On this point Ewald and Gesenius express no doubt. It is possible, but it seems entirely superfluous, to suppose, with Kuenen (iii. 149) that the festival in question was that described by the Byzantine historian Menander ten centuries afterwards under the name of Furdigan.

Books was the consecration which it gave to the Jews of the dispersion. Alone of all the Books of the Old Testament it contains no reference to the Holy Land. When Haman is asked to describe the objects of his hostility, he replies in words which every Israelite through all the hundred and twenty satrapies, from India to Ethiopia, must have applied to himself.[1] 'There is a 'certain people scattered and dispersed in all the provinces of 'thy kingdom and their laws are diverse from all people.' Along the banks of the Euphrates and Tigris, already renowned for their schools of learning; high up in the mountains of Kurdistan, where, perchance, their descendants linger still; all the dispersed settlers were included in those words, which might stand as the motto of the larger part of the Jewish race ever since—which might have been said of them by Tacitus in the Roman Empire, or by the Arabian or English chroniclers of the Middle Ages. The line of beacon-lights kindled from hill to hill along the whole route from Jerusalem to Babylon,[2] 'from Olivet to Sartaba, from Sartaba to Grophinah, from 'Grophinah to Haveran, from Haveran to Beth Baltin, waving 'the torches upwards and downwards, till the whole country 'of the Captivity appeared a blazing fire'—was an apt emblem of the sympathetic links which bound all these settlements together. Of this vast race, for whom so great a destiny was reserved when the nation should fail, the Book of Esther recognised, as by a prophetic instinct, the future importance. Every Jew throughout the world felt with Mordecai, and has felt in many a time of persecution since, as he raised in the city his loud and bitter cry, and stood wrapped in sackcloth and sprinkled with ashes before the Royal Gate. Every Jewess felt, and may have felt ever since, with Esther as she prepared herself for the dreadful venture.

The Book of the Dispersion.

It was this which gave a significance to the long succession of idle coincidences, as it seemed, on the failure of any one of which the catastrophe would have taken place; culminating

[1] Esther iii. 8.

[2] Mishna (Rosh Hashanah, ii. 4).

in the fortunate chance that when the enemy of their race, after the manner of the East, cast lots to secure a propitious day for the vast enterprise of extermination, he was compelled, beginning with the first month of the year, by the failure of the lots, to go on, day after day, and month after month,[1] until he was driven to the 13th day of the very last month as the only auspicious time for the commencement of the massacre; thus leaving, between the issuing of the decree and the arrival of that fatal day, eight months for the posts to carry the King's warrant to the ends of the Empire, and for every Jewish settlement in every village, however remote and however defenceless, to stand at bay against the hunters of their lives. The 'Feast of the Lots' became the Passover of the Dispersion. It preceded the Paschal Feast by only a month, and, to make the parallel complete, was celebrated, not on the predestined and triumphant day, the 13th, but on the 14th and 15th of Adar, corresponding[2] to the 14th and 15th of the Paschal month, Nisan.

The Feast of Purim.

The continuance of that bitter animosity in the Jewish nation renders the Feast of Purim the least pleasing of their festivals. It was long retained in all its intensity as the natural vent of their hatred to their heathen or Christian oppressors in each succeeding age. On that day, at every mention of Haman's name in the worship of the synagogue, it was long the custom to hiss and stamp and shake the clenched fist and say: 'Let 'his name be blotted out, Let the name of the wicked perish.' The boys who were present with a loud clatter rubbed out the detested name, which they wrote for the purpose on pieces of wood or stone. The names of Haman's ten sons were read in one breath, to express the exulting thought that they all died in one instant.[3] They were written in the Book of Esther in three perpendicular lines, to signify that they were hanged on three parallel cords. It was added that his seventy surviving sons fled, and, according to the curse of the 109th Psalm,

[1] See Bertheau on Esther iii. 7

[2] This is ingeniously worked out by Ewald, v. 231.

[3] See Prideaux, i. 355. *Dict. of the Bible*, 'Esther,' and 'Purim.'

begged their bread from door to door. At the conclusion the whole congregation exclaimed: 'Cursed be Haman, blessed be 'Mordecai;[1] cursed be Zeresh, blessed be Esther; cursed be 'all idolaters, blessed be all Israelites; and blessed be Harbonah, 'who hanged Haman.'[2]

Such a spirit reminds one inevitably of the union of fear and cruelty felt by those, not alone of Jewish descent, who find themselves in foreign lands exposed to the attacks of hostile populations. It is the same sentiment as that which caused the English nation to cling, for so many generations, to the celebration of the deliverance from the Gunpowder Plot; and, if the Jewish festival has lasted longer, it is because of the more continual sense of danger, acting on even a more tenacious instinct of nationality.

The Book of Esther.

It was natural that a book thus bound up with one of the strongest sentiments of the Hebrew race should be raised to a high place in their sacred volume. Late as its introduction was, it mounted up at once, if not to the first rank, yet to be the first amongst the second. It was believed that it would outlast all the Hebrew Scriptures except the Pentateuch; more precious than Prophets, or Proverbs, or Psalms. Amongst[3] the five Hagiographical rolls ('Megilloth') it was emphatically '*the* roll,' 'the Megillah.' In the Christian Church its fate has been just the reverse. Of all the Canonical Books of the Old Testament it is the one which lingered longest on the outskirts, and which has provoked the most uneasy suspicion since. Melito of Sardis, Gregory of Nazianzus, Athanasius of Alexandria hesitated to permit its reception. Luther, even if he did not, as was once commonly believed,

[1] The power of distinguishing between the curse and the blessing was laid down as the limit to the hilarity of the revels which accompanied the feast.

[2] It is still the case that the eyes of the aged sparkle, the younger members clasp in their hands a rattle; and the outburst of stamping, knocking of desks, and springing of rattles compel the reader to stop till it subsides. (*Jewish World*, March 18, 1881.) These violent expressions are said now to be discontinued in all the more civilised Jewish communities, as the Greek Church has, to a large extent, abandoned the anathemas of Orthodox Sunday, as the Latin Church has surrendered the detailed excommunications of Holy Thursday, as the English Church has disused its vindictive political services, and, in many instances, the recital of the Athanasian Creed.

[3] See Surenhusius' *Mishna*, ii. 387–402.

'toss the Book of Esther into the Elbe,' yet wished that 'it did 'not exist, for it hath too much of Judaism, and a great deal 'of heathenish naughtiness.'[1]

These two expressions well describe the natural objection of the civilised—we may add, of the Christian—conscience, to the Book of Esther and the Feast of Purim. The exclusive spirit which breathes through them—the wild passion of Esther's revenge in the impalement of Haman's innocent family—are too closely allied to the fierce temper of Jael or of Jezebel, or of the cruel Queen of Xerxes, whose name[2] Amestris is perilously like that of Esther, to win the favour of the modern Jewish, still less the modern Christian, reader. And, yet further, it is so entirely confined to an earthly horizon that, alone of all the sacred books, it never names the name of God from first to last. Whether this absence arose from that increasing scruple against using the Divine Name, which we have already noticed, or from the instinctive adoption of the fashion of the Persian Court, this abstinence from any religious expressions was so startling that the Greek translators thrust into the narrative long[3] additions containing the sacred phrases which, in the original narrative, were wanting.

But there is a sense in which these peculiarities of the Book of Esther are most instructive. Within that Judaic 'hardness 'of heart,' behind that 'heathenish naughtiness,' burn a lofty independence, a genuine patriotism, which are not the less to be admired because Mordecai and Esther spoke and acted without a single appeal by name or profession to the Supreme Source of that moral strength in which they dared the wrath of the Great King and laboured for the preservation of their countrymen. It is necessary for us that in the rest of the

[1] *Table-Talk*, clix. 6. *Bondage of the Will* (Works, iii. 182). Archdeacon Hare conclusively proved (Notes to the *Mission of the Comforter*, vol. ii. 819) that what Luther 'tossed into the Elbe' was not the Book of *Esther*, but the Apocryphal Book of *Esdras*. On the other hand, Sir W. Hamilton (*Discussions*, p. 519) has shown not less conclusively that the incontestable expressions of the great Reformer's aversion to the Book of Esther are quite as strong as those contained in the popular though mistaken rendering of his words.

[2] Herod. ix. 108–113.

[3] 'The rest of the Book of Esther,' x. 9, 10, 11, 12, 13; xi. 10; xiii. 9–18; xiv. 3–9; xv. 28; xvi. 4, 16.

sacred volume the name of God should constantly be brought before us, to show that He is all in all to our moral perfection. But it is expedient for us no less that there should be one book which omits it altogether, to prevent us from attaching to the mere name a reverence which belongs only to the reality. In the mind of the sacred writer the mere accidents, as they might seem, of the quarrel of Ahasuerus, the sleepless night, the delay of the lot, worked out the Divine Will as completely as the parting of the Red Sea or the thunders of Sinai. The story of Esther, glorified by the genius of Handel and sanctified by the piety of Racine, not only affords material for the noblest and the gentlest of meditations, but is a token that in the daily events—the unforeseen chances—of life, in little unremembered acts, in the fall of a sparrow, in the earth bringing forth fruit of herself, God is surely present. The name of God is *not* there, but the work of God *is*. Those who most eagerly cling to the recognition of the Biblical authority of the book ought the most readily to be warned by it not to make a man an offender for a word or for the omission of a word. When Esther nerved herself to enter, at the risk of her life, the presence of Ahasuerus—'I will go in unto the King, and if I 'perish I perish'—when her patriotic feeling vented itself in that noble cry, 'How can I endure to see the evil that shall 'come unto my people? or can I endure to see the destruction 'of my kindred?'—she expressed, although she never named the name of God, a religious devotion as acceptable to Him as that of Moses and David, who, no less sincerely, had the sacred name always on their lips.

Esther is, in this sense, the Cordelia of the Bible.

> Thy youngest daughter does not love thee least,
> Nor are those empty-hearted whose low sounds
> Reverberate no hollowness. . . . .

The Influence of Zoroaster.

2. It remains for us to ask the perplexed and perplexing question whether, behind the splendour of the Persian Court, and the struggle of the Dispersion for existence, we can trace any higher influence of the Persian dominion on the Jewish nation.

There is one great religious name which, even in the less instructed days of Christendom, was always acknowledged, with a reverential awe, as bound up with the beginnings of sacred philosophy. In Raffaelle's 'School of Athens' the only Eastern sage admitted is Zoroaster the Persian. By the theological inquirers of the seventeenth century, the likeness of this theology to that of the Old Testament was so fully acknowledged as to drive them to the theory that he must have been the pupil of Daniel.[1] The research of modern times has dispelled this hypothesis, by the allegation that he and his career preceded even the earliest date of Daniel by centuries, but it has not therefore dissolved the connexion between Judaism and the Zendavesta.

'Let us picture to ourselves' (we adopt the eloquent words of Bunsen) 'one of the holy hills dedicated to the worship of 'fire, in the neighbourhood of the primeval "city of marvels" 'in Central Asia—Baktra "the glorious," now called Balkh, '"the mother of Cities." From this height we look down in 'imagination over the elevated plateau, which lies nearly 2,000 'feet above the level of the sea, sloping downwards towards 'the north, and ending in a sandy desert, which does not even 'allow the streams of Bactria to reach the neighbouring Oxus. 'On the southern horizon the last spurs of the Indian Caucasus 'rear their lofty peaks of 5,000 feet high. Out of those hills, 'the Parapomisus, or Hindu-kush, springs the chief river of 'the country, the Bactrus or Delias, which divides into hun-'dreds of canals, making the face of the country one blooming 'garden of richest fruits. To this point converge the caravans, 'which travel across the mountains to the land of marvels, or 'bring treasures from thence. Thither, fifteen centuries before 'the Babylonian Captivity, on occasion of the peaceful sacrifice 'by fire, from whose ascending flame auguries were drawn, 'perhaps also with the customary interrogation of the earth-'oracle by means of the sacred bull, Zoroaster or Zarathustra 'had convened the nobles of the land that he might perform a 'great public religious act. Arrived there, at the head of his

[1] Prideaux, i. 236-257.

'disciples, the seers and preachers, he summons the Princes to 'draw nigh and to choose between faith and superstition.'[1]

He was willing to retain those outward symbols of adoration, but only as signs of the worship of the true God, who is the God of the good and truth-loving, and, strictly speaking, can be honoured alone by truthfulness in thought, word, and deed, by purity of motive and a strictly veracious life. Accounted by his contemporaries a blasphemer, atheist, and firebrand worthy of death; regarded even by his own adherents after some centuries as the founder of magic, by others as a sorcerer and deceiver, he was nevertheless recognised already by the earliest Greek philosophers as a spiritual leader of the primeval ages of mankind.

This identification of Truth with the Supreme Being is, as it would seem, the fundamental article of the Zoroastrian creed; dimly indicated in the veneration of fire and of the sun, as the emblem of the Divinity; practically enforced in the summary of the moral education of the Persian youth:—'to speak the 'truth;' reflected in the Jewish apologue of Zerubbabel's speech in the Court of Persia,[2] that 'truth is great and shall prevail.' That this creed should at once have drawn the conqueror Cyrus near to his Jewish subjects, as we have already seen, was inevitable. Then comes the confused story of its admixture with the Magian system, and of its temporary subversion under the domination of that system in the reign of the usurper Smerdis. Nor can it be altogether accidental that, when Darius Hystaspis overthrew the Magians and re-established,[3] as he himself records, the true Zoroastrian worship, the favour to the Jewish race which had been suspended during the Magian supremacy was once more restored. And thus, although it may be that Zoroaster himself lived long before, he[4] rose, as it were, from the grave, in this middle period of the Persian dominion, with renewed force; but yet with elements which, if not foreign to his original creed, were

Revival of Zoroastrianism, B.C. 521.

[1] Bunsen's *God in History*, i. 280-290.

[2] 1 Esdr. iv. 35. See Lecture XLIII.

[3] Behistun Inscription, Rawlinson's *Herodotus*, App. to Book I., Essay V.

[4] See Malcolm's *Persia*, i. 58.

strengthened by the Magian influence that henceforth coloured it—and of which the Jewish, no less than all the surrounding religions, felt the effect. 'Magic'—of which the very name dates from this epoch—that is, the belief in the use of natural and material objects to control or to supersede moral acts—entered from henceforth deeply into the vitals, if not of Jewish faith, yet certainly of Jewish practice. The veneration for the holy fire, which was kindled from the sacred naphtha fountains of Persia by the Caspian Sea, penetrated into the Jewish traditions in the story that, when Nehemiah rekindled the consecrated fire of the Temple from the stones of the altar, he called it 'napthar,' giving it a Hebrew meaning, 'a cleansing,' 'though many call it nephi.'[1] Although the returning Jews, as we have seen, were not influenced by the Persian repugnance to temples, and strictly maintained the exclusive sanctity for sacrificial worship of the sanctuary at Jerusalem, yet it was in accordance, and probably through contact, with the Persian system of allowing sacrifice to be performed in all places and on every holy hill that there sprang up, side by side with the Temple service of Jerusalem, the more spiritual worship of the synagogue.[2] The Persian doctrine of the Unity and the Invisibility of the Divinity, of a celestial and infernal hierarchy, which had never before received, so to speak, the sanction of the Imperial Powers of the earth, was substantially the counterpart to the corresponding elements of the Hebrew faith.

Connexion with Judaism.

The conclusion, therefore, is that whilst these doctrines and practices sprang up indigenously in the Israel of this period, from reasons adequate to account for their growth at this particular juncture, yet they must, in all probability, have received an immense stimulus from the consciousness that the whole atmosphere of the vast neighbouring and surrounding Empire was impregnated with the same ideas. The small band of exiles must, if they were not exempt altogether from the weakness and strength of human motives, have felt that their con-

[1] 2 Macc. i. 36; Ewald, v. 163; Herder, vol. v. 75.
[2] Kuenen, iii. 35. See Lecture XLIV.

fident trust in the Unity of the Divine Will, their belief in the multiplied subordinate ministers of that Will, their intense horror and gradual personification of the principle of Moral Evil, had acquired new form and bone and substance by the sympathy of an older, vaster frame of worship, inspiring and encouraging ideas which they themselves had been led to foster with a new and exclusive zeal. Even in detail it is not possible to avoid the conviction that the mystical number of the seven lamps, the seven watchers before the throne of God, were derived directly from the seven Amshaspands ('the unsleeping 'ones'), who, like the seven Counsellors of the Persian King, encircled the presence of Ormuzd ; and the name of the demon Asmodeus in the Book of Tobit is unquestionably the Persian 'Aeshma-Deva,' [1] the spirit of concupiscence, who at times rose to the rank of the Prince of Demons.

But here we must pause. Not only is there no trace of Ahriman by name, but the idea of the separate co-equal existence of the Evil with the Good Spirit is unknown to the Judaic creed, and even at the very moment of the first contact between the two systems the Prophet of the Captivity meets the doctrine of an eternal Dualism of Good and Evil—so natural in itself, and so deeply rooted in the Zoroastrian theology—by the announcement, as if in express antithesis : 'I form the light 'and create darkness. I make peace and create evil. I the 'Eternal do all these things.' [2] And not only are the 'watchers,' the good and evil spirits of the Books of Daniel, of Tobit, and of Enoch (with the single exception of Asmodeus), called by Hebrew not by Persian names, but their functions are different. The beneficent 'messengers' are far more closely bound up with human joys and sorrows than the hierarchy which fills the vacant space of the Persian heaven, and the malevolent accusers far more completely subordinate to the over-ruling power of the same Divine Master, to whom both good and evil are as ministers.[3]

[1] Kuenen, iii. 40. Compare the names of the demons in the Book of Enoch, c. 6. Müller's *Chips from a German Workshop*, i. 148 ; Kalisch's *Commentary*, i. 310, 311, 316.

[2] Isa. xlv. 1–7.

[3] See Kalisch's *Commentary*, ii. 292–294.

There is, in short (such seems to be the result of the most recent[1] investigation), a close affinity between the forms which the two religions assumed; but it is the affinity—with the exception of a few details—rather of a common atmosphere of lofty truths, of a simultaneous sympathy in their view of earthly and heavenly things, than the affinity of direct lineage and discipleship.[2] It is a kinship, however, which did not cease with this period of the Jewish history. One great doctrine which, though mainly fostered from another quarter, was to be held in unison by the ancient followers of Zoroaster and the later followers of Moses and of Isaiah, is yet to be noticed—the immortality of the soul. One vast influence the Persian religion was still to exercise, if not over the Jewish Church itself, yet over that which sprang from its bosom, through the subtle invasion of Manicheism, which in the early centuries of Christendom was, partly as an ally, partly as a foe, to colour the growth of its ritual and its creed. But this is far in the future. The connexion of Judaism with the faith of Zoroaster, however explained, is not without instruction. Whatever there be of permanent truth in the substance of any of these beliefs will not lose in value if it was allied or be even traced to a religion so pure and so venerable as that of the Zendavesta. Whatever there is of transitory or excessive in the forms of any of these may be the more contentedly dropped if it can be shown to be derived from a faith which, however once powerful, now lingers only in the small sect of the Fire-worshippers of Bombay, who alone carry on[3] the once formidable name of 'Parsee' or 'Persian.'

Influence of China.

3. If the influence even of Zoroaster and Cyrus on Judaism be open to question, it will not be expected that with the remoter Eastern regions any direct connexion can be discovered. Once, and once only, in the Hebrew records we catch a doubtful glimpse of that strange race, which

[1] Kuenen, iii. 35-44; Ewald, v. 184; Max Müller's *Chips from a German Workshop*, i. 142-159.

[2] 'The germs which lay hidden in 'Judaism were fertilised by contact with 'a religion in which they had arrived at 'maturity.' Kuenen, iii. 63. The same view, substantially, is maintained in Hardwick's *Christ and other Masters*, pp. 545-570.

[3] See Müller's *Chips*, i. 161.

has been eloquently described to be at the eastern extremity of Asia [1] what Judæa is at the western, 'a people dwelling alone 'and not reckoned among the nations.' When the Evangelical Prophet is calling the scattered exiles to return from the uttermost parts of the earth he extends his cry even to those that 'come from the land of Sinim.' In that solitary word,[2] if so be, the Empire of China rises on the religious horizon of the historic world. Not a vestige of its influence can be traced even on the outer circumference of the theatre on which the movement of mankind was then advancing. Yet, having in view the ultimate scope of that movement, it is impossible not to be struck by the coincidence that in the period which was close within the ken of the Prophet of the Captivity—in the very years in which Ezra was preparing for his mission to Palestine—there drew to its close the career of one whose impression on his own nation was deeper than that of the mighty Scribe on the Jewish race. In the year 478 Confucius [3] died, the Ezra rather than the Moses of his race; 'the transmitter, not the maker of belief, born not in 'possession of [4] knowledge, but loving antiquity, and 'in it seeking knowledge—for 2,000 years the supreme and 'undisputed teacher of this most populous [5] land'—leaving a memory of himself which is still perpetuated even in the very [6] manners, gestures, and dress of the Chinese of our day—leaving maxims which, though stamped with that homely and pedestrian character belonging to the whole religion of his race, yet still secure for him a place amongst the permanent teachers of mankind. 'The superior [7] man is catholic and no partisan—'the mean man is a partisan and not catholic.' 'It is only the 'truly virtuous man who can love or who can hate others.' 'Virtue is not left alone.[8] He who practises it will have 'neighbours.' 'To be able to judge of others by what is in 'yourselves may be called the Art of Virtue.' 'When you are 'labouring for others, labour with the same zeal as if it were

Death of Confucius, B. C. 478.

[1] Quinet, *Génie des Religions*, 293.

[2] Isa. xlix. 12; Ewald doubts, Gesenius affirms, the identification of *Sinim* with China.

[3] Müller's *Chips*, i. 311.

[4] Legge's *Life of Confucius*, p. 87.

[5] *Ibid.* p. 95.

[6] *Ed Rev.* cxxxix. p. 315, 316.

[7] Legge, 95.

[8] *Ibid.* 138.

'for yourself.' 'The man of perfect virtue, wishing to be 'established himself, seeks also to establish others; wishing to 'be enlarged himself, he seeks also to enlarge others.' 'Is 'there one word which may serve as a rule for one's whole life? 'Is not Reciprocity such a word?' 'What you wish not to be 'done to yourself, do not to others.'[1]

In those words we cannot doubt that 'an incense of pure 'offering went up,' as Malachi proclaimed, 'to the Eternal God; 'even from the rising of the sun.' To ask how and why the religion, the empire, the morality of China have not reached as far as and beyond the level from which they sprang would lead us too far away from this period.

Influence of India.

4. There was another career yet wider and nobler than that of Confucius—unknown to him and unknown to Ezra and Malachi—in that vast country, which also is now for a moment, and for the first time, distinctly brought within the view of the Jewish world, although[2] its products had penetrated thither even in the reign of Solomon. 'From '*India*[3] even to Ethiopia'—this was the extreme verge of the dominion of the Persian King, as it appears in the Book of Esther, in describing the struggles of the Persian Court, almost in the very year in which, following close upon the death of the great sage of China, there passed away[4] the greater sage of India, Sakya Muni, more commonly known as Buddha, 'the 'Buddha,' the Enlightened. That extraordinary personage, whose history was wrapped in uncertainty, and whose very existence was doubted, till within our own generation, has suddenly been received as amongst the foremost characters of the world. 'I hesitate[5] not to say 'that, with the single exception of Christ, there is, amongst the 'founders of Religions, no figure purer or more affecting than 'that of Buddha. His life is blameless. His constant heroism 'equals his conviction; and if the theory which he announces 'is false, the personal example that he gives is irreproachable.

Death of Buddha, B.C. 747.

[1] Legge, 226.
[2] See Lecture XXVI.
[3] Esther i. 1; viii. 9.
[4] St. Hilaire places Buddha's death in B.C. 543 (*Bouddha*, p. ii.). But Professor Müller, with more precision, fixes it in B.C. 477 (*Chips from a German Workshop*, i. 311).
[5] St. Hilaire, *Bouddha*, p. v.

'He is the finished model of all the virtues that he preaches;
'his self-denial, his charity, his unchangeable sweetness, do not
'betray him for a single moment. He abandons at the age of
'twenty-nine the court of his aged father to make himself an
'ascetic, a beggar. He prepares in silence for his doctrine by
'six years of retreat and meditation; he propagates it, by the
'sole power of argument and persuasion, for more than half a
'century; and when he dies, in the arms of his disciples, it is
'with the serenity of a sage, who has done good all his life, and
'who has the assurance of having found the truth.'

Wonderful as is the appearance of so sacred a person on the scene, it must be confessed that even in the East, widely as his doctrines and institutions have been spread, the impress of his own character has been slight, compared with other founders of religious systems, and certainly with that One to whom, without irreverence, he has been more than once likened; and outside the sphere of his own wide communion his influence, direct or indirect, is almost nothing. One single Buddhist[1] is known to have travelled westward in ancient times—he who in the reign of Augustus burned himself alive at Athens. It is true that Buddha has been canonised as a saint in the Roman Catholic Church, under the name[2] of S. Josaphat; but this singular deviation from the exclusive rules of that Church was the result of one of those inadvertencies into which the Church of Rome has so often fallen in directing the faith of its members. Still, it is difficult for those who believe the permanent elements of the Jewish and Christian religion to be universal and Divine not to hail these corresponding forms of truth or goodness elsewhere, or to recognise that the mere appearance of such saint-like or godlike characters in other parts of the earth, if not directly preparing the way for a greater manifestation, illustrates that manifestation by showing how mighty has been the witness borne to its value even under the most adverse discouragement and with strangely inadequate effects.

[1] See the whole story in Professor Lightfoot's edition of *St. Paul's Epistle to the Colossians*, p. 155.

[2] Müller, *Chips from a German Workshop*, v. 182.

5. But the history that opens upon us in the ensuing struggles of the Jewish nation compels us to take into account another sphere of intellectual and moral influence, which, unlike those prodigious appearances in the far East, has worked with direct and potent energy on Judaism and Christianity, and been incorporated in some form or other into the essence of both.

The influence of Greece.

We have seen the results of the contact of the Jewish race with the Persian monarchy and the Persian religion; we have seen also the rise of the two greatest teachers of China and India, who yet stand apart from the stream of historic movement of which Judaism was the centre. We are about to enter on a blank of three centuries, of which in Palestine we know almost nothing. We have looked towards 'the rising of the 'sun' and gathered what we can of the true incense, of the pure offering, which went up from thence. Is there any similar or any greater accession of new forces such as the Prophet anticipated to appear from the 'going down of the sun'? Hardly, with the exception of those two or three prophetic utterances which have already been quoted, and which were literally 'before their time,' was any eye of Judæan Priest or Teacher turned in that direction. If an Israelite or Syrian looked over the Mediterranean Sea from the heights of Lebanon, the whole Western world seemed to him summed up in the one object within his ken, the distant range of the island of Cyprus or Chittim.[1] It may be that Phœnician traders had brought back from that complex medley of seagirt coasts and promontories, known as the 'isles of the sea,' a few Ionian slaves, from whom the name of Ion or Javan became familiar to Hebrew ears.[2] It may be that a few Jewish seamen[3] from Joppa or Accho had served in the army of the Great King and shared the struggle in the Bay of Salamis. But no voice yet reaches us from those distant regions. Of the first twelve years[4] of the reign of Xerxes, so teeming with interest for all the world that lay

[1] Num. xxiv. 24; Isa. xxiii. 1, 12; Jer. ii. 10. See *Sinai and Palestine*, c. xi.

[2] Joel iii. 6; Isa. lxvi. 19; Ezek. xxvii. 13; Zech. ix. 13.

[3] Herod. vii. 8, 9; Hitzig, 279. They may, however, have been the Philistine occupants of Ashdod, Gaza, and Ashkelon (Rawlinson).

[4] Esther i. 1, 2.

beyond the Hellespont, the Jewish account contains not a word to indicate aught that should ruffle the splendour and frivolity of the Court of Susa. Yet not the less had come the hour when an influence more penetrating than any that we have yet touched is about to burst upon the development of the Jewish Church. Already, at the opening of this period, contemporaneous with Confucius and Buddha in China and India, had arisen the first fathers of Greek Philosophy, Pythagoras and Xenophanes and Solon. Already the Jews must have heard the first[1] accents of that Grecian tongue which was soon to take its place as the language of their own sacred books, side by side with their native Hebrew. And now, at the very same date as the last of the Judæan Prophets, arose, if not the earliest yet the most enduring, name among the Prophets of the European world.

> Not by Eastern windows only,
> When daylight comes, comes in the light;
> In front the sun climbs slow—how slowly!
> But Westward look—the land is bright.[2]

[1] The earliest Greek words in the Hebrew Scriptures are the names of the musical instruments in Dan. iii. 7. But see note at the end of Lecture XLII.

[2] Clough's *Poems*, ii. 195.

THE GRECIAN PERIOD.

LECTURE XLVI. SOCRATES.—B.C. 468–399.

AUTHORITIES.

'The Memorabilia' of Xenophon; Plato's 'Dialogues,' especially the 'Apologia,' the 'Crito,' and the 'Phædo,' in Professor Jowett's excellent edition of Plato. The narrative has, wherever it was possible, been taken from the eighth volume of Grote's 'History of 'Greece,' which appeared by the keenness of its insight and the vividness of its representation to supersede all other accounts.

THE GRECIAN PERIOD.

LECTURE XLVI.

SOCRATES.

We have arrived at the point when the influence of Greece is to make itself felt so deeply on the history both of Judaism and of the religion which sprang from Judaism as to constrain us to pause for a time, in order to bring clearly before our minds the strong personality and the quickening power of the one Grecian character who, beyond dispute, belongs to the religious history of all mankind, and whose example and teaching—unlike that of the Eastern sages whom we have just noticed—struck directly on the heart and intellect, first of Hebrew Palestine, and then of Christian Europe. The solemn pause at which the last utterances of Malachi leave us in Jerusalem corresponds, in some respects, to the pause which meets us in Grecian history when we transport ourselves to the same period in Athens. It was not merely that at the close of the Peloponnesian War the long struggle between the contending States had just been brought to an end, but that the eminent men who bore their part in it had been themselves called away from the scene. It is the Grecian 'Morte of heroes.' Every one of the great statesmen of Athens had passed away by the close of the fifth century before the Christian era ; and not the statesmen only, but the great writers also, whose career had run parallel to the tragedy of actual life. Thucydides, the grave recorder of the age, had left its exciting tale unfinished in the middle of a sentence. Euripides, the most philosophical and sceptical of the dramatic poets, had already met a fate stranger than that of his own Pentheus in the hunting-grounds of his royal patron in Macedonia. Sophocles in the fulness of years had been called away from the midst of his labours and his honours by an end as peaceful and as glorious as that of his own Colonean Œdipus. One man there still remained to close this funeral procession—he whose death alone of all the characters of Athenian history is an epoch in the annals not only of Greece but of the world.

Socrates.

With the mention of the name of Socrates we seem to pass at once from the student's chamber into the walks of common life—from the glories of Hellenic literature into the sanctities of Biblical religion. He, and he alone, of the sons of Javan, finds a place in the Fathers of Christian, as well as in the moralists of Pagan, antiquity; in the proverbs of modern Europe, as well as in the oracles of classical Greece. The prayer 'Sancte Socrates, ora pro nobis,' by whomsover said, has won a more universal acceptance than that of many a prayer addressed to the dubious saints of the Byzantine or of the Latin Church. If the canonisation of Buddha, though formal, was the result of inadvertence, the canonisation of Socrates, though informal, has been almost accepted. And the peculiar circumstances of his career, and its contrasts and affinities with the events and characters of the Sacred History both before and after the date of his appearance, make its description an almost necessary element in the course of the story on which we have been hitherto and shall be henceforth engaged.

His universality.

It is not on the public stage of Greek events that Socrates is most familiar to us. Yet for that very reason there is a peculiar interest in first approaching him, as in a purely historical point of view we must approach him, on the larger and more complex sphere of war and politics. When we meet such characters at moments where one least expects to find them, especially (as in this case) on occasion-

His public life.

which illustrate and call forth some of their most remarkable qualities, it is the surprise of encountering a friend in a strange country—it is the instruction of seeing a character which we have long known and admired in private put to a public test, and coming through the trial triumphantly. In the winter campaign at Potidæa, when the Athenian army was struck down by the severity of the Thracian frosts, we start with a thrill of pleasure as we recognise, in the one soldier whose spirits and strength continued unbroken by the hardship of that northern climate, the iron frame and constitution of the great philosopher. We survey with renewed interest the confused flight from the field of Delium,[1] when we remember that from that flight the youthful Xenophon was borne away on the broad shoulders of his illustrious friend. In the iniquitous condemnation of the Ten Generals—when 'the magistrates were so intimidated by the 'incensed manifestations of the assembly that all of them, 'except one, relinquished their opposition and agreed to put 'the question, that single obstinate officer whose refusal no 'menace could subdue, was a man in whom an impregnable 'adherence to law and duty was only one amongst many titles 'to honour. It was the philosopher Socrates—on this trying 'occasion, once throughout a life of seventy years discharging a 'political office among the fifty senators taken by lot from his 'own native district.'[2] Once, or it may be twice again, was he allowed to exhibit to the world this instructive lesson. In the Athenian Reign of Terror, after the oligarchical revolution of Lysander, 'pursuant to their general plan of implicating un-'willing citizens in their misdeeds, the Thirty Tyrants sent for 'five citizens to the government-house, and ordered them, with 'terrible menaces, to cross over to Salamis, and bring back as 'prisoner one of the innocent objects of their resentment. Four 'out of the five obeyed: the fifth was the philosopher Socrates, 'who refused all concurrence, and returned to his own house.'[3]

This was the last time that Socrates appeared in the political

[1] For every Englishman the plain of Delium (now Delisi) has a melancholy interest, as the scene of the death of the young Englishmen who perished there, with a spirit not unworthy of ancient Greeks or of Christian Englishmen, in 1870.

[2] Grote's *Greece*, viii. 272.

[3] Grote, viii. 332.

transactions of the country, unless we may believe the later traditions which represent him as present at that 'most striking 'and tragical scene,' when Theramenes sprang on the sacred hearth of the Athenian senate-house for protection against his murderers, like Joab at the horns of the altar of Jerusalem, or Onias in the consecrated grove of Daphne,[1] and when, as we are told, Socrates and two of his friends alone stood forward to protect him, as Satyrus, the executioner, dragged him by main force from the altar.

Such was the political life of Socrates—important in a high degree as proving that, unlike many eminent teachers, his character stood the test of public no less than of private morality, as exemplifying also the principle on which a good man may serve the State not by going out of his way to seek for trials of his strength, but by being fully prepared to meet them when they come. Had nothing more been handed down to us of his life than these comparatively trifling incidents, we should still have dwelt with peculiar pleasure on the scenes in which his name occurs, as, in fact, amidst 'the naughty world' of Grecian politics we dwell on 'the good deeds' of the humane Nicomachus, or of the noble Callicratidas : we should still have desired to know something more of the general character and pursuits of so honest and fearless a citizen.

That desire is gratified almost beyond example in the ancient world, by what is left us of the individual life of Socrates, which even in his own time made him the best-known Athenian of his day, and in later times has so completely thrown his political acts into the shade that not one in ten thousand of those to whom his name is a household word has any knowledge whatever of the few passages in which he crossed the path of the statesman or the soldier.

His personal appearance.

It is not often that the personal appearance of a great man has been so faithfully preserved. In the Jewish history we have hardly, except in the case of David, and perhaps of Jeremiah, been able to discern a single lineament or colour of outward form or countenance. In the famous picture of the School of Athens we look round on the

[1] Lectures XXVI., XLVIII.

faces of the other philosophers, and detect them only by their likeness to some ideal model which the painter has imagined to himself. But the Socrates of Raffaelle is the true historical Socrates of Xenophon and Aristophanes. Could we transport ourselves back to the Athenian market-place during the Peloponnesian war, we should at once recognise one familiar figure, standing, with uplifted finger and animated gesture, amidst the group of handsome youths or aged sophists, eager to hear, to learn, and to refute. We should see the Silenic features of that memorable countenance—the flat nose, the thick lips, the prominent eyes—the mark of a thousand jests from friends and foes. We should laugh at the protuberance of the Falstaff stomach, which no necessary hardships, no voluntary exercise, could bring down. We should perceive the strong-built frame, the full development of health and strength, which never sickened in the winter campaign of Potidæa, nor yet in the long plague and stifling heats of the blockade of Athens; which could enter alike into the jovial revelry of the religious festivities of Xenophon and Plato, or sustain the austerities, the scanty clothing, the naked feet, and the coarse fare of his ordinary life. The strong common-sense, the humour, the courage of the man were conspicuous at his very first outset. And everyone knows the story of the physiognomist who detected in his features the traces of that fiery temper which for the most part he kept under severe control, but which, when it did break loose, is described by those who witnessed it as absolutely terrible, overleaping both in act and language every barrier of the ordinary decorum of Grecian manners.[1]

But we must go back into his inner life, and into his earlier youth, before we can apprehend the feelings with which the Athenians must have regarded this strange apparition among them, and understand some of the peculiarities of the teachers with whom we have had to deal in the Semitic world. He was still young, perhaps stilll in his father's workshop, labouring at his group of Graces, and seeking inspirations from the ancient founder of his house, the hero-artist Dædalus, when the first

[1] See *Fragments of Aristoxenus*, 27, 28, as quoted by Grote, vol. viii. p. 548.

intimation of his mission dawned upon him. It is evident that Socrates partook largely of that enthusiastic temperament which is so often the basis of a profound character, but which is rarely united with a mind so remarkable for its healthy and vigorous tone in other respects. His complete abstraction from outward things reminds us partly of the ecstatic condition of the Hebrew Prophets or leaders, partly of some of the great scientific minds both in ancient and modern times. We have seen how Ezekiel lay stretched out like a dead corpse [1] for more than a year, or how Ezra [2] sat crouching in the court of the Temple from dawn till evening in his horror at the violation of the law. In like manner 'Archimedes would forget to 'eat his meals and require compulsion to take him to the bath.' In such a moment of abstraction it was that he rushed out of the bath into the streets of Syracuse, exclaiming *Eureka! Eureka!* In such another moment he fell a victim to the sword of the Roman soldier, too intent on his problem to return the answer which would have saved his life. In such a mood it was that Sir Isaac Newton sat half-dressed on his bed for many hours in the day while composing the 'Principia.' [3] And so we are told of Socrates, that he would suddenly fall into a reverie, and then remain motionless and regardless of all attempts to interrupt or call him away. On such an occasion, when in the camp at Potidæa, he was observed to stand thus transfixed at the early dawn of a long summer day. One after another the soldiers gathered round him, but he continued in the same posture, undisturbed by their astonishment or by the noon-day heat which had begun to beat upon his head. Evening drew on, and still he was to be seen in the same position, and the inquisitive Ionians in the camp took their evening meal by his side, and drew out their pallets from their tents to watch him. And the cold dews of the Thracian night came on, and still he remained unmoved, till at last the sun rose above Mount Athos, and still found him on the same spot where he had been since the previous morning. Then at last he started

His abstraction.

[1] See Lect. XL.

[2] See Lect. XLIV.

[3] Life of Archimedes, by Professor Donkin, in Smith's *Classical Biographical Dictionary.*

from his trance, offered his morning prayer to the Sun-god, and retired.[1]

Abstraction from the outer world so complete as this would of itself prepare us for the extraordinary disclosures which he has himself left of that '*divine sign*,' which by later writers was called his 'dæmon,' his 'inspiring genius,' but which he himself calls by the simpler name of his prophetic or supernatural 'voice.' It is impossible not to be reminded by it of the language in which the Hebrew Prophets, both by themselves and by the historians of their race, are said to have heard in the midnight silence of the sanctuary or in the mountain cave, or on the outskirts of the desert, the gentle 'call,' the still small whisper, the piercing cry, of the Divine Word.[2] It recalls to us 'the voices' by which the Maid of Orleans described herself to be actuated in her great task of delivering France from the English yoke, and to which, in the anguish of her last trial, she confidently appealed against the judgment of Bishop, Council, or Pope. As in the case of some of the Jewish seers, like Samuel or Jeremiah, or of that French maiden, so in the case of Socrates, this mysterious monitor began to address him when he was a child, long before the consciousness of his powers or the conception of his mission had been realised in his mind, and continued down to the very close of his life; so that even his conduct on his trial was distinctly based upon its intimations:—

His 'inspiring genius.'

'He was accustomed not only to obey it implicitly, but to 'speak of it publicly and familiarly to others, so that the fact 'was well known both to his friends and to his enemies. It 'had always forbidden him to enter on public life: it forbade 'him, when the indictment was hanging over him, to take any 'thought for a prepared defence: and so completely did he 'march with a consciousness of this bridle in his mouth, that 'when he felt no check he assumed that the turning which 'he was about to take was the right one. Though his per-'suasion on the subject was unquestionably sincere, and his 'obedience constant—yet he never dwelt upon it himself as

[1] Plato, *Symp.* pp. 175 B, 220 C. [2] 1 Sam. iv. 4, 6, 8, 10; 1 Kings xix. 12; Isa. xl. 3, 6.

'anything grand, or awful, or entitling him to peculiar deference; 'but spoke of it often in his usual strain of familiar playfulness. 'To his friends generally it seems to have constituted one of 'his titles to reverence, though neither Plato nor Xenophon 'scruples to talk of it in that jesting way which, doubtless, they 'caught from himself.'[1]

Another mode which Socrates seemed to himself to enjoy, of intercommunion with the invisible world, was by dreams—in this respect also, as even the cursory insight of the Gentiles remarked, resembling some of the intuitions of the leaders[2] of Israel and of the surrounding tribes. 'Often 'and often' (so he related one such instance in his last hours) 'have I been haunted by a vision in the course of my past life; 'now coming in one form, now in another, but always with the 'same words—*Socrates! let* music *be thy work and labour.*' In his last hours he endeavoured literally to comply with this injunction by trying even at that solemn moment to versify the fables of Æsop.

His dreams.

But the most important preternatural influence—more important even than the restraining voice of his familiar spirit—was that which acted upon him, in common with the rest of his countrymen, and to which, owing to the singular detachment of even the most sacred localities of Palestine from Prophetic influences, the Jewish history furnishes no parallel—the Oracle of Delphi. Who that has ever seen or read of that sacred spot—the twin cliffs overhanging the sloping terraces which descend to the deep ravine of the Plistus—terraces now bare and untenanted, but then crowned by temples, rising tier above tier with a magnificence the more striking from the wild scenery around—can fail to enter in some degree into the reverence paid to the mysterious utterances which issued from beneath those venerable rocks? It was a remarkable proof of the sincere belief which the Greek world reposed in the oracle that it was consulted not only for state purposes, but

The Oracle of Delphi.

[1] Grote, viii. 559.

[2] Strabo, xvi. 710. See Lecture V. and the vision in Job iv. 13. Compare Solomon, 1 Kings iii. 5, 10 (Lecture XXVI.); Nebuchadnezzar, Dan. ii. 1 (Lecture XLI.); Judas Maccabæus, 2 Macc. xv. 11 (Lecture XLVIII.).

to solve the perplexity which was felt with regard to individual characters. Even so late as the time of Cicero this belief continued. We are told that when the Roman orator, as a young man, went to Rhodes to complete his education, and consulted the oracle concerning his future career, the Pythia advised him to live for himself, and not to value the opinion of others as his guide. 'If this be an invention,' says Niebuhr, in relating the incident with his usual liveliness, 'it was certainly made by one 'who saw very deep, and perceived the real cause of all Cicero's 'sufferings. If the Pythia did give such an answer, then this is 'one of the oracles which might tempt one to believe in an 'actual inspiration of the priestess.' This is one instance, and assuredly another is the answer made to the faithful disciple, who went to inquire whether anyone was wiser than the son of Sophroniscus. The priestess replied, and Chærephon brought back the reply, that Socrates was the wisest of men. It was this oracle which was the turning-point of the life of Socrates.

His Call.

It would be curious, had we the materials, to delineate the struggles of that hour, to trace the homely common-sense of the young statuary, confounded by the words of the response, contrary to all that he knew of his own wisdom, as he then counted wisdom, yet backed by what he believed to be an infallible authority, and pressed upon him, doubtless, by all the enthusiasm of his ardent friend. There was an anguish of distressing perplexity, like that which is described at the like crisis in the call of some of the greatest of the Jewish Prophets—Isaiah, Jeremiah, and Ezekiel.[1] The Athenian craftsman resolved to put the oracle to the test by examining into the wisdom of others ; and from this seemingly trivial incident began that extraordinary life, which, in its own peculiar vein, 'is without parallel among contemporaries or 'successors,'[2] although indirectly furnishing and receiving instructive illustrations along the whole pathway of the Jewish history, which, from its deeper seriousness, supplies resemblances that in Grecian history would be sought in vain.

[1] Isa. vi. 3–8 ; Jer. i. 6–9 ; Ezek. ii. 9, iii. 3. See Lectures XXXVII., XL.
[2] Grote, viii. 561.

He was in middle age when this call came upon him, and at once he arose and followed it. From that time for thirty years he applied himself to 'the self-imposed task of teacher, 'excluding all other business, public or private, and neglecting 'all means of fortune.' For thirty years—for those thirty years which extend through the whole period of the Peloponnesian war—in the crowded streets and squares, when all Attica was congregated within the walls of Athens to escape the Spartan invasions—during the horrors of the plague—amidst the excitements of the various vicissitudes of Pylus, of Syracuse, of the revolution of the Four Hundred, of the tyranny of the Thirty, of the restoration of the democracy, Socrates was ever at his post, by his presence, by his voice, by his example, restraining, attracting, repelling every class of his excitable countrymen:—'Early in the morning he frequented the public walks, the 'gymnasia for bodily training, and the schools where youths 'were receiving instruction; he was to be seen in the market-'place at the hour when it was most crowded, among the 'booths and tables, where goods were exposed for sale: his 'whole day was usually spent in this public manner. He 'talked with anyone, young or old, rich or poor, who sought 'to address him, and in the hearing of all who chose to stand 'by: not only he never either asked or received any reward, 'but he made no distinction of persons, never withheld his 'conversation from anyone, and talked upon the same general 'topics to all.'[1]

Under any circumstances such an apparition would have struck astonishment into a Grecian city. All other teachers, both before and afterwards, 'either took money for their lessons, 'or at least gave them apart from the multitude in a private 'house to special pupils, with admissions or rejections at their 'own pleasure.' Plato's retreat in the consecrated grove of *Academus*, Epicurus in his private *Garden*, the painted *Portico* or cloister of Zeno, the *Peripatetics* of Aristotle in the shaded walks round the *Lycean* sanctuary of Apollo, all indicate the prevailing practice. The philosophy of Socrates alone was

[1] Grote, viii. 554.

in every sense the philosophy of the market-place. Very rarely he might be found under the shade of the plane-tree [1] or the caverned rocks of the Ilissus, enjoying the grassy slope of its banks, and the little pools of water that collect in the corners of its torrent bed, and the white and purple flowers of its agnus castus shrubs. But ordinarily, whether in the city, in the dusty road between the Long Walls, or in the busy mart of Piræus, his place was amongst men, in every vocation of life, living not for himself, but for them, rejecting all pay, contented in poverty. Whatever could be added to the singularity of this spectacle was added by the singularity, as already indicated, of his outward appearance. Amidst the gay life, the beautiful forms, the brilliant colours of an Athenian multitude and an Athenian street, the repulsive features, the unwieldy figure, the bare feet, the rough thread-bare attire of the philosopher must have excited every sentiment of astonishment and ridicule which strong contrast can produce. And if to this we add the occasional trance, the eye fixed on vacancy, the total abstraction from outward objects—or again, the momentary outbursts of violent temper—or lastly (what we are told at times actually took place) the sudden irruptions of his wife Xanthippe to carry off her eccentric husband to his forsaken home—we shall not wonder at the universal celebrity which he acquired, even irrespectively of his singular powers or of his peculiar objects. An unusual diction or even an unusual dress secures attention for a teacher, so soon as he has once secured a hearing. Such was the natural effect of the hair-cloth wrappings, or at times the nudity, of the Jewish Prophets. [2] When Socrates appeared it was (so his disciples described it) [3] as if one of the marble satyrs which sat in grotesque attitudes with pipe or flute in the sculptors' shops at Athens had left his seat of stone, and walked into the plane-tree avenue or the gymnastic colonnade. Gradually the crowd gathered round him. At first he spoke to the tanners, and the smiths, and the

His teaching.

[1] Plato, *Phædrus*, c. 9. The exact spot described in this dialogue can still be verified.

[2] See Lectures XIX., XXX., XXXVII.

[3] Plato, *Symp.* c. 39.

drovers, who were plying their trades about him; and they shouted with laughter as he poured forth his homely jokes. But soon the magic charm of his voice made itself felt. The peculiar sweetness of its tone had an effect which even the thunder of Pericles failed to produce. The laughter ceased—the crowd thickened—the gay youth whom nothing else could tame stood transfixed and awestruck in his presence; there was a solemn thrill in his words, such as his hearers could compare to nothing but the mysterious sensation produced by the clash of drum and cymbal in the worship of the great Mother of the Gods—the head swam, the heart leaped at the sound—tears rushed from their eyes; and they felt that, unless they tore themselves away from that fascinated circle, they should sit down at his feet and grow old in listening to the marvellous music of this second Marsyas.

But the excitement occasioned by his appearance was increased tenfold by the purpose which he had set before him, when, to use the expressive comparison of his pupils, he cast away his rough satyr's skin and disclosed the divine image which that rude exterior had covered. The object to which he thus devoted himself with the zeal 'not simply of a 'philosopher, but of a religious missionary doing the work of 'a philosopher,' was to convince men of all classes, but especially the most distinguished, that they had the 'conceit of 'knowledge without the reality.'

'Should you even now offer to acquit me' (these were his own words in his defence at his trial) 'on condition of my 'renouncing this duty, I should reply with all respect: If you 'kill me you will find none other such. Men of Athens, I 'honour and love you; but I shall obey God rather than you, 'and while I have life and strength I shall never cease from 'the practice and teaching of philosophy, exhorting anyone 'whom I meet after my manner, and convincing him, saying: '"O my friend, why do you, who are a citizen of the great 'and mighty and wise city of Athens, care so much about 'laying up the greatest amount of money and honour and 'reputation, and so little about wisdom and truth and the

'greatest improvement of the soul, which you never regard
'or heed at all?"

'And this I should say to everyone whom I meet, young
'and old, citizen and alien, but especially to the citizens,
'inasmuch as they are my brethren. For this is the command
'of God, as I would have you know; and I believe that to this
'day no greater good has ever happened in the State than my
'service to God. For if you kill me you will not easily find
'another like me, who, if I may use such a ludicrous figure of
'speech, am a sort of gadfly, given to the State by God; and
'the State is like a great and noble steed who is tardy in his
'motions owing to his very size, and requires to be stirred into
'life. I am that gadfly which God has given the State, and all
'day long and in all places am always fastening upon you,
'arousing and persuading and reproaching you.'[1]

Never has the Socratic method of instruction been described
in language so vivid and forcible as in the words of the last and
greatest historian of Greece.

'To him the precept inscribed in the Delphian Temple—
'*Know thyself*—was the holiest of all texts, which he constantly
'cited, and strenuously enforced upon his hearers; interpret-
'ing it to mean, "Know what sort of a man thou art and what
'are thy capacities in reference to human use." His manner
'of enforcing it was alike original and effective, and though he
'was dexterous in varying his topics and queries according to
'the individual person with whom he had to deal, it was his
'first object to bring the hearer to take just measure of his own
'real knowledge or real ignorance. To preach, to exhort, even
'to confute particular errors, appeared to Socrates useless, so
'long as the mind lay wrapped up in its habitual mist, or
'illusion of wisdom: such must be dissipated before any new
'light could enter. Accordingly, the hearer being usually
'forward in announcing positive declarations on those general
'doctrines, and explanations of those terms, to which he was
'most attached, and in which he had the most implicit confi-
'dence, Socrates took them to pieces, and showed that they

[1] Jowett's *Plato*, i. 344, 345.

'involved contradiction and inconsistency; professing himself 'to be without any positive opinion, nor ever advancing any 'until the hearer's mind had undergone the proper purifying 'cross-examination. It was this indirect and negative proceed-'ing, which, though only a part of the whole, stood out as his 'most original and most conspicuous characteristic, and 'determined his reputation with a large number of persons 'who took no trouble to know anything else about him. It 'was an exposure no less painful than surprising to the persons 'questioned, and produced upon several of them an effect of 'permanent alienation, so that they never came near him again, 'but reverted to their former state of mind, without any 'permanent change. But, on the other hand, the ingenuity 'and novelty of the process were highly interesting to hearers, 'especially youthful hearers, sons of rich men, and enjoying 'leisure, who not only carried away with them a lofty admira-'tion of Socrates, but were fond of trying to copy his negative 'polemics. His constant habit of never suffering a general 'term to remain undetermined, but applying it at once to 'particulars—the homely and effective instances of which he 'made choice—the string of interrogatories, each advancing 'towards a result, yet a result not foreseen by anyone—the 'indirect and circuitous manner whereby the subject was turned 'round and at last approached and laid open by a totally 'different face—all this constituted a sort of prerogative 'in Socrates, which no one else seems to have approached. 'What is termed his *irony*—or assumption of the character 'of an ignorant learner asking information from one who knew 'better than himself—while it was essential as an excuse for 'his practice as a questioner, contributed also to add zest and 'novelty to his conversation; and totally banished from it both 'didactic pedantry and seeming bias as an advocate, which, 'to one who talked so much, was of no small advantage.'[1]

That a life of thirty years so spent should have created animosities similar to those excited at Jerusalem against Jeremiah, and at times Isaiah[2]—that the statesmen, poets,

[1] Grote, viii. 605.

[2] Lectures XXXVII., XL.

and lawyers should have thought him insufferably vexatious—that 'the Sophists,' like the Priests and hired Prophets, should have hated the man whose disinterested pursuance of his vocation without pay seemed to cast a slur upon their profession—that the multitude should have regarded, partly with dislike, partly with awe, a man whose aims were so lofty, whose life was so pure, and yet whose strange behaviour seemed to indicate something wild and preternatural, was only too intelligible; and we cannot be surprised that 'so violent 'was the enmity which he occasionally provoked, that there 'were instances in which he was struck or maltreated, and 'very frequently laughed to scorn.'

'In truth, the mission of Socrates, as he himself describes 'it, could not but prove eminently unpopular and obnoxious. 'To convince a man that—of matters which he felt confident 'of knowing, and had never thought of questioning or even of 'studying—he is really profoundly ignorant, insomuch that he 'cannot reply to a few pertinent queries without involving 'himself in flagrant contradictions, is an operation highly 'salutary, often necessary to his future improvement; but an 'operation of painful surgery, in which, indeed, the tem'porary pain experienced is one of the conditions almost indis'pensable to the future beneficial results. It is one which few 'men can endure without hating the operator at the time; 'although, doubtless, such hatred would not only disappear, 'but be exchanged for esteem and admiration, if they perse'vered until the full ulterior consequences of the operation 'developed themselves. But we know (from the express 'statement of Xenophon) that many who underwent this 'first pungent thrust of his dialectics, never came near 'him again; he disregarded them as laggards, but their 'voices did not the less count in the hostile chorus. What 'made that chorus the more formidable, was the high quality 'and position of its leaders. For Socrates himself tells us 'that the men whom he chiefly and expressly sought out to 'cross-examine were the men of celebrity, as statesmen, 'rhetors, poets, or artisans; those, at once, most sensitive to 'such humiliation, and most capable of making their enmity 'effective.'[1]

We may wonder, not that the thirty years' 'public, notori-'ous, and efficacious discoursing' was finally interrupted, but that it was not interrupted long before. Why, then, it may be asked, did he fall at last? Why should he have been prosecuted at seventy years of age for persevering in an occupation precisely the same in manner and in substance as he had followed for so many years preceding? The answer is to be found in the general history of Athens at that time, and the general character of the Athenian people, but it is of such universal application that it deserves record in its connexion with the triumphs and defeats of the truth everywhere, in Palestine and in modern Europe as well as in Greece It was the moment of a strong reaction. The most galling tyranny to which Athens had ever been exposed had just been overthrown. A restoration of the old democracy had just been effected, under circumstances singularly trying; and in the jubilee of that restoration the whole people of Athens were entirely absorbed. Every association with the dreadful period of the eight months' dominion of the Thirty was now viewed with the darkest suspicion. Every old institution was now cherished with double affection, reminding them, as it did, of the free and happy days which those eight months had suspended, securing them, as it did, from the return of the lawless cruelty and self-indulgence which had been established in the interval. All the suspicions and excitements which Thucydides describes, with a master hand, as the result of the mere traditional recollections of the tyranny of the Pisistratides, were now let loose with so much the greater force from the freshness of the recollections of the tyranny of Critias and his associates. All the undefined, mysterious panic which ran through the city after the mutilation of the Hermes-busts was now, although in a less concentrated form, afloat again to vindicate the majesty of the ancient institutions of their forefathers so unexpectedly, so providentially restored to them.

His fall.

[1] Grote, viii. 634.

It was in this state of public feeling that on the walls of the portico of the King Archon—that ancient vestige of primæval usage, which long preserved at Athens the recollection of the Gate of Judgment, in which the Kings of the East presided over the trial of their subjects, from the Porch of Solomon[1] down to the Sublime Porte at Constantinople and the Tower of Justice in the Alhambra—there appeared in the presence of the Athenian people the fatal indictment, memorable for all future ages :—'Socrates is guilty of crime, first, 'for not worshipping the gods whom the city worships, but 'introducing new divinities of his own ; next for corrupting the 'youth. The penalty due is—death.'

His trial.

These two accusations at once concentrated upon Socrates the indefinite odium which had, perhaps for years, but certainly for months past, been gathering in the minds of the people. Three men only had spoken, Melitus, Anytus, and Lycon; but they spoke the feeling of hundreds. The charge of innovation on the national religion, as it was one which, especially at that moment, roused the 'too much superstition'[2] of that sensitive populace almost to madness, was one to which, however unjustly, his manner and his conversation eminently exposed him. It recalled, too, and Melitus the poet would not suffer the recollection to sleep, the great spectacle which twenty-four years ago had been exhibited in the Dionysiac Theatre, when Socrates had been held up to ridicule and detestation as the representative of the Sophist school in the 'Clouds' of Aristophanes ; and although many who had sat on the tiers of the theatre at that time were now in their graves, and, possibly, the long and blameless course which had followed might have cleared away some misundersandings, yet the very appearance of Socrates would suggest the laughter which that hideous mask had called forth ; the very words of the charge would bring before their minds the most striking of the Aristophanic scenes.

Still more sharply was the second count in the indictment pointed by the events of the time—'He has corrupted the youth.' Two men, the most distinguished of the pupils of his earlier

[1] See Lecture XXVI.

[2] Acts xvii. 22 (Greek).

years, had just been cut off, in the very height of their fame and of their crimes. The two most hateful names at Athens at this moment were Alcibiades and Critias—Alcibiades, both for his individual licentiousness and insolence, and also for the public treason, which more than any one cause had precipitated the fatal termination of the war—Critias, as 'the chief director 'of the spoliations and atrocities committed by the Thirty.' And yet both these dreadful characters—for so they must have been regarded—had in former times been seen hanging on the lips of Socrates in public and in private; for Alcibiades his affection had been stronger than he had felt to any other man; of Critias it was enough to say that he was the uncle of the philosopher's most admiring disciple, Plato. And the odium which would be incurred by this connexion must have been enhanced by the presence of his accuser Anytus. Anytus had suffered with Thrasybulus during the late usurpation—with him had taken refuge in the mountain fastnesses of Phyle—with him had shared the danger and the glory of the return. As the aged accuser and the aged prisoner stood before the Athenian court, the judges could hardly fail to be reminded that in one they saw the faithful supporter, through evil report and good report, of their greatest benefactor—in the other, the master and friend of the arch-traitor and the arch-tyrant.

It was to feelings such as these, added to the long-accumulated jealousy and suspicion which intellectual and moral eminence, when accompanied either by eccentricity or by hostility to existing opinions or practice, always provokes, that we must ascribe the unfavourable attitude assumed by the Judicial Assembly of Athens towards Socrates. Amongst the five hundred and fifty men of whom that assembly was composed there must have been ample room for the entrance of all those irregular and accidental influences to which a numerous court of justice in such a case must always be exposed—there must have been many who had formerly smarted under his questions in the market-place—many who had been disturbed by the consciousness of something beyond their ordinary powers of understanding or appreciation.

It is due alike to him and to them to remember that by 276 out of that number he was acquitted. A majority of six turned the scale in the most momentous trial which down to that time the world had witnessed. There was still, however, a chance of escape. The penalty for which the Athenians had called was death. But, according to the form of the Athenian judicature, it was always in the power of the accused, after the verdict had been pronounced, to suggest some lesser penalty than had been proposed, such as fine, imprisonment, or exile. Had Socrates done this simply and purely, the very small majority by which the condemnation had been pronounced affords sufficient proof that the judges were not inclined to sanction the extreme penalty against him. But the lofty tone which he had assumed in the previous part of the trial, and which to many of the judges 'would appear to betray an insolence not without analogy to Alcibiades or Critias, with whom 'his accuser had compared him,' now rose to a still higher pitch. His own words must be given, as alone conveying an impression of the effect which must have been produced.

'And what shall I propose on my part, O men of Athens? 'Clearly that which is my due. And what is that which I 'ought to pay or to receive? What shall be done to the man 'who has never had the wit to be idle during his whole life; 'but has been careless of what the many care about—wealth, 'and family interests, and military offices, and speaking in the 'assembly, and magistracies, and plots, and parties? Reflecting 'that I was really too honest a man to follow in this way and 'live, I did not go where I could do no good to you or to 'myself; but where I could do the greatest good privately to 'every one of you, thither I went, and sought to persuade every 'man among you that he must look to himself, and seek virtue 'and wisdom before he looks to his private interests, and look 'to the State before he looks to the interests of the State; and 'that this should be the order which he observes in all his 'actions. What shall be done to such an one? Doubtless 'some good thing, O men of Athens, if he has his reward; and 'the good should be of a kind suitable to him. What would 'be a reward suitable to a poor man who is your benefactor, 'who desires leisure that he may instruct you? There can be 'no more fitting reward than maintenance at the expense of the 'State in the Prytaneum.'

It is easy to conceive the indignation with which this challenge must have been received by the judges, as a direct insult to the court—the bitter grief and disappointment with which it must have been heard by his friends, as throwing away the last chance of preserving a life to them so inestimably precious. To us, it invests the character of Socrates with that heroic dignity which would else perhaps have been wanting to his career, from its very simplicity and homely usefulness. At the same time it has a further and peculiar interest in enabling us to form a distinct conception of that determined disregard of time and place and consequences which constitutes so remarkable a feature of Socrates' individual character, and harmonises completely with that stern religious determination which recalls and illustrates so many a solitary career in the history we have traversed from Moses down to Malachi. It is the same intent devotion to his one object of life, as appeared when he remained transfixed in the camp at Potidæa—as when he looked back with calm majesty on his pursuers at Delium—as when he argued through long days and months in the public places of Athens—as when he refused in the raging assembly after the battle of Arginusæ to be turned one hair's breadth from the strict rule of law and duty.

His death.

The closing scenes which Plato has invested with such surpassing glory can never be forgotten. The Hebrew prophet, the Christian martyr, might well have couched their farewells to the audiences before which they, like him, often pleaded in vain, almost in the same words: 'The 'hour of departure has arrived, and we go our ways. I go to 'to die, and you to live. Which is better God only knows.' Then ensue the long thirty days which passed in prison before the execution of the verdict—the playful equanimity and unabated interest in his habitual objects of life amidst the uncontrollable emotions of his companions, after they knew of the return of the sacred ship, whose absence had up to that moment suspended his fate. Then follows the gathering in of that solemn evening, when the fading of the sunset in all its variety of hues on the tops of the Athenian hills was the signal that the last hour was at hand.[1] Then the fatal hemlock enters; we see the immovable countenance, the firm hand, the wonted 'scowl' of stern defiance at the executioner;[2] we hear the burst of frantic lamentation from all his friends, as, with his habitual 'ease and cheerfulness,' he drained the cup to its dregs;[3] we watch the solemn silence enjoined by himself—the pacing to and fro—the cold palsy of the hemlock creeping from the extremities to the heart, and the gradual torpor ending in death.

We trace also how he chose, or how his disciple has chosen for him, these last moments for some of his most characteristic arguments. Now comes out his ruling passion strong in death suggesting to him the consolation, as natural to him as it seems strange to us, that when in the world beyond the grave he should, as he hoped, encounter the heroes of the Trojan war, he should then 'pursue with them the business of mutual cross-'examination, and debate on ethical progress and perfection' —how he confidently (as the event proved, mistakenly in the letter, truly in the spirit) predicted that his removal would be the signal 'for numerous apostles putting forth with increased 'energy that process of interrogatory test and spur to which 'he had devoted his life, and was doubtless to him far dearer 'and more sacred than his life'—how his escape from prison was only prevented by his own decided refusal to become a 'party in any breach of the law'—how deliberately, and with matter-of-fact precision, he satisfied himself with the result of the verdict, by reflecting that the Divine voice of his earlier years had 'never manifested itself once to him during the whole 'day of the trial; neither when he came thither at first nor at 'any one point during his whole discourse'—how his 'strong

[1] ἀλλ' οἶμαι ἔτι ἥλιον εἶναι ἐπὶ τοῖς ὄρεσι και οὔπω δεδυκέναι. *Phædo*, c. 116.
[2] ὥσπερ εἰώθει, ταυρηδὸν ὑπολέψας. *Ib.* b. 117.
[3] μαλα εὐχερῶς καὶ εὐκόλως εξέπιε. *Ib.* c. 117.

'religious persuasions were attested by his last words addressed 'to his friend immediately before he passed into a state of 'insensibility:' 'Crito, I owe a cock to Æsculapius; will you 'remember to pay the debt?'

His religious character.

Perhaps in the powerful modern narrative of the career of Socrates—perhaps in our own as condensed from it—the readers of ancient history, as it has hitherto been familiar to us, will have felt something like a jar against the solemn and majestic associations with which the life and death of Socrates have always been invested. To a large extent this is merely the inevitable result of the sudden exhibition, in its true historical light, of a great character usually regarded with almost ideal indistinctness. It is very seldom that the first sight of an eminent man exactly corresponds to our preconceived impression; and the disturbance of that impression, especially if the impression is tinged by moral or religious awe, has the effect of disappointment and depreciation beyond what is justified by the facts of the case. It is for this reason, amongst others, that it has been thought good to introduce at length the contemplation of the whole historical position of Socrates. It illustrates precisely the like difficulty which we experience in dealing with the characters of the yet more consecrated story of the Jewish sages and prophets. But on second thoughts we shall recognise, as in other matters, so in this, that truth and reality, so far from being inconsistent with a just reverence, tend to promote it. The searching analysis of the modern English scholar has taught us more exactly wherein the greatness of Socrates consisted, and we are therefore the better able truly to honour, and, so far as in us lies, to imitate it. We know better than we did wherein lay the true secret of his condemnation, and we are therefore the better able not merely to compassionate, but to take warning by the error of his judges.

We have pointed out in the story of 'the wisest of Greeks' how curiously his claims, his expressions, even his external mode of life, illustrate, and are in turn illustrated by, the utterances and acts of the Hebrew seers. But there is yet more than this. As in the cases of David and Jeremiah, we have felt ourselves entitled to see the forecastings—the preludings—of that supreme event which gives to the earlier Jewish history its universal interest, so, in the case of Socrates, it is not less remarkable to trace the resemblances which bring that final consummation of the Jewish history into connexion with that Western World for which the great Prophet of the Captivity already had anticipated so important a part [1] in the fortunes of his own race.

Likeness to the Christian History.

In studying the character and life of Socrates we know that we are contemplating the most remarkable moral phenomenon in the ancient world; we are conscious of having climbed the highest point of the ascent of Gentile virtue and wisdom; we find ourselves in a presence which invests with a sacred awe its whole surroundings. We feel that here alone, or almost alone, in the Grecian world, we are breathing an atmosphere, not merely moral, but religious, not merely religious (it may be a strong expression, yet we are borne out by the authority of the earliest Fathers of the Church), but Christian. Difficult as it was to escape from these associations under any circumstances, the language of the latest Greek historian has now rendered it all but impossible. The startling phrases which he uses, as alone adequate to the occasion, are dictated by the necessity of the case; and when we are told that Socrates was a 'cross-examining *missionary*'—that 'he spent 'his life in public *apostolic* dialectics'—that he was habitually actuated by 'his persuasion of a special *religious* mission,' [2] we are at once carried forward from the time of Socrates himself to that more sacred age from which these expressions are borrowed, and by which alone we are enabled fully to appreciate what Socrates was and did.

The comparisons which have often been drawn between the Galilean Teacher and the Athenian sage may have been at times exaggerated. There are in the accompaniments of the character of Socrates dark shadows, grotesque incidents, unworthy associations, which render any such parallel, if pressed

[1] See Lectures XL. and XLI.

[2] Grote, viii. 553, 566, 588.

too far, as painful and as untrue as the like parallels that have sometimes been found in Jacob or David, or, yet more rashly, in Jephthah or Samson. Still, if viewed aright, there are few more remarkable confirmations of the reality of the Gospel history than the light which, by way of contrast or likeness, is thrown upon it by the highest example of Greek antiquity. It is instructive to observe that there, almost alone, outside of the Jewish race is to be found the career which, at however remote a distance, suggests whether to friends or enemies a solid illustration of the One Life, which is the turning-point of the religion of the whole world. We do not forget the marvellous purity of the life of Buddha;[1] nor the traces of contact between the rise of Islam[2] and the rise of Christianity. But there are points of comparison where these fail, and where the story of Socrates is full of suggestions. When we contemplate the contented poverty, the self-devotion, the constant publicity, the miscellaneous followers of Socrates, we feel that we can understand better than before the outward aspect at least of that Sacred Presence which moved on the busy shores of the Sea of Galilee, and in the streets and courts of Jerusalem. When we read of the dogged obstinacy of the court by which he was judged—the religious or superstitious prejudices invoked against him—the expression of his friend when all was finished—'Such was the end of the 'wisest and justest and best of all the men that I have ever 'known'—another Trial and another Parting inevitably rush to the memory. When we read the last conversations of the prisoner in the Athenian dungeon, our thoughts almost insensibly rise to the farewell discourses in the upper chamber at Jerusalem with gratitude and reverential awe. The differences are immense. But there is a likeness of moral atmosphere, even of external incident, that cannot fail to strike the attention. Or (to turn to another side), when we are perplexed by the difficulty of reconciling the narrative of the first three Evangelists with the altered tone of the fourth, it is at least a step towards the solution of that difficulty to remember that there is

Likeness to the Gospel History.

[1] See Lecture XLV. [2] See Lecture VIII. on the Eastern Church.

here a parallel diversity between the Socrates of Xenophon and the Socrates of Plato. No one has been tempted by that diversity to doubt the substantial identity, the true character, much less the historical existence of the master whom they both profess to describe. The divergences of Plato from Xenophon are incontestable; the introduction of his own colouring and thought undeniable; and yet not the less is his representation indispensable to the complete ideal which mankind now reveres as the picture of Socrates. Nor, when we think of the total silence of Josephus, or of other comtemporary writers, respecting the events which we now regard as greatest in the history of mankind, is it altogether irrelevant to reflect that for the whole thirty years comprised in the most serious of ancient histories, Socrates was not only living, but acting a more public part, and, for all the future ages of Greece, an incomparably more important part, than any other Athenian citizen; and yet that so able and so thoughtful an observer as Thucydides has never once noticed him directly or indirectly. There is no stronger proof of the weakness of the argument from omission, especially in the case of ancient history, which, unlike our own, contained within its range of vision no more than was immediately before it for the moment.

Likeness to the Apostolic History.

If we descend from this higher ground to those lower but still lofty regions, which belong to the closing epoch of the Jewish history, the illustrations supplied by the life of Socrates are still more apposite and instructive. When we are reminded of the 'apostolic' self-devotion of Socrates a new light seems to break on the character and career of the teacher of Tarsus from whose life that expression is especially derived; and the glowing language in which the English historian of Greece describes the energy and the enthusiasm of the Athenian missionary enables us to realise with greater force than ever 'the pureness, and knowledge, and 'love unfeigned,' of the missionary of a higher cause, who argued in the very market-place where Socrates had conversed more than four centuries before, and was, like him, accused of being a 'vain babbler' and a 'setter-forth of strange gods.'[1]

[1] Acts xvii. 18.

And even in minute detail there are some passages of the Apostle's life which are singularly elucidated by the corresponding features in the career of the philosopher. How much more vividly, for example, do we understand the relation of St. Paul, himself a Rabbi, to the teachers of his time, at once belonging to them and distinct from them, when we contemplate the like relations of Socrates to the Sophists! How striking is the coincidence between the indignant refusal of St. Paul in these very cities of Athens and Corinth to receive remuneration for his labours, and the similar protest of Socrates, by precept and example, against the injurious effect produced on teachers by direct dependence on the casual contributions, on the voluntary or involuntary payment of their hearers![1] And how remarkably is the vulgar feeling of the Roman world towards the Apostles and their converts illustrated by the vulgar feeling of the Athenian world towards Socrates and his pupils! In the attack which was made at two distinct periods on Alcibiades and on Socrates we see the union of the great mass of Athenian society, both democratical and aristocratical, against what they conceived to be revolutionary, and against men who were obnoxious because they towered above their age. As in the alleged plot of the mutilation of the Hermæ, Thessalus, the son of the aristocratic Cimon, and Androcles, the demagogue, both united against Alcibiades in the charge of overthrowing the constitution and establishing a tyranny—so Aristophanes, the poet of the aristocracy, and Anytus, the companion of the exiled leader of the popular party, combined in bringing against Socrates the charge of overthrowing mythology and establishing atheism. In each case there was a real danger to be discovered—if the prosecutors could have discerned it. Alcibiades was at work on designs which might have dissolved the existing bonds of society at Athens, and perhaps made him its tyrant and destroyer. Socrates was at work on designs which would ultimately tend to place the religion and morality of Greece on a totally new foundation. They failed to convict Alcibiades, because his plans were not yet fully developed;

[1] Grote, viii. 482. Comp. 1 Cor. ix. 1–18.

they failed to convict Socrates justly, because his design was one which none but the noblest minds could understand. So far there was a resemblance between the two cases—a resemblance of which the enemies of Socrates made the most. But, as everyone now recognises, the difference was far wider. Alcibiades was really what he was taken to be, the representative of all that was worst in the teaching of the Sophists—of all that was most hostile to faith and virtue. Socrates, whilst formally belonging to the Sophists, was really the champion of all that was best and truest in that time; and he fell a victim to the blindness which in all great movements has again and again confounded two elements intrinsically dissimilar, because externally they both happened to be opposed to the prevailing opinion of the time.

There is no passage in history which more happily illustrates the position which was taken up against the Christian apostles and missionaries of the first and second centuries—a position which has not unfrequently been overlooked or misapprehended. 'Christianity,' as has been well remarked, 'shared the common lot of every great moral change which 'has ever taken place in human society, by containing amongst 'its supporters men who were morally the extreme opposites of 'each other.'[1] No careful reader of the Epistles can fail to perceive the constant struggle which the Apostles had to maintain, not only against the Jew and the heathen external to the Christian society, but against the wild and licentious doctrines which took shelter within it. The same confusion which had taken place in the Athenian mind in the case of Socrates and Alcibiades, took place in the first century of the Christian era with regard to the Apostles and the fierce fanatics of the early Church, who were to all outward appearance on the same side, both equally bent on revolutionising the existing order of civil society. As Aristophanes could not distinguish between the licentious arguments of the wilder class of sophists and the elevating and inspiring philosophy of Socrates, so Tacitus could not distinguish between the anarchists whom St. Paul and St.

[1] Arnold's *Fragment on the Church*, 85.

Peter had laboured to repress, and the pure morality and faith which they had laboured to propagate. He regarded them both as belonging to 'an execrable race,' 'hateful for their 'abominable crimes;' and as the Greek poet could see nothing but an atheist in Socrates, so the Roman historian would have joined in the cry, 'Away with the atheists,' which was raised against the first Christians. In each case there were some who even at the time judged more calmly and more wisely. Socrates was by his illustrious disciples justly appreciated, and the gross mistake which Tacitus had made with regard to Christianity was not shared by his friend and contemporary the younger Pliny. But these warnings are instructive for every age; and it is because the two cases, amidst infinite diversity, tend to explain each other, that we have ventured thus far to anticipate the story of coming events, and to bring them together as combining to read the same indispensable lesson of religious wisdom.

Besides these indirect illustrations of the Hebrew annals in the life of Socrates there are also indications in the Platonic representations of his teaching which bring it directly within the prophetic scope of the Sacred History. Not only in the hope of a Prince of the House of David, or an Elijah returning from the invisible world, who should set right the wrong and deliver the oppressed, but in the still small voice that was heard by the Ilissus or on the quays of the Piræus was there a call for another Charmer who when Socrates was gone might come even amongst the barbarian races[1] —one who should be sought for far and wide, 'for 'there is no better way of using money than to find such an 'one.' Not only in the Man of Sorrows, as depicted by the Evangelical Prophet, but in the anticipations of the Socratic dialogues, there was the vision, even to the very letter, of the Just Man, scorned, despised, condemned, tortured, slain, by an ungrateful or stupid world, yet still triumphant.[2] And yet a higher strain is heard. No doubt the Egyptian monuments speak of another life, and the Grecian mythology and poetry

General anticipations of a higher revelation.

[1] *Phædo*, 78; *Politicus*, 262.

[2] Plato's *Republic*, 362.

spoke of Tartarus and Elysium and the Isles of the Blessed. No doubt the Hebrew Psalmists and Prophets contained aspirations for a bright hereafter, and also dim imagery of the under-world of the grave. But in the dialogue of Socrates in the prison, the conviction of a future existence is urged—whatever may be thought of the arguments—with an impressive earnestness which has left a more permanent mark on the world,[1] and of which the Jewish mind, hitherto so dark and vacant on this momentous topic, was destined henceforth to become the ready recipient and the chief propagator. There was also the double stream of the two philosophies which have since flowed from the teaching of Socrates; each of which has in turn dominated in some measure the Jewish Church, in a still larger measure the Christian Church—the 'world un-'realised' of Plato, the counterpart, in Hellenic phrase and form, of the anticipations of the Hebrew Prophets; the 'world 'explored' of Aristotle, as we have already indicated, and shall have occasion again to notice, the counterpart, on a colossal scale, of the boundless knowledge and practical wisdom, as it was believed, of Solomon[2] and his followers.

The general influence of Socrates.

These details belong to a later stage of the history, and are connected with Socrates himself more or less remotely. It is true that he founded no school, that he refused the title of master. No definite system of opinions or of doctrines can be traced to his instructions. Some of his chief admirers fell into courses of life or adopted theories of philosophy which he would have highly disapproved. But not the less from him came the general impulse, of which the effects were henceforth evident to a certain extent in every province touched by the Greek intellect, and which bear, therefore, on the future prospects of the Jewish Church as clearly as the teaching of Isaiah or of Ezra. That which cannot be questioned, and which places him at once in the midst of the pathway of the development of the Jewish religion, is that his appearance exercised an influence over the whole subsequent history of

[1] Alger's *Doctrine of a Future Life*, pp. 185-193. See Lectures XLVII. and XLVIII.

[2] Lectures XXVIII. and XLVII.

European speculation: that he stands at the very fountain-head of philosophical thought.

Although, as in the case of the Hebrew predictions of the glory of the restored Commonwealth of Israel, there was no literal fulfilment of the hopes of Socrates that his own peculiar weapons of instruction would be taken up by his successors, yet, like those same predictions, in a larger and higher sense these hopes were accomplished by the lasting results which his mighty originality achieved. The moral sciences then first took the place in philosophy which they have never since lost. 'Out 'of other minds he struck the fire which set light to original 'thought, permanently enlarging the horizon, improving the 'method, and multiplying the ascendant minds of the specu-'lative[1] world' for all subsequent generations.

Again, Socrates stands conspicuous as the first great example of the union between vigorous inquiry and profound religious relief. There was nothing in the Hebrew Scriptures to prevent such an alliance. But there is hardly any positive instance of its realisation. In the Book of Job and the Book of Ecclesiastes there is anxious inquiry, but it is united rather with religious perplexity and despair than with religious faith. In the Psalms there is unshaken confidence in the laws of God and of nature; but the restless curiosity of the modern world is absent. In the Proverbs there is an ample glorification of Wisdom; but it is rather of practical sagacity and common sense, than of active speculation. But in Socrates, for the first time, we see that complete union which many have doubted to be possible, but after which the best of later times have ardently aspired. 'Socrates,' so speaks the impartial voice of the modern historian, 'was the reverse of a sceptic: no man ever looked upon life 'with a more positive and practical eye; no man ever pursued 'his mark with a clearer perception of the road which he was 'travelling: no man ever combined, in like manner, the ab-'sorbing enthusiasm of a missionary with the acuteness, the 'originality, the inventive resource, and the generalising com-'prehension of a philosopher.'[2]

[1] Grote, viii. 621.

[2] *Ibid.* viii. p. 669.

Amidst the controversies of modern times it is a rare satisfaction to know that the boldest philosophical enterprise ever undertaken was conceived, executed, and completed, in and through a spirit of intense and sincere devotion. The clash between religion and science was discerned by him, no less clearly than by us; his course was more difficult than ours, in proportion as Paganism was more difficult to reconcile with reason than Judaism or Christianity—yet to the end he retained his hold equally on both; and no faithful history can claim his witness to the one without acknowledging his witness to the other also.

Lastly, there is the especial, the singular prerogative of Socrates—his faculty, his mission, his life, of cross-examination. The points which we have just enumerated have been shared with him by others; but in this his own favourite, life-long method of pursuing or suggesting truth—

'Where are we to look for a parallel to Socrates, either in 'or out of the Grecian world? The cross-examining disputa- 'tion, which he not only first struck out, but wielded with such 'matchless effect and to such noble purposes, has been mute 'ever since his last conversation in the prison; for even his 'great successor Plato was a writer and lecturer, not a colloquial 'dialectician. No man has ever been found strong enough 'to bend his bow; much less, sure enough to use it as he did. 'His life remains as the only evidence, but a very satisfactory 'evidence, how much can be done by this sort of intelligent 'interrogation; how powerful is the interest which it can be 'made to inspire; how energetic the stimulus which it can 'apply in awakening dormant reason and generating new mental 'power.'

True it is that the re-appearance of such a man in subsequent stages of society is all but impossible. The modern privacy of domestic life, the established order of social intercourse, the communication through books rather than through speech, render that perpetual dialogue wholly impracticable, which in the open out-of-door life of Greece needed only courage

[1] Grote, viii. p. 614.

and resolution to be adequately sustained. But though the remedy is impossible, the need for it cannot be said to have diminished :—

'However little that instrument may have been applied 'since the death of its inventor, the necessity and use of it 'neither have disappeared, nor ever can disappear. There are 'few men whose minds are not more or less in that state of 'sham knowledge against which Socrates made war : there is 'no one whose notions have not been first got together by 'spontaneous, unexamined, unconscious, uncertified association, 'resting upon forgotten particulars, blending together disparities 'or inconsistencies, and leaving in his mind old and familiar 'phrases, and oracular propositions, of which he has never 'rendered to himself account : there is no man who, if he be 'destined for vigorous and profitable scientific effort, has not 'found it a necessary branch of self-instruction, to break up, 'disentangle, analyse, and reconstruct these ancient mental 'compounds—and who has not been driven to do it by his 'own lame and solitary efforts, since the giant of colloquial 'philosophy no longer stands in the market-place to lend him 'help and stimulus.'

He no longer stands amongst us. Yet we can fancy what would result were he now to visit the earth—were he once more to appear with that Silenic physiognomy, with that grotesque manner, with that indomitable resolution, with that captivating voice, with that homely humour, with that solemn earnestness, with that siege of questions—among the crowded parties of our metropolis, under the groves and cloisters of our universities, in the midst of our political, our ecclesiastical, our religious meetings, on the floor of our legislative assemblies, at the foot of the pulpits of our well-filled churches. How often in a conversation, in a book, in a debate, in a speech, in a sermon, have we longed for the doors to open and for the son of Sophroniscus to enter—how often, in the heat of angry accusations, in the tempest of pamphlets, in the rabbinical subtleties or in the theological controversies, that have darkened counsel by words

[1] Grote, viii. p. 670.

without knowledge for eighteen centuries and more, in Judaic or Christian times, might souls, weary with unmeaning phrases and undefined issues, have been tempted to exclaim: 'O for 'one hour of Socrates!' O for one hour of that voice which should by its searching cross-examination make men see what they knew and what they did not know—what they meant, and what they only thought they meant—what they believed in truth, and what they only believed in name—wherein they agreed, and wherein they differed! Differences, doubtless, would still remain, but they would be the differences of serious and thinking men, and there would be a cessation of the hollow catchwords and empty shibboleths by which all differences are inflamed and aggravated. The voice of the great Cross-examiner himself is indeed silent, but there is a voice in each man's heart and conscience which, if we will, Socrates has taught us to use rightly. That voice, more sacred than the divine monitor of Socrates himself, can still make itself heard; that voice still enjoins us to give to ourselves a reason for the hope that is in us—'both hearing and asking questions.' He gave the stimulus which prepared the Western world for the Great Inquirer, the Divine Word which should 'pierce even 'to the dividing asunder of soul and spirit, and of the joints 'and marrow' of the human mind, 'and discern the thoughts 'and intents of the heart.'[1] For that fancied repose, which the spirit of inquiry, whether from within or without, disturbs, the example of Socrates, and of the long line of his followers in Christendom, encourages us to hope that we shall be more than compensated by the real repose which it gives instead. 'A wise 'questioning' is indeed 'the half of knowledge.' 'A life without 'cross-examination is no life at all.'

[1] **Heb. iv. 12.**

LECTURE XLVII.

ALEXANDRIA, B.C. 333–150.

JEWISH AUTHORITIES :—

Josephus, *Ant.* xi. 8-xii. 4. A.D. 70.
3 Maccabees.
Wisdom of the Son of Sirach (Ecclesiasticus) :
In Hebrew, B.C. 200.
In Greek, B.C. 132.
Wisdom of Solomon, *Qu.* B.C. 50 ?
Aristobulus, B.C. 180, in Eusebius, *Præp. Ev.* vii. 13 ; viii. 9 ; ix. 6 ; xiii. 12.

HEATHEN AUTHORITIES :—

Hecatæus of Abdera, B.C. 320 (Joseph. *c. Apion*, i. 22).
Agatharchides (ibid.).
Clearchus (ibid.).

CHRONOLOGY.

ALEXANDER THE GREAT, B.C. 336–323.

Kings of Egypt	Jewish High Priests	Kings of Syria
Ptolemy I. (Soter), B.C. 322.	Jaddua, B.C. 333.	Seleucus I. (Nicator), B.C. 312.
Ptolemy II. (Philadelphus), B.C. 285.	Simon I., B.C. 310.	Antiochus I. (Soter), B.C. 280.
Ptolemy III. (Euergetes I.), B.C. 246.	Eleazar, B.C. 291.	Antiochus II. (Theos), B.C. 261.
Ptolemy IV. (Philopator), B.C. 221.	Manasseh, B.C. 276.	Seleucus II. (Callinicus), B.C. 246.
Ptolemy V. (Epiphanes), B.C. 205.	Onias II., B.C. 250.	Seleucus III. (Keraunos), B.C. 226.
Ptolemy VI. (Philometor). B.C 181.	Simon II. (the Just), B.C. 219.	Antiochus III. (The Great), B.C. 224.
Ptolemy VII. (Physcon) (Euergetes II.), B.C. 146.	Onias III., B.C. 199.	Seleucus IV. (Philopator), B.C. 187.
	Jason, B.C. 175.	Antiochus IV. (Epiphanes), B.C. 175.

PALESTINE IN THE GREEK AND ROMAN PERIOD

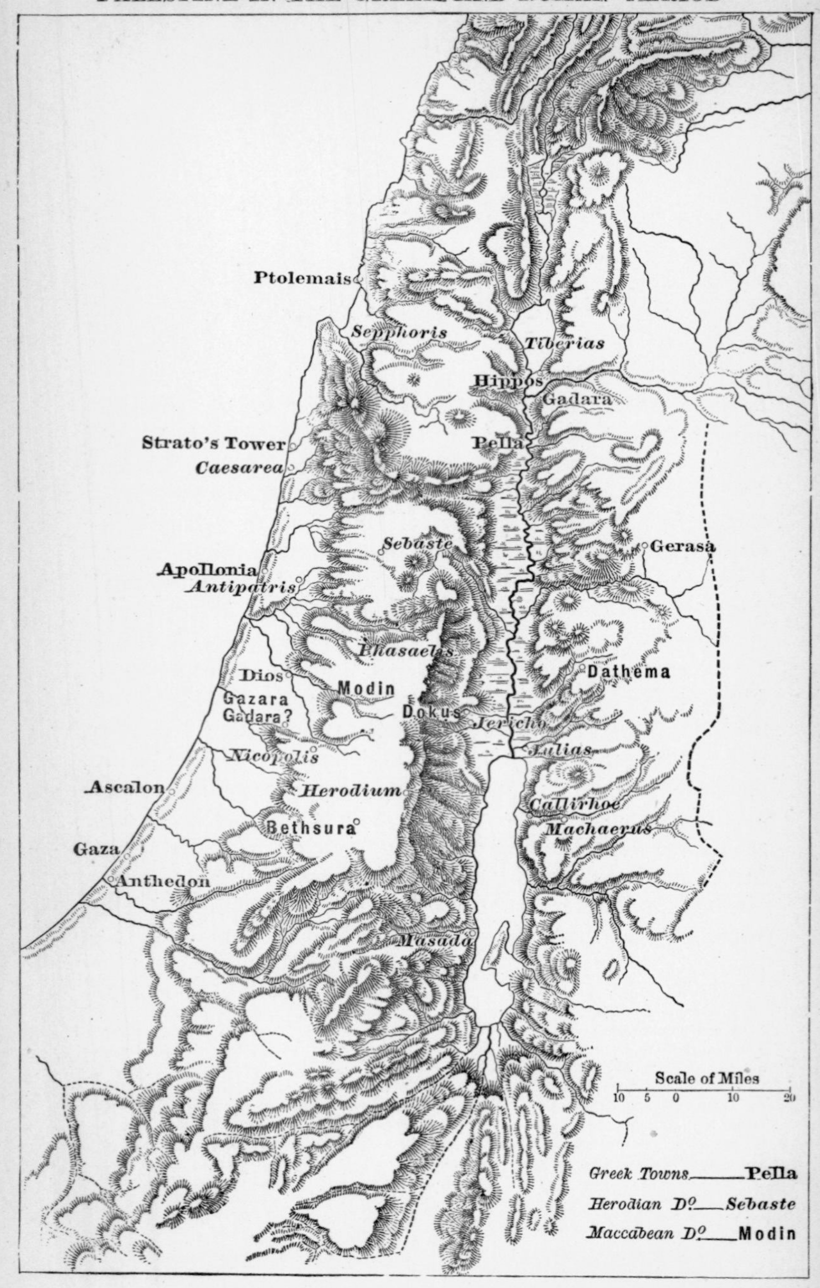

LECTURE XLVII.

ALEXANDRIA.

It was a striking remark[1] of Hegel that Greece, the youthful prime of the world, came in with the youth Achilles, and went out with the youth Alexander. But if Grecian history died with Alexander, Grecian influence was created by him. If Hellas ceased, Hellenism, the spirit of the Greek race throughout the Eastern world, now began its career. In the Prophets of the Captivity we felt the electric shock produced by the conquest of Cyrus. There is unfortunately no contemporary prophet in whom we can in like manner appreciate the approach of Alexander. Yet that was no inapt vision which, in the Book of Daniel, pictured the marvellous sight[2] of the mountain goat from the Ionian shores, bounding over the face of the earth so swiftly as not to touch the ground—with one beautiful horn, like the unicorn on the Persepolitan monuments, between his eyes—which ran in the fury of his power against the double-horned ram, the emblem[3] of the Kings of Media and Persia, 'and there was no power in the ram to stand 'before him, but he cast him down to the ground, and stamped 'upon him, and there was none to deliver the ram out of his

Alexander.

[1] *Philosophy of History*, p. 233.

[2] Dan. viii. 5.

[3] I confine the illustrations from the Book of Daniel to those which are certain. The arrangement of the two visions of the four empires is so difficult to combine with any single hypothesis that it belongs to the commentator on the several passages rather than to a general historical survey. On the one hand the brass of Dan. ii. 39 agrees in order with the leopard of Dan. vii. 6, which agrees with the Grecian monarchy, particularly in regard to the swiftness, of the animal 'and the four 'heads.' On the other hand, the last horn of the fourth beast (Dan. vii. 8) must almost certainly be identified with the last horn of the he-goat (Dan. viii. 9), and this (Dan. viii. 11) must be Antiochus Epiphanes (Dan. xi. 36). For the chronological enigma of Dan. xi. 24-27; xii. 12. see note at the end of Lecture XLVIII.

'hand.' So it was in a yet wider sense than the ancient seer had discerned: 'Asia beheld with astonishment and awe the 'uninterrupted progress of a hero, the sweep of whose con- 'quests was as wide and as rapid as that of her own barbaric 'kings, or of the Scythian or Chaldæan hordes; but, far unlike 'the transient whirlwinds of Asiatic warfare, the advance of the 'Macedonian leader was no less deliberate than rapid; at 'every step the Greek power took root, and the language 'and civilisation of Greece were planted from the shores 'of the Ægean to the banks of the Indus, from the Caspian 'and the great Hyrcanian plain to the Cataracts of the 'Nile; to exist actually for nearly a thousand years, and in 'their effects to endure for ever. In the tenth year after he 'had crossed the Hellespont, Alexander, having won his vast 'dominion, entered Babylon, and, resting from his career in that 'oldest seat of earthly empire, he steadily surveyed the mass of 'various nations which owned his sovereignty, and revolved in 'his mind the great work of breathing into this huge but inert 'body the living spirit of Greek civilisation. In the bloom of 'youthful manhood, at the age of thirty-two, he paused from 'the fiery speed of his earlier course; and for the first time 'gave the nations an opportunity of offering their homage 'before his throne. They came from all the extremities of the 'earth, to propitiate his anger, to celebrate his greatness, or to 'solicit his protection.'[1]

Amongst those various races two nations are said, either then or in the earlier stages of his advance, to have approached the Grecian conqueror. Both interviews are wrapt in doubtful legend; yet both may have an element of truth, and both certainly represent the enduring connexion of that career with the two other most powerful currents of human history.

'Later writers,[2] yielding to that natural feeling which longs 'to bring together the great characters of remote ages and 'countries and delights to fancy how they would have regarded 'one another, asserted expressly that a Roman Embassy did 'appear before Alexander in Babylon; that the King, like

[1] Arnold's *Rome*, ii. 169. [2] *Ibid.* ii. 173.

'Cineas afterwards, was struck with the dignity and manly 'bearing of the Roman patricians, that he informed himself 'concerning their constitution, and prophesied that the Romans 'would one day become a great power. This story Arrian 'justly disbelieves: but history may allow us to think that 'Alexander and a Roman ambassador did meet at Babylon; 'that the greatest man of the ancient world saw and spoke with 'a citizen of that great nation which was destined to succeed 'him in his appointed work, and to found a wider and still 'more enduring empire. They met, too, in Babylon, almost 'beneath the shadow of the temple of Bel—perhaps the earliest 'monument ever raised by human pride and power—in a city 'stricken, as it were, by the word of God's heaviest judgment, 'as the symbol of greatness apart from and opposed to goodness.'

A like scene was recounted in various forms by the Jewish writers when, after the battle of Issus, Alexander arrived at the other oldest seat of Asiatic power—Tyre. That ancient queen of the Mediterranean had, as we see by this account, survived the destruction anticipated by Ezekiel two centuries before. Her impregnable island fortress, her king, her worship of Melcarth or Moloch, probably with only a shadow of her former grandeur, still remained, like the stately colony of Venice after the fall of the Roman empire—a relic of the Old World long passed away. Thither came embassies from the rival cities of Jerusalem and Shechem, each claiming his protection—the Jewish settlement, if we may believe their account, still faithful[1] to their Persian benefactors; the Samaritans still smarting from the insult inflicted on their second founder, the High Priest Manasseh. At last the Phœnician capital fell before that stupendous mole, which for ever destroyed its insular character, and Alexander marched on to reduce the fortress of Gaza, which on its sandy eminence defied him in the south. It was on his return from his savage triumph over the gallant defender of that last stronghold of the old

Alexander at Tyre. B.C. 333.

[1] The fidelity of the Jews to their oaths of allegiance even when contracted with heathen Princes is much dwelt upon, see Jos. *Ant.* xii. 1, 1; and compare the severe condemnation of Zedekiah, Lecture XL

Philistine power that he is represented as marching on the only remaining fortress that had refused to submit. It may have been that, like the French conqueror of later times, he may have thought that 'Jerusalem did not lie within the lines 'of his operations;' and such is the effect of the silence of the Greek historians, and after them of some of the most critical of modern historians likewise. But there is nothing incredible in the occurrence of some such event, as, in divers forms, has entered into the Jewish annals. The Samaritan version concentrated the whole interest of the story in their High Priest Hezekiah [1]—the Jewish version fluctuates between the Talmud and Josephus. Alexander had come—so the Rabbinical account runs—to Antipatris [2] at the entrance of the mountains, or, according to Josephus, mounted by the pass of Beth-horon, and found himself standing with Parmenio on the eminence long known as 'the watch-tower'—in earlier days by its Hebrew name of Mizpeh,[3] in later times by the corresponding Greek name of Scopus. There, before the conquest of Jebus, Samuel had held his assemblies; there, as in a commanding place of oversight, the Chaldæan and the Persian Viceroys had their habitations; there was the Maccabæan wailing-place; and there Sennacherib, and afterwards Titus, had their first view of the holy city; and there, with Parmenio at his side, the Grecian conqueror now stood, with the same prospect spread before him. Suddenly from the city emerged a long procession—the whole population streamed out, dressed in white. The priestly tribe, in their white robes; the High Priest, apparently the chief authority in the place, in his purple and gold attire, his turban on his head, bearing the golden plate on which was inscribed the ineffable name of Jehovah. It was Jaddua, the grandson [4] of the indulgent Eliashib, the son of the murderer John, who, as it was said in his agony of fear at Alexander's approach, had been warned in a dream to take this method of appeasing the conqueror's wrath. 'Who are these?'

Alexander at Jerusalem.

[1] Derenbourg, 43.

[2] *Ibid.* 42.

[3] See Mr. Grove on Mizpeh, *Dictionary of the Bible*, 389.

[4] In the Talmud, Simon the Just (Derenbourg, p. 42). But this is against all chronology.

said he to the Samaritan guides, who had gained from him the promise of the destruction of the Temple and the possession of Mount Moriah. 'They are the rebels who deny your 'authority,'[1] said the rival sect. They marched all night, in two ranks, preceded by torches, and with the band of priestly musicians clashing their cymbals. It was at the sunrise of a winter[2] morning, long afterwards observed as a joyous festival, when they stood before the king. To the astonishment of the surrounding chiefs[3] Alexander descended from his chariot and bowed to the earth before the Jewish leader. None ventured to ask the meaning of this seeming frenzy, save Parmenio alone. 'Why should he, whom all men worship, worship the High 'Priest of the Jews?' 'Not him,' replied the King, 'but the 'God, whose High Priest he is, I worship. Long ago, when at 'Dium in Macedonia, I saw in my dreams such an one 'in such an attire[4] as this, who urged me to undertake 'the conquest of Persia and succeed'—'or,' added the Rabbinical account,[5] 'it is the same figure that has appeared to me 'on the eve of each of my victories.' Hand in hand with the High Priest, and with the priestly tribe running by his side, he entered the sacred enclosure,[6] and offered the usual sacrifice, saw with pleasure the indication of the rise of the Grecian power in the prophetic books,[7] granted free use of their ancestral laws, and specially of the year of jubilee inaugurated so solemnly a hundred years before under Nehemiah, promised to befriend the Jewish settlements of Babylonia and Media, and invited any who were disposed, to serve in his army, with the preservation of their sacred customs.

'And who are these' (so added the fiercer tradition of the Talmud, in which theological legend has even more deeply coloured the historical event),[8] asked Alexander, 'who have 'threatened to take away your Temple?' 'They are the

[1] Derenbourg, 42.

[2] 21st of Chisleu (Dec.), Derenbourg, 41.

[3] Derenbourg, 42.

[4] Compare the dream in which he saw the God of Tyre inviting him to take the city (Plutarch, *Alex.* 24), and the satyr near the fountain—no doubt the Râs-el-Ain.

[5] Derenbourg, 42.

[6] Jos. *Ant.* xi., ἱερόν, not ναός.

[7] Josephus, as before, in his account of Cyrus, so now in his account of Alexander, mentions the book of Daniel by name (*Ant.* xi. 5). See Lecture XLIII.

[8] Derenbourg, 43.

'Cutheans now standing before you,' replied the Jewish High Priest, pointing to the hated Samaritans. 'Take them,' said the King, 'they are in your hands.' The Jews seized their enemies, threw them on the ground, pierced their heels, fastened them to the tails[1] of horses, which dragged them over thorns and briars till they reached Mount Gerizim. A ploughshare was driven over the Temple of Gerizim, and the day was henceforth observed as sacred to joy and festivity.

These narratives are obviously mixed with fable, but it is probable that Alexander visited Jerusalem; that he paid his homage to the God of the Jews as he had paid it to the God of the Tyrians; that the rivalries of the Jews and Samaritans then, as of the Greeks and Latins now, grasped alike at the protection of this new Imperial power granted alternately to each. In a higher point of view, the romance of the story is not unworthy of the importance of this first meeting of the Greek and the Hebrew on the stage of history.

His place in religious history.

Henceforth, Alexander the Great became the symbol of their union. His name came into common Jewish use as a translation of Solomon.[2] The philosophy of Aristotle was believed to have sprung from Alexander's gift of the works of Solomon. The friend of Jaddua becomes a Jewish proselyte. The son of Ammon, with the twisted horns appearing beneath his clustering locks, was transformed in the Mussulman legends into the saintly 'Possessor[3] of the Two Horns' and reckoned among the Apostles of God. These legends or fancies were not without their corresponding realities. The Orientals were not so far wrong when they treated Alexander not only as a conqueror but a prophet. That capacious mind, which, first of the Greeks, and with a wider grasp than even his mighty master Aristotle, conceived the idea of the universal Fatherhood of God, and the universal communion of all good men,

[1] This is probably a distortion of the story of Alexander's brutal treatment of Batis, the brave defender of Gaza (Grote's *Greece*, xii. 195).

[2] See Lecture XXVI. Another explanation of the frequency of the name of Alexander is given in Raphall, i. 50.

[3] 'He never allowed anyone to shave 'his head, lest the horns should be seen— 'at last they were seen, and the man, to 'keep the secret, whispered it into the 'well, round which stood the reeds which 'revealed it' (Mussulman legend).

was 'not far' from the realm of those with whom the Jew and Mussulman have placed him. 'God,' he said,[1] 'is the common 'Father of all men, especially of the best men.' He came inspired[2] with the belief that he was the heaven-sent reconciler and pacificator of the whole world. These ideas bore fruit in two immense consequences. One was the union of the European and Asiatic races under one Empire, leading to the spread of the Greek language as the common vehicle of communication in the Eastern, ultimately of the whole civilised, world; of Greek ideas, partly for evil, and partly for good, into the very recesses of the Semitic mind. Of this we shall trace the course as we proceed. The other fact was the foundation of Alexandria. It became at once the capital of the East, the centre of the three continents of the ancient earth, and the point in which Greek philosophy and Hebrew religion were to meet in an indissoluble union.

In the little fishing-town of Rhacotis, the discerning eye of Alexander, on his rapid journey to the Oasis[3] of Ammon, saw the possibility of creating that which hitherto the Eastern shores of the Mediterranean had entirely lacked—a magnificent harbour. The low level reef of the isle of Pharos[4] furnished the opportunity—when connected with the mainland by a mole—of such a shelter for ships as neither Tyre nor Sidon nor Joppa had ever been able to afford.

Foundation of Alexandria.

The first Ptolemy did well to name the city not after himself, but after Alexander. Not Constantine was more identified with the city on the shores of the Bosphorus than was Alexander with that at the mouth of the Nile. His friend Hephæstion became its guardian hero. The military cloak of Alexander supplied its outline. It was his own plan for Babylon resuscitated; even the rectangular streets of the

[1] Plutarch, *Alex.* 27.

[2] κοινὸς ἥκειν θεοθεν ἁρμοστὴς καὶ διαλλακτὴς τῶν ὅλων νομίζων (Plutarch, *Alex. Fort.* i. 6). I owe this quotation to Bishop Lightfoot.

[3] Sharpe's *Egypt*, i. 220, 226, 241.

[4] Here, again, as at Tyre and Jerusalem, he was guided by a dream. Homer, he said, had appeared to him, repeating the lines which describe the island of Pharos (Plutarch, *Alex.* 26).

Asiatic capital were reproduced. In the later Jewish phraseology it even bore the name of Babylon.[1] No funeral was ever seen more splendid than that which conveyed the remains of the dead[2] King from Chaldæa in the golden car drawn by sixty-four mules, each with its golden cover and golden bells, across desert and mountain, through the hills and vales of Palestine, till they were deposited in the tomb which gave to the whole quarter of Alexandria where it stood the name of 'the Body.' That tomb has gradually dwindled away to a wretched Mussulman chapel, kept by an aged crone, who watches over a humble shrine, called 'The Grave of Iskander 'of the Two Horns, founder of Alexandria.' But 'the whole 'habitable earth was long filled,' according to the coarse saying of Demades, 'with the odour of that interment.'[3] 'The horn 'was broken,' as the Book of Daniel expressed it, 'and the 'four horns' of the four successors came in its place; and for the long wearisome years through which History passes with repugnance, and which form perhaps the most lifeless and unprofitable page in the whole of the Sacred Volume, Asia, Europe, and Africa resounded with their wrangles.

In this world's debate Palestine was the principal stage across which 'the kings of the South,' the Alexandrian Ptolemies, and 'the kings of the North,'[4] the Seleucidæ from Antioch, passed to and fro with their court intrigues and incessant armies, their Indian elephants, their Grecian cavalry, their Oriental pomp. It was, for the larger part of the century-and-half that succeeded Alexander's death, a province of the Græco-Egyptian kingdom.

Greek cities in Palestine.

It was now that new constellations of towns, some of which acquired an undying fame in Jewish and Christian history, sprang up, bearing in their names the mark of their Grecian origin.[5] Judæa itself still remained entirely Semitic. But in a fringe all round that sacred centre the Ptolemies or the Seleucidæ, but chiefly the Ptolemies, left their foot-prints, if not to this day, at least for centuries.

[1] Surenhusius' *Mishna*, v. 240.
[2] Diod. Sic. xviii. 21, 27.
[3] Grote's *Greece*, xii. 346.
[4] Dan. xi. 1–29.
[5] Reland, *Palestina*, p. 806.

On the sea-coast Gaza sprang from its ashes, now no more a Philistine, but a Grecian city. Close by we trace, in Anthedon and Arethusa, a Hellenic City of Flowers with the reminiscence of the famous Dorian fountain. The seaport of Joppa became to the Alexandrian sailors the scene of the adventure of Perseus and Andromeda. On another rocky headland rose the Tower of Strato, some Grecian magnate now unknown. Chief of all, the old Canaanitish fortress of Accho was transformed by Ptolemy Philadelphus or his father into 'Ptolemais,' a title which for centuries overlaid the original name, once more to reappear in modern times as Acre.[1] Beyond the Jordan a like metamorphosis was effected in the ancient capital of Ammon, when Rabbah, after the same Prince, was called Philadelphia. In its neighbourhood sprang up the new town of Gerasa, so called, according to tradition, from the aged men (*gerontes*) whom Alexander left there as unable to keep up with his rapid march. Further north were two towns, each with its Macedonian name[2]—one Dium, so called from the Thracian city, where, according to the legend, Alexander had seen in his dream the figure of Jaddua; the other Pella,[3] from the likeness of its abundant springs to the well-watered capital of Macedonia. Round the southern extremity of the Lake of Gennesareth the Canaanite Bethshan, from the reminiscence of its Scythian conquerors, became Scythopolis, with a new legend ascribing its foundation to Bacchus; and Sus[4] easily changed itself into the corresponding Greek name of Hippos. High up beyond Dan, the romantic cave which overhangs the chief source of the Jordan became the Sanctuary of Pan, and the town which clustered at its foot acquired, and has never lost (except for the period of the Roman occupation), the name of Paneas.

Grecian travellers.

Through these Hellenic settlements it is not surprising that ever and anon some story reached the outer world from the Jewish settlement which they enclosed. At one time it was Hecatæus of Abdera, the indefatigable

[1] Reland, 918.

[2] *Ibid.* 458.

[3] *Ibid.* 924. There was another Pella in Moab. *Ibid.* 101.

[4] The Hebrew word for 'horse.' Clermont Ganneau, *Revue Archéologique*, July 1875.

traveller, who in his vast researches had included the British Islands and the Egyptian Temples.[1] He travelled with the first Ptolemy into Palestine, and saw with admiration the sanctuary at Jerusalem ; and there heard how the Jews in Alexander's army refused to join in rebuilding the Temple of Bel at Babylon ; he long remembered the Jewish bowman, Mosollam, most famous of all the archers in his day, who acted as the guide of Hecatæus' party[2] by the shores of the Red Sea, and showed at once his professional skill, his national courage, and his religious superiority to the superstition of all around him, by shooting the bird from which the soothsayers were drawing their auguries. At another time it was Agatharchides who was struck with a mixture of awe and contempt at the rigid observance of the Sabbath which led them to leave their city unguarded to be taken when on that same expedition Ptolemy invaded Judæa and captured Jerusalem.[3] Most memorable of all, 'the great master 'of all the peculiarities of nature and of men, and the eager 'investigator of all the varieties then pouring out of Asia, the 'mighty Aristotle himself, met with a Jew who had descended[4] 'from his mountain fastnesses to the Hellenised sea-board of 'his country, and thus in his travels encountered and conversed 'with Aristotle on the philosophy of Greece, and himself replied 'to the great master's inquiries on the wonders of his own people.' Questions and answers are alike unrecorded. But no 'ima'ginary dialogue' can be conceived more instructive than this actual conversation of which the bare fact alone remains in the fragment of Clearchus, to whom it was repeated by Aristotle himself.

Within that inner circle of mountain fastnesses, for the long period from Alexander the Great to Antiochus Epiphanes, there are but few events which throw any light on the religious history of this now secluded people. We discern the fact, slightly, yet certainly indicated, that the last book of the Jewish annals which has come down to us in the Hebrew tongue was now finally concluded in its present form. The Book of Chronicles, including, as it doubtless did,

The Chronicles.

[1] Diod. i. 46 ; ii. 47. [2] Jos. *c. Ap.* i. 22. [3] *Ibid.* [4] Ewald, v. 247.

in the same group the Books of Ezra and Nehemiah, received at this time its latest touches. 'Darius the Persian' is mentioned as belonging to an Empire which had by that time ceased to exist, and the priestly and royal lines are continued down to the contemporaries of Alexander.[1] Of the peculiarities of the Chronicler we have already spoken.[2] But it is a marked epoch in the story of the Jewish race, when we catch a parting glimpse of one who has accompanied us so long and with such varying interest. We bade farewell to the compiler of the prophetical Book of Kings on the banks of the Euphrates. We bid farewell to the compiler of the priestly 'Chronicles' under the shadow of the Grecian dominion in the fastness of Jerusalem.

The priestly office still continued in the same corrupt condition as under the Persian dominion. The highest ambition of its occupants seems to have been the making of colossal fortunes by the farming of the revenues of the country, of which, as chief magistrate, the High Priest was made the collector, for the tribute[3] to the Egyptian King. Out of this there grew a rival ambition of the head of a powerful clan, which, under the name of 'The Sons of Tobiah,' long exercised sway both in the Alexandrian court and in the Temple of Jerusalem. It would seem that they claimed some descent from the House of David, and the cleverness of their representative at this time—Joseph, nephew of the High Priest Onias —established him in high favour with Ptolemy IV.[4] It is needless to follow the course of this earlier Anastasius. One permanent monument remains of his family. His youngest son, Hyrcanus,[5] inheritor of his fortunes, deposited them in the bank,[6] which, as in Greece, so in Judæa, was established in the Temple, and then settled himself as an independent freebooting chief in a fastness beyond the Jordan. It was a castle of

The Sons of Tobiah.

[1] Neh. xii. 11–22; 1 Chron. iii. 22, 23, 24.

[2] See Lecture XXXVI.

[3] The tribute to the foreign Kings was made up from the yearly poll-tax of the half-shekel, called in Greek the didrachma. Sharpe's *Egypt*, i. 328.

[4] Jos. *Ant.* xii. 4, 2.

[5] Herzfeld (ii. 435) supposes the 'sons of mischief' and the 'visions' in Daniel xi. 14, to refer to the troubles and the pretensions of Hyrcanus. The name he regards as the Hellenic equivalent of Johanan (ii. 191).

[6] 2 Macc. iii. 11.

white marble, carved with colossal figures, and surrounded by a deep moat, and in face of it was a cliff honeycombed with a labyrinth of caverns. It was named 'the Rock.'[1] In this fantastic residence he reigned as an independent magnate amongst the neighbouring Arabs, till at last he was hunted down by the Syrian Kings. But the castle and the rock still remain, and preserve the name of Hyrcanus, the semi-Arabian chief, in the modern appellation of *Arak-el-Emir*.[2] The fosse, the fragments of the colonnade, the entrance-gateway, with the colossal lions sculptured on its frieze, the mixture of Greek Ionic capitals with the palm-leaved architecture as of the Ptolemaic temples at Philæ, the vast stables hewn out of the adjacent rock, all attest the splendour of this upstart Prince—this heir, if so be, of the lineage of David.

Simon the Just.

Amidst these intrigues and adventures there rises one stately figure, the High Priest,[3] Simon the Just, towering above all who came before him and all who came after him in that office, from the time of Zerubbabel to the time of the Maccabees. According to one legend it was he who encountered Alexander the Great. According to another he was the last survivor of the members of the Great Synagogue. According to another it was he who warned Ptolemy Philopator—the one exception to the friendly character of the Ptolemæan princes—not to enter the Temple. The expression of his intention had thrown (so it was said) the whole city into consternation. From the densely packed multitude there went up a cry so piercing that it would have seemed as if the very walls and foundations of the city shared in it. In the midst of the

[1] Josephus (*Ant.* xii. 4, 11) calls it 'Tyre.' This surely must be the Hebrew *Tsur*, which is 'rock.' See *Sinai and Palestine*, 278, 488.

[2] Tristram's *Land of Israel*, 529. Palestine Exploration Fund, *Quarterly Statement*, April 1872. *Travels* of Irby and Mangles, p. 473.

[3] There are two High Priests in this period, both Simons and both sons of Onias. It is a question which of the two was Simon the Just and which of the two was the Simon described in Ecclesiasticus. Derenbourg has conclusively established (47–51) that the Simon of Ecclesiasticus was Simon the Just, and that this Simon was Simon II. That Josephus, who identifies Simon the Just with Simon I., should have been mistaken is no more surprising than his like error in confounding Ahasuerus with Artaxerxes, or transferring Sanballat from the time of Nehemiah to the time of Alexander.

tumult was heard the prayer of Simon, invoking the All-seeing God. And then, like a reed broken by the wind, the Egyptian King fell on the pavement [1] and was carried out by his guards.

All the traditions combine in representing Simon as closing the better days of Judaism. Down to his time it was always the right hand of the High Priest that drew the lot of the consecrated goat: after his time the left and right wavered and varied. Down to his time the red thread round the neck of the scape-goat turned white, as a sign that the sins of the people were forgiven; afterwards, its change was quite uncertain. The candlestick at the entrance of the Temple burned in his time without fail: afterwards it often went out. Two faggots a day sufficed to keep the flame on the altar alive in his time: afterwards piles of wood were insufficient. In his last year he was said to have foretold his death, from the omen that whereas on all former occasions he was accompanied into the Holy of Holies on the Day of Atonement to the entrance only by an old man clothed in white from head to foot, in that year his companion was attired in black, and followed him as he went in and came out. These were the forms in which the later Jewish belief expressed the sentiment of his transcendent worth, and of the manifold changes which were to follow him. But the more authentic indications convey the same impression. The very title of 'the Just' [2] expressed the feeling, as always, that he stood alone in an untoward age. The description which has come down to us by his contemporaries, in whose judgment [3] he worthily closed the long succession of ancient heroes, is that of a venerable personage, who belonged to a nobler age and would be seen again no more. They remembered his splendid appearance when he came out from behind the sacred curtain of the Holy of Holies into the midst of the people as they crowded the Temple on the Great Fast-day. I

[1] 3 Macc. i. 28, 29; ii. 1, 21, 24. Comp. 2 Macc. iii. 25. An exactly similar story was related to me by the Imam of the Mosque of Hebron of another Egyptian potentate — Ibrahim Pacha — who was struck down in like manner on attempting to enter the shrine of Isaac.

[2] Thus Noah, Gen. vi. 9; Joseph in the Koran xii. 76, James in Josephus (in Eus. *H. E.* ii. 23). Derenb. 47.

[3] Ecclus. l. 1 21.

was like the morning star bursting from a cloud, or the moon in her fulness. It was like the sunlight striking the golden pinnacles of the Temple, or the rainbow in the stormy cloud. It was as the freshly blown rose, or the lilies clustering by the stream, the olive laden with fruit, or the fir-tree reaching to the sky, with the fragrance as of frankincense, with the refinement as of a golden vessel set with gems. Every gesture was followed with admiration. To the gorgeous robes of his office he gave additional grace by the way he wore them. When he stood among the priests he towered above them like a cedar in a grove of palms. When he poured out the libations or offered the offerings, the blast of the silver trumpets, the loud shout of the people, the harmony of the various voices, the profound prostrations, were all in keeping, and his final benediction was an event in the memory of those who had received it.

On the material fabric of the city and Temple he left his permanent traces in the repairs and fortification and elevation of the walls, in its double cloister, and the brazen plates with which he encased the huge laver of ablutions. The respect which he won from Antiochus[1] the Great procured from him the timber and stone for the work. The precept which survived of his teaching was: 'There are three foundations of the 'world—the Law, the Worship' (and herein consisted his peculiar teaching), 'and Benevolence.' In accordance with this gentle humanity is the one anecdote handed down of his private thoughts. 'I never,' he said, 'could endure to receive the 'monastic dedication of the Nazarites. Yet once I made an 'exception. There came a youth from the south to consecrate 'himself. I looked at him—his eyes were beautiful, his air 'magnificent, his long hair fell clustering in rich curls over his 'face. "Why," I asked him, "must you shave off these splendid 'locks?" "I was a shepherd of my father's flocks," he re'plied, "in my native village. One day, drawing water at the 'well, I saw with undue complacency my reflection in the 'water. I should have given way to a wicked inclination and 'have been lost. I said: 'Wicked one, wilt thou be proud

[1] Derenbourg, 47.

'of that which does not belong to thee, who art but worms 'and dust? O God, I will cut off these curls for the honour of 'heaven.'"' Then, said Simon, 'I embraced his head and 'exclaimed: "Would that there were many such Nazarites in 'Israel!"'[1]

There was yet one other character of the Ptolemæan period of Palestine, Joshua, the son of Sirach—contemporary or nearly contemporary of Simon—who was conspicuous in his time at once as the great student of the sacred Hebrew literature, as the collector of the grave and short sentences of the wise men who went before him, and as himself uttering 'some things of 'his own, full of understanding and judgment.' But the characteristics of his work must be reserved for its appearance in the Greek form in which alone it is now known.

We turn from these brief and disjointed notices of the internal history of Palestine under the Ptolemies to the important Jewish settlement more directly connected with them in Egypt. It was directly to the east of Alexandria—close along[2] the sea-shore, probably with a view to the convenience of their ablutions in the Mediterranean—that the Jewish colonists chiefly resided; and to this day the burial-ground of their race is on the sandy hillocks in the same situation. They were in such numbers as to be known by the name of 'The Tribe.'[3] They retained the privileges alleged to have been granted by Alexander, as on a level with the Macedonian settlers. The commercial enterprise of the race, never since extinct, now for the first time found an outlet. They gradually became a separate community under their own chief, entitled Ethnarch or Alabarch, and represented more than a third of Alexandria, with a council corresponding to that which ultimately ruled at Jerusalem.[4]

Jewish colonies in Egypt.

This was the only settlement of permanent interest. Other colonies may be traced here and there, under the Ptolemæan rule, in insulated fragments. One was the band of Samaritans,[5] who, still keeping up their deadly feud, retired to the Thebaid.

[1] Derenbourg, 47.
[2] Josephus, *c. Ap.* ii. 4.
[3] *Ibid.*
[4] See Herzfeld, *Geschichte*, iii. 437, 438, 445, 446.
[5] Jos. *Ant.* xi. 8.

Another was the group of anchorites by the lake Mareotis, the forerunners of the parents of Christian monasticism. Another powerful community was settled at Cyrene—just become a dependency on Egypt—destined to react on the nation in Palestine [1] by their special synagogue at Jerusalem.

Leontopolis.

Another, still in the future, but drawn by the same friendly influence of the Græco-Egyptian dynasty, was the settlement at Leontopolis. When, in the subsequent troubles of Palestine, it seemed that the Temple itself would perish, one of the High Priestly family, Nechoniah or Coniah, in Greek Onias—fled to Egypt, and begged the loan of a deserted temple of Pasht,[2] the Cat-Goddess, in the neighbourhood of Heliopolis. There, with the military experience which he may have acquired in heading a band of troops in one of the Egyptian civil wars, he built a fortress [3] and a temple, which, although on a smaller [4] scale, was to rival that of Jerusalem, where he and his sons, keeping up the martial traditions of the Levitical tribe, formed a powerful body of soldiery, and assumed the name and habits of a camp.[5] The general style of the sanctuary was (apparently) not Jewish but Egyptian. A huge tower—perhaps equivalent to the great gateway of Egyptian temples [6]—rose to the height of sixty cubits. There were no obelisks, but it was approached by the usual long colonnades [7] of pillars. The altar alone resembled that of the Jewish temple. But instead of the candlestick a golden chandelier was suspended from the roof by a golden chain. A circuit of brick walls, as in the adjacent sanctuary of Heliopolis, enclosed it, and the

[1] Acts ii. 1; vi. 1; Herzfeld, iii. 321.

[2] The name of *Leontopolis*, in connexion with the Temple of Onias, probably arose from this. Every Temple of Pasht (called by the Greeks Bubastis) was (as is familiar to every visitor to Thebes) a menagerie of cats, living, embalmed, or in stone. This to the Greeks, as to the Arabs, who give one name to the two animals, may well have caused this sanctuary of Pasht to have been called the City of Lions, and therefore we have no need to seek the locality in any other part of Egypt. This solution had occurred to me before I saw it worked out in Herzfeld, iii. 562. It is possible, however, that it may have been so called from sacred lions, which, at the more certainly ascertained Leontopolis, were kept in separate houses and had songs sung to them during their meals. Ælian, xii. 7; Wilkinson, v. 173; iv. 296.

[3] Jos. *c. Ap.* ii. 5.

[4] Jos. *Ant.* xiii.

[5] Herzfeld, iii. 462.

[6] Jos. *B. J.* vii. 10, 3.

[7] This must be the origin of the statement of Apion (Jos. *c. Ap.* ii. 2) and of Strabo, xvii.

ruins of these it is that still form the three rugged sandhills known by the name of 'the Mounds of the Jews.' It was a bold attempt to form a new centre of Judaism; and the attempt was supported by one of the earliest efforts to find in the poetic language of the ancient prophets a local, prosaic, and temporary application. In the glowing prediction [1] of the homage which Egypt should hereafter pay to Israel, Isaiah had expressed the hope that there should be five cities in Egypt speaking the language of Canaan and revering the Sacred Name, and that one of these should be the sacred City of the Sun. What had been indicated then as the most surprising triumph—the conversion of the chief sanctuary of the old Egyptian worship to the true religion—was seized by Onias as a proof that in the neighbourhood, if not within the walls, of the Sun City—which the Greeks called Heliopolis, and which the Egyptians called On—there should rise a temple of Jehovah. The very Name of On was a likeness to his own name of Onias. The passage in Isaiah was yet further changed to give the city a name more exactly resembling the title of Jerusalem. As the City of the Palestinian sanctuary was called the Holy City, the City of Holiness, so this was supposed to have been foreseen as the Righteous City—the City of Righteousness.[2] It was, moreover, close within the view of that sacred college where, according to Egyptian tradition, Moses himself had studied. But a worship and a system so elaborately built up on doubtful etymologies and plays on ambiguous words was not destined to long endurance; and, although an ample patrimony was granted by the Egyptian kings for the endowment of this new Pontificate, and although the territory round was long called the 'Land 'of Onias,'[3] and the sanctuary lasted for three centuries, it passed away under the pressure of the Roman[4] government,

[1] Isa. xix. 18, 19. 'The city of the sun'—wrongly translated in the A.V. 'the city 'of destruction.' Herzfeld (iii. 561) gives the explanation as above. Gesenius (on *Isaiah*, iii. 639) has doubts of the genuineness of the passage. Whiston (on Jos. *Ant.* xiii. 3, 1) with his usual honesty and eccentricity, supposes Onias's interpretation to be correct.

[2] This appears in the LXX. translation of Isa. xix. 18, 19, πόλις Ἀσεδέκ.

[3] The whole question is ably discussed in Herzfeld, iii. 556-564.

[4] Jos. *B. J.* vii. 10, 4.

and left no permanent trace even on the Alexandrian Jews. The failure of such a distorted prediction is a likeness of what may be in store for equally fanciful applications of sacred words and doubtful interpretations in more modern times.

It may be that round[1] this centre of ancient Jewish traditions, secluded on the border of the desert from the great world of Alexandria, was gathered the opposition to the Grecian learning which we faintly discern in the next century. But it had only a local and sectarian existence. The flow of the religious life of the new story of 'Israel in Egypt' rolled on regardless of this artificial and insulated sanctuary. The presiding genius of Egyptian Judaism was not the priestly house of Onias, but the royal house of Ptolemy.

Over these Jewish colonists, as over their native Egyptian subjects, the Ptolemies, at least for the first four reigns, ruled with beneficent toleration. The Egyptian priesthood, after the hard dominion of the Persian iconoclasts, welcomed them as deliverers. The temples were restored or rebuilt after the antique model. The names of the Grecian Kings and Queens were carved in hieroglyphics, and their figures painted on the Temple walls in the disguise of the Pharaohs. They became as Egyptians to the Egyptians, and so to the Jews they became almost as Jews[2]—sending their accustomed sacrifice to the Temple of Jerusalem, and patronising with lands and privileges the Temple of Leontopolis. The Museum with its unique Library, the scholars who frequented the court—Euclid the geometrician, Apelles the painter, Eratosthenes the grammarian—brought the Grecian learning to the very doors of the Israelite community.[3] In this fostering atmosphere there sprang up those influences which Alexandria

The Ptolemies.

[1] Nicolas, p. 842.

[2] The one exception is Ptolemy Philopator, whose endeavour to enter the Temple, and whose employment of the Indian punishment of trampling under the feet of enraged elephants, is the subject of the third Book of Maccabees. But even these incidents terminate happily for the Jews. He is restrained from entering the Temple by Simon the Just; he is compelled to acknowledge the rights of the Alexandrian Jews by the reluctance of the elephants; and this was commemorated by a festival like that of Purim. See Ewald, v. 468.

[3] Herzfeld, iii. 446-458. See Sharpe's *Egypt*, chap. vii.

exercised over the Jewish, and thus over the Christian, Church for ever.

The first was the translation of the Hebrew Scriptures into Greek—the rise of what may properly be termed the Greek Bible.

As the meeting of the Greek Empire with the Jewish nation is presented to us in the legend of Alexander's interview with Jaddua, so the meeting of the two sacred languages of Greek and Hebrew is presented to us in the legend of the Seventy Translators. It was believed two centuries later—and, however much the details have been shaken by recent criticism, the main fact is not doubted—that in the reign of the second Ptolemy the translation of the Pentateuch into Greek was undertaken at Alexandria. It is, perhaps, most probable that it sprang up spontaneously to supply the wants of the Alexandrian Jews. But the Jewish community would not be satisfied with this homely origin. The story took two forms. One was that King Ptolemy Philadelphus, wishing to discover the difference between the Jews and the Samaritans, summoned [1] five translators—three representing the Samaritans, one Jew, and one assessor. The Samaritans undertook the Pentateuch, the Jew the later Books, and the King approved the Samaritan version. This was, doubtless, the Samaritan tradition. It points to the gradual growth of the work. It also may connect itself with the venerable High Priest [2] Hezekiah, whom Hecatæus met in Egypt, and who appears to have been the chief of the sacerdotal order not in Jerusalem but in Samaria.

The Septuagint (LXX.)

The larger story is [3] that of which the full account is given in the letter ascribed to Aristeas, a courtier of Ptolemy II. This account rose above the level of the sectarian differences

[1] The number 5 also appears in the Talmudic traditions (Sopherim, i. 7) quoted in Herzfeld, iii. 536. Two names were connected with the work by tradition, Aristobulus with Exodus, Lysimachus with Esther (Grätz, iii. 35).

[2] Jos. *c. Ap.* Herzfeld (iii. 538) founds this conjecture on the facts (1) that no Jewish Hezekiah is known at this time; (2) that the Samaritan High Priest in Alexander's time was Hezekiah; 3) that Hecatæus never distinguishes between the Jews and Samaritans.

[3] 'The letter of Aristeas to Philocrates' is given in Hody, *De Bibliorum Textibus Originalibus*, p. i.-xxvi. For the discussion of details see *ibid.* 1-9, Ewald, v. 249, Kuenen, iii. 171, Herzfeld iii. 545.

of Jew and Samaritan, and attached itself to the wide sympathies of the great patrons of Gentile literature. Ptolemy Philadelphus (thus ran the tale) was resolved to enrich his new library by so important a treasure as an intelligible version of the sacred books of so large a class of his subjects. Seventy or seventy-two delegates were sent from the High Priest at Jerusalem—it may be, as in the story, so as to give six from each of the twelve tribes, or in order to correspond to the sum total of the Jewish Council, or in accordance with the mystic number which pervades this and other Eastern stories.[1] A long catalogue existed of the splendid tables, cisterns, and bowls, which Josephus[2] describes as if he had seen them, and which are said to have been sent by Ptolemy at this time as presents to conciliate the Jewish High Priest to the work. A local tradition long pointed out the island of the Pharian lighthouse as the scene of their labours. There, it was believed, they pursued their work, withdrawn in that seagirt fortress from the turmoil of the streets of Alexandria, and with the opportunity of performing every morning their religious ablutions in the sea which washed their threshold—and on the shore of which, as late as the second century, were shown the remains of the seventy[3] or the thirty-six cells in which the translators had been lodged, and in which (so the later Alexandrian tradition maintained) each produced by miracle exactly the same inspired version as all the rest, without one error or contradiction.

Like all such incidents of the contact between a narrower and a broader civilisation, the event itself was by different portions or at different times of the Jewish community invested with totally contrary aspects.

On the one hand, it was regarded as a great calamity, equal to that of the worship of the Golden Calf. The day[4] on which

[1] See Ewald, v. 252.

[2] Jos. *Ant.* xii. 2, 7, 8, 9.

[3] Justin (*Cohort. ad Græcos*, c. 34) saw the 70 cells. Epiphanes (*De Pond. et Mens.* c. vii., viii.) speaks of 36 cells, in which they were lodged, two and two, with two scribes in each (Comp. Irenæus, *Adv. Hær.* iii. 24).

[4] The fast-day was the 8th of Tebet (January). See the quotations from the Talmud and the arguments upon their date in Kuenen, iii. 214-216. The Samaritans took the same view, on account of their hatred of the Jewish translation (Herzfeld, iii. 537).

it was accomplished was believed to have been the beginning of a preternatural darkness of three days' duration over the whole world, and was commemorated as a day of fasting and humiliation. It needs but slight evidence to convince us that such a feeling more or less widely-spread must have existed. It is the same instinct which to this hour makes it a sin, if not an impossibility, in the eyes of a devout Mussulman to translate the Koran ; which in the Christian Church assailed Jerome with the coarsest vituperation for venturing on a Latin version which differed from the Greek ; which at the Reformation regarded it as a heresy to translate the Latin Scriptures into the languages of modern Europe ; and which in England has in our own days regarded it in the English Church as a dangerous innovation to revise the authorised version of the seventeenth century, or in the Roman Church to correct the barbarous dialect of the Douay translation of the Vulgate, or to admit of any errors in the text or the rendering of the Vulgate itself. In one and all of these cases the reluctance has sprung from the same tenacious adherence to ancient and sacred forms —from the same unwillingness to admit of the dislodgment even of the most flagrant inaccuracies when once familiarised by established use. But for all these venerable texts, even in some instances the Koran, this sentiment has been compelled to yield to the more generous desire of arriving at the hidden meaning of sacred truth, and of making that truth more widely known. So it was in the most eminent degree in the case of the Septuagint. The very story,[1] fictitious as it may be, of the splendour of the reception of the translators at Alexandria indicates the pride which was taken in the work. The eagerness of the tradition to connect the translation with the Grecian king and his universal library shows how gladly it was welcomed as a bridge between the Jewish and the Gentile world ; the fantastic addition which was made in Christian times of the preternatural inspiration of the seventy translators, shows how

[1] The probability, amounting almost to certainty, is that the Pentateuch alone was translated under Ptolemy Philadelphus. For this and for its connexion with the Samaritans see Ewald, v. 253.

readily the new takes the place of the old, and exhibits in the most striking form the transference, which has again and again occurred, of the same reverence, it may be even of the same superstition, for the new version as had formerly clung with exclusive attachment to the old.

If ever there was a translation which, by its importance, rose to a level with the original, it was this. It was not the original Hebrew but the Septuagint translation through which the religious truths of Judaism became known to the Greek and the Roman. It was the Septuagint which was the Bible[1] of the Evangelists and Apostles in the first century, and of the Christian Church for the first age of its existence, which is still the only recognised authorised text of the Eastern Church, and the basis of the only authorised text of the Latin Church. Widely as it differs from the Hebrew Scriptures in form, in substance, in chronology, in language; unequal, imperfect, grotesque as are its renderings, it has nevertheless, through large periods of ecclesiastical history, rivalled, if not superseded, those Scriptures themselves. This substitution was, no doubt, in great measure based on the fable of the miraculous accuracy of the translation, and has led to the strangest theological confusions in the treatment of the Bible by the older Churches—which thus claim for two contradictory texts the same authority, and avowedly prefer the translation to the original. But still, on the whole, in the triumph of the Septuagint the cause of freedom, of criticism, of charity triumphed also. No rigid requirement of literal exactness can stand in the presence of the fact that apostles or apostolic men appealed for their arguments to a translation so teeming with acknowledged mistakes. No criticism need fear to handle freely the Sacred Volume, in which the Alexandrian translators ventured on such bold variations, accommodations, omissions, and insertions, with the applause of the Christian world from Irenæus to Augustine. Whatever religious scruple is felt at circulating occasional errors in the hope of inculcating the general truth with which they have been entangled should dis-

Its importance.

[1] See Roberts, *Discussion on the Language of Palestine*, p. 292.

appear before the example of the authoritative and universal use, in early times, of the Septuagint, which differs far more widely from the original, and is far more deeply imbued with the natural infirmity of translators, than any other version of the Bible that has ever since appeared.

Again, the gradual completion of the translation, dragging its slow length along for at least two centuries, is an encouragement to the laborious efforts of modern scholars, each adding something to the knowledge of the preceding time. The use to which the Seventy turned their knowledge of Egyptian localities and customs is a faint, yet sufficient stimulus, in the interpretation of the Scriptures, to the duty of seeking light far and near. The honest silence with which, when the Greek translators stumble upon Hebrew words, such as those describing the furniture of the Temple or the tunes of the Psalms, they hold their pens, and leave the unintelligible phrases in their native obscurity unexplained, is an example of the modest love of truth, capable of confessing its own ignorance—a modesty such as many interpreters have grievously lacked. If 'the noble army of translators,' as they have been sometimes called, may look with affectionate veneration on Jerome's cell of Bethlehem, on Luther's study in the Castle of the Wartburg, on the Jerusalem Chamber, where once and again the majestic language of the English Bible has been revised, yet the goal of their most sacred pilgrimage should be the narrow rocky islet of the Alexandrian harbour, where was kindled a brighter and more enduring beacon in the intellectual and religious sphere even than the world-renowned Pharos, which in the maritime world has been the parent of all the lights that from shore to shore and sea to sea have guided the mariners for two thousand years.

Its peculiarities.

We do not propose to follow their labour into detail, or to give the various instances of the liberties taken with the sacred text, lengthening the chronology to suit the more exacting claims of Egyptian science, softening the anthropomorphic representations of the Divinity to meet the requirements of Grecian philosophy.

One example alone shall be given of the connexion of the translation with the Alexandrian Court and with Hellenic culture. There was a tradition in the Talmud that in the Pentateuch,[1] in rendering the word *Arnebeth* ('hare') not by *lagos* (the usual Greek word for hare) but by *dasypus* (hairy-foot), the Greek translators were influenced or controlled by the desire to avoid so homely a use of the name of *Lagus*, the father of the Ptolemæan dynasty. The mere supposition of such a courtly concession on so minute a point implies a dependence on the Greek sovereign, which far exceeds even the dedication of the Authorised English Version to King James I., or Sixtus V.'s imperious preface to the Vulgate. But, though it is hardly necessary to resort to so strange an hypothesis, the real explanation leads us to the intervention of another influence on the text more reasonable and equally curious. The substitution of the word *dasypus* for *lagos* was not uncommon at this time, but for its frequency there was a cause more interesting than the power of the Lagidæ. The conquests of Alexander had contributed to the production of a more permanent monument of his progress than the dynasty of the Ptolemies. On the specimens sent home to his great teacher had been founded and published the greatest scientific work of ancient times, Aristotle's 'History of Animals.' In it the modern word *dasypus* had almost entirely superseded the older word *lagos*, and the translators at Alexandria might therefore well have been expected to catch the new fashion. But there was an even yet more striking example of Aristotle's influence on this passage. In that same context the hare in the Hebrew Scriptures is described as a ruminating animal. In the ancient world, before the birth of accurate observation, that which had the appearance of rumination had been taken for the reality and was so considered. But by the time that the Greek translators approached this text, the secret of the habits of the hare had been disclosed by the natural history of Aristotle, and, accordingly, on this

[1] Lev. xi. 6; Deut. xiv. 7. See Kuenen, iii. 212. There is, however, some confusion here. *Dasypus* is the translation of the word for *coney* in Lev. xi. 5. The word translated 'hare' in the English of Lev. xi. 6, is by the LXX. translated *chærogryllus*. In either case, however, there is a deviation from *lagos*.

minute point arose the first direct conflict, often since repeated, between Theology and Science. The venerable translators who were at work, if so be, on the Pharos island, were too conscientious to reject so clear an evidence of the fact; but they were too timid to allow the contradiction to appear, and they therefore, with the usual rashness of fear, twice over[1] boldly interpolated the word NOT into the sacred text, and thus, as they thought, reconciled it to science by reversing the special point of the passage. There have since that time been many falsifications of Science to meet the demands of theology. This is the first instance of many like falsifications of Scripture to meet the demands of Science.

The appearance of the Septuagint translation was important not only in itself, but as affording a new opening for constant additions to the sacred volume. The Hebrew Literature had come nearly to an end. If here and there a fresh Hebrew book or a fresh Hebrew Psalm might be added, their entrance was more or less covert, ambiguous, and questionable. But the Greek literature was still abounding, and into that vast world the Jewish race was now entering. From this time forward, with very few exceptions, any new sacred book which should win its way must be part not of the Hebrew, but of the Greek Bible. The tents of Shem were closed, but the doors of Japheth were expanded with a never-ending enlargement. The first pages of this Greek volume began with the Grecian translation of the Pentateuch; but its last pages were not closed till they had included the last of the writings which bore the name of St. John. This was the chief outward bond between the Jewish and the Christian Scriptures. By this unity of the sacred language the beginning and end of the sacred literature were indissolubly linked together, and not only so, but by its intervention was filled the gap between the Old and the New Testament, and their differences were veiled under the common garb of Greek. Into that vacant space, clothed in the same language, stole in those Grecian books, which in the Latin Church have been called Deuterocanonical,

The Apocrypha.

[1] Lev. xi. 5, 6. (LXX. ed. Van Ess.)

and in the Protestant Churches Apocryphal, but which in the early ages of Christianity were blended, under the common sanction of the Septuagint, with the earlier books which closed with Malachi, the Chronicles, or Daniel, according to the varying order in which the Hebrew books were arranged.[1]

The introduction of these[2] writings into the very heart of the ancient Scriptures has had wider consequences than is often recognised.

In some respects, no doubt, it has had a debasing effect on the religious systems which have been founded on the mixed volume resulting from such additions. The books of this second Canon partook largely of the enfeebled style, the exaggerated rhetoric, the legendary extravagance, and, on the other hand, the rigid exclusiveness, which characterised the history and literature of the nation after the return from the Captivity. It was, thus far, a true instinct which has caused the Rabbinical schools to denounce the perusal of these writings with a severity like that of the Roman Index. 'He 'who studies the uncanonical books will have no portion in the 'world to come.' 'He who introduces into his house more 'than the twenty-four introduces confusion.'[3] And the like condemnation has been felt, if not expressed, by those Protestant Churches or teachers who have most eagerly excluded from use any Bible or Calendar that contains them. But there is another side to the question. These writings, if not deserv-

[1] See Lecture XLVIII.

[2] It may be necessary to give briefly the history of the generic title of these books.

1. By the early Church they were (when not reckoned as Canonical) called 'Ecclesi-'astical,' *i.e.* books read in public services of the Church.

2. By the Roman Catholic Church, at least since the Council of Trent, they have been called 'Deuterocanonical,' a title of inferiority which well expresses their relation in regard to the Hebrew books, but is hardly consistent with the entire equality with the Canonical books to which they have been raised by the Councll of Trent and more recently by the Council of the Vatican.

3. By the Protestant Churches they have been called 'Apocryphal,' a name which has passed through three phases:— (*a*) A title of praise bestowed by the Gnostics on their own books of 'hidden 'wisdom.' (*b*) A title of reproach bestowed by the early Church on the spurious Gospels and the like literature, with the view of stigmatising them with the same name as that applied to the Gnostic books. (*c*) The title of the Deuterocanonical Books of the Old Test., first given by Wycliffe, and finally adopted by the Protestant Churches at the Reformation (see Professor Westcott's *The Bible in the Church*; Professor Plumptre in the *Dictionary of the Bible*, art. 'Apocrypha').

[3] Kuenen, iii.

ing to be called 'Canonical,' as by the Church of Rome, or 'inspired,' though not 'canonical,'[1] Scriptures, as by the Church of England,[2] are invaluable as keeping alive, not only the continuity of the sacred literature, but the sense of the gradations of excellence even in sacred books; and thus serving as a perpetual protest against the uniform, rigorous, rigid, levelling theory, which has been the bane of all theology, and which has tended so greatly to obscure the true meaning and purpose even of the earlier Hebrew Scriptures. It is humorously told in a famous romance[3] of our day how the pious peasant, who read through the whole Bible regularly, though he felt a certain disappointment on reading the Apocrypha, yet rejoiced in the freedom which it afforded of innocent criticism from which he had been hitherto withheld. That sentiment and that advantage are not confined to the English peasant. The free thought which thus played around the Apocryphal books nurtured a spirit of inquiry from which the whole Bible has gained. When Jerome attacked the improbabilites in the Song of the Three Children in the Greek part of Daniel, he was using exactly the same weapons which Porphyry used against the early date of the Hebrew part of the same book. The more enlightened members of the Roman Church, who have been familiarised with the admixture of legendary matter in the Books of Tobit and Judith, have been more ready, though in defiance of the usages of their communion, to recognise the like elements in the Books of the Pentateuch or of the Judges. And even to those who (as in many Protestant Churches) refuse to concede any rank to the Books of the Apocrypha, a solid advantage has accrued from involuntary familiarity with writings so nearly Biblical in tone and spirit, and yet by the traditions of their sect or family excluded from the Bible. In an affecting passage in his autobiography John Bunyan relates how he was for a long period at once comforted and perplexed by finding deep inward relief from words for which he vainly sought within the four corners of his Bible:[4] '*Look at the generations of old and see; did ever*

[1] Canons of Trent; Canons of the Vatican.

[2] Homilies (Oxford ed. 1859), pp. 100, 107, 242, 248, 389.

[3] *Adam Bede*, c. 51.

[4] *Grace Abounding*. § 62, 63, 64, 65.

'*any trust in the Lord and was confounded?*' 'Then I 'continued,' he says, 'above a year and could not find the 'place; but at last, casting my eyes upon the Apocrypha 'books, I found it in the tenth verse of the second chapter of 'Ecclesiasticus. This at the first did somewhat daunt me; 'because it was not in those texts that we call holy or canonical. 'Yet, as this sentence was the sum and substance of many of 'the promises, it was my duty to take the comfort of it, and I 'bless God for that word, for it was of good to me. That word 'doth still oft-times shine before my face.'

The discovery which Bunyan thus made of a source of consolation outside the 'canonical texts' has a far wider application than the particular instance which so moved him. It opens as it were a postern-door into the charmed circle of the sacred books. It calls our attention to the fact that there were writings which, though denied a place in the Canonical Scriptures, yet shade away from the outskirts of those Scriptures into the Grecian philosophy and poetry, and have been acknowledged by grave theologians, and by Protestant Churches, to be inspired by the same Divine Spirit that breathed, though in fuller tones, through Isaiah or through David.

The instruction involved in this process is enhanced by the fact that these Books are themselves of such varying character and value. Some of them, like the Book of Judith, are apparently mere fables; some, like the additions to the Books of Ezra, Esther, and Daniel, are examples of the free and facile mode in which, at that time, the earlier sacred books were 'improved,' modified, enlarged, and corrected, by the Alexandrian critics. Some, like the Books of the Maccabees, are attempts, more or less exact, at contemporary or nearly contemporary history. Some, like the Psalter of Solomon, have never gained an entrance even into this outer court of the sacred writings. Some, like the Second Book of Esdras and the Book of Enoch, have attained a Biblical authority, but only within a very limited range. But there are two which tower above the rest, and which, even by those who most disparage the others, are held in reverential esteem. The one is the recommendation of the theology of Palestine to Alexandria, 'the Wisdom of the Son of Sirach;' the other is the recommendation of the theology of Alexandria to Palestine, 'the 'Wisdom of Solomon.'

These books are both in the same class of literature. They both attach themselves in the Hebrew Scriptures, not to the Prophetical or Historical or Poetical portions, but to those writings on which the influence of the external world had already made itself felt, the books which bear the name of Solomon.[1] They both furnish links which connect the earlier Hebrew literature with that final outburst of religious teaching which is recorded in the Gospels and Epistles. The Parables and Discourses beside the Galilean Lake, the Epistles of James, of John, and of the unknown author of the Epistle to the Hebrews, have hardly any affinity with the style of Daniel or Malachi, of Tobit or of the Rabbinical schools, but they are the direct continuation, although in a more exalted form, of those two Apocryphal Books of Wisdom.

The Wisdom of the Son of Sirach. B.C. 180.

The Wisdom[2] of Joshua (or as the Greeks called him, Jesus), the Son of Sirach, was the first of those writings which, from the sanction given to them by the Church, were called 'Ecclesiastical' as distinct from 'Canonical,' and thus took to itself the name 'Ecclesiasticus,' which properly belonged to them all. It was for the Jews of Alexandria first, and then for the Christians, '*The Church Book*;' 'the favourite book of ecclesiastical edification;'[3] 'the Whole 'Duty of Man,' 'the Imitation'—the 'summary of all virtues,'[4] as it was called in its original title.

[1] See Lecture XXVII.

[2] It is strange that any doubt should have ever arisen on the date of Ecclesiasticus. The comparison of Haggai i. 1; ii. 1; Zech. i. 7; vii. 1; 1 Macc. xiii. 42; xiv. 27, makes it certain that the words ἐν τῷ ὀνδοῷ καὶ τριακοστῷ ἔτει ἐπὶ τοῦ Εὐεργέτου βασιλέως in the Prologue can only mean 'in the thirty-eighth year of 'King Euergetes;' and as the first Euergetes only reigned twenty-five years; the date of the translation is thus fixed to the thirty-eighth year of the second Euergetes, B.C. 132. The indication from the mention of Simon in chap l. 1 is less certain. But the great probability in favour of identifying him with Simon II. agrees with the conclusion to be drawn from the interval between the grandfather who wrote and the grandson who translated, and this would place the original work about B.C. 180.

[3] A fierce attack upon it, as favouring Arianism, necromancy, and Judaic error was published by Reynolds in 1666.

[4] *Panaretos.*

It must have early acquired this reputation. The grandson of its author arrived in Alexandria in the close of the troubled reign of Ptolemy Physcon—the second of those kings who were renowned among the Gentiles for bearing, seriously or ironically, the name of 'benefactor' (Euergetes). When, amongst his countrymen in a foreign land, he discovered 'no slight difference of education,' and at the same time a keen desire to become instructed in the customs of their fathers, he found no task more worthy of his labour, knowledge, and sleepless study than to translate into Greek this collection of all that was most practical in the precepts and most inspiring in the history of his people.

B.C. 132.

It is, perhaps, the only one of the Deuterocanonical[1] books composed originally, not in Greek, but in Hebrew; and the translator well knew the difficulty of rendering the peculiarities of his native tongue into the fluent language of Alexandria. It is the first reflection which we possess on the Old Testament Scriptures after the commencment of the formation of the Canon. 'The Law and the Prophets' were already closed. 'The other books' were, as the phrase implies, still regarded as an appendix, capable of additions, yet already beginning to be parted by an intelligible though invisible line from those of later date.[2] The Son of Sirach had given himself much to their perusal; he was, as we may say, the first Biblical student; but he felt that he had still something new to add, something old to collect. He was, like a great teacher of later times, as one born out of due time.[3] He had awakened up 'last of 'all, as one that gathereth after the grape-gatherers;[4] by the 'blessing of the Lord he profited,' and 'filled his wine-press 'like a gleaner of grapes.' It was a noble ambition, alike of the grandfather and the grandson, to carry into the most minute duties of daily life the principles of their ancient law—'labouring not only for himself only, but for all who seek 'learning.'

It is one of the largest books in the whole Bible. It con-

[1] The First Book of Maccabees and Judith may also perhaps be exceptions.

[2] Ecclus., Prologue. See Lect. XLVIII.

[3] 1 Cor. xv. 8.

[4] Ecclus. xxxiii. 16.

tains the first allusions to the earlier records of the Jewish race. The Psalms, and occasionally the Prophets, had touched on the history of Abraham, Jacob, Moses, Samuel. But neither in Psalms nor Prophets, neither in Proverbs nor history, is there the slightest reference to the mystic opening of the Book of Genesis, which in Christian times has been the battle field of so many a strife, theological, scientific, and critical. It is the Son [1] of Sirach, in his passing allusions to the creation of Adam, and to the old giants, who is the first precursor of the Pelagian controversy, of the 'Paradise Lost,' of the Elohistic and Jehovistic theories.

Jerusalem [2] is still the centre, and Palestine the horizon, of his thoughts. The Priesthood,[3] with their offerings, their dues, and their stately appearance, are to him the most prominent figures of the Jewish community. Nor is the modern institution of the Scribes forgotten.[4] He draws his images of grandeur from the cedars of Lebanon and the fir-trees that clothe the sides of Hermon, from the terebrinth [5] with its spreading branches—his images of beauty from the palm-trees in the tropical heat of Engedi, or from the roses and lilies and fragrant shade by the well-watered gardens of Jericho. The drops of bitterness which well up amidst his exuberant flow of patriotic thanksgiving are all discharged within that narrow range of vision which fixed his whole theological and national animosity on the three hostile tribes that penned in the little Jewish colony—the Edomites on the south, the Philistines on the west, and the Samaritans on the north.[6] And in accordance with this local and almost provincial limitation is the absence of those wider Oriental or Western aspects which abound in other Canonical or Deuterocanonical books of this period. It is, after Malachi, the one specimen of a purely Palestinian treatise during this period.

But the grandson, through whose careful translation alone

[1] Ecclus. xiv. 17; xvi. 7; xvii. 1; xxxiii. 10; xliv. 16, 17.

[2] *Ibid.* xxiv. ii.; xxxvi. 13; l. 26.

[3] *Ibid.* vii. 30; xiv. 11; xlv. 7-20.

[4] *Ibid.* x. 5.

[5] *Ibid.* xxiv. 13-19; l. 8-12.

[6] *Ibid.* l. 26. For *Samaria* read *Seir,*' and possibly for 'the foolish people' (μωρός) read 'the Amorites' (Grimm, *ad loc.*)

it has been preserved, was not wrong in thinking that it had a sufficiently universal character to make it suitable for the vast complex world in which he found himself in the capital of Alexander's dominions. Even although hardly any direct Alexandrian influence can be detected in its style, yet it is evident that the breath of the Grecian spirit has touched it at the core, and raised it out of its Semitic atmosphere. The closed hand of the Hebrew proverb has opened (thus to apply a well-known metaphor) into the outstretched [1] palm of Grecian rhetoric. The author, although his birthplace and his home were Jerusalem, was yet a traveller in foreign lands; he knew the value, even if he had not had the actual experience, of 'serving among great men and before princes;' he had 'tried 'the good and the evil among men.' [2]

In some respects the Book of the Son of Sirach is but a repetition of the ancient writings of Solomon. In some of its maxims it sinks below the dignity of those writings by the homeliness of its details [3] for guidance of behaviour at meals,[4] of commercial speculations, of social advancement. But its general tone is worthy of that first contact between the two great civilisations of the ancient world, and breathes a spirit which an Isaiah would not have condemned, nor a Sophocles or a Theophrastus have despised. There is not a word in it to countenance the minute casuistries of the later Rabbis, or the metaphysical subtleties of the later Alexandrians. It pours out its whole strength in discussing the conduct of human life, or the direction of the soul to noble aims. Here first in the sacred books we find the full delineation of the idea of education through a slow, gradual process. 'At first by crooked 'ways, then will she return the [5] straight way, and comfort him, 'and show him her secrets.' 'At the last thou shalt find her 'rest, and that shall be turned to thy joy. Then shall her 'fetters be a strong defence for thee, and her chains a robe of 'glory.' [6] Here is a pointed warning against spoiled children:

[1] See especially Ecclus. xxxviii. 24; xxxix. 11.

[2] Ecclus. xxxix. 4; li. 13.

[3] *Ibid.* viii. 11–19; xi. 10; xiii. 2; xix. 1; xxix.; xxxvii. 11.

[4] *Ibid.* xxxi. 16.

[5] *Ibid.* iv. 17.

[6] *Ibid.* vi. 28.

'Cocker thy child, and he shall make thee afraid, play with 'him and he will bring thee to heaviness.'[1] Here is the measure of true nobleness: 'It is not meet to despise a poor man 'that hath understanding, neither is it convenient to magnify a 'sinful man. Great men and judges and potentates shall be 'honoured, yet is there none of them greater than he that 'feareth the Lord. To the slave that is wise shall they that are 'free do service, and he that hath knowledge will not grudge 'when he is reformed.'[2] Here is the backbone of the honest love of truth: 'In nowise speak against the truth, but be 'abashed of the error of thy ignorance.' 'Be not ashamed to 'confess thy faults, nor swim against the stream of conviction.' 'Strive for the truth unto death and the Lord shall fight for 'thee.'[3] Here is a tender compassion which reaches far into the future religion of mankind: 'Let it not grieve thee to bow 'down thine ear to the poor and give him a friendly answer 'with gentleness. Be as a father to the fatherless, and instead 'of a husband to the widow; so shalt thou be as the son of 'the Most High and He shall love thee more than thy mother 'doth.'[4] If there is at times the mournful and hopeless view of life and of death[5] which pervades the earlier 'Preacher,' yet on the whole the tone is one of vigorous, magnanimous action.

He must have been a delightful teacher who could so write of filial affection[6] and of friendship[7] in all its forms, and so rise above the harshness of his relations with his slaves.[8] He must have seen deep into the problems of social life who could contrast as keenly as Bacon or Goethe the judgments of the uneducated many and the highly-educated few.[9] Yet in the midst of these homely and varied experiences, which belong only to the imitator of the wise King, a voice as of the Prophet and the Psalmist is still heard. Again and again the strain is raised, such as Amos and Isaiah had lifted up, not the less impressive for the quiet soberness with which it is urged. It is the same

[1] Ecclus. xxx. 9.
[2] *Ibid.* x. 23, 24.
[3] *Ibid.* iv. 25.
[4] *Ibid.* iv. 8, 10.
[5] *Ibid.* xli. 1.
[6] *Ibid.* iii. 12–15; vii. 28.
[7] *Ibid.* vi. 14, 15; ix. 10; xii. 8; xix. 13; xxxvii. 2.
[8] *Ibid.* iv. 30; vii. 21; x. 25; xxxiii. 24.
[9] *Ibid.* xxxviii. 24–xxxix. 11.

doctrine of the substitution of the moral duties for the ceremonial. The true 'atonement' for sins is declared to be, not the dumb sacrifices in the Temple courts, but 'the honour to 'parents,' the giving of 'alms.' The trust in 'oblations,' the recklessness of reliance on the mere mercy of God are solemnly discountenanced. 'He that requiteth a good turn offereth fine 'flour; and he that giveth alms sacrificeth praise. To depart 'from unrighteousness is propitiation.'[1] And underneath all this there still burns the gentle flame of hope and resignation. 'Look at the generations of old and see' (it is the passage which 'shone before the face' of Bunyan) 'did ever any 'trust in the Lord and were confounded? As His majesty 'is so is His mercy.'[2] Both by example and by definition there is no more exalted description of the true greatness of prayer.[3]

But there is yet another characteristic of the Son of Sirach, more peculiarly his own. As the philosophy of the Hebrew Scriptures is contained in the larger part of the book—possibly from older documents—so their poetry finds a voice in the conclusion, which is beyond question original. It is the song of praise[4] which, beginning with the glories of the Creation, breaks forth into that 'Hymn of the Forefathers,' as it is called in its ancient title, to which there is no parallel in the Old Testament, but of which the catalogue of the worthies of faith in the Epistle to the Hebrews is an obvious imitation. Here and here only is a full expression given to that natural instinct of reverence for the mighty dead, which has in these striking words been heard from generation to generation in the festivals of the great benefactors of Christendom, or when the illustrious of the earth are committed to the grave.

'Let us now praise famous men and the fathers that begat 'us.'[5] 'Their bodies[6] are buried in peace, but their name 'liveth for evermore.' It begins with the unknown sages of antiquity; it closes with the 'Ultimus Judæorum' as it seemed,

[1] Ecclus. iii. 3, 4, 30; v. 5, 6; vii. 9, 10; xxxv. 1-7.

[2] *Ibid.* ii. 4-18.

[3] *Ibid.* xxiii. 1-6; xxxv. 17.

[4] *Ibid.* xlii. 15—l. 29.

[5] *Ibid.* xliv. 1. Read on all Founders' days.

[6] *Ibid.* xliv. 14. Sung in Handel's Funeral Anthem.

of his own generation, Simon the Just. Well might the grandson delight to render into Greek for the countrymen of Pindar and Pericles a roll of heroes more noble than were ever commemorated at the Isthmian games or in the Athenian Ceramicus.

The Book of Wisdom.

The 'Wisdom of the Son of Sirach' was followed, at how long an interval we know not, by 'the Wisdom of Solomon.' As the former book was the expression of a sage at Jerusalem with a tincture of Alexandrian learning, so the latter book was the expression of an Alexandrian sage presenting his Grecian ideas under the forms of Jewish history. We feel with him the oppressive atmosphere of the elaborate Egyptian idolatry.[1] We see through his eyes the ships passing along the Mediterranean waters into the Alexandrian harbour.[2] We trace the footprint of Aristotle in the enumeration, word by word, of the four great ethical virtues.[3] We recognise the rhetoric of the Grecian sophists in the Ptolemæan Court;[4] we are present at the luxurious banquets and lax discussions of the neighbouring philosophers of Cyrene.[5] But in the midst of this Gentile scenery there is a voice which speaks with the authority of the ancient prophets to this new world. The book is a signal instance of the custom prevalent in the two centuries before the Christian era, both in the Jewish and the Grecian world, of placing modern untried writings under the shelter of some venerable authority. No name appeared for this purpose so weighty as that of the master of the wisdom of Israel. Solomon is evoked from the dead past to address the living rulers of mankind. 'Love righteousness ye that are judges of the earth. Hear, 'therefore, O ye kings, and understand; for your power is 'given unto you of the Lord, and your dominion from the 'Most High, who shall try your works and search out your 'counsels. Being ministers of His kingdom [torn] have not 'judged aright, nor kept the law, nor walked af[torn] 'of God.'[6] It is the first strong expression, u[torn]

[1] Wisdom xiii. 2–19; xv. 17–19.
[2] *Ibid.* xiv. 1–6.
[3] *Ibid.* viii. 7.
[4] *Ibid.* v. 9–12; x[torn]
[5] *Ibid.* ii. 1–7.
[6] *Ibid.* i. 1; vi. [torn]

combined force of Greek freedom and Hebrew solemnity, not of the Divine right, but of the Divine duty, of kings; and it might well be provoked by the spectacle of the corrupt rulers whether of the Egyptian or Syrian dynasties. The importance of wisdom and the value of justice had been often set forth before, both by Jew and Greek. But there is a wider and more tender grasp of the whole complex relation of intellectual and moral excellence, and therefore of the whole ideal of true religion, in the indications which this Book contains of the universal workings of the Divine Mind in the heart of man. 'Love[1] is the care of education; love is the keeping of wisdom. 'The just man maketh his boast that God is his father, and that 'he is the son of God.[2] The Spirit of the Lord filleth the 'world.[3] Thou sparest all, for they are thine, O Lord, thou 'lover of souls.[4] Thine incorruptible Spirit filleth all things. 'Thy providence, O Father, governeth the world.[5] Yet they 'were unto themselves more grievous than the darkness.'[6] 'The Holy Spirit of education.' 'An understanding spirit, 'holy, one only, manifold, subtile, flexible, transparent,[7] undefiled, plain, not subject to hurt, loving the thing that is good, 'quick, which cannot be hindered, ready to do good, kind to 'man, steadfast, sure, free from care, having all power, overseeing all things and going through all spirits however pure, 'intelligent and subtile, more moving than any motion, passing 'through all things by reason of her pureness; for she is the 'breath of the power of God, and an influence flowing from the 'genuine glory of the Almighty; therefore no defiled thing can 'fall into her: the lightness of the everlasting light, the unspotted mirror of the energy of God, and the image of His 'goodness; being but one, she can do all things: and, remaining in herself, she maketh all things new, and, in all ages 'entering into holy souls, she maketh them friends of God and 'prophets.'[8]

The conception of 'Wisdom' as 'the personified idea of

[1] Wisdom, vi. 17, 18; ἀγάπη.
[2] *Ibid.* ii. 16–18.
[3] *Ibid.* i. 7.
[4] *Ibid.* xi. 26.
[5] *Ibid.* xii. 1.
[6] *Ibid.* xvii. 21.
[7] *Ibid.* i. 5.
[8] *Ibid.* vii. 22–27.

'the mind in God, in creation—a mirror in which the world 'and mankind are ever present to him'[1]—is in part derived from the ancient Solomonian theology, but it is coloured by the Platonic doctrine, and lends itself to the wide development opened by the doctrine of 'the Word' in Christian theology, and by the doctrine of 'Law' in European philosophy. The very phrases, 'Love or Charity,' 'Holy Spirit,' 'only begotten,' 'manifold,' 'philanthropic,' 'Providence,' 'the Fatherhood of 'God,' occur here in the Greek Bible, some of them in the Greek language, for the first time; and appear not again till we find them in the New Testament. No wonder that this singular book has been ascribed to Philo, the famous contemporary of the Apostles,[2] or to that other Jew of Alexandria,[3] who was 'eloquent and mighty in the Scriptures,' and in whom Luther saw the author of the mysterious Epistle to the Hebrews. No wonder that Ewald, with his usual insight, declares that 'in the 'deep glow which, with all its apparent tranquillity, streams 'through its veins, in the nervous energy of its proverbial style, 'in the depths of its representations, we have a premonition of 'John; and in the conception of heathenism a preparation for 'Paul, like a warm rustle of spring, ere the time is fully come.'[4] No wonder that in that elaborate description of Wisdom an eminent statesman of our day, in one of his most generous moods, should have seen an exact anticipation of the liberal aspect of true Religion 'which alone can flourish, not by a policy of 'isolation, but by filling itself with a humane and genial warmth, 'in close sympathy with every true instinct and need of men, 'regardful of the just titles of every faculty of his nature, apt 'to associate with and make its own all, under whatever name, 'which goes to enrich and enlarge the patrimony of the race.'[5]

These preludings of a high philosophy and faith, whether two centuries before or close upon the dawn of the new era, are, in any case, the genuine product of Alexandrian Judaism, of the union of Greek and Hebrew thought. And in one

[1] Döllinger, *Gentile and Jew*, ii. 384.
[2] Jerome, Pref. in *Lib. Salom.*
[3] Acts xviii. 24.
[4] Ewald, v. 484.
[5] Mr. Gladstone's Address to the University of Edinburgh on the Influence of Greece, 1865.

special quarter of the religious horizon there is a revelation which this unknown author is the first to proclaim, with the authority of firm conviction and deep insight, whether to the Gentile or the Jew, namely, the revelation of 'the hope full 'of immortality,' 'the immortality of righteousness.'[1] In the Psalmists and Prophets there had been bright anticipations of such a hope, inseparable from their unfailing assurance of the power and goodness of the Eternal.[2] But it rarely took the form of a positive, distinct assertion. In the Grecian world[3] a vast step forward was taken in the Platonic representations of the last teachings of Socrates. At last the seed thus sown by the doctrine of Athenian philosophy fell on the prolific soil of a Hebrew faith, and struck root downward to a depth from which it has never since been eradicated, and bore fruit upward which has sustained the moral life of Christendom to this hour. Nor is it only the force and pathos with which this truth of a future existence is urged, but the grounds on which it is based, that fill the soul and intensify the teaching of this Jewish Phædo. It is founded on those two convictions, which, alike to the most philosophic and the most simple minds, still seem the most cogent—the imperfection of a good man's existence if limited to this present life, and the firm grasp on the Divine perfections. 'The souls of the righteous are in the hand of 'God.' 'In the sight of the unwise they seemed to die; but 'they are in peace.' 'He, being made perfect in a short time, 'fulfilled a long time.' 'God created man to be immortal, 'and made him an image of His own eternity. To know God 'is perfect righteousness. To know His power is the root of 'immortality.'[4]

Aristobulus.

There is yet one more expansion of the limits of sacred literature into the world of general culture. The Hebrew antagonism to the Gentile polytheism is still brought out strongly in Baruch and the Greek Daniel. But we now first see clearly not only the imperceptible influence of one upon the other, but the avowed recognition of the religious

[1] Wisdom iii. 4; i. 15.
[2] See Lectures VII. and XXV.
[3] See Lecture XLVI.
[4] Wisdom iii. 2; iv. 13; v. 15; xv. 3.

excellence of each. This tendency is summed up in one name, now almost forgotten, possibly used as a mask for writings of a somewhat later[1] age, but of the highest eminence at the time, and standing at the fountain-head of two vast streams of thought, of which the effects on theology have never ceased. In a critical moment[2] in the fate of the Jews of Palestine they are represented as addressing a letter to 'Aristobulus, master of King Ptolemy, and of the 'stock of the anointed priests.' This was Aristobulus,[3] first of that name which afterwards became so common, himself the chief of the Jewish community at Alexandria, in the time of Ptolemy VII., whose instructor he had become. He is one of those mysterious personages, of whom history speaks but little, yet whose importance is beyond all proportion to the small space which they appear to occupy. Others, no doubt, there were, who endeavoured to blend in one the two literatures that met under the shadow of the Alexandrian Museum.[4] Some rewrote the story of Israel in the verse of Grecian epic or tragedy. Some interwove with the sacred narrative the traditions of Egypt and Chaldæa. But it was Aristobulus who, as far as we know, first made this reconciliation his deliberate and avowed object.

B.C. 180.

Unlike most of the later Alexandrian scholars, he was a disciple, not of Plato, but of Aristotle. The master of Alexander still held sway in Alexander's city.[5] Under this potent influence Aristobulus was determined to find the Hebrew religion in the Greek philosophy. He was determined also to find the Greek philosophy in the Hebrew Scriptures. In each of these enterprises there

His endeavour to Hebraise the Grecian literature.

[1] For the arguments against the genuineness of the Aristobulian writings, see Kuenen, iii. 207.

[2] 2 Macc. i. 10.

[3] His Hebrew name was probably Judas. See Lecture XLIX.

[4] The Jewish historians of this period at Alexandria were :—1. Demetrius (Clem. Alex. *Strom.* i. 21 ; Jerome, *Cat. Ill. Script.* 38). 2. Eupolemus (Clem. Alex. *Strom.* i. 21). 3. Artapanus (Eus. *Præp. Ev.* ix. 18, 23, 27). 4. Cleodemus (Malchus) (Jos. *Ant.* i. 15). 5. Jason of Cyrene (2 Macc. ii. 23 ; Jos. *c. Ap.* i. 23). The Jewish poets were :—1. Ezekiel, a tragedy on the Exodus (Eus. *Præp. Ev.* ix. 28, 29). 2. Philo the Elder, poem on Abraham (*ibid.* ix. 21–24). 3. Theodotus, poem on the story of Dinah (*ibid.* ix. 22). (See Grätz, iii. 40, 438 ; Herzfeld, iii. 517.)

[5] See Nicolas, *Doctrines Religieuses des Juifs*, pp. 129–140.

was a noble motive, but a dangerous method. In the attempt to find the Hebrew truth in the Greek he was fired, as many a devout Jew may well have been fired, with the desire to claim in that glorious literature, now for the first time opening on the Oriental horizon, an affinity with that which was deemed most sacred in the Jewish faith. It was like the Renaissance of the same literature after the night of the Middle Ages. The Jewish priest, like the mediæval ecclesiastic, was ravished with the beauty of the new vision, and longed to make it his own. But the means by which he endeavoured to cross the gulf which parted them was

> A fatal and perfidious bark,
> Built in th' eclipse, and rigged with curses dark.

Under a delusion probably unconscious, he, like many Jewish and Christian theologians afterwards, persuaded himself that the identity between some of the most characteristic features of the two literatures sprang, not from the native likeness which exists between all things true and beautiful, but from the fact, as he alleged, that the one was borrowed from the other; that the sages and poets of Grecian antiquity had but plagiarised their best parts from Moses [1] or Solomon or Jeremiah. And then, with the facile descent of error, he, not alone of his age, but foremost in this special department, laboured to strengthen his cause by the deliberate falsification of Greek literature, sometimes by inventing whole passages, sometimes by interpolating occasional fragments, in which the ancient Gentile poets should be made to express the elevated sentiments of Hebrew monotheism. Of the venerable names that which lent itself most easily to this deception was Orpheus,[2] lost in the mists of mythology, yet still living by the natural pathos and the inherent wisdom of his story. He, it was alleged, had met Moses—the Greek Musæus—in Egypt, and hence the Orphic poems which contained so much of the Mosaic cosmogony. Deeply as the course of true philosophy and history was coloured and perverted by this double false-

Orpheus.

[1] Eus. *Præp. Ev.* vii. 14. [2] *Ibid.* xiii. 12.

hood, yet, as stated before, it contained within it the profound truth which in after times gradually faded away, to be revived only in our own age, that the comparison of the mythologies of different ages reveals to us the same Divinity, the same morality, 'in sundry times and in divers manners,' throughout all their various forms. And that beautiful legend which Aristobulus chose as representing their union—the figure of Orpheus taming the savage and bestial natures by the celestial harmony of his lyre—passed into the imagery of the first Christians to express almost without a figure the reconciliation of the Pagan to the Christian World, as was seen represented in the paintings of the Roman Catacombs, or in the Chapel of Alexander Severus.

Another name, which, if not Aristobulus himself, a contemporary or successor borrowed for the purpose of winning the favour, not only of the Greek, but of the now rising Roman world, was that of the Sibyls. Either under the seventh or the eighth Ptolemy there appeared at Alexandria the oldest of the Sibylline oracles, bearing the name of the Erythræan Sibyl, which, containing the history of the past and the dim forebodings of the future, imposed alike on the Greek, Jewish, and Christian world, and added almost another book to the Canon. When Thomas of Celano composed the grandest hymn of the Latin Church he did not scruple to place the Sibyl on a level with David; and when Michel Angelo adorned the roof of the Sixtine Chapel, the figures of the weird sisters of Pagan antiquity are as prominent as the seers of Israel and Judah. Their union was the result of the bold stroke of an Alexandrian Jew; but it kept alive, till the time when comparative theology claimed for the old Creeds of the world their just rights, the important truth which a more isolated theology overlooked, that those rights existed and must not be ignored.[1]

The Sibyls.

B.C. 165, or B.C. 124.

In like manner the wish to find the grace and freedom of

[1] The 2nd and 4th portions of the 3rd Sibylline book are the oldest parts of the collection and belong either to B.C. 165 (Alexandre, *Oracula Sibyllina*, ii. 320) or to B.C. 124 (Ewald, v. 360; *Abhandlung über die Sibylinische Bücher*, 10–15). They are quoted as genuine and authoritative by Josephus, Justin, and Clement.

Grecian literature in the Hebrew Scriptures was prompted by the natural desire to make the True Religion embrace all that was best in the ideas now for the first time revealed to Israel from beyond the sea. Here again Aristobulus embarked on a method of reconciliation, which, although in his hands, so far as we know, it rarely passed the limits of reasonable exposition, was destined to grow into disproportionate magnitude, and exercise a baneful influence over the theology of nearly two thousand years. He was the inventor of allegorical interpretation. For himself it was little if anything more than the sublime maxim that the spirit and not the letter is the essence of every great and good utterance; and that, especially in treating of the Divine and of the Unseen,[1] metaphors must not be pressed into facts nor rhetoric transformed into logic. This just principle, in the hands of his followers, was perverted into a system by which the historical, and therefore the real, meaning of the Sacred Books was made to give way to every fanciful meaning, however remote, which could be attached to the words, the numbers, or the statements contained in them. Aristobulus was the mental ancestor of Philo, and Philo,[2] though with a yet wider spiritual insight, was the immediate parent of that fantastic theology which to most of the Fathers and of the Schoolmen took the place of the reasonable and critical interpretation of all the Scriptures of the Old Testament and of much of the New. Yet still even here it must be borne in mind that the first origin of the allegorical interpretation lay in the sincere and laudable effort to extract from the coarse materials of primitive imagery the more elevated truths which often lay wrapt up in them, to draw out the ethical and the spiritual elements of the Bible, and to discard those which were temporary and accidental. In this sense, if Aristobulus is responsible for the extravagances of Philo, of Origen, or of Cocceius, he may also claim the glory of having first led the way in the road trodden long afterwards by his own country-

His endeavour to idealise the Hebrew Scriptures.

[1] Eus. *Præp. Ev.* viii. 10: especially in reference to the Hand of God, the Voice of God, the descent on Sinai.

[2] See Professor Jowett's Essay on Philo (*Commentary on St. Paul's Epistles*, vol. ii. 468–472).

men Maimonides and Spinoza, and by the Christian followers of the rational theology of Hooker, and Cudworth, and Coleridge, of Herder, Schleiermacher, and Hegel. He was the first to start what has been[1] called '*the* great religious problem—
'the discovery, if possible, of a test by which we may discern
'what are the eternal and irrepealable truths of the Bible, what
'the imaginative vesture, the framework, in which those truths
'are set forth in the Hebrew and even in the Christian
'Scriptures.'

[1] Milman's *Annals of St. Paul's*, 467.

LECTURE XLVIII.

JUDAS MACCABEUS. B.C. 175–163.

AUTHORITIES.

HISTORICAL.

(1) 1 Maccabees—Greek translation of a lost Hebrew original, which bore the name of Sarbath Sar Beni El, B.C. 120. It contains the history from the accession of Antiochus to the death of Simon.

2 Maccabees—Greek abridgment of a lost work of Jason of Cyrene, B.C. 160, in five books. B.C. 100–50. It contains the history from the accession of Antiochus to the death of Judas, with legendary additions.

3 Maccabees—Greek. No Latin Translation, and therefore in the Greek Bible, but not in the Roman, Lutheran, or English Bible. B.C. 50? It contains the account of the persecutions by Ptolemy Philopator.

4 Maccabees—Greek—wrongly ascribed to Josephus, but printed in his works. B.C. 4? It contains an amplification of 2 Macc. vi. 18, vii. 42.

5 Maccabees—A late work, certainly after A.D. 70—known only in Arabic and Syriac. It contains the history both of the Asmoneans and of Herod.

These five books were published in one English volume by Archdeacon Cotton, 1832.

(2) Josephus, *Ant.* xii. 5-11, *B. J.* i. 1, A.D. 71.

PROPHETIC AND POETICAL.

(1) Daniel—probably B.C. 167–164. (See Note on Lecture XLII.)
(2) Psalms lxxiv., lxxix.
(3) Psalter of Solomon (Fabricius, *Codex Pseud.* v. i., p. 914–999)—B.C. 167–162?
(4) Sibylline Books, iii. 2, 3, B.C. 165, or B.C. 124.

GENTILE.

(1) Diodorus Siculus, xxxiv. 4, xl. 1.
(2) Polybius, xxvi. 10, xxxi. 3, 4.
(3) Livy, xli. 21.

LECTURE XLVIII.

JUDAS MACCABÆUS.

THE close connexion between the Jews of Palestine and the Ptolemæan dynasty received a rude shock in the outrage of Ptolemy[1] Philopator ; and, as at the same time they had been on friendly terms with Antiochus III.,[2] from the time of his victory over the Egyptian forces by the source of the Jordan at Paneas, their allegiance was gradually transferred to the Syrian kingdom. At this point, therefore, we turn from Alexandria to Antioch, from Egypt to Syria.

Antioch.

In the northern extremity of Syria, where[3] 'the fourth 'river' of the Lebanon ranges, after having risen from its abundant fountain in the centre of those hills, bends through the rich plains to escape into the Mediterranean out of the pressure of the ridges of Mount Casius and Mount Amanus, the first Seleucus founded the city to which, after his father Antiochus, he gave the name of Antioch —a city destined to owe its chief celebrity not to its Grecian, but its Semitic surroundings, by a sacred association which in one sense will outshine Jerusalem itself.[4]

It would almost seem as if Alexandria and Antioch had divided between them the two characteristics of the old metropolis of the primeval world. If Alexandria represented the learning and commerce of Babylon—the nobler elements of ancient civilisation—Antioch represented its splendour, its luxury, its vanities. And, accordingly, whilst the relations of the Ptolemies to Israel are almost all pacific and beneficent,

[1] Raphall, i. 186. Jos. *Ant.* xii. 3, 3. See Lecture XLVII.

[2] His reign is briefly described in Dan. xi. 11–19.

[3] *Sinai and Palestine*, ii. xiv.

[4] Acts xi. 26.

the relations of the Seleucidæ towards it are almost all antagonistic and repulsive.

Sometimes the thought occurs whether it was possible for the Judaism of Palestine to have absorbed the genial and artistic side of the Grecian polytheism, as, in fact, the Judaism of Alexandria did to a large extent absorb the speculative and spiritual side of the Grecian Philosophy. An honoured name appears at the opening of the struggle on which we are now entering—Antigonus of Socho, who was regarded as the founder of some such attempt to combine a broader view of religion with the Judaic austerity handed down from Ezra. One saying of his alone remains, but it is full of significance and shows how a seed of a future faith had already borne fruit in that dark and troubled time. 'Be not 'like those servants who busy themselves to serve their masters 'in the hope of reward, but be like those servants who busy 'themselves to serve their masters without expectation of re-'compense, and the favour of Heaven be over you.'[1]

Antigonus of Socho. B.C. 198.

But whatever was the higher aspect of the Grecian party in Judæa was speedily cast into the shade by the deadly struggle which was now to be waged between the accursed 'kingdom of Javan,'[2] as the Syrian dynasty was called, and the stern patriots who saw in its policy the attempt to suppress all that had sanctified and ennobled their national existence. In this struggle two parties only were recognised by its historian, the 'Chasidim' or 'pious,'[3]—a name already familiar in the Psalter—and their opponents, to whom was given the opprobrious designation, also borrowed from the Psalter, 'sinners,' 'lawless,' 'impious.'[4]

Conflict of Hellenists and the Chasidim.

The aggression on the part of the Syrian kings had already begun in the reign of Seleucus IV., with the encouragement of the Hellenising party, for the moment headed by one of the mischievous clan[5] known as the sons of

B.C. 188.

[1] Ewald, v. 275; comp. Luke xvii. 10.

[2] Derenbourg, 56.

[3] ὅσιοι, εὐσεβεῖς, Psalms xxx. 5; xxxi. 24; xxxvii. 28; lxxix. 2; cxxxii. 9. It means 'kind,' and is, therefore, in this sense (like *pius* in Latin), attentive, as with filial piety, towards God. The Grecised form is 'Assidean.' 1 Macc. ii. 42; vii. 13; 2 Macc. xiv. 6.

[4] 1 Macc. i. 11; iii. 6, 8; vi. 21; vii. 5; ix. 23.

[5] See Lecture XLVII.

Tobias. The first attempt was on the Temple treasures, including the private deposits, which as in a bank had been laid up for the widows and orphans under the shelter of the sanctuary.[1] Then it was that occurred the scene portrayed in the liveliest colours in the traditions of the next century,[2] when Heliodorus the king's treasurer [3] came with an armed guard to seize it. It is a complete representation of what must have been the general aspect of a panic in Jerusalem. The Priests in their official costume are prostrate before the altar. The High Priest is in such 'an inward agony 'of mind that whoso had looked at his countenance and 'changing colour, it would have wounded his heart.' The Temple courts are crowded with supplicants; the matrons, with bare bosoms, running frantically through the street; the maidens, unable to break their seclusion, yet peering over walls, and through windows, and at every door to catch the news; the pitiless officer bent on discharging his mission. Then the scene changes. A horse with a terrible rider in golden armour dashes into the Temple precinct, and tramples Heliodorus under foot, whilst on either side stood two magnificent youths, who lash the prostrate intruder to the very verge of death, from which he is only rescued by the prayers of Onias. The story lives only in the legends of the time, and was passed over [4] alike by the contemporary and the later historians. But when Raffaelle wished to depict the triumph of Pope Julius II. over the enemies of the Pontificate he could find no fitter scene to adorn for ever the walls of the Vatican than that which represents the celestial champions, with the vigour of immortal youth, trampling on the prostrate robber.

Heliodorus.

Whatever may have been the actual incident thus enshrined, it was the natural prelude to the undoubted history which followed. It was reserved for the successor of Seleucus IV. to precipitate the crisis which had been long expected.

Antiochus IV. was one of those strange characters in whom

[1] 2 Macc. iii. 4.

[2] *Ibid.* iii. 15–21.

[3] The chief Syrian officer in Palestine was called the Tax-gatherer, ἄρχων τῆς φορολογίας. 1 Macc. i. 29; iii. 10; 2 Macc. v. 24. Jos. *Ant.* xii. 5, 5 (7, 1); Herzfeld, ii. 197.

[4] It is briefly touched in Dan. ix. 21.

an eccentricity touching insanity on the left and genius on the right combined with absolute power and lawless passion to produce a portentous result, thus bearing out the two names by which he was known—*Epiphanes*—'the Brilliant,'[1] and *Epimanes*, 'the Madman.' On the one hand, even through the terrible picture drawn by the Jewish historians, traits[2] of generosity and even kindness transpire. And in his splendid buildings,[3] his enlargement and almost creation of Antioch as a magnificent capital—his plans for joining it with the bay of Scanderoon and thus making it a maritime[4] emporium—his munificence throughout the Grecian world—his determination, however mischievous in its results, of consolidating a homogeneous Eastern Empire against the aggressions of the newly-rising Empire of the West—there is a grandeur of conception which corresponds to the contemporary Prophetic delineation of 'the king of an invin-'cible countenance, understanding dark sentences, and full of 'high swelling[5] words.' On the other hand, there was an extravagance, a littleness, in all his demeanour, which agrees with the unintelligible madman of the Gentile writers, 'the vile 'person' of the Hebrew poets and historians. They saw, instead of the godlike Alexander or the literary Ptolemies, a fantastic creature without dignity or self-control, caricaturing in a public masquerade the manners and dress of the august Roman magistrates, playing practical jokes in the public streets and baths of Antioch, startling a group of young revellers by bursting in upon them with pipe and horn; tumbling with the bathers on the slippery marble pavement,[6] as they ran to receive the shower of precious ointment which he had prepared for himself. The contradiction of the two sides of his character was wound up to its climax in the splendour of the procession which he organised at Daphne, in the most stately style,

Antiochus Epiphanes. B.C. 175.

[1] Niebuhr, *Lectures on Ancient History*, iii. 446. But the origin of the name seems to have been his sudden appearance from his Roman captivity (Appian, *De Rebus Syr* c. 45). 'The Apparition'—'like '*præsens* Deus;' see Mangey's notes on *Philo ad Caium*, 1039.

[2] 2 Macc. iv. 37; vii. 12, 24; comp. Diod. Sic. xxxiv. 1.

[3] Liv. xli. 21.

[4] 2 Macc. v. 21.

[5] Dan. xi. 36. See Ewald, v. 293; who sees this in the Rabbinical Æpystomus—'swelling mouth.'

[6] Diod. Sic. xxxi. 3, 4.

to outshine the most magnificent of the Roman triumphs, but in which he himself appeared riding in and out on a hack pony, playing the part of chief waiter,[1] mountebank, and jester.

It was a union of lofty policy and petty buffoonery, of high aspirations and small vexations, which reminds us of the attempts of Peter the Great to occidentalise Russia: as in the opposition of the old Muscovite party and of the Rascolniks we have a resemblance[2] of the determined antagonism of the 'Chasidim' to the Hellenisation of their race. But Peter's attempt was founded on a far-seeing principle—that of Antiochus on a short-sighted fancy. The resistance of the Russian Dissenters was the mere tenacity of ancient prejudice. The resistance of the Jewish patriots was the determination of a superior faith.

To bring into a uniform submission to himself and the Gods of Greece, amongst whom he claimed to be reckoned, the various creeds and usages which he found under his sway, became his fixed idea, fostered in part by his own personal vanity, partly by the desire to imitate the Roman policy, which he had studied whilst a hostage in Italy. In this design he was assisted by the Grecian party, of which we have spoken, in Palestine itself. The passion for Grecian connexions showed itself in the desire to establish a claim of kindred with the Lacedæmonians, amongst whom a Jewish colony seems to have been established,[3] and with whom a correspondence was alleged, as if Sparta too, in her fallen state, was eager to cultivate friendly relations with them. The names of the Macedonian[4] months, hitherto unknown, were adopted either beside or instead of those in the Hebrew or Chaldæan calendar. The fever of Grecian fashions manifested itself in the Grecian nomenclature by which the ancient Hebrew names were superseded or corrupted. We have already seen how the central Judaic settlement had been surrounded by a fringe of Grecian towns. We now encounter the same tendency

The Grecian party.

[1] Polyb. xxvi. 10.

[2] Lecture IX. on the Eastern Church.

[3] 1 Macc. xiv. 16–29: 2 Macc. v. 9; 1 Macc. xii. 5, 23; Jos. *Ant.* xiv. 10, 22. See Herzfeld, ii. 202, 216–219.

[4] Clinton's *Fasti Hellenici*, iii. 376.

in the heart of every Jewish family.[1] Jehoiakim becomes Alcimus; Solomon, from supposed analogy between the great Jewish and the great Gentile King, becomes Alexander; Salome, Alexandra; Onias, or Joseph, is transformed into Menelaus; Judas becomes Aristobulus; Mattathias, Antigonus; John or Jonathan, Hyrcanus or Jannæus;[2] Joshua sometimes becomes Jesus, sometimes the Argonautic hero Jason, sometimes (in the etymological sense of Champion) Alexander. The era observed by the Jews in their civil contracts,[3] even till A.D. 1040, was the era of the Seleucidæ, still observed by Eastern Christians as the era of Alexander, and adopted by the Syrian kingdom from October, B.C. 312—when the world seemed to begin again from the victory by which Seleucus wrested from Antigonus the ancient capital of Chaldæa, which even in its ruin was the prize of the East.

The High Priesthood, like the modern Patriarchates of the Eastern Church, was sold by the Government, in the needy condition of the Syrian finances, to the highest bidder, and amongst the various rivals Jason succeeded, adding to his bribes the attempt to win the favour of Antiochus by adopting the Gentile usages. It is startling to think of the sudden influx of Grecian manners into the very centre of Palestine. The modesty of the sons and daughters of Abraham was shocked by the establishment of the Greek palæstra, under the very citadel[4] of David, where, in defiance of some of the most sensitive feelings of their countrymen, the most active of the Jewish youths completely stripped themselves and ran, wrestled, leaped in the public sports, like the Grecian athletes, wearing only the broad-brimmed hat, in imitation of the headgear of the God Hermes, guardian[5] of the gymnastic festivals. Even the priests in the Temple caught the infection,[6] left their sacrificial duties unfinished, and ran down from the Temple court to take part in the spectacle as soon as they heard the signal for throwing

[1] So in the endeavour to approach the usages of Russia to Western Europe, Andrew is Henry, Demetrius is Edward, Basil is William, &c.

[2] Derenbourg, 53.

[3] Raphall, i. 98.

[4] ὑπὸ τὴν ἀκρόπολιν, 2 Macc. iv. 12.

[5] *Ibid.* ὑπὸ τὴν πέτασον. So in the Panathenaic frieze. So Suidas (*in voce* περιαγυρόμενοι), 'The athletes wore hats 'and sashes.'

[6] 2 Macc. iv. 14.

the quoit, which was to lead off the games. The sacred names of Jerusalem and Judæa were laid aside in favour of the title of 'citizens of Antioch.'[1] A deputation[2] of these would-be Greeks was sent by 'the hateful Jason' to a likeness[3] of the Olympian festival celebrated in the presence of the King at Tyre, in honour of the ancient sanctuary of Moloch[4] or Melcarth, now transformed into the Grecian Hercules; though here, with a curious scruple which withheld the pilgrims from going the whole length with their chief, they satisfied their consciences by spending the money[5] intended for the sacrifice in the building of the war-galleys of the Syrian navy. With these lax imitations of the Pagan worship, the corruptions of the Priesthood became more and more scandalous. Menelaus outbid Jason for the office. Their brother Onias took refuge from his violence in the sanctuary of Apollo at Daphne, near Antioch, and was thence dragged forth and killed, with a sacrilegious perfidy which shocked Jew and heathen alike, and called out almost the only sign of human feeling which the Jewish annalist allows to the Syrian King.[6] Onias himself, like a Becket or a Stanislaus, was transformed by a popular apotheosis into the celestial champion[7] of his nation; and a long-standing monument of the horror created by his murder was the rival temple at Heliopolis, built by his son Onias, who fled from Palestine on hearing of his father's death, as though there were no longer a home or a sanctuary for him in Palestine.[8] Jason himself, after a momentary victory over his brother Menelaus in Jerusalem, was expelled, and closed a wandering exile by dying amongst the Spartan mountains. 'And he that had cast out many unburied had none to

B.C. 172.

[1] Coins exist with Ἀντιοχέων τῶν ἐν Πτολέμαιδι, as though there was also such a corporation of 'Antiochians' at Ptolemais. Grimm on 2 Macc. iv. 18.

[2] θεωρός, the usual word for religious deputations, like that sent to Delos.

[3] 2 Macc. iv. 18. Five-yearly games like the Olympians.

[4] Comp. Herod. ii. 44. He was equally the God of Carthage. Compare Hannibal's vision, Liv. xxi. 22.

[5] 2 Macc. iv. 19, 20. 300 drachms. This seeming too small a sum, some MSS. read 3,000. But, as an Egyptian Jew, the writer reckons by the Alexandrian drachm, which was twice as much as the Athenian (Grimm).

[6] 2 Macc. iv. 34–37.

[7] *Ibid.* xv. 12. He is, perhaps, the Prince of the Covenant, Dan. xi. 22.

[8] See Lecture XLVII.

'mourn for him, nor any solemn funerals at all, nor sepulchre 'with his fathers.'[1]

In the midst of this dissolution of Jewish society it is no wonder that to the tension of imagination which such a time produces portents should have appeared—such as we find not only in the final siege of Jerusalem, but in the Gothic invasion of ancient Rome, in the plague of Papal Rome, in the fall of the Empire of Montezuma in Mexico, in the Plague of London, in the French war of 1870. It happened that 'through[2] all the 'city, for the space almost of forty days, there were seen horse- 'men galloping through the air, in cloth of gold, and armed 'with lances like a band of soldiers, and squadrons of cavalry in array, and charges, and encounters, and shaking of shields, 'and multitude of pikes, and drawing of swords, and glittering 'of golden ornaments, and harness of all sorts.' The prayer 'that this apparition might turn for good' was presently answered by the approach of the most startling catastrophe which the Jewish colony had experienced since its return from Babylon, and which yet, with a fine moral sense of a deserved Nemesis, the nobler spirits among them acknowledged to be the just retribution for their crimes.

It was after completing his conquest of Egypt that Antiochus, in pursuit at once of his political and religious ambition, seized upon Jerusalem. The terrified population fled before him. They were hewn down in the streets; they were pursued to the roofs of their houses.[3] But that which even more than this widespread massacre thrilled the city with consternation was the sight of the King, in all the pomp of royalty, led by the apostate[4] Menelaus into the sanctuary itself. It was believed by the Greek world that he reached the innermost recess and there found (as they imagined) the statue of the founder of the nation, the great lawgiver Moses, with the long flowing beard which tradition assigned to him,

Attack on Jerusalem.

[1] 2 Macc. v. 5–10.

[2] *Ibid.* v. 2–4. Compare Plutarch, *Marius*, c. 75; Humboldt, *Kosmos*, i. 145. Dean Milman (i. 461) compares with this the description of the Aurora Borealis in his own *Samor*, to which we may add the striking picture of a like phenomenon in Italy in Lord Lorne's *Guido and Lita*.

[3] 1 Macc. i. 20–27; 2 Macc. v. 11–16.

[4] Diod. Sic. xxxiv. 1; see Lecture IV.

and seated on the Egyptian ass, which from the Exodus down to the second century of our era the Gentile world regarded as the inseparable accompaniment of the Israelite. With characteristic rapacity he laid hands on the sacred furniture which the wealthy Babylonian Jews had contributed through the hands of Ezra—the golden altar of incense, the golden candlestick, the table of consecrated bread, and all the lesser ornaments and utensils. The golden candlestick, which was an object of especial interest from its containing the perpetual light, was traditionally believed to have fallen to the share of the renegade High Priest Menelaus.[1] The great deposits which had escaped the grasp of Heliodorus, and which, but for the national depravity, would, it was thought, have been again defended by celestial champions, were seized by the king himself.

Then came another sudden attack under Apollonius the tax-gatherer, successor of Heliodorus, who took occasion to attack them on their day of weekly rest, scattering them or dragging them off to the slave-market from the midst of their festivities.[2] It is a stratagem which occurs so often at this time as to lose its point, but which shows how rigidly since Nehemiah's time the observance of the Sabbath had set in. The rest, both of the seventh day and of the seventh year, had now become a fixed institution, guarded with the utmost tenacity, and carried into the most trivial and, at times,[3] impracticable details.

There was a short pause, during which consternation spread through the country. In every home there was desolation as if for a personal sorrow. The grief of the women was even more affecting than the indignant sorrow[4] of the men; and showed how completely they shared the misfortunes of their country. The Holy City was transformed into the likeness of a Grecian garrison. The walls that Nehemiah had built with so much care were dismantled; the houses in their neighbourhood were burnt; another massacre and another captivity

[1] See Derenbourg, 53.
[2] 1 Macc. i. 29-37; 2 Macc. vi. 24.
[3] 1 Macc. vi. 49; Jos. *Ant.* xiv. 10, 6; see Farrar's *Life of Christ*, i. 431, 432.
[4] 1 Macc. i. 26-27.

followed. The blood ran through the streets and even in the Temple courts. The hill on which had stood the Palace of David was fortified with a separate wall, took the name of 'The 'Height' ('Acra'), and was occupied with the Greek or Grecian party, the more irritating to those who still adhered to their country and their faith because it overlooked the Temple itself. It was regarded as a perpetual tempter, an adversary [1] or devil in stone, as a personal enemy. And over this fortress presided Philip, of rough Phrygian manners, and, more odious than all, the High Priest Menelaus, 'who bore a heavy hand over all 'the citizens, having a malicious hatred against his countrymen 'the Jews.'

But the worst was still to come. As soon as the entanglements of Antiochus in his Egyptian war allowed him a respite for his Syrian projects, he determined on carrying out his fixed plans of a rigid uniformity throughout the land—'that all should be one people and that everyone 'should hear his laws.' There was not a corner of Judæa which was not now invaded by the emissaries of Polytheism, rendered yet more hateful by the assistance received from renegade Israelites. A special commissioner was sent to preside over this forced conversion; it is uncertain whether from Antioch, or, as if to introduce the new worship from its most genuine seat, from Athens.[2] Under him, adopting the existing framework of the Jewish constitution for the purpose, 'over-'seers' (as we have already seen [3] expressed in the Greek original by the word which has passed into 'Bishops') were sent throughout the several districts both of Judæa and Samaria. The Divinity to whom the Holy Mount of Jerusalem was to be dedicated was the Father of Gods and men—Jupiter Olympius, in whose honour Antiochus had already begun at Athens the stately temple, even in his own age a wonder of the world,[4] of which the magnificent ruins still stand on the banks of the Ilissus. On Mount Gerizim—apparently because the Samari-

B.C. 168.

[1] 1 Macc. i. 36, διάβολον πονηρόν, the translation of the Hebrew word *Satan*. See Lecture XLV.

[2] 2 Macc. vi. 1. Ewald, v. 298.

[3] See Lecture XLIV.

[4] Polyb. xxvi. 10.

tans gave the new worship a more hospitable welcome—was planted the sanctuary of the patron of hospitality—Jupiter Xenius.[1]

The gay Dionysiac festival was also established, and the grave Israelites were compelled to join in the Bacchanalian processions with wreaths of ivy round their heads—sometimes with the mark of the [2] ivy-leaf branded into their skins. The King's own special deity was not of his Grecian ancestry, but one borrowed from Rome—whether the War-God Mars, Father of the Roman people, or Jupiter of the Capitoline Rock, to whom he began to build a splendid temple at Antioch—in either case, filling even the Jews, to whom all these divinities might have been thought equally repugnant, with a new thrill of sorrow, as indicating a disrespect even of the religions of his own race; and introducing a strange and terrible name. 'He 'regarded not the God of his fathers,[3] he honoured the God 'of forces, a God whom his fathers knew not'—a God whose temples were fortresses.

In every town and village of the country were erected altars at which the inhabitants were compelled to offer sacrifices in the heathen form, and on the King's birthday to join in the sacrificial feast. The two chief external marks of Judaism—the repose of the Sabbath and the proud badge of ancient civilisation, the rite of[4] circumcision—were strictly forbidden on pain of death. And at last the crowning misery of all, which sent a shock through the whole community, was the deliberate desecration of the Temple, not only by adapting it to Grecian worship, but by every species of outrage and dishonour, The great gates were burned. The name of the officer who had charge of setting fire to them was known and marked [5] out —Callisthenes. Its smooth and well-kept courts were left to be overgrown by rank vegetation, in the shelter of which, as in the groves of Daphne, the licentious rites of Antioch were carried on.[6]

[1] Jos. *Ant.* xii. v. 5, says 'Jupiter 'Hellenius.' But this, as the name of the local Jupiter worshipped at Ægina, seems less likely.

[2] 2 Macc. vi. 7; 3 Macc. ii. 29.

[3] Dan. xi. 38, 39.

[4] See Lectures I., XL.

[5] 2 Macc. viii. 33.

[6] *Ibid.* vi. 4; 1 Macc. iv. 38.

And now came the culminating horror. It[1] was the 23rd of the month Marchesvan (November) that the enclosure was broken between the outer and inner court; in after days the breaches were pointed out in thirteen places.[2] On the 15th of the next month (Chisleu—December) a small Grecian altar was planted on the huge platform of the altar of Zerubbabel in honour of the Olympian Jupiter. On the 25th the profanation was consummated by introducing a herd of swine and slaughtering them in the sacred precincts. One huge sow was chosen from the rest. Her blood was poured on the altar before the Temple and on the Holy of Holies within. A mess of broth was prepared from the flesh, and sprinkled on the copies of the Law.[3] This was the 'abomination of desolation'—the horror which made the whole place a desert. From that moment the daily offerings ceased, the perpetual light of the great candlestick was[4] extinguished—the faithful Israelites fled from the precincts. When in the last great pollution of Jerusalem under the Romans, a like desecration was attempted, no other words could be found more solemn than those already used in regard to the Syrian distress.[5] But this persecution was not confined to the extirpation of the national worship. Every Jew was constrained to conform to the new system. The children were no longer to receive the initiatory right of circumcision. The swine's flesh was forced into the mouths of the reluctant worshippers, who were compelled to offer the unclean animal on altars erected at every door and in every street. The books of the Law, multiplied and treasured with so much care from the days of Ezra, were burnt. Many assisted and bowed before the oppressor. One example was long held in horror, which shows that there were some who welcomed the intrusion with delight. There was a daughter of the priestly order of Bilgah, Miriam, who had married a Syrian officer, and with him entered the Temple, and, as they approached the altar, she struck the altar

The Abomination of Desolation.

December, B.C. 168.

[1] For these dates see Derenbourg, 60-64; Grätz, iii. 419-420. [2] Dan. ix. 27

[3] Diod. Sic. xxxiv. 1; Jos. *Ant.* xii. 5, §4.

[4] Diod. Sic. xxxiv. 1. Probably this took place in the earlier outrages of 1 Macc. i. 21.

[5] 1 Macc. i. 54; Dan. ix. 27; xii. 11; Matt. xxiv. 15; Mark xiii. 14.

with her shoe, exclaiming, 'Thou insatiable wolf, how much 'longer art thou to consume the wealth of Israel, though thou 'canst not help them in their hour of need?' It was the remembrance of the rapacity of her family,[1] so it was said, that drove her into this fierce reaction. When the worship was restored, the disgrace which she had brought on the order was perpetuated, and they alone of the priestly courses had no separate store-room, or separate rings for their victims. But others dared the worst rather than submit. Some concealed themselves in the huge caverns in the neighbouring hills, and were there suffocated by fires lighted at the mouth. Two mothers were hanged on the wall, with their dead babes at their breasts, whom they had circumcised. A venerable scribe[2] of ninety years of age, Eleazar, steadily refused to retain the hated swine's flesh in his mouth; stripped of his clothes, but, as the latest version finely[3] expresses it, wrapped in the dignity of old age and piety, like a fine athlete in the Grecian games, he walked boldly to the[4] rack, on which he was scourged to death. 'I will[5] show myself such an one 'as mine age requireth, and leave a notable example to such as 'be young to die willingly and courageously for the honourable 'and holy laws.' Most memorable was the slow torture by which the mother and her seven sons expired. It was told in a narrative couched, like the martyrologies of Christian times, in exaggerated[6] language, and disfiguring the noble protestations of the sufferers by the invocations of curses on the persecutors, but still forcibly expressing the living testimony of conscience against the interference of power, the triumph of the spirit over outward suffering. The very implements of torture are the same which have lived on through all the centuries in which theological hatred and insane cruelty have overborne the

The Persecution.

[1] Raphall, i. 232.

[2] 'A lawyer,' νομικός, 4 Macc. v. 4.

[3] 4 Macc. vi. 2.

[4] See Grimm on 2 Macc. vi. 28.

[5] 2 Macc. vi. 27, 28. Compare the fine speech of an aged theologian of our time, who sacrificed, not life, but office and peace, rather than accept an historical falsehood. 'I am an old man, and I cannot go into the presence of God with a lie 'in my right hand.'

[6] Compare the savage remarks on the scent of the roasted flesh with the jests of St. Laurence, and the introduction of Antiochus on the scene (against all probability, see Grimm on 2 Macc. vi. 2, 12, 18, ii. p. 130), with the appearance of the Roman Emperors in all Christian martyrologies.

natural affections of the human heart. The rack, the wheel, the scourge, the flame, have been handed on from Antiochus to Diocletian, to the Council of Constance, to Philip II., to Calvin, to Louis XIV.

These are the first of the noble army of martyrs to whom history has given a voice. 'Vixere fortes ante Agamemnona.' Those who were slain by Jezebel or Manasseh may have nourished in their deaths a courage as high and a faith as firm. But they passed to their reward in silence. In the earlier account even of those who fell under the tyranny of Antiochus, their end [1] is described with a severe brevity, which for solemn impressiveness leaves nothing to be desired, 'So then they 'died.' But the later account places in the mouths of the sufferers the words destined to animate the long succession of the victims of religious intolerance, whether heathen against Christian, Christian against Jew, Catholic against Protestant, Protestant against Protestant. 'What wouldst thou ask or learn? 'We are ready to die rather than transgress the laws of our 'fathers. It is manifest unto the Lord that hath the holy 'knowledge that whereas I might have been delivered from 'death, I now endure grievous pains in body, but in soul I am 'well content to suffer these things because I fear Him.' In this sense Eleazar was justly honoured in the ancient Church as the Proto-Martyr. The seven brothers were, by a bold fiction of ecclesiastical law, entitled 'Christian Martyrs'—*Christianum nomen, postea divulgatum, factis antecesserunt.*[2]

The Maccabæan Psalms.

In this terrible crisis it is not surprising that whatever sparks of the spirit of the Psalmist and the Prophet still lingered should once more have been evoked from the depths of the national heart. There are two Psalms at least—the 74th and the 79th—which can hardly be the expressions of any period but [3] this. They describe with

[1] 1 Macc. i. 63.

[2] Grimm on 2 Macc. p. 133. The traditional scene of their death was Antioch, where a Basilica was erected in their honour. Their relics (?) are now exhibited in Rome, and their day is celebrated on August 1. Their traditional names are, Maccabæus, Oberus, Machiri, Judas, Ahaz, Jacob; or else Ablis, Gurias, Antonius, Isleazar, Marcellus; their mother's name, Salome; their father's, Archippus or Maccabæus.

[3] It is possible that these two Psalms may belong to the Chaldæan capture, but

passionate grief the details of the profanation of the sanctuary, the gates in flames, the savage soldiers hewing down the delicate carved work, with axe and hatchet, like woodmen in a forest, the roar of the irreverent multitude, the erection of the heathen emblems ; they sigh over the indignity of the corpses slain in the successive massacres, left outside of the walls of the city to be devoured by vulture and jackal—they look in vain for a Prophet to arise—they console themselves with the recollection of the overthrow of the huge monsters of the earlier empires, and with the hope that this crisis will pass in like manner.

The Psalter of Solomon.

Another burst [1] of anguish was in the eighteen Psalms ascribed to Solomon, but probably of this epoch. In them we see the battering-ram beating down the walls, the proud heathens stalking through the Temple courts, not so much as taking off their [2] shoes ; we hear the bitter curses on those who endeavour to please men, and who dissemble their [3] own convictions ; we see those who frequented the synagogues wandering in the deserts ; [4] we watch the expectation of some anointed [5] of the Lord who should, like David, deliver them from their enemies.

The Book of Daniel.

But there was a yet more important addition to the sacred literature of this period. Even those who would place the composition of the Book of Daniel at an earlier time will not deny that this was the exact date—to be measured almost by the year and the month—when as a whole or piecemeal it made its appearance and significance felt throughout the suffering nation. 'Antiochus was on his way 'northward from Egypt. The [6] complete suppression of the 'Temple sacrifices might then have lasted a twelvemonth, and

the arguments are strongly in favour of the Maccabæan time. 1. The profanation rather than the destruction is insisted upon, lxxiv. 3. 2. The synagogues are mentioned, lxxiv. 8. 3. The details exactly coincide with the description in the Books of Maccabees. Compare Psalm lxxiv. 7 ; 1 Macc. iv. 38 ; 2 Macc. viii. 33 ; i. 8. Psalm lxxix. 2, 3 ; 1 Macc. i. 44 ; vii. 16 ; 2 Macc. v. 12, 13. Psalm lxxix. 9 ; 1 Macc. ix. 46 ; ix. 47 ; xiv. 61.

[1] The date of the Psalter of Solomon is variously given by modern critics ; but this is the earliest period to which it can be assigned.

[2] Comp. Psalms of Solomon, in Fabricius, *Cod. Pseudepig.* Ps. ii. 1, 2.

[3] *Ibid.* iii. 21, 22.

[4] *Ibid.* xvi. 19.

[5] *Ibid.* xviii. 6–10.

[6] Ewald, v. 303.

'everything had reached that state of extreme tension when the 'ancient religion upon its sacred soil must either disappear 'from view completely for long ages, or must rise in fresh 'strength and outward power against enemies thus im-'moderately embittered. It was at this crisis, in the sultry heat 'of an age thus frightfully oppressive, that this book appeared 'with its sword-edge utterance, its piercing exhortation to 'endure in face of the despot, and its promise, full of Divine 'joy, of near and sure salvation. No dew of heaven could fall 'with more refreshing coolness on the parched ground, no 'spark from above alight with a more kindling power on the 'surface so long heated with a hidden glow. With winged 'brevity the book gives a complete survey of the history of the 'kingdom of God upon earth, showing the relations which it 'had hitherto sustained in Israel to the successive great heathen 'empires of the Chaldæans, Medo-Persians, and Greeks—in a 'word, towards the heathenism which ruled the world; and 'with the finest perception it describes the nature and indi-'vidual career of Antiochus Epiphanes and his immediate pre-'decessors so far as was possible in view of the great events 'which had just occurred. Rarely does it happen[1] that a book 'appears as this did, in the very crisis of the times, and in a 'form most suited to such an age, artificially reserved, close and 'severe, and yet shedding so clear a light through obscurity, 'and so marvellously captivating. It was natural that it should 'soon achieve a success entirely corresponding to its inner 'truth and glory. And so, for the last time in the literature of 'the Old Testament, we have in this book an example of a 'work which, having sprung from the deepest necessities of the 'noblest impulses of the age, can render to that age the purest 'service; and which by the development of events immediately 'after, receives with such power the stamp of Divine witness 'that it subsequently attains imperishable sanctity.'

Whether the narrative of the faithful Israelites in the court of Nebuchadnezzar and of Darius had been handed down from the Exile, or whether they were then produced for the first time,

[1] Ewald, v. 305.

the practical result must have been the same. As the seven sons are the first examples of the heroic testimony of martyrs' words, so the narrative of the Three Children in the Fire and of Daniel in the Lions' Den is the first glorification, the first canonisation, so to speak, of the martyr spirit. And accordingly at this time we first find them cited as encouragements and consolations.[1]

'At this stage[2] of its history, when Israel rises once more, 'even though but for a brief period, to the pure elevation of its 'noblest days, it was fitting that the first beginning of 'a serious resistance should come about involuntarily, 'as it were by a higher necessity, almost without the 'co-operation of human self-will and human passion; still less 'with any aid of human calculation, yet, by the force of human 'courage and skill and perseverance, working as if without any 'Divine interposition.' The Psalter of Solomon had expressed its hope that an anointed or priestly hero[3] should arise to save the people. The expectation of Daniel was that, after the monster forms of Empires, tearing and rending each other to pieces, there should rise a Deliverer in human form, 'A son of 'man,'[4] with all the gentle and noble qualities of man. They were not deceived. Such an one was at hand.

The Asmonean family.

There was a priestly family known by the unusual name[5] of its chief of four generations back, Chasmon or *Asmon*, 'The 'Magnate.' Its present head was advanced in years, Mattathias, with five sons in the prime of life. At the beginning of the persecution the whole family retired from Jerusalem to their country residence in the town of Modin or Modein, on the slope of the hills which descend from the passes of Judæa into the plains of Philistia or Sharon. 'Who can encounter the sun at mid-'summer? Everyone escapes and seeks a shelter. So everyone

[1] 1 Macc. ii. 59, 60. The earliest quotation from Daniel.

[2] Ewald, v. 306.

[3] Psalms of Solomon vi. 1 2; xvii. 23 24; xviii. 8, 9.

[4] Dan. vii. 14. (Heb.) See Note at end of this Lecture.

[5] It only occurs in Psalm lxviii. 32, 'fat' —with large means and retinue. Herzfeld, ii. 264, renders it 'a temperer of steel,' so as to be the equivalent of *Maccabee*, and both then would be like the English *Smith* or *Marshall* (Marechal), and as the Cabiric demigods and Scandinavian heroes were 'blacksmiths.' Hitzig (426) derives the names from a town in the south of Judæa, Joshua xv. 27, and connects the origin of the family with Engedi and the Essenes.

'fled from the Grecian kingdom and its armies. Only the Priest 'Mattathias and his sons remained faithful to God, and the 'armies of Antiochus were dispersed before them, and were ex-'terminated.'[1] Such is almost the sole notice in the later Talmudic literature of this return of the heroic age of Israel. But the vacancy is amply filled by the treble account which the three generations immediately near the time supplied.

The war of independence began, as often, from a special incident. At Modin, as elsewhere through Palestine, an altar had been erected on which the inhabitants were expected to join in the Greek sacrifices. Mattathias, who had himself indignantly refused to take part, was so enraged at the sight of the compliance of one of his countrymen that 'his reins 'trembled, neither could he forbear to show his anger accord-'ing to[2] judgment.' Both sacrificer and royal officer fell victims to this sudden outburst of indignation, which the historian compares to that of the ancient Phinehas. The die was cast. It was like the story of Wat Tyler in Kent, or of Tell in Switzerland, or of the Sicilian Vespers. Mattathias raised his war-cry of 'Zeal,' and of 'the Covenant,' and dashed with his whole family into the adjacent mountains. There they herded like wild animals in the limestone caverns, protected against the weather by the rough clothing of the Syrian peasants, taken off the backs of the white sheep or black goats on which they fed,[3] together with such roots and vegetables as they could find, so as to avoid the chance of the polluted food of the heathen.

Whenever they encountered a heathen altar they destroyed it. Whenever they found a neglected child they circumcised it. Their spirit rose with the emergency. 'The venerable leader 'felt his soul lifted by the higher need above the minute 'precepts of the Scribes,' and determined to break the sabbatical repose which had so often exposed them to ruin. 'If we all do as our brethren have done, and fight not for our 'lives and laws against the heathen, they will now quickly root

[1] Derenbourg, p. 57.

[2] Or 'breathing fury through his nos-'trils,' 1 Macc. ii. 24.

[3] 2 Macc. v. 27; vi. 11; x. 6, and (for this must be the chief reference) Heb. xi. 37. Comp. Psalt. Sol. xviii. 19.

'us out of the earth. Whosoever shall come to make battle 'with us on the Sabbath day, we will fight against him; neither 'will we all die as our brethren that were murdered.'[1] For a moment even the rigid party of 'the Chasidim' threw in their lot with the loftier patriotism of Mattathias; and when he sank under the weight of age and care, in the first year of the revolt, the whole nation joined in interring him in the ancestral tomb at Modin, which henceforth became a sacred place, to which child after child of that renowned family was borne. 'If it was 'a stroke of rare fortune that the insurrection thus broke out 'undesignedly and was set on foot by such a blameless character, 'it was no less fortunate that he left behind him a heroic band of 'five sons, who were ready to carry on the contest without an 'instant's delay. Seldom has the world seen an instance of five 'brothers animated by the same spirit, and without mutual 'jealousy sacrificing themselves for the same cause, of whom 'one only survived another in order to carry it on, if possible, 'with more zeal and success, while not one had anything in 'view but the great object for which his father had fallen.'[2]

Each of the five sons succeeded in turn to the chieftainship of the family, and each had a separate surname to distinguish him from the many who bore the like names amongst the Jewish people. The eldest, John, was 'the Holy' or 'the 'Lucky;' the second, Simon,[3] was 'the Burst of Spring,' or 'the Jewel;' the fourth, Eleazar,[4] was 'the Beast-sticker;' the fifth, Jonathan, was 'the Cunning.' But of all these surnames, whether given in their lifetimes or afterwards from their exploits, the only one which has survived to later times and covered the whole clan with glory, is that of the third brother Judas, who, like Charles the 'Martel' of the Moors, and Edward the 'Malleus Scotorum,' received the name of the 'Hammer,' *Maccab*[5]—possibly connected with the name of the ancestor of

[1] 1 Macc. ii. 41, 42.

[2] Ewald, v. 308.

[3] Grimm, ii. 266, on 1 Macc. ii. 1-5.

[4] One tradition represented the origin of the insurrection to have been an outrage on Eleazar's wife, Hannah, the beautiful daughter of John. On their wedding-day, the seventeenth of the month Elul, she was seized by a Syrian officer. The bridegroom killed him on the spot (Raphall, i. 241). May it not have been from this that Eleazar's surname was first derived?

[5] This derivation of *Maccabi* is the one adopted by Ewald, Herzfeld, and Hitzig

the family *Asmon*—possibly also commemorated in the original Hebrew name of the book which described his fame—'The 'Avenging Rod of the Prince of the Sons of God.'[1]

Judas Maccabæus.

He it was whom Mattathias in his last moments recommended as the military leader—'as mighty and strong from his 'youth up. Let him be your captain and fight the 'battle of the people.' At once he took the vacant place. At once he became the Jewish ideal of 'The Happy 'Warrior.' There was 'a cheerfulness' diffused through the whole army when he appeared. His countrymen delighted to remember the stately appearance, as of an ancient giant, when he fastened on his breast-plate, or tightened his military sash around him, or waved his protecting sword—a sword itself renowned, as we shall see, both in history and legend—over the camp of his faithful followers. They listened with delight for the loud cheer, the roar as of a young lion—the race not yet extinct in the Jordan valley[2]—with which he scented out the Israelite renegades, chasing them into their recesses, and smoking or burning them out. They exulted in his victory over the three, 'the many,' kings. But the lasting honour which they pathetically regarded as the climax of all was that with a true chivalry 'he received such as were ready to perish.'[3]

B.C. 166. Battle of Samaria.

Three decisive victories in the first two years of the campaign secured his fame and his success. The first was against the Syrian general Apollonius, apparently near Samaria. The trophy which Judas retained of the battle was the sword of the distinguished general, which he carried, as David did that of the Philistine giant, to the end of his life.[4] The second was in the mountains near his native place, and on the spot already ennobled by the overthrow of the Canaanite kings by Joshua in the Pass of Bethhoron.

Battle of Bethhoron.

Another, which rests on no authority, is that it is formed from the initials of the Hebrew words, *Who is like unto thee, Jehovah?* Another is that of Dr. Curtiss (Leipsic), to the effect that the original spelling of the word is *Machabee*, as in Jerome (*Prolog. Galeat.* p. xxviii.), and that, if so, it is derived from *chabah*, 'to 'extinguish,' and that it was applied to Judas as 'the extinguisher' of the Pagan worship.

[1] This seems the most probable explanation (Ewald, v. 463) of '*Sarbath sar Bene* '*El*,' as given by Origen in Eus. *E.H.* vi. 25.

[2] 1 Macc. iii. 4.

[3] *Ibid.* iii. 9.

[4] *Ibid.* iii. 12.

The third and most decisive struggle brings before us in a lively form the various elements of the war. The King was absent on an expedition into Persia, but no less than three generals, Ptolemy, Nicanor, and Gorgias, are mentioned by name under Lysias, the Governor of the whole Syrian province, and the young Antiochus, the heir of the throne. Their head-quarters were at Emmaus, 'the 'hot baths' in the Philistine plain; and the interest of the merchants in the seaport towns of Philistia was engaged by the hope of the sale of the Israelite insurgents for slaves. In this crisis Judas led his scanty host over the mountains to the ridge of Mizpeh, the spot where Alexander had met Jaddua, where, after the Chaldæan capture of Jerusalem, the pilgrims had come to wail over the holy city. It was a mournful scene. They could see from that high, rocky platform the deserted streets, the walls and gates closed as if of a besieged town, the silent [1] precincts of the Temple, the Greek garrison in the fortress. Before that distant presence of the holy place, to which they could gain no nearer access, the mourners come wrapt in tatters of black hair-cloth, with ashes on their heads. They spread out the copies of the Law, on which the Greeks had painted in mockery the pictures of heathen deities. They waved the sacerdotal vestments, for which there was now no use. They showed the animals and the vegetables due for firstfruits and tithes. They passed in long procession the Nazarites [2] with their flowing tresses, who were unable to dedicate themselves in the sanctuary. And at the close of this sorrowful ceremony there was a blast of trumpets, and the army was sifted of its timid or pre-engaged members. To the gallant remainder Judas addressed his stirring harangue. He reminded them of their ancient and their recent deliverances amongst those same hills and vales—in ancient days of the overthrow of Sennacherib—in recent days of the battle in which the comparative prowess of the Israelite and the Macedonian troops was tested by an encounter with the Celtic invaders of Asia, in which the Jews turned the fortunes of the day when the Greeks fled. The

The Battle of Emmaus.

1 Macc. iii. 45.

[2] *Ibid.* iii. 46-49.

army was placed in four parts under himself and his three brothers Simon, John, and Jonathan, whilst the fifth, Eleazar, was commissioned to recite 'the Holy Book' and to proclaim[1] his own name as the watchword—Eleazar, 'the help of God.' After these preparations, Judas descended from the hills by night, and, leaving his empty camp as a prey to Gorgias, the commander of the garrison at Jerusalem, suddenly attacked the forces of Nicanor at Emmaus. Once more was heard the well-known trumpet-blast of the Israelite host, and a complete rout followed. Nothing could stand the enthusiastic ardour of the insurgents, slightly armed as they were. It was a Friday afternoon, and Judas gave the command to halt from pursuing the flying enemy. From the ridge of the mountain which overlooked the plain, the Grecian army[2] saw the columns of smoke rising from the plains, which announced that their countrymen's camp had been stormed. The Sabbath, on whose eve the battle closed, had now set in; and as the gorgeous spoils of gold, and silver, and blue silk, and Tyrian purple were spread out, they sang the hundred and thirty-sixth Psalm—the national anthem, it may be called, of the Jewish[3] race, which enumerates the examples of the never-ending goodness of God. It would hardly have been in keeping with the national character if this day had passed without some terrible vengeance. One of the subordinate officers[4] was caught and slain. Callisthenes, who had set fire[5] to the gateways of the Temple, they forced into a village hut and there burned him alive.

B.C. 165. Battle of Beth-zur.

Yet another victory was needed to secure their entrance into Jerusalem. It was won in the course of the next year over Lysias himself, in the immediate vicinity of the capital, at Beth-zur—'the House of the Rock'—a fort which commanded the Idumæan border, possibly represented by the lonely tower which now overhangs the stony passes on the way to Hebron. From that moment they were

[1] 2 Macc. viii. 23.

[2] 1 Macc. iv. 20.

[3] Compare 1 Chron. xvi. 41; 2 Chron. xx. 21; Jer. xxxiii. 11; Song of the Three Children, 67; Psalms cvi. 1; cvii. 1, cxviii. 1.

[4] φυλάρχης, 'an officer of the tribes,' not (as in A. V.) Philarches. 2 Macc. viii. 32.

[5] 2 Macc. viii. 33.

masters of Jerusalem. The desolation, which before could only be seen from the height of Mizpeh, they now were able to approach without impediment. The Greek garrison was still in the fortress, but the Temple was left open. They entered, and found the scene of havoc which the Syrian occupation had left. The corridors of the Priests' chambers which encircled the Temple were torn down; the gates were in ashes, the altar was disfigured, and the whole platform was overgrown as if with a mountain jungle or forest glade.[1] It was a heart-rending spectacle. Their first impulse was to cast themselves headlong on the pavement, and blow the loud horns which accompanied all mournful as well as all joyous occasions —the tocsin as well as the chimes of the nation. Then, whilst the foreign garrison was kept at bay, the warriors first began the elaborate process of cleansing the polluted place. Out of the sacerdotal tribe those were chosen who had not been compromised with the Greeks. The first object was to clear away every particle which had been touched by the unclean animals. On the 22nd of Marchesvan they removed the portable altar which had been erected. On the 3rd of Chisleu they removed the smaller altars from the court in front of the Temple, and the various Pagan statues.[2] With the utmost care they pulled down, as it would seem, the great platform of the altar itself, from the dread lest its stones should have been polluted. But, with the scrupulosity which marked the period, they considered that stones once consecrated could never be entirely desecrated, and accordingly hid them away in a corner of the Temple (it was believed in one of the four closets of the fireroom of the Priest[3] at the north-west corner), there to remain till[4] the Prophet—it may be Elijah, the solver of riddles,—should come and tell what was to be done with them. How many stones of spiritual or intellectual edifices excite a like perplexed fear lest they have been so misused that they cannot be employed again —at least till some prophet comes to tell us how and when!

The Dedication.

[1] 1 Macc. iv. 38.

[2] 2 Macc. x. 2, 3. *Sigura*, grate. *Simoth*=σημεῖα. Derenbourg, 62.

[3] Middoth, Mishna iv. 46.

[4] 1 Macc. iv. 46.

For the interior of the Temple everything had to be furnished afresh,—vessels, and candlesticks, and tables, and curtains, and incense altar. At last all was completed, and on the 25th of Chisleu, the same day that three years before the profanation had occurred, the Temple was re-dedicated. It was the very[1] time, either predicted or commemorated in the Book of Daniel. The three years and a half from the time of the first beginning of the sacrilege was over, and the rebound of the national sentiment was in proportion. 'It was the feast of the dedication 'and it was winter,' but the depth of the winter could not restrain the burst of joy. From the first dawn of that day for the whole following week there were songs of joy sung with cymbals and harps. In the Psalms ascribed to Solomon there are exulting strains which echo the words of the Evangelical Prophet and welcome the return into Jerusalem.[2] The smoke once more went up from the altar; the gates and even the priestly chambers were fumigated. The building itself was studded with golden crowns and shields, in imitation of the golden shields which in the first Temple had[3] adorned the porch. What most lived in the recollection of the time was that the perpetual light blazed again. The golden candlestick was no longer to be had. Its place was taken by an iron chandelier cased in wood. But this sufficed.[4] It was a solemn moment when the sacred fire was once again kindled on the new altar, and from it the flame communicated to the rest of the building. As in the modern ceremony of the 'Sacred Fire' in the Church of the Holy Sepulchre, so this incident was wrapt in mystery[5] and legend. The simple historical account is that they procured the light by striking the fresh unpolluted stones against each other. But later representations, going back to the like

[1] Dan. vii. 25; ix. 24–27; xii. 6, 7: Jos. *B. J.* i. 1. 1; Ewald (v. 305) and Herzfeld (ii. 416) suppose the Book of Daniel to have appeared in B.C. 167, thus about three years before the coincidence of the time had been realised. If so, it was a prediction which, in the hands of a hero like Maccabæus, tended no doubt to fulfil itself.

[2] Psalms of Solomon xi. 2, 3, 7.

[3] Shields (probably in imitation of the Temple) were hung up in the Alexandrian synagogues (Philo *ad Caium*, 994).

[4] Derenbourg, 54. It is possible that this was the origin of the name 'Judas 'light' as applied to the central light in the candelabrum, or ancient rood-screen. (See the Rev. C. B. Pearson, *A Lost Chapter in the History of Bath*, p. 11.)

[5] *Ibid.* 62.

events of Nehemiah's life, imagined some preternatural origin of the fire itself. It was further supposed that one unpolluted cruse was found which furnished the oil for the lighting of the Temple during the whole week of the festival; in remembrance of which every private house was illuminated, beginning, according to one usage, with eight candles, and decreasing as the week went on; according to the other usage, beginning with one and advancing to eight. Partly, no doubt, from these traditions, or (as Josephus thinks) from the returning joy of the whole nation, the festival in after days bore the name of the 'Feast of Lights.' This would receive yet a fuller significance in connexion with another aspect of this great day. Though latest of all the Jewish festivals, it took rank at once with the earlier holy days. It won for itself a sanctity which neither the dedication of Solomon nor of Zerubbabel[1] had acquired. Both of these consecrations had been arranged to coincide with the great autumnal Feast of the Tabernacles, the most festive of the Jewish solemnities. That season had already passed while the patriots were hiding in the mountains; and, therefore, if celebrated at all, had been shorn of its general gaiety, or defiled by an attempted combination with the Bacchanalian[2] festival, to which its peculiarities lent themselves. Now, however, it was determined to make this new solemnity a repetition, as it were, of the Feast of Tabernacles.[3] It was called in after days 'The 'Tabernacle Feast of the Winter;' and on this, its first occasion, there were blended with it the usual processions of that gay autumnal holiday, brandishing their woven branches of the palm,[4] and other trees whose evergreen foliage cheered the dull aspect of a Syrian December. And we can hardly doubt that they would, in accordance with the name of the 'Feast of 'Lights,' add to its celebration that further characteristic of the Feast of Tabernacles—the illumination of the whole precincts of the Temple by two great chandeliers placed in the court, by the light of which festive dances were kept up all through the night.[5]

[1] Edersheim, *The Temple*, 294.

[2] Plutarch (*Quæst. Conv.* v. 6, 2) dwells on the thyrsi, the gilt kidskin of the High Priest, the bells and the trumpets, as signs of identity. Compare Tac. *Hist.* v.

[3] 2 Macc. vi. 7.

[4] *Ibid.* x. 5.

[5] See Wetstein on John viii. 12.

There was an additional propriety in the transference of the natural festival of the vintage to this new feast because it coincided with the natural solemnity of welcoming the first light kindled in the new year. The 25th of December was at Tyre, as at Rome in after times, celebrated as the birthday of the Sun, the Hercules, the Melcarth of the Phœnician theology, dying on his funeral pyre, and reviving, phœnix-like, from his own ashes.[1] It was the revival—the renewal—the Encænia of man and of nature.

The Temple was the kernel of Judæa, and having won that, the Maccabæans might be said to have won everything. Still it was surrounded by a circle of enemies. Close at hand was the fortress occupied by the Syrian garrison. Against this Judas took the precaution[2]—apparently for the first time in Jewish history—of surrounding the whole of the Temple mount with high walls and strong towers, which remained as a permanent feature of the place. The two hostile parties stood entrenched in their respective positions, without mutual interference, like the rival factions in Jerusalem during the siege of Titus, or in Paris during its great insurrections.

B.C. 164. Campaign against Edom.

But on the further circumference there were three distinct sources of alarm. On the south was Edom, whose territory now reached within a few miles of Jerusalem. On the east were the malignant tribes of Ammon and Moab. And on the north and west was that fringe of Grecian colonies which had been established chiefly in the ancient Canaanite or Philistine cities, by the Ptolemæan or Syrian kings. The year following on the dedication of the Temple was entirely occupied with repelling the intrusion of these hereditary enemies. The first effort of Judas was in the south against the old hereditary foe, the race of Esau. On the frontier of that territory was the craggy fortress commanding the pass and, from its situation called the House of the Rock (Beth-zur), already contested in the battle with Lysias. This was occupied by Judas as an outpost against Edom, and from this he attacked the whole of the hostile race. Now, if ever, began to be fulfilled the hope expressed in the bitterness of the

[1] Raoul Rochette (*Mémoires de l'Académie*, xvii. Part II., p. 25); Ewald, v. 312.
[2] 1 Macc. iv. 60.

Babylonian Exile, that a conqueror should return from those hated fastnesses, wading knee-deep in the blood[1] of Edom, and with his garments stained as if from the red winepress of the battle-fields of Bozra. From their entrenchments at the head or foot of the Pass of Akrabbim he swept eastward and drove a tribe, terrible then, unnamed before or since, 'the children of 'Bean,' into their 'towers' or 'peels,' which, in the savage spirit of Jewish retaliation, he burned with all their occupants; and thus, still pressing onwards, in skirmish after skirmish routed the Ammonites, under their Greek commander Timotheus, and returned in triumph. But the campaign was only half completed. The widespread magic of the name Judas is wonderfully attested by the entreaties for succour which pursued him into his[2] brief repose at Jerusalem. One came from the Transjordanic district which he had just left, announcing that Timotheus had rallied his forces, and driven the Israelites of the district into the fortress of Dathema, of site now unknown; another, borne by messengers with their clothes torn in expression of the extremity of their distress, to announce that the Grecian settlers in the north and west had risen against the inhabitants of Galilee. Instantly Judas made his arrangements. To the north he sent his eldest brother Simon, whose exploits are briefly told, but who succeeded in[3] driving back the Grecian armies across the plain of Esdraelon to the very gates of Ptolemais. He himself took the ground already familiar to him in the Transjordanic forests, reserving for his assistance his brother 'Jonathan the Cunning.' As travellers now, so then, he gained the alliance of a friendly Arabian tribe. Throughout the district the inhabitants had shut themselves up for refuge in the numerous towns which of old had been renowned for the high walls which acted as defences against the Bedouins of the adjacent desert. The Greek leader had laid his plans for a simultaneous attack on all those fortresses on the same day. But at the very moment

Beyond Jordan.

[1] Isa. lxiii. 1–6.

[2] 1 Macc. v. 3. The same campaign is told, though in different order and with different details, in 2 Macc. xii. 1–45.

[3] 1 Macc. v. 23. Arbattis—*i.e.* the upper part of the Araboth or Arboth, or valley of the Jordan. See *Sinai and Palestine*, Appendix, § 10.

when at early dawn the scaling-ladders were planted, and the battering-rams prepared against one of the most important, there broke through the stillness of the morning the well-known trumpet-blast which the Grecian general recognised as the signal that the Hammer of the Gentiles was at hand, and the siege was raised, and the besiegers fled. Another fight followed on the banks of one of the mountain torrents that descend from the hills of Gilead to the Jordan. Judas dashed across the stream whilst his adversaries wavered, and down the way before him to the great sanctuary of Atargatis with the Two Horns,[1] and there destroyed them. This was the crowning act of his series of victories, gained, as we are assured, without the loss of a single Israelite, and the victor returned laden with spoil, and followed by vast masses of the Transjordanic population. On his way, in the pride of conquest, he destroyed the tower of Ephron, which refused them admittance. He crossed the Jordan, at the ford by which Gideon had returned from a like victorious expedition, to celebrate[2] the Feast of Pentecost in triumph at Jerusalem. And, now that all was thus secured, he completed his successes by one more more sally into Edom, reducing the ancient Hebron,[3] since the Exile converted into an Idumæan fortress, and destroying the last stronghold of the old Philistine worship at Ashdod.

Death of Antiochus Epiphanes, B.C. 164.

In this climax of the resistance of Israel there came the tidings that King Antiochus was suddenly dead. Alike in Greek and Jewish records fable gathered round the end of this splendid but wayward prince. Even to his own co-religionists there was a strange significance in his sudden disappearance. It seemed to them as if it was a judgment for his reckless attack on the Temple[4] of Nanea, or the Moon-Goddess, in Persia; and even one of the Jewish[5] accounts represented him as having perished in his assault on the shrine. But the Hebrew historians not unnaturally connected the unexpected close of their persecutor's career with

[1] Atargatis Carnion, 1 Macc. v. 44; 2 Macc. xii. 26; possibly the same Carnaim as *Asteroth Carnaim*, Gen. xiv. 5.

[2] 2 Macc. xii. 32.

[3] 1 Macc. v. 65.

[4] Polyb. xxxi. 11.

[5] 2 Macc. i 16.

his mortification at the reception of the tidings of their hero's victories; and it agrees with their occasional recognition of some sparks of generous feeling in his capricious courses that they give him the credit of a death-bed repentance for his misdeeds—in the latest account even a complete revocation of his tyrannical edicts.[1] It was, no doubt, the crisis of the contest. Whether the mysterious counsellor who, under the name of the Babylonian seer, had sketched in such minute detail the fortunes of the struggle till the moment of the desecration of the Temple, saw or foresaw the death of the persecutor, is doubtful. There are in the Book of Daniel dim anticipations of his end; but none of the frightful details with which the historians of the next generation [2] abound.

From this moment the struggle, although it still continued, becomes more complicated, and its fluctuating results more difficult to follow, the more so as the ultimate success of the insurgents was now assured. On both sides there was the entanglement of a civil war. Alcimus,[3] Eliakim, or Jehoiakim, with a large body of adherents, maintained his position in Jerusalem as High Priest, by the influence of the Syrian Court against the Maccabæan warrior; and Antiochus, the young prince, with Lysias as his guardian, had to fight for his crown against his uncle Demetrius. But, leaving the details which obscure the main thread of events, we may fix our attention on the conflict which raged in the closest quarters between the two rival fortresses in Jerusalem itself. The Temple mount was occupied by the insurgents; the ancient citadel of David was occupied by the Greeks. To secure this position a vast army was sent by Lysias down the Jordan valley, which then besieged the Judæan outpost, already taken and retaken, of Beth-zur. It was here that a battle took place of which the unprecedented circumstances left a deep impression on the Jewish mind. It was one of the peculiarities of Alexander's remote conquests that,

Second Battle of Beth-zur.

[1] 1 Maccabees vi. 1-16; 2 Maccabees ix. 1-28.

[2] Dan. xi. 45. Possibly Dan. vii. 11 may refer to the diseases by which Antiochus was consumed.

[3] See Lecture XLIX.

during this century, for the first and last time in Western history, the Indian and African elephants were brought into play in military achievements. The Syrian and Alexandrian kings especially prided themselves on their display of these vast creatures. One of them had been known as 'the 'elephant-master'[1] on account of this passion, and had given five hundred as a wedding-present to his daughter. On this occasion the elephants were distributed among the army ranged, in Macedonian fashion, in phalanxes or columns. Each animal rose like a mountain from a troop of 1,000 infantry and 500 cavalry, of which it was the centre. The animals were roused to fury by showing them the red juice of grapes and mulberries. Their advance was magnificent. The attendant soldiers were dressed in chain armour, their helmets were of bright brass, their shields of brass or of gold. Huge wooden towers rose on the backs of the elephants, fastened on by vast trappings. The black Indian driver was conspicuous on the neck of each animal, with a group of two or three soldiers round him, which the Israelites magnified into a whole troop.[2] Those who have seen the effect even of an ordinary military escort defiling through the grey hills and tufted valleys of Judæa can imagine the effect of this vast array of splendour. When 'the sun 'shone on the shields and helmets of gold and brass,' the whole range of the rocky ridges and of the winding glens 'glistened therewith around, and shined like blazing torches.' The noise of the multitude, the tramp of the huge beasts, the very rattling of the armour and caparisons was portentous. Fantastic traditions of this fight lingered in various forms—a heavenly champion in white and gold—a charge like the spring of lions against walls of steel—the watchword, 'Victory is of 'God.'[3] But the sober fact was that for once the small band of Judas's indomitable infantry failed in the face of such tremendous odds—not, however, before the achievement of

[1] *Revue des Deux Mondes*, 1874, iv. 483.

[2] 32 is the impossible number in the text of 1 Macc. vi. 37. Possibly it is a confusion with the thirty-two elephants, or with 'three or two,' or else a curious instance of the enormous exaggerations of the Jewish enumeration.

[3] 2 Macc. xi. 8, 11; xiii. 15.

one memorable deed. Eleazar, the fourth of the illustrious brothers, singling out an elephant which, from its towering howdah, he imagined to bear the young Prince, determined to sacrifice his life. He found his way through the hostile ranks, crept under the elephant, and by one thrust brought down the enormous beast upon him—perishing, but winning by his daring act the perpetual name which he desired. He was known to the next generation as Avaran, 'the Beast-'sticker.'[1]

The next decisive move was the victory over Nicanor, who was chosen to make an attack on Jerusalem, from the fanatical hatred he bore against the insurgents, and whose name accordingly long survived the memory of Lysias, Bacchides, Timotheus, and the rest, who come and pass like shadows.

B.C. 162. Nicanor.

He had already taken part in the conflict at the time of the battle of Emmaus,[2] and a peculiar pathos is given to his history by the circumstance that of him alone, amongst all their opponents at this period, there remained a tradition—difficult, perhaps, to reconcile with the hard language in which he is generally described, but quite consistent with human character—that, whatever might be his animosity against the Jewish nation, he had, perhaps from admiration of the earlier prowess displayed in their first encounter, conceived a strong personal admiration and affection for Judas Maccabæus. The momentary consternation by which his sudden appearance checked the insurgents under Simon, gave him the opportunity of opening friendly communications with Judas himself. There was a natural suspicion. But Judas came to Jerusalem, and for the first time the two foes came face to face, and in a moment each appreciated the other. It was the meeting of Claverhouse and Morton.

His meeting with Judas.

They sat side by side on chairs of state,[3] like the curule seats of the Roman magistrates. The Syrian general was

[1] 1 Macc. vi. 43-46; ii. 5.

[2] If he is the same as the Nicanor of 1 Macc. But the incident recorded in Jos. *Ant.* xii. 10, 4, and Polyb. xxxi. 22, makes this doubtful.

[3] 2 Macc. xiv. 21.

completely fascinated. He could not bear to have Judas out of his sight—'he loved the man from his heart.' He entered into his future plans. He entreated him to lay aside this wandering course, to have a wife and children of his own. He held out the picture of marriage, and a quiet and settled home. The High Priest's office was apparently suggested as the haven of the warrior's stormy career. If we may trust the brief sentence[1] which follows, Judas accepted the advice so cordially that the long-delayed event took place—that he married, and for a time settled quietly and happily in domestic life. Suddenly all was changed. The jealous rival Alcimus saw in this friendship the ruin of his own hopes, denounced Nicanor to the King, and procured an order that Judas should be sent as prisoner to Antioch. Nicanor was deeply hurt. He could not break his plighted troth to his friend. He could not venture to disobey the royal order. His uneasy conscience showed itself in the fierceness of his temper and the roughness of his manners. Judas boded no good and escaped. A skirmish took place between him and some of the royal troops at Capharsalama in the plain of Sharon. The two friends parted to meet no more.

The excited tradition of the next generation represented the furious Greek as standing in the great outer[2] court of the Temple—the priests and chiefs of the people vainly endeavouring to propitiate him by showing him the offering prepared on the altar for the welfare of the Syrian king. With an insulting gesture Nicanor stretched out his hand to the Temple and swore that unless Judas was given up to him he would level the building, break down the altar, and erect on its site a Temple to the Grecian Bacchus. The terrified hierarchy, as in the old days, took up their position between the altar and the Temple, and invoked the Divine aid for their sanctuary so recently purified. Amongst those who were specially obnoxious to Nicanor was Rhazis, a Jew conspicuous for his austere

[1] 2 Macc. xiv. 25, ἐγάμησεν, εὐστάθησεν, ἐκοινώνησε βίου. It almost looks as if this were a mistranslation of part of Nicanor's advice.

[2] 2 Macc. xiv. 31, 33. The passage well illustrates the difference of ἱερόν and ναός.

patriotism. He was determined not to give the enemy the chance of insulting him by capture, and, rather than yield, endeavoured to destroy himself, first by falling on his sword in the tower where he had taken refuge, then springing from the tower to the ground, and then, despite his ghastly wounds, throwing himself headlong from one of the precipitous cliffs of the city. All this stamped the memory of Nicanor with additional horror.[1]

At last the vengeance came, in the fitting place and from the fitting man. In that same memorable pass of Beth-horon where Judas had gained his first victory, he was now to gain his last. There, amongst his native hills, he was encamped, at a village at the foot of the Pass. He felt that it was again one of the critical moments of his life ; and his address (so it was believed in the next generation) partook of that strong historic enthusiasm which marked his character. He told his army that in his dreams he had seen Onias,[2] the last blameless High Priest before the disorders of the time began, whose intercessions had called down the ministers of Divine wrath on Heliodorus, and who had fallen a victim to the sacrilegious jealousy of his rivals in the laurel groves of Daphne. The venerable man had appeared as in life, the true dignified Priest, the true Israelite nobleman,[3] with his reverend demeanour, his gentle manners, his gracious utterance, the model of virtuous training from his youth upwards. As of old in the Temple, so had he seemed to be standing, with his hands outstretched in prayer for the whole host of Judæa. Suddenly, in answer to the High Priest's supplication, there started into view the apparition of a magnificent, hoary-headed figure, of lofty stature and commanding presence. 'This,' said Onias, 'is the lover of our brethren, the intercessor for our people and our holy city. This is Jeremiah, the Prophet of God.' In that age of silent expectation this welcome vision of the Suffering Servant of the Eternal, who had come to be regarded almost as the Patron Saint of

Battle of Beth-horon, B.C. 161.

[1] 2 Macc. xiv. 37-46. [2] *Ibid.* xv. 12-17.
[3] καλὸν καὶ ἀγαθόν. The Greek expression for 'gentleman.' 2 Macc. xv.

Palestine, might well have presented itself to the devout warrior's sleeping thoughts. The Prophet seemed to stretch out his right hand, as if with a pledge of support, and gave to Judas a golden sword. It was not merely like the short[1] weapon which he had hitherto wielded from the day when he took it from the dead hand of his earliest foe Apollonius, but the huge broadsword of the Macedonian phalanxes. 'Take this holy 'sword,' said the Prophet, 'and with it thou shalt crush thine 'enemies.'[2]

The battle was felt to be decisive, especially for the Temple,[3] which ran the risk of another defilement or destruction that would undo all the labour and joy of the recent dedication. Alike in the mountain pass, and in Jerusalem, from which the hills which encompass Beth-horon are visible, the 'agony' was intense. The intrepid chief with his small band saw the huge and variegated host approach, the furious elephants snorting in the centre, the cavalry hovering on the wings. It was, if ever, a time and place to invoke the Divine aid which supports the few against the many. It was not only the spot where Joshua had defeated the kings of Canaan, but where tradition fixed the more[4] recent deliverance from Sennacherib. With these thoughts (and in this both the earlier and later narratives substantially agree) Judas raised his hands to heaven, and called on the All-seeing, Wonder-working God. 'Thou, O Lord, sentedst thine angel in the reign of Hezekiah 'and didst destroy from the camp of Sennacherib an hundred 'and fourscore and five thousand. Now, O Ruler of the 'Heavens, send a good angel before us and strike terror and 'trembling, and with Thy mighty arm may they be struck 'down, who have come with blasphemy against Thy Holy 'Temple!' The army of Nicanor came on with trumpets sounding in accord with their triumphal heathen[5] war-songs. The army of Judas advanced (the expression reminds us of the Ironsides) 'fighting with their hands and praying with

[1] ῥομφαία in 2 Macc. xv. 16 as distinct from μάχαιρα in 1 Macc. iii. 12.

[2] Philo (*De Execratione*) regards the venerable seer of the past as παράκλητος πρὸς τὸν πατέρα (Grimm on 2 Macc. xv. 16)

[3] τοῦ καθηγιασμένου ναοῦ, 2 Macc. xv. 18.

[4] See Lightfoot, ii. 18.

[5] 2 Macc. xv. 25 (παιάνων).

'their hearts.' The rout was complete. The neighbouring villages [1] and the surrounding hills were roused by the horn of the Maccabee, as of another Roland, to intercept the passes and cut off the fugitives. There was a later tradition still, that when Judas encountered his former friend in the battle he called out, 'Take care of thyself, Nicanor [2]—it 'is to thee that I come!' But in the earlier version it was not by the hand of Judas that Nicanor was slain; he fell in the first onset of the battle, and it was only after its close that his corpse was found, recognised by his splendid armour. Wild was the exultation, loud the shout, with which in their own Hebrew tongue the Jewish army blessed their Divine Deliverer. Then (it is no unfitting conclusion) laden with spoil, they came in triumph to Jerusalem. Amongst the trophies the most conspicuous were the head of Nicanor and his right hand and arm from the shoulder downwards, which they had severed from the body as it lay on the battlefield. The Priests assembled before the altar to receive them. The head and hand (like Hasdrubal's in Hannibal's camp) were held up before the Greek garrison in the fortress. The head was fastened to the fortress itself. The hand, which had been so proudly stretched forth in defiance against the Temple, was nailed to the main eastern entrance of the inner court, known long after as the Gate Beautiful, but also as 'the Gate of [3] Nicanor' from this terrible reminiscence. The tongue with which the insults were spoken was cut into small pieces and thrown for the birds to devour. It was a savage revenge—so savage, and, in the sacred precincts, approaching so nearly to a profanation, that neither Josephus nor the earlier historian ventures to mention it; but told in such detail and so confirmed by long tradition, and (alas!) by analogous usage in so many a Christian country, that there seems no reason to doubt it. One further honour was to be bestowed on the victory. It was a day already auspicious,

B.C. 161.

Death of Nicanor.

[1] Jos. *Ant.* xii. 10, 5.

[2] 5 Macc. v. 16.

[3] Another explanation, but probably of a later date, was given, that Nicanor, an Alexandrian Greek, had brought the gate from Alexandria; that it was thrown over in a storm to lighten the ship, that a sea-monster swallowed it and threw it out on the shore at Joppa, where he found it on his arrival (see the various Rabbinical quotations collected by Herzfeld, ii. 345).

the 13th of the month Adar—the eve of the Feast of Purim—or, as the historian calls it, the eve of 'Mordecai's Day;' and the anniversary itself was to be hereafter[1] called 'Nicanor's 'Day.'

This was the crowning success of Judas. A wider sphere seemed opening before him, a new and powerful ally was on the point of joining his cause, when he was suddenly cut off. The Syrian army under Bacchides advanced down the Jordan valley to avenge the defeat of Nicanor. From a cause which the historian does not explain, but which incidental illustrations will enable us presently to indicate with fatal precision, Judas found a difficulty in mustering his forces. A veil, as it were, is drawn over his last effort. Even the place is uncertain.[2] We cannot be sure whether he encountered the enemy in his old haunts in the valleys branching into the hills from his native village, or whether he had been decoyed away into the far north by the sources of Jordan, or by the caverned rocks which overhang the Lake of Gennesareth. In the latest traditions[3] he is represented as advancing to the fight with the lion-like port of his earlier days, and brandishing his sword, whether that which he had won from Apollonius, or that which he had received from the Prophet in the vision at Beth-horon. The famous trumpet sounded for the last time. From morning till night the conflict lasted. One wing of the Syrian army fled before the charge, but the other pursued the pursuers, and between the two the gallant champion was caught. His watchword before the battle was cherished as his latest utterance.[4] When he saw the odds against which he had to fight, 'God forbid that 'I should do this thing and flee away from them; if our time 'be come, let us die manfully for our brethren, and let us not 'leave behind a stain upon our honour.' His dead body was

Battle of Eleasa and Death of Judas. B.C. 161.

[1] Herzfeld, ii. 345. See Lecture XLV.

[2] 1 Macc. ix. 2. *Galgaga* is *Galilee* in Jos. *Ant.* xii. 11. *Arbela* also points to the fortress above the Lake of Gennesareth, *Masaloth* possibly to its well-known caves (Herzfeld, ii. 346), (see Lecture L.), and in that case *Eleasa* might be Laish near Dan. But on the other hand it seems improbable that he should have ventured so far from Judæa.

[3] 5 Macc. v. 17, 3.

[4] 1 Macc. ix. 18–20.

found by the two worthiest of his brothers; they laid him in the ancestral sepulchre at Modin, and a dirge went up from the whole nation for him, like that of David over Saul and Jonathan: 'How is the valiant man fallen, the deliverer of Israel!'

With the death of Judas ends the first stage of the struggle for independence. Hardly any character of the later days of Judaism so strikes the imagination as the hero who, of all military chiefs, accomplished the largest ends with the scantiest means, who from the brink of extermination raised his nation to a higher level of freedom than they had enjoyed since the fall of the Monarchy. 'He had been ever 'the chief defender of his countrymen both in body and 'mind; he had maintained his early love for his people un- 'broken to the end.'[1] No conflict in their history has been more frequently recorded. Even David's story is told but twice; the story of the Maccabæan struggle is repeated at intervals of successive generations in no less than four separate versions. And around the struggle revolves the mysterious book which still exercises the critic, which still stirs the conscience, which filled the whole imagination of the coming centuries of the Jewish people. When some good men regard it as a disparagement of the Book of Daniel that it should have been evoked by the Maccabæan conflict, it is because they have not adequately conceived the grandeur of that crisis, nor recognised the fact that, when the final agony of the nation approached, two centuries later, there was no period which so naturally supplied the imagery for its hopes and fears as that which was covered by the blows and counter-blows between Antiochus the Brilliant Madman and Judas the Hammer of the Heathen. If in the visions of Daniel the anticipations of the deliverance are thought worthy of being announced by the Archangel Gabriel,[2] if the hero who shall accomplish the deliverance is summoned to receive his reward by myriads of ministering spirits, not less in the poetic accounts of the Second Book of Maccabees does the valiant ruler with his little band appear surrounded by angelic champions.

His career.

[1] 2 Macc. xv. 30. [2] Dan. vii. 14; ix. 27 (*Speaker's Commentary*, vol. vi. 336).

Sometimes, when he is marching out of Jerusalem on a sudden there starts up a horseman clothed in white, who heads the little band, brandishing his shield and spear[1] of gold. Sometimes in the thick of the fray five splendid horsemen start as if from the sky, rattling their golden bridles, as if the celestial guardians of the five gallant brothers. One gallops before, and on each side of Maccabæus ride, two and two, the other four, protecting him with shield, and spear, and sword, and darting lightnings at their enemies.[2]

Such apparitions—the counterparts of the Twin Gods at the battle of the[3] Lake Regillus, of St. Iago in the Spanish armies, of the angels of victory and defeat which even now hover before the eyes of Russian[4] soldiers in the crisis of the combat, of St. Nicholas who caught in the air the bombs of the British fleet at the holy fortress of Solowetsky in the White Sea—are the outward expressions of the deep moral significance of the Maccabæan struggle. The sober style of the contemporary account is content with the moral qualities of the human hearts and hands by which the victory is won. But the interest is not less vivid, nor the glory of that 'Son of Man' less transparent, in the solid prose than in the radiant poetry of the period. Let us consider some of the characteristics from which this interest is derived.

Narrowness of conflict.

1. There may be a momentary disappointment when we reflect that the special objects which provoked the contention were such as the highest religious minds of subsequent times have regarded as trivial or temporary. The rite of circumcision, for which the choicest spirits of the nation fled into the caverns and hills of Palestine, was two centuries later regarded by Saul of Tarsus as absolutely indifferent.[5] The sabbath and the sabbatical year, for the sake of which they exposed themselves to defeat and ruin, were pronounced by him to be amongst the beggarly elements of the world—shadows and not realities.[6] One of them has been

[1] 2 Macc. xi. 7.

[2] διαπρεπεῖς, πανοπλία. 2 Macc. x. 29, 30 (Grimm).

[3] Preface to Macaulay's *Lays of Ancient Rome*.

[4] Kinglake's *Crimean War*, i. 458.

[5] 1 Cor. vii. 19; Gal. vi. 15.

[6] Gal. iv. 9; Col. ii. 16.

abandoned altogether by the Jewish race itself, the other has been so modified in the Christian world as to have almost ceased to bear the same name or serve the same end. The distinctions of food, which to the martyrs of the Maccabæan age were the tests for which they endured the most cruel torments, were declared in the vision to Peter by the seashore[1] at Joppa to be of not the slightest importance in the sight of God. The sacrifices, of which the sudden extinction under the pressure of Antiochus seemed to be the cessation of the very pulse of religion, have vanished, and the neglect which once seemed to be the most terrible of desolations now reigns through every church and through every synagogue. Even the hated statues and pictures of heathen divinities, which filled with horror the mind of every pious Israelite at that time, now stand unchallenged at the corners of the streets and adorn the walls of the houses in every capital of Europe. Doubtless, as was urged by the Alexandrian Jew Philo[2] at a later epoch, these usages each contributed to the support of the Jewish nationality, so that (to use his own homely illustration) 'if one brick were 'taken out the whole house would have fallen to pieces.' Yet still the fact remains that there was a narrowness in the conflict which in time was destined to make itself felt. And even without looking further than the career of Judas Maccabæus, we see that the true interest of the struggle rose above these external watchwords, and that the heroic family which fought for them had a wider and deeper insight than belonged to any mere ceremonial forms.

Elevation of Spirit.

2. In this instance the danger lay in the absorption of Judaism not into the higher spirit of Athens or Alexandria, but into that basest and most corrupt form of heathenism of which the very name 'Syrus' or 'Syrian' was the byword. And the stern resistance to it is a signal example of the 'stubbornness and stiffness of neck' which, says the Rabbinical[3] tradition, Moses mentioned as a fault, but knowing in a prophetic spirit that it would be not the

[1] Acts x. 15. [2] *Ad Caium*, p. 99. [3] Raphall, i. 232.

ruin but the salvation of the people against force, and fraud, and persecution.

It might have been thought, that with such an excessive tenacity to these outward symbols, the nation would have felt that in their loss all was lost, and resigned itself to despair. Not so. With that inextinguishable fire of spiritual faith which burned beneath the superficial crust, it was recognised, even in that contention for the framework of things which so soon were ready to wax old and vanish away, that there was something better and more enduring even than Temple or sacrifice. That strain which we hear at the moment of the profanation of the sanctuary is the prelude of a higher mood. 'God did 'not choose the people for the place's sake, but the place for[1] 'the people's sake.' The calamities which befell them were felt to be the consequence of their having been 'wrapped in 'many sins.'[2] The tendency, so natural at such moments, to throw the blame on others was kept in check by the genuine[3] and generous sentiment of self-accusation which breathes through the histories and devotions of this period.

Of this elevation of religion the Maccabæan family were the main representatives, and thus an insensible undercurrent of divergence sprang up between them and the more fanatical of their followers. 'The 'Pious'[4] or 'the Chasidim' are constantly mentioned as a party on whom the true patriots were obliged to count for support, but on whom they could not securely reckon. The unreasoning abstinence from self-defence[5] on the Sabbath was put aside by Mattathias with a disdainful impatience—according to one account, with a fine insight into the spirit[6] of the ancient Law, in which he seemed to see that its purpose was not to destroy life, but to save it. The Priests on more than one occasion brought dishonour on the cause by a fanatical foolhardiness, which the wise leader of the insurgents vainly strove to check.[7] There was a secret reluctance in the stricter party to break altogether with the

[1] 2 Macc. v. 19.
[2] *Ibid.* v. 18.
[3] Dan. ix. 4–19; Psalm lxxix. 9; 2 Macc. vi. 12–16.
[4] 1 Macc. ii. 42.
[5] *Ibid.* ii. 40.
[6] Lev. xviii. 5. See Raphall, i. 242.
[7] 1 Macc. v. 67; vii. 13.

legitimate successor of Aaron, as represented in the renegade Priest Alcimus,[1] and, although it is not expressly mentioned, we can hardly doubt that the elevation[2] of the Maccabæan family to the High Priesthood, of which the first attempt was discerned in the case of Judas, though not realised till after his death in the person of his brother, must have been a rude shock to many a cherished prejudice. The race of Joarib from which they sprang was studiously disparaged ; the very names of Modin and Maccabee were twisted into words of ignominy, signifying 'rebellion,' or 'revolt.'[3] It would almost seem as if the enlarged policy of Judas in seeking allies from the outside world was the object of suspicion to the Muckle-wraths and Macbriars of this older Covenant, and thus one of the causes of that sudden defection of his troops which cost him his life at the close of his career.[4]

Nor did this alienation of the narrow spirit of the religious world of Judaism from the heroic chief to whom was due the restoration of the sanctuary and the nation terminate with the disaffection against which he had to contend in his lifetime. It is a striking fact which can hardly be accidental that, enshrined as was his memory in the popular histories which live in the successive books called after him, it is almost entirely disregarded in the traditions of the Talmudic schools. Not one of his exploits—not even his name—occurs in the Mishna. In the annual thanksgiving which commemorates the deliverance from Antiochus the name of Judas is not mentioned, and even the intervention of the family is veiled under the

[1] 1 Macc. vii. 14.

[2] 2 Macc xiv. 26. Raphall, i. 325.

[3] Raphall, i. 345.

[4] In Grätz (iii. 10), copied by Raphall (i. 345) without verification, there professes to be given a direct proof of this from the Midrash Hanuka. 'Johanan, the leader of 'the Pious, was wroth, and said to the 'Asmonean: Is it not written, Cursed is the 'man that putteth his trust in thee while 'his heart departeth from the Lord ; but 'blessed is he that trusteth in the Lord, 'for the Lord will be his trust? Thou 'and thine, I and mine, we represent the 'twelve tribes of the Lord, and through 'us I am assured the Lord will have 'wrought wondrously.' But I am informed by Professor Neubauer that this is an incorrect quotation, and that the passage from the Midrash—itself of a very late date, the twelfth century—is of no authority. It may possibly represent some earlier tradition, but as it stands it is a mass of confusion. It is *Mattathias the High Priest* who addresses the Asmonean, in the name not of the Chasidim, but of the congregation ; and the protest precedes not a defeat, but a victory. The Gentiles in question are not the Romans but the Parthians.

unhistorical name of Mattathias the High Priest.[1] As Columba in Ireland, as Joan of Arc in France, as Robert the Bruce in Scotland, as Simon de Montfort in England, so Judas Maccabæus, neglected or disparaged by the ecclesiastical authorities, received his canonisation only from the popular voice, and from the judgment of posterity. Yet in a certain sense this disparagement was from their point of view more just than he or they could have discerned at the time; even as the real grandeur of his cause by a strange irony is derived in large measure from the nobler side of the Grecian influences which he devoted his life to oppose.

Patriotism.

3. That spirit of patriotism which had been developed by the longings of the Captivity and the joy of the Return assumed at this epoch a form and style which, more than any previous incidents of the Jewish history, recalls the maxims of Greek and Roman history. 'We fight 'for our lives and our laws.' 'The jeopardising of a gallant 'soldier is to the end that he might deliver his people and 'win himself a perpetual name.' 'Let us die manfully for our 'brethren and not stain our honour.' 'I will show myself 'such as mine old age requireth, and leave a notable example 'to such as be going to die courageously for the honourable 'and holy laws.' These are expressions which are Gentile rather than Jewish, which remind us of Leonidas and Horatius Cocles more than of Moses or David. The career of Judas exemplifies the profound truth of the Scottish poet's invocation,

> The Patriot's God peculiarly Thou art,
> His Friend, Inspirer, Guardian, and Reward.

It is precisely because the name of Maccabæus has a national and warlike rather than a theological savour, that he has deserved a special place amongst the heroes of mankind, as combining in one, in a preeminent degree, the associations of the patriot and the saint. For this reason the old mediæval romancers and artists did well when they placed him, not in the

[1] Raphall, i. 345.

exclusive circle of Jewish or Christian hagiology, but in the larger sphere of the Nine Worthies drawn from every nation and land, not only with Joshua and David, but with Alexander and Cæsar, with Arthur and Charlemagne. For this reason the greatest of modern musicians, when he wished to celebrate with the grandest military strains the return of a youthful Prince from the victorious[1] campaign in which he had, as was believed at the time, delivered his country from the bondage of tyranny and superstition, chose as the framework of his oratorio the exploits of Judas Maccabæus, and made his triumph over Nicanor the occasion for the chorus which has greeted every British warrior since, 'See the Conquering Hero comes.'

Gentile Philosophy.

4. But the broader aspect of the Maccabæan history is not confined to its patriotic fervour. In the very language of the descriptions the Greek rhetoric has mingled with the Hebrew simplicity so strongly as to show how the zeal against Hellenism failed to resist its subtle and penetrating influence. The first book of Maccabees, indeed, retains on the whole the ancient style. The lament and the parting counsels of Mattathias are such as might have come from the life of Jeremiah or Ezra. But even then the military and geographical details have a tincture of Polybius; and when we read the second book, the speeches and conversations have all the flow of the orations which Greek and Latin historians place in the mouths of their heroes. And yet further, when we arrive at the fourth book—of uncertain date, and probably the last native offshoot of the literary stimulus of the Maccabæan age—it is not merely the form, but the substance of the philosophy of Aristotle and Zeno which reigns supreme. It is, as Ewald says,[2] our only specimen of a Jewish sermon. But it is a sermon without a sacred text, or rather its text is the government of the Passions by the supremacy of Reason or Principle. It is Butler's Discourse on Human Nature illustrated, with all the turgid eloquence of the Alexandrian school, by the story of Eleazar and the seven martyrs. The Four Cardinal Virtues figure in the place of the Mosaic Law, the Law itself is

[1] The Duke of Cumberland's return from Culloden in 1745.

[2] Ewald, v. 485

transfigured in the light of Greek Philosophy. The imagery[1] is drawn, not from the mountains or forests of Palestine, but from the towers and reefs that guard the harbour of Alexandria, from the legends of the Dying Swan and of the voices of the Sirens.

Belief in Immortality.

5. There was a still more definite connexion between the faith of the Maccabees and that of the Gentile world against which they were contending. We have watched the gradual growth of the hope of immortality along the progress of the Jewish race, enkindled by the aspirations of the Psalmists, deepened by the misfortunes of the Captivity, coloured, perchance, by the contact with Zoroastrianism.[2] We have seen its deliberate expression[3] in the teaching, if not of Socrates, yet of his greatest disciple. We have witnessed, though at what date we know not, the clear and vivid statement of the Greek and Hebrew belief combined in the culminating revelation of Alexandrian Judaism, 'the Wisdom of Solomon.'[4] In Palestine the prospect of futurity had still for the people at large remained under the veil that had rested on it from the time of Moses; though with occasional glimpses furnished in some of the bolder utterances of Psalmist or Prophet,[5] who for themselves, if not for others, claimed a share in the eternal communion with the Eternal. The one great teacher who had appeared in Judæa since Malachi—the son of Sirach—was entirely silent on the world beyond the grave. 'O death, how 'bitter is the remembrance of thee to a man that liveth at rest 'in his possessions! . . . O death, how acceptable is thy sen-'tence unto the needy and unto him whose strength faileth! '. . . Fear not the sentence of death; remember them that 'have been before thee, and that come after; for this is the 'sentence of the Lord over all flesh.'[6] In this calm but gloomy resignation is summed up the experience of the most gifted sage in Palestine twenty years before the Maccabæan insurrection. But in the course of that insurrection—or, at least, in the records

[1] 4 Macc. xiii. 7; *ibid.* xv. 14.
[2] Lecture XLV.
[3] Lecture XLVII.
[4] Lecture XLVI.
[5] See Ewald, *Lehr. von Gott.* ii. 442.
[6] Ecclus. xli. 1, 2, 3.

of it—'the belief in immortality' which the Grecian philosophy had communicated to the Jewish schools of Alexandria started into a prominence which it had never achieved before, and which it never lost afterwards. 'It is true that in the trans-'figured form in which they correspond to the true Religion 'these hopes had long been established in Israel as one of the 'highest and most enduring fruits which its thousand years' ex-'perience had brought forth upon its sacred soil. Not till now, 'however, can it be said that this fruit was so natural that it would 'never again disappear; and if the immovable hope of immor-'tality and resurrection is the true and only weapon that cannot 'be wrested from us, by which in the spiritual struggles of 'humanity all the sufferings of the time can be victoriously 'endured, all the tyranny of the earth broken, and all imperish-'able happiness attained—it must be admitted that, through 'the deep surging storm of the age, there was sent from above, 'in this faith which nothing could take away, the only sword 'of salvation, against whose edge the most fatal terrors [1] would 'strike in vain.' It is not only that in the Book of Daniel, with a precision sharpened by the intensity of conflict, it is announced that 'many of them that sleep in the dust of the 'earth shall awake; some to everlasting life, some to shame 'and everlasting contempt. And they that be wise shall shine 'as the brightness of the blue sky, and they that help many to 'righteousness shall shine as the stars for ever and ever.' [2] It is not only that in the Psalter of Solomon [3] we are told that 'whoso fear the Lord shall rise to eternal life, and their life is 'in the light of the Lord and shall no longer fail.' It is into the very tissue of the history that the belief is interwoven, and in forms which, whilst they show its Western origin, show also that it had struck root in the Jewish heart with all the tenacity of an Eastern faith. The earliest version of the story, indeed, is still silent, like the Son of Sirach. But the traditions of the time, as handed down in the second and fourth books [4] of the

[1] Ewald, v. 306. [2] Dan. xii. 2, 3 (Heb.)

[3] *Ibid.* iii. 16.

[4] 2 Macc. vii. 9. This book, no doubt, as being abridged from a work written in Cyrene, may have been more easily filled with Greek ideas. Still, the connexion with the Palestine insurrection implies that the belief had reached thither.

Maccabees, relate distinctly and firmly how the seven brothers and their mother trusted that 'the King of the world would 'raise up them who had died for His laws unto everlasting life.' And not only in the words but in the deeds recorded is the new doctrine exemplified. The desperate effort of Rhaziz to destroy himself 'manfully' rather than be dishonourably treated by his enemies, in the very Paganism of its depreciation of life,[1] implies a new form of contempt for death, in the mind of the historian, evidently based on his confidence of another state. And, yet further, an incident is recorded, too circumstantial to be set aside, which indicates that the belief not only existed, but had already begun to run into those curious speculations which have themselves in turn darkened the hope that engendered them. After one of the battles of Judas in the plains of Philistia, when, according to custom, they rested on the following Sabbath, and took up the corpses of their killed, to lay them in their ancestral tombs, it was found that underneath the inner clothing of each dead man were amulets in the form of the small idols found in the Temple of Jamnia.[2] It was the last lingering trace of the ancient Philistine practice of taking into battle figures of their divinities as charms against danger.[3] The victorious soldiers of the Maccabæan army, with a superstition hardly less excusable than that of their unfortunate[4] comrades, sprang to the conclusion that these amulets had been the destruction of those who had worn them. After the first triumphant exultation that they had not fallen into the same snare as others, Judas, with the generous[5] sympathy which characterised him, was struck with the fear, still tinged with the same confusion of ideas, lest the gallant survivors should, by the common partnership of war and nationality, share the guilt of the crime of their fellow-soldiers, and accordingly caused a collection to be made, man by man, which amounted at least to the sum of 2,000 Greek coins, for a sacrifice which should efface the

Offerings for the Dead.

[1] The peculiar characters of Samson and Saul give a different colour to the act, in 1 Sam. xxxi. 4, Judg. xvi. 30.

[2] 2 Macc. xii. 39-45.

[3] 2 Sam. v. 21; 1 Chron. xiv. 12.

[4] 'Those on whom the tower of Siloam 'fell, were they sinners above all men?' (Luke xiii. 4.)

[5] γενναῖος Ἰούδας, 2 Macc. xii. 42.

memory of the sin of the fallen combatants. The act was regarded as one of peculiar significance ; there was something in it 'noble,' 'becoming,' and 'thoughtful,'[1] like a chief who felt that his soldiers were part of himself, and who cast his glance forward to their future in another world. The offering which they thus made, collecting for the whole army, might, perchance, benefit even those who had perished with the idolatrous images on their bosoms ; it would still more benefit those who had no direct share in the guilt ; and if any such had fallen or might fall in the conflict, it might even be considered as an offering of thankful gratitude.

The whole incident is full of characteristic traits ; the last flicker of the old Canaanitish idolatry, the inborn superstition of the Jewish race, the gracious act of the leader, rising above the transitory terror of the moment, and endearing himself to the troops by his care that they should not, even unconsciously, have incurred the danger which he apprehended. But it is most remarkable as exhibiting what has been truly called 'the 'earliest distinct assertion of a Jewish belief in the resurrection,'[2] and that belief, as it was derived in the first instance from the Greek world, so now expressed itself in a practice unknown before to Israel, but common in Greece, of making offerings at the graves of the dead, which should divert from them any glance of Divine displeasure that might rest upon them. In the Gentile usage it took the form of libations or sacrifices to the departed spirits themselves. In the Maccabæan practice this was modified, in accordance with the nobler religious feeling of Judaism, by addressing them not to the dead but for the dead to God. In this form it passed into the early Christian Church, but with the further change of substituting the simple aspirations of prayer for the cumbrous sacrifices of Jewish and Pagan rites. This innocent thought, based on the natural religious instinct alike of heathen and of Jew, at last culminated in the elaborate system of buying and selling of

[1] This seems to be the meaning of the whole passage, 2 Macc. xii. 40–45. Observe the words καλῶς—ἀστείως—διαλογιζόμενος, and again, προπεπτωκότων (= fallen in battle)—χαριστήριον—in LXX. only used here, but common in classical authors for a 'thankoffering.'

[2] Milman's *Hist. of Jews*, ii. 8.

prayers, regardless of the reasonable devotion alike of Jew or of Christian. But the practice itself belongs to the earliest and simplest endeavour to unite the dead and the living in one spiritual communion, and the circumstance that this is the one solitary example of it in the whole range of the Greek or Hebrew Scriptures has caused the name of 'Maccabee' to pass into a synonym, in a large part of Christendom, for funereal celebrations.[1]

It will thus be seen what was the peculiarity of the superstitious dread which Judas sought to allay, what the beauty of his act as it seemed to his Cyrenian biographer, what its connexion with the glorious doctrine of Grecian philosophy, which, in spite of his stubborn resistance to Grecian tyranny, he thus solemnly celebrated at the altar in Jerusalem. Never before had the existence of the departed in the unseen world assumed so tangible a form. 'Resurrection,' the great word of the New Testament, first comes prominently forward in the mouths of the Maccabæan martyrs and heroes. It was as though the resurrection of the nation gave a solid shape to the belief which henceforth was never to be lost.

6. There is one more aspect of the Maccabæan struggle which has left a decisive mark on the religious history of the nation. For the first time the attack of their enemies was directed, not only (as in the invasions of the Assyrian or Babylonian kings) against the people, the city, and the Temple, but against the sacred books which—thanks to the exertions of Ezra and Nehemiah—had now taken their place amongst the treasures of the nation. It had been the object of the Syrian persecutors to destroy the copies of the Law whenever found, or to render them valueless in the eyes of the nation by painting on their margins the figures of heathen divinities. Such an attempt, as in the parallel case of Diocletian's persecution of the Christians, must have had the natural effect of causing

[1] It has been pointed out to me that the 'Danse Maccabre,' as an expression for the Dance of Death, is supposed to have its origin in the use of 2 Macc. xii. in the funeral offices of the Latin Church (Tylor's *Primitive Culture*, i. 359). For the same reason probably the register of the Morgue was called 'Le Livre des Maccabées,' and the French slang word for a drowned man is 'Macchabée.'

the Jews to cling more closely to these monuments of their faith, and to gather up whatever fragments might be lost. Such a feeling, as we have seen, had already manifested itself in the compilations of ancient documents during the Exile, and in the time of Nehemiah produced the first definite attempt at a complete collection. That collection consisted, according to the earliest extant tradition, of the Pentateuch, the Prophets, the histories of the Kings, the writings of David (whatever may have been included under that term), and the royal letters or donatives of the Persian kings. The same tradition that ascribes this work to the great reformer of the fifth century before the Christian era records a corresponding work of the great[1] hero of the second. As Nehemiah had agglomerated round the Law the works which had gradually taken form by his time, so, 'in like manner' Judas Maccabæus and his companions eagerly gathered[2] round Nehemiah's group of sacred literature the scattered remains which had escaped, like fragments of a wreck or survivors of a battle,[3] or 'brands plucked from the fire,' out of the ruin of the Syrian war.

The additions to the Canon.

It was[4] the last instalment of the Hebrew Bible, and was a work well worthy of the last leader who commanded the unchallenged reverence of the Hebrew race. It may, perhaps, be too much, on this single testimony, to ascribe the collection to himself personally; though we would fain imagine the noble-hearted warrior, in the days which followed the dedication of the Temple, or in the brief interval of domestic peace during his friendship with Nicanor, recovering and rearranging the precious scrolls which, from

The Hagiographa.

[1] This is on the assumption (as generally received) that 'Judas' in 2 Macc. ii. 14 is the Maccabee. Herzfeld (ii. 444) supposes him to be another Judas, the possible author of the Epistle in 2 Macc. i. 10. But it can hardly be doubted, that it was intended to be Maccabæus.

[2] ἐπισυνήγαγε, 2 Macc. ii. 13, 14.

[3] διαπεπτωκότα, *ibid.*, mistranslated 'lost.' See Schleusner *in voce*. Comp. 1 Macc. ix. 49; Judith vi. 9. See the striking passage in Deutsoh's *Remains*, 13.

[4] It is said that one result of the extermination of the Law—*i.e.* the Pentateuch—by Antiochus was that, in order to supply its place in the synagogues was introduced the Haphtara, *i.e.* the reading of lessons from the Prophets and some of the Hagiographa, which thus *liberated* (from *Phatar*, to liberate) the faithful from the obligation of reading the Pentateuch. See Dr. Ginsburg, in his article on the Haphtara. Kitto, ii. 227, 228.

broken vault or limestone cavern, were brought to his care to be lost no more. But in his time doubtless the work was done. The letters of the Persian kings, as having lost their interest, were now laid aside. And in their place, clinging to the skirts of 'the things of David,' were added those later writings which had either accumulated since Nehemiah's time, or by him, for whatever reason, had not been admitted. There was the historical work of the Chronicler, completed shortly after the invasion of Alexander, which carried with it the Book of Ezra, not yet divided into its twofold parts of Ezra and Nehemiah; and the comparatively recent book of Esther, so especially needed for the Feast of Purim. There was the Book of Job already venerable, and the three Hebrew works bearing the name of Solomon, the latest, as we have seen, probably composed between the time of Nehemiah and the Maccabees. Finally there were, if so be, the Psalms which had sprung up in the Maccabæan struggle, and the great work of the period, almost the Gospel of the age, the Book of Daniel.

Other books were still floating to and fro, the Wisdom of the Son of Sirach, the Psalter of Solomon. These, for reasons unknown to us, were not accepted by the Maccabæan compiler. But the inestimable additions made by him were now secured to the sacred volume in a far more enduring sense than was thought of by the historian who described their annexation in the subsequent[1] century. 'They' do indeed 'remain with us.' The Hebrew Canon henceforth consisted, not only of 'the Law 'and the Prophets,' but also of this third instalment, which, from the roll to which they were appended, took the name of 'the Psalms,'[2] or more generally, from their own indeterminate character, 'the Writings,' 'the Sacred Writings,' 'the Books,' 'the other Books.' That is to say, inferior as their place was compared with the older volume, they took the name, which, little as it could have been then anticipated, was destined afterwards to comprehend and throw into the shade the titles borne even by the venerated Law and the inspired Prophets. They were emphatically 'the Scriptures,' the 'Hagiographa,' 'the Holy

[1] 2 Macc. ii. 14. [2] Luke xxiv. 44.

'Scriptures,' 'the Bibles,' the 'Biblia Sacra' of the Jewish Church. Already in the Book of Daniel there is a slight trace of the name 'Book' or 'Bible,' including the writings of Jeremiah. But, as a general rule, the name, naturally appropriate to more purely literary productions, belonged only to these later additions, and it was not till long afterwards that it ascended to its higher level and embraced with an iron grasp the whole multifarious volume of the Old and the New Covenant.

The door was closed, and, as far as the Church of Palestine was concerned, no new intruder was ever admitted. But there were several modifications still possible, so difficult is it even for the strictest rigour to fetter those books, 'which are 'like living creatures with hands and feet.' The Word of God, whether written or unwritten, cannot be bound with earthly chains. First, they were divided and subdivided afresh, in order to assimilate them to the fancy which sprang up of making their number exactly equal to the twenty-two letters of the Hebrew alphabet. For this purpose the Law was disintegrated into five parts. The two large groups, under the name of 'the Prophets,'—'the former,' containing the historical books of Joshua and Judges, and the Book of Kings, and 'the 'hinder,' containing Jeremiah, Ezekiel, and Isaiah, and the Lesser Prophets all in one—were now broken up. Joshua and Judges became two books. The 'Book of Kings' was divided into four, and the Prophets into fifteen component parts. Ruth was reckoned as part of 'Judges,' and the Lamentations as one with Jeremiah. Again, either for the purposes of public reading or from doubt as to their character, five were taken out of the whole collection, and ranged on separate rolls, called 'Megilloth.' These were Ruth, Esther, Canticles, Ecclesiastes, and Lamentations. Secondly, the arrangement of the Books, as they issued from the hands of the Maccabæan leader, had preserved on the whole the order in which the successive accretions had been formed. At the head was the Pentateuch; then came the Books which, whether of the earlier histories, or of the Prophets, properly so called, were comprised under the common title of Prophetical. And last were 'the Scriptures,' ending with the Chronicles. This was to the Jews of that age the last book of the Canon. But all this time-honoured arrangement was pulled to pieces by the Alexandrian critics, whose labours we have already indicated. They determined to disregard entirely the redactions of Nehemiah and Judas Maccabæus, and placed the books as far as possible according to their subjects and chronology. The collection of 'the Prophets' was torn asunder, and into the midst of it, following on the last book of the Kings, were inserted the three later historical books from the Hagiographa —the Chronicles, Ezra now broken into two parts, and Esther. These were followed by the poetical books, according to the supposed order of their authorship—Job, the Psalms, the Proverbs, the Canticles, and Ecclesiastes; and then followed at last the second part of Nehemiah's collection of the Prophets, preserving the priority of the twelve Lesser Prophets, and thus, with a true instinct of the latest book of the whole series, closing with Daniel, followed by the three kindred books of the Maccabees. This was the arrangement which prevailed more or less till it was once more disturbed by the Churches of the Reformation, which have combined by a rough compromise the Maccabæan Canon with the Alexandrian order. The Greek Bible kept the entrance open for the admission of yet newer books, for which Judas Maccabæus had left no place, and which, as we have indicated, were to exercise a still wider influence. But it is to him that we owe the distinction between the Hebrew and the Grecian books, to which the Reformers returned, and which remains a lasting monument of the victory of the holy Hebrew cause over the Græco-Syrian kingdom, though in quite another sense than he intended it. In later ages, both in the Jewish and the Christian Church, not only has this hard line of demarcation been questioned, but several of the books which he admitted—Ezekiel, the Canticles, Esther, and Ecclesiastes—have been challenged. Yet on the whole his judgment has been confirmed. The Greek additions, at least down to the last unexpected burst of Israelite prophecy, in the writings of the Evangelists and Apostles, have always borne, even when most admired, a stamp of inferiority. The original Hebrew books, even when most open to censure, have yet a native vigour and conciseness which belongs to the old Palestinian atmosphere—'the Rock of Abraham, from whence 'they were hewn.' Even as a theologian, Judas 'has fought 'the battle of Israel.'

NOTE ON ACRA AND MOUNT ZION.

Zion and Acra.

Without embarking on the intricate question of the interior topography of Jerusalem, there are two points which are clear in the Maccabæan time:—

1. 'Mount Zion' in 1 Macc. iv. 37, 60; v. 54; vi. 62; vii. 33; xii., is the Temple Hill—that which in 2 Chron. iii. 1 and in later times has been called Mount Moriah.
2. The 'city or citadel of David' (1 Macc. i. 33; xiv. 36) is that which was occupied by the Syrian fortress, and usually known by the name of 'Acra' (with the definite article) 'the Height' (1 Macc. iv. 2; ix. 52; x. 32; xiii. 52; xiv. 7; 2 Macc. xv. 31, 35).

From this it follows:—

1. That 'Mount Zion' had changed its meaning since 2 Sam. v. 7, 9 (1 Chron. xi. 5), when it was identical with the citadel of David.
2. That 'Acra' afterwards changed its meaning, when it was identified by Josephus, *Ant.* xii. 5, 4; xiii. 6, 7; *B. J.* v. 4, 1. I. 22, with the Lower Hill.
3. That both were different from the *Baris* or tower occupied by the Persian garrison, close to the Temple (Neh. ii. 8, vii. 2) and apparently on the site of the later Tower of Antonia.

NOTE ON THE FEAST OF THE DEDICATION.

The Hanucah.

I am indebted to the kindness of a modern Hebrew scholar for the accompanying description of the present celebration of the Hanucah or Feast of the Dedication:—

'The Feast of Lights is observed as an eight days' holiday, 'on which, however, all manner of work is allowed without 'restriction. At home on each evening, as soon as possible as is 'consistent with their arrangements, the lights are lit, commencing 'with one green taper on the first night, the number increasing by 'one every evening, eight being used on the last occasion. Tapers 'are the ordinary custom, but the more orthodox people use oil and 'wick; but either is allowable. The prescribed formula of bless-'ing[1] is said over these lights, and they burn for half-an-hour, 'during which all work is at a standstill. Latterly, that is to say, 'in modern times, a very pretty hymn has been added, written as 'an acrostic by one Mordecai. The tune is popular, not only in 'England, but throughout the world where Jews are to be found. 'This is about the whole of the home service, except that at every 'meal, when grace is said, a special prayer is added commemora-'tive of God's mercies in rescuing the nation from the hands of 'their Greek oppressors. This prayer is also said in synagogue 'every morning, noon, and night, being introduced among the 'eighteen Benedictions, which are repeated three times daily 'throughout the year.

'In the synagogue the feast is likewise observed with some 'solemnity. There is usually a large gathering on the first night, 'but this falls off during the remainder of the week. Every even-'ing during the week the officiating minister ascends a platform 'and lights the candles as at home *exactly*. Here large wax candles 'are employed; oil is allowed, but I have never seen it. The 'hymn referred to before is *not* said in synagogue, but Psalm xxx. 'is repeated instead, more stress being laid upon the opening 'evening's service than the others. In the more important metro-'politan synagogues, the service on the first night is stirring and 'choral.

'Ordinarily, on Mondays and Thursdays, a scroll of the Law is 'taken from the Ark and a small portion of the Pentateuch is read 'to the congregants, varying from a dozen to two dozen verses, 'but during *Hanucah* the Law is read *every* morning.[2] As, how-'ever, here is naturally no allusion to the Feast of Dedication to 'be found in the Pentateuch, the history of the Dedication of the 'Tabernacle is read in lieu of it, as being the readiest reminder; 'and this is subdivided into eight sections, one for each day. On 'the Sabbath of the feast (there may be two Sabbaths if the first

[1] 'Blessed art Thou, O Lord our God, 'King of the world, Who hast sanctified us 'with Thy commandments and enjoined 'upon us to light the lamps of the Feast 'of the Dedication.' (*Jewish World.*)

[2] There is also read an account of the deliverance by the Maccabees which is repeated 66 times in 8 days. (*Jewish World.*)

'day is Saturday) this section is read in addition to the Lesson of 'the day, so that two scrolls are removed from the Ark; the reading from the Prophets, common to every Sabbath, is selected from 'Zechariah ii. 14 to iv. 7, as being most appropriate. The sermon 'of the day is usually devoted to the events being commemorated. 'The period is marked by an extra half-holiday or so being given 'in schools during the week, a festive entertainment being often 'added.'

NOTE ON THE CHRONOLOGICAL STATEMENTS OF DANIEL IX. 24-27.

'I know,' said St. Jerome, 'that this passage has been much 'disputed amongst the most learned men. Each has spoken the 'opinions suggested by his own mind. And, therefore, because I 'consider it dangerous to pass judgment on the views of the 'Doctors of the Church, and invidious to prefer one to another, 'I will state what each one has thought, and leave it to the option 'of the reader whose interpretation he shall follow.'

Such is the statement prefixed to the elaborate summary of the contradictory opinions in the 'Speaker's Commentary' on the Book of Daniel, pp. 360-365, which concludes with the words, 'It is impossible at present to explain the passage satisfactorily.'

It is not in accordance with the plan of this work to discuss these several opinions. But it is permissible, and may be useful, to state the view which is commended to us by the nearest contemporary authority and by the nearest coincidence of fact.

According to this view, 'the commandment to rebuild Jerusalem' in Dan. ix. 25 is the prophecy of the seventy years in Jeremiah, B.C. 588 (Dan. ix. 2); the Anointed Prince is Cyrus, as in Isaiah xlv. 1, B.C. 536. More doubtfully, in Dan. ix. 21, 'the 'death of the Anointed one without a successor' (Heb.) is Onias the high priest (2 Macc. iv. 35), which is substantially the explanation of Eusebius (*H. E.* i. 6, *Demonst. Ev.* viii. 391). 'The Prince 'who shall destroy the city and sanctuary, whose end shall be 'sudden,' in Dan. ix. 26, is Antiochus Epiphanes (1 Macc. vi. 8). In Dan. ix. 27 (compare viii. 11, xii. 12) the cessation of the daily sacrifice is the cessation described in 1 Macc. i. 54, and the Abomination of Desolation (Dan. xi. 31, xii. 12) is the desecration of the altar by Antiochus as described under that same phrase in 1 Macc. i. 54. The three years (Dan. viii. 14, xii. 11, 12) relate to the interval between the desecration and the re-consecration of the altar (1 Macc. ii. 54, iv. 52).

The only illustrations from any other part of the Bible are to be found in the application of the words 'the Abomination of 'Desolation' in Matt. xxiv. 15, Mark xiii. 14, to the desecration of the Herodian temple by the Roman Government. Such a secondary application is in accordance with the well-known usage of the New Testament, as, for example, Matt. ii. 15, 18, Acts vii. 43, Rev. xi. 11, xviii. 2.

The expression, 'One like to a Son of Man,' in Dan. vii. 13 [1] (Heb.) is explained in Dan. vii. 27 to be 'the people of the saints.' The phrase 'Son of Man,' in the only other place in which it occurs in Daniel (viii. 17), agrees with its universal signification in the Old Testament, viz., as representing man, collectively or individually, in his mortal and fragile aspect. See especially Psalm viii. 4, lxxx. 17, and the forty-seven times in which it is applied to Ezekiel. It is in the Book of Enoch that it is first applied to the Chosen One who is to judge the world (xlv. 3, 5; xlvi. 3, 6; xlvii. 3; lxii. 2, 5; lxii. 27, 29; lxx. 1). The references are given at length in Dr. Pusey's 'Daniel the Prophet,' 382–385.

That numerous *applications* of these passages may be made to the events of Christian history, past or future, is obvious. The purpose of these remarks is to point out—what is admitted by almost all scholars (see *Speaker's Commentary*, iv. 337, 365)—that their *primary* and *historical* reference is to the Maccabæan age.

[1] 'The Authorised Version: "*The* Son 'of Man," however accurate as a mode 'of expressing a Christian truth, must, if 'literally rendered, be altered into "*A* 'son of man."'—*Speaker's Commentary*, vol. vi. 328.

THE ROMAN PERIOD.

B.C. 160 TO A.D. 70.

LECTURE XLIX.

THE ASMONEAN DYNASTY.

AUTHORITIES.

(1) 1 Macc. ix. 23—xvi.
(2) Joseph. *Ant.* xiii. 1–16.
(3) 5 Macc. xviii.–xxxiv.
(4) Book of Judith, B.C. 130?
(5) Sibylline Books (iii. 828) B.C. 120, see Lecture XLVII.

(6) Book of Enoch, B.C. 115? which is found (1) in Epistle of Jude, verses 14, 15; (2) Fragments preserved by Georgius Syncellus, A.D. 792, and discovered by Scaliger; (3) in the Ethiopic Bible, discovered in 1773 by Bruce, the Abyssinian traveller, and translated into English by Archbishop Laurence, 1838, and into German, with notes and discussions, by Dillmann, 1853.

(7) The Book of Jubilees? Probably B.C. 100-1? quoted in Clem. *Recog.* xxx., xxxii., perhaps in 2 Peter ii. 4, Jude 6, and in various later authors, collected in Fabricius' *Codex Pseudep.* v. i. 849–863 under the name of 'Little Genesis;' originally in Hebrew, translated into Greek, and found in an Ethiopic version in 1844 by Kraff, and first brought to notice by Ewald (Dr. Ginsburg, in Kitto, ii. 669-670). Its date and origin are, however, too uncertain to justify much remark.

(8) The Talmudical traditions, given in Derenbourg, *Histoire de la Palestine*, ch. iv. v. vi. vii. viii.

THE ROMAN PERIOD.

LECTURE XLIX.

THE ASMONEAN DYNASTY.

THE chief offence which alienated from Judas Maccabæus the fanatical spirits amongst his countrymen seems to have been an act of which he did not live to reap the fruits, but which indicates the opening of a new epoch in Palestine. He had heard of a mighty people in the far West who might assist his country in her struggles. There had been during his father's time in Syria one who could have told more of the prowess of Rome than any other man living. It was only thirty years before the Maccabæan insurrection that Hannibal came from Carthage to the cradle of his race at Tyre and thence to Antioch[1] in the fond hope of rousing the East against his ancient foe, and thus fulfilling to the last his own early vow of eternal enmity against the Roman State, which is known to us only through his own conversations in this his latest journey. A confused story of a letter from two Roman Consuls occurs in the doubtful legends of the campaign against Lysias.[2] Whether from these or other sources had come accounts of the rising nation in the latest days of the Maccabee which commanded the whole attention at once of his powerful intellect and his lofty soul. He had heard of their rapid[3] growth and their astounding valour. He was full of their recent victory over the Galatian or Celtic tribes of Asia Minor who had assisted the Syrian

[1] Polyb. iii. 11 ; Liv. xxxiii. 45.

[2] 2 Macc. xi. 34.

[3] 1 Macc. viii. 1–16.

monarch in his war against them. He had been deeply impressed by the tidings that they had made themselves masters of Spain, with its mines of gold and silver—that distant dependency, the America of the old Eastern world—even then so hard to conquer and so difficult to keep. He had heard of their victories over the kings of Greece, still veiled to his eyes under the name of Chittim or Cyprus, and naturally, with all details, of their successful encounters with the foremost prince of the Asiatic kingdoms in these latter days—Antiochus the Great. But, most of all—and here the Israelite hero rises at once to the fullest appreciation of the true majesty of Rome, and also gives us the fullest insight into the simple dignity of his own elevated spirit—he knew that 'whom 'they would help to a kingdom, they reign; whom, again, they 'would, they displace;' 'finally, that they were highly exalted: 'yet for all this' (so unlike the Princes, great and small, in Asia, past or present) 'none of them wore a crown or was clothed in 'purple to be magnified thereby.' Moreover, 'how they had 'made for themselves a senate-house, wherein' (the inaccuracies[1] of detail only confirm the general faithfulness of the impression) 'three hundred and twenty men sat in council daily, 'consulting always for the people to the end that they might be 'well ordered; and that they committed their government to 'one man every year, who ruled over all their country, and 'that they were all obedient to that one' (and here we mark how untarnished still remained the ideal of 'the brave days of 'old,' when 'none were for a party and all were for the State'), 'there was neither envy nor emulation amongst them.' It is a moment impressive in the retrospect, and must have been so even at the time, before the consequences of the act could be apprehended, when, in the Roman Senate there appeared two ambassadors from the insurgents of Palestine, asking in the

The Treaty with Rome. B.C. 162.

[1] The inaccuracies in the account are as follows: 1. Spain was not wholly reduced till the reduction of Cantabria, B.C. 19. 2. The elephants at the Battle of Magnesia were not 120, but (Liv. xxxviii. 39) 54. 3. Antiochus was not taken prisoner. 4. His dominions did not include India. 5. The conquest of Ætolia was fifteen years later. 6. The Senate was not 320, but 300. 7. One consul is substituted for two. 8. The Roman factions are ignored.—The total omission of the conquest of Carthage is difficult to explain.

name of Judas Maccabæus for an alliance with the Imperial Commonwealth—the first occasion on which the representatives of the two nations met face to face. From their Greek names, Jason and Eupolemus, it may be inferred that Judas, with his usual sagacity, had chosen his envoys, not from the stricter, but the free-minded section of his nation. The journey had been 'long exceedingly.' The august assembly, according to their custom, received them in their full sitting. A treaty offensive and defensive was agreed upon, and written on two sets of brazen tablets. One was deposited, as usual, in the Tabularium beneath the Capitol.[1]

The copy was sent to Jerusalem; its opening words, though known to us only in Greek, betray the fine old Roman formula —'Quod felix faustumque sit populo Romano[2] et genti Judæ-'orum.' Before it arrived, its bold contriver had paid on the battle-field the penalty of his enlarged policy. But its fruits remained, and from henceforth, for good or evil, the fortunes of the Jewish State were inextricably bound up with those of its gigantic ally—at first on terms of friendly equality, soon of complete dependence, then of violent conflict, finally of the profoundest spiritual relations—each borrowing from each the peculiar polity, teaching, superstitions, vices, and virtues of the other. When Antiochus Epiphanes was negotiating with[3] Popilius Lænas on the seashore of Egypt, the Roman envoy drew with his staff a boundary in the sand out of which he forbade the Syrian king to move. Like to this was the invisible circle within which from henceforth Judæa was enclosed by Rome; within which, we may add, the power of Rome was henceforth enclosed by the religion of Judæa. Into the Tiber, to use the expression of the later Roman poet, henceforth flowed the Orontes. The Jordan, as in the early Roman mosaics, henceforth assumed the attitude[4] and physiognomy of Father Tiber.

With this thought ever before us we return to the history of

[1] Jos. *Ant.* xii. 10, 6.
[2] Grimm, on 1 Macc. viii.
[3] Liv. xlv. 12.
[4] Even the Roman name of God, 'Deus 'optimus maximus,' was at last taken by the Jews (5 Macc. xvi. 26).

the struggle in Syria. From this time it enters on a new phase, for the understanding of which a brief retrospective survey is required.

So long as the heat of the contest with Antiochus continued, there could be no recognised government of the nation. The commanding character and magic spell of the Maccabee's name was sufficient. But now after he was gone, having secured by his victory the independence of his country, it becomes necessary under these altered circumstances to review the position of the ancient institutions.

The Jewish Institutions.

Since the death of Zerubbabel, the High Priest had become virtually the representative of the people. The investment of Ezra and of Nehemiah [1] with the office of the Persian Governor gave them for the time supreme authority. One momentary chance had opened for the rise of a prince [2] of the Royal line in the questionable claim of the sons of Tobias. But these were exceptions. The descendants of Aaron took their natural place at the head of the nobles, in the absence of any other authority. Many of their ancient prerogatives were gone. The oracular breast-plate had never returned from Babylon. The sacred oil had never been recovered [3]—and in consequence the profuse unction which had enveloped their whole persons in its consecrating fragrance, through hair, and beard, and clothes down to their feet, had been long discontinued. The elaborate ceremonial of the sacrifice of the bullock had also been dropped. In the place of these the sanctity of the office was now wrapped up in the blue robe with its tinkling bells, the long golden sash, the high blue turban, in which at his accession the new High Priest was clothed, and in which, whatever might be his ordinary dress, he discharged his public offices. One relic of the ancient insignia had been preserved, which was probably prized as the most precious of all. It was the golden plate affixed to the turban, inscribed 'Holiness 'to Jehovah,' which was believed to have come down from the time of Aaron, and which, treasured through all [4] the

The Pontificate.

[1] See Lecture XLIII.
[2] See Lecture XLVII.
[3] Reland, *de Rebus et Locis Sacris*.
[4] Jos. *Ant.* iii. 3, 6; vii. 3, 8; *Dictionary of the Bible*, i. 807.

vicissitudes of the Jewish State, was carried to Rome by Titus, and seen there by a great Jewish Rabbi in the time of Hadrian. Whosoever had these paraphernalia in his possession had virtually the appointment to the office. There have been many later occasions in ecclesiastical history in which excessive importance has been ascribed to vestments, but the conveyance of the sacerdotal succession through the dress of the High Priest is the highest point to which this peculiar form of veneration has reached. Still, down to the troubles of the Syrian war, the post of High Priest was rigidly confined to the lineal descendants of Joshua, the Pontiff of the Return, and so remained, even through all the violence and disorder which, first in the family of Eliashib and then of Onias, marked its occupants. Of these the last was Menelaus, in the Jewish nomenclature Onias, the renegade who had led Antiochus into the temple, and secured for himself the golden candlestick. After long struggles to maintain his office, sometimes in the Temple, more usually in the Syrian fortress, he was represented in varying traditions to have met with the fitting reward of his misdeeds. According to one he was thrown headlong into a tower full of ashes—as if to requite him for his profanation of the sacred ashes [1] on the altar. According to another, which clung to the hope that the High Priest, wicked as he was, had repented at last, he was sawn asunder for refusing to participate further in the plunder [2] of the Temple. The Syrian Government appointed in his place Eliashib or Jehoiakim, more usually known by his Greek name of Alcimus. He, according to a popular legend just mentioned, was the nephew of the chief Rabbi of that time, Joseph, son of Joazar, who was impaled by the Syrian persecutor. Alcimus rode by in state as he saw his uncle hanging on the instrument of torture. 'Look at the 'horse which my master has given to me,' he said, 'and look 'at that which he has given to thee.' 'If those,' said the venerable martyr, 'who have fulfilled the will of God are thus 'punished, what shall be the fate of those who have broken it?' The words shot like a viper's fang into the breast of Alcimus.

[1] 2 Macc. xiii. 5–8. [2] Derenbourg, p. 53.

And the tradition went on to say that he had proceeded to destroy himself by the accumulation of all manner of punishments provided by the Jewish law—stoning, burning, beheading, hanging.[1] Another more authentic version described him as struck by palsy for having endeavoured, in pursuance of his Hellenising policy, to take down the partition which since the Return [2] separated the outer from the inner court of the Temple.

But whatever may be the reconciliation of these conflicting stories, which betray the same lurking tenderness towards the successor of Aaron as we have seen in the case of Menelaus. Alcimus still played a conspicuous part for at least two years before his end. He paid his homage to the Syrian Government by a golden crown and the branches of palm and olive used in the Temple processions, and represented that 'so long as Judas 'at the head [3] of "the Chasidim," or "Pious," was left, it was 'not possible that the state should be quiet.' Accordingly he was at once invested with the office which it was felt would carry weight into the heart even of the insurgent nation. The calculation was correct. The fanatical party, to whom every Grecianising tendency was an abomination, and the name of Alcimus a byword, yet, in their excessive tenacity for the letter above the spirit, when they heard [4] that a genuine 'son of Aaron' was advancing on Jerusalem, could believe no harm of him, and placed themselves in his hands, to find themselves miserably betrayed. In the massacre which followed, and in which probably Joseph the son of Joazar perished, their contemporaries seemed to see the literal fulfilment of the words of the seventy-fourth [5] Psalm. But Alcimus succeeded in his ambition. He entered on his office in the Temple, and it was he [6] who, when Nicanor had for a moment been won over by the magnanimity of the Maccabee's bearing, fearing that he might be supplanted by that formidable rival, sowed discord between the two friends, and brought on the final struggle, which terminated, as we have seen, in the

Alcimus. B.C. 162.

[1] Derenbourg, p. 54.
[2] 1 Macc. ix. 54–56; Jos. *Ant.* xii. 10, 6.
[3] 2 Macc. xiv. 6.
[4] 1 Macc. vii. 14.
[5] 1 Macc. vii. 17
[6] 2 Macc. xiv. 26.

destruction of both. For the moment, on the fall of Judas, the party of Alcimus was in the ascendant. Bacchides took Nicanor's place. A confused struggle ensued. Jonathan, the youngest of the Asmonean brothers, appeared to be marked out for the supreme command by the peculiar dexterity which gave him his surname of 'the cunning.' There was a skirmish [1] beyond the Jordan—a fray with the Arabs—a sudden inroad on the wedding-party of a tribe that had carried off the quiet eldest brother John—a close encounter with Bacchides, which Jonathan and his party escaped by plunging into the Jordan, like the Gadite [2] warriors of old times. For a time all the fruits of the victories of Judas seemed to be lost. Bacchides occupied all the Judæan fortresses and Alcimus reigned supreme in the Temple. Jonathan meanwhile entrenched himself in the Pass of Michmash, in the haunts of his illustrious namesake, the friend of David. The sudden death of Alcimus, and the disgust of Bacchides at the excesses of his party, finally cleared the prospect, and, after a long and doubtful conflict, Jonathan gradually vindicated his claim to be the successor of his glorious brother. The rivalry between the two claimants to the throne of Antioch, Alexander Balas, the pretended son of Antiochus, and his cousin Demetrius, gave to the Jewish chief the opportunity of siding with Alexander, who in return struck the critical blow alone wanting to Jonathan's success, by investing him with the office of High Priest, and adding to it the dignity of 'the 'King's Friend,' with a golden crown and purple robe—the mark of adoption into the regal circle.

It was a decisive step in the relations of the Syrian Government to the Jewish insurgents, as the first recognition of their independence. But it was a decisive step also in the internal history of Israel. It was a break in the succession of the High Priests, such as had only taken place twice before, once when Eli, from some unexplained cause, superseded the elder house of Eleazar; again when Zadok was placed by Solomon in the place of Abiathar. But in the elevation of Jonathan to the High Priesthood, the interruption was more serious. Regarded

[1] 1 Macc. ix. 35-48. [2] See Lecture XXII.

from a purely ceremonial point of view, it was a complete departure from that hereditary descent which had hitherto marked the whole previous series.

The last unquestioned representative of the unbroken line was the murdered Onias, and his legitimate successor was the youth who had fled to Egypt. But even Jason, Menelaus,[1] and Alcimus, although covered with popular obloquy, were yet all more or less members of the same sacred family. As such they were venerated even by those who most abhorred their policy. The extinction, therefore, of the house of Josedek, whether with Onias, Jason, or Alcimus, was regarded as the close of 'the 'Anointed Priests' of those (so it would seem) who belonged to that direct succession which had shared in the consecrated oil of the ancient[2] Priesthood.

Seven years had now passed, in which the functions of the great office had been altogether suspended; and it might have seemed as if from excess of regard for the exact hierarchical lineage, the Pontificate itself would expire. But here, as in other critical moments of the Jewish history, the moral force of the higher spirits of the nation overrode the ceremonial scruples. As in Russia, after the civil wars which brought to an end the ancient dynasty of Ruric,[3] the nation chose for their new Prince the child of the Romanoff Prelate, who had with his whole order suffered in the struggle against the Polish oppressor, so the Jewish people could not but turn to the gallant family who had saved them and their faith from destruction. Even in the lifetime of Judas the idea of investing him with the High Priesthood had been entertained, though never fulfilled. And now

[1] This is doubted by Herzfeld, ii. 218. But that Menelaus was the brother of Onias III. and of Jason, is stated by Josephus, *Ant.* xii. 5, 1, xx. 10, 3 (his Hebrew name being Onias, *ibid.* and Hegesippus, ii. 13). That Alcimus was the nephew of Menelaus, according to the Rabbinical tradition, is almost certain (Derenbourg, 53, 54), and both statements are confirmed by 1 Macc. vii. 14. The natural tendency of the Jewish traditions would have been to illegitimatise these heretical Pontiffs.

[2] This is one probable explanation of Dan. ix. 25, whether 'the Anointed One' be Onias, or (as Herzfeld, ii. 430) Jason (comp. 2 Macc. i. 10). So (in general terms) the passage is interpreted by Eusebius, *H. E.* i. 6, *Demonst. Ev.* viii. p. 391 —'It means nothing else than the succes- 'sion of anointed High Priests' (compare Tertullian and Theodoret). (See Rosenmüller *ad loc.*)

[3] See *Lectures on the Eastern Church,* Lecture X.

came the time for its accomplishment. To modern nations the selection of a warlike deliverer for a sacred post, of raising a Charles Martel to the Papacy, a Cromwell to the office of Moderator, a Gustavus Vasa or a Wellington to the Primacy, is curiously incongruous. But the Jewish Priesthood was so essentially military in its character, so entirely mechanical[1] in its functions, that there was no shock to its associations in the same hand grasping the sword or spear of Phinehas and the censer or rod of Aaron. The Asmonean family brought to it more than it gave to them—a moral elevation and grandeur, which it had long lost, and which, after they had gone, it did not retain. One indispensable outward qualification there was to be and one only, the nomination, by the Syrian Government, stepping as it did into the place and authority formerly occupied by Moses, by Solomon, and by Cyrus. It was for this benefit, no less than for his friendly relations generally, that the name of Alexander Balas was so studiously cherished by the Jewish Annals. For this they ignore his doubtful birth, his questionable surname; they rejoice in his wedding festivity; they describe with pride how their own chief sat by him in purple and ruled as a Syrian officer over the troops and over a district[2] in the south of Palestine, how he received from the king a golden brooch, and the appanage of Ekron.

The Pontificate of Jonathan. B.C. 153.

The entrance of Jonathan on the Pontificate was conducted with due solemnity. It was on the joyous Festival of the Tabernacles, so often chosen for inaugurations of this kind, that Jonathan dressed himself in the consecrated clothes, surmounting the blue turban with the golden[3] crown which he wore as 'the King's Friend,' and at the same time (it is characteristically added) collected his forces and his arms. From this time the union of the sacerdotal and the political supremacy was completed, and the language in which that union is described in the 110th Psalm is more exactly applicable to the Pontificate of the Asmonean warriors than to any period since the age of

[1] See Lecture XXXVI.

[2] στρατηγὸν καὶ μεριάρχην. The latter word is only found again in Jos. *Ant.* xii. 5, 5.

[3] 1 Macc. x. 21, 22.

David. The military career of Jonathan himself was not for a moment interrupted. He fortified the Temple mount afresh 'with square stones,' intending, apparently, in despair of removing the Syrian fortress, to make it a completely separate town, erecting a large mound on the side towards the fort, and repairing the ruinous parts of the wall overhanging the Kedron.[1] He accepted the challenge of the general of the rival Syrian king Demetrius into the Philistine plain, 'where there was 'neither stone nor pebble nor place to flee unto,'[2] beat back with his archers the cavalry on which the Syrians relied, secured Joppa and Askalon, and burned the old sanctuary of the Philistine Dagon at Ashdod. The temple was left in ruins, and the scorched corpses of those who perished in it lay all around. The succession first of Demetrius to the throne, then of the son of Alexander Balas. made no difference in Jonathan's position. From each he received the confirmation of the government to his sacerdotal office, and the annexation of the three outposts of Apherema, Ramathaim, and Lydda from the borders of Samaria. Less attractive than his brother Judas, worthy of his name 'the crafty,' he went on balancing the various pretenders against each other, till at last he was caught by the Syrian general Tryphon, carried off in a deep snowstorm, and killed in an obscure village beyond the Jordan.[3]

Simon. B.C. 143.

One still remained of the gallant five—he whom Mattathias on his death-bed had designated alike by his superior wisdom and his age (next to the retiring John he was the eldest) 'as the father of them all.' He rose at once to the occasion. His appeal to his countrymen and their response are indeed the models of the generous spirit which can alone fill the vacancy caused by 'a lost leader.' 'When 'Simon saw that the people was in great trembling and fear, 'he went up to Jerusalem, and gathered the people together; 'and gave them exhortation, saying, "Ye yourselves know 'what great things I, and my brethren, and my father's house,

[1] 1 Macc. xii. 37, 38. Caphenatha is only mentioned here.

[2] An excellent description of the Shephela, 1 Macc. x 73. Compare, for the contest of the Syrian cavalry and the Israelite infantry on the plains 1 Kings xx. 25.

[3] 1 Macc. xi. 34.

'have done for the laws and the sanctuary, the battles also 'and troubles which we have seen, by reason whereof all my 'brethren are slain for Israel's sake, and I am left alone. 'Now therefore be it far from me, that I should spare mine 'own life in any time of trouble: for I am no better than 'my brethren. Doubtless I will avenge my nation, and the 'sanctuary, and our wives, and our children: for all the 'heathen are gathered to destroy us of very malice." Now 'as soon as the people heard these words, their spirits revived. 'And they answered with a loud voice, saying, "Thou shalt 'be our leader instead of Judas and Jonathan thy brother. 'Fight thou our battles, and whatsoever thou commandest 'us, that will we do."'[1] His name of itself struck terror into the Syrian army. His first act was to recover his brother's bones, to inter them in the ancestral cavern at Modin. On that ridge overlooking the Philistine plain, the scene of so many of their glorious deeds, and visible from the Mediterranean Sea, beyond which, alone of the rulers of Israel, they had ventured to seek for allies from the western world, Simon, with the consciousness that he was the last of a family of heroes, built a monument, in that mixed Græco-Egyptian style which is to be seen at Petra, in the valley of the Kedron, and on the Appian Way. It was a square structure, surrounded by colonnades of monolith pillars, of which the front and back were of white polished stone. Seven pyramids were erected by Simon on the summit for the father and mother and the four brothers who now lay there, with the seventh for himself[2] when his time should come. On the faces of the monument were bas-reliefs, representing the accoutrements of sword and spear and shield, 'for an eternal memorial' of their many battles. There were also the sculptures of 'ships'—no doubt to record their interest in that long seaboard of the Philistine coast, which they were the first to use for their country's good. A monument at once so Jewish in idea, so Gentile in execution, was worthy of the combination of patriotic fervour and philosophic enlargement of soul which raised the Maccabæan heroes so high above their age.

Monument at Modin.

[1] 1 Macc. xiii. 2–9.

[2] *Ibid.* xiii. 27; Jos. *Ant.* xiii. 6, 1.

The monument remained in all its completeness till the first century, and in sufficient distinctness till the fourth century, of the Christian era. Then all trace of its existence and even of the name of the place disappeared, and it is only within the last three years that the joint labours of Polish, French, and English explorers have discovered 'Modin' in the village of Medieh, and, possibly, the tomb of the Maccabees in the remains of large sepulchral[1] vaults and broken columns in its neighbourhood, corresponding in general situation and, as far as the few traces left can indicate, in detail, with the only tomb among the existing remains of Palestine (except the patriarchal sanctuary at Machpelah) which can be clearly identified.

Conquest of the Syrian fortresses.

But Simon was to raise a nobler monument to the memory of his brethren than the sepulchre of Modin. Far advanced as he was in years, three crowning achievements fell to his lot which neither of his more stirring brothers had been able to accomplish. There were three strongholds of the Syrian party, which, after all the successes of Judas and Jonathan, had remained in their hands. One was Gezer,[2] the ancient Canaanite fortress in the south-western plain, which after long vicissitudes had passed into the hands of the Israelites, and now again in these later days had become the chief garrison of the Syrians in the thoroughfare of Philistia. This was attacked with the newly-invented[3] Macedonian engine of war, and the terrified inhabitants surrendered at discretion; the images in the temples were cleared out, and a colony of Jews was established there under Simon's son John, now for the first time winning his renown.

The second outpost was the oftentimes taken and retaken rock-fortress on the road to Hebron, Beth-zur. This, whether captured by Simon at this or at some earlier period, was now

[1] Mr. Sandrecsky and Mr. Conder (*Palestine Exploration Fund*, 1873, 93), M. Forner and M. Guérin (*Description de la Palestine*, i. 403).

[2] In 1 Macc. xiii. 43. Gaza is a misreading for Gazara, which is preserved in Jos. *B. J.* i. 2, 2; *Ant.* xiii. 6, 7. Comp. 1 Macc. xiii. 53, xii. 34, xv. 28, 35 (see Ewald, v. 335). Gezer was discovered in 1873 at Tell el-Jezer, six miles SSE. of Ramleh, by M. Clermont-Ganneau.

[3] 1 Macc. xiii. 43, 'Helepolis,' invented by Demetrius Poliorcetes (Plutarch, *Demetr.* c. 21).

for the first time secured and garrisoned[1] with Jews, and the day of its occupation, the 17th of Sivan (May–June), was celebrated as a festival.[2]

But the decisive victory was the expulsion of the Syrian occupants—'the sons of Acra,' as they were called—from the citadel that had so long overlooked the sanctuary. B.C. 142. It had been, as the historian calls it, the incarnate Enemy,[3] the Satan of Jerusalem. Now at last its doom was come. The day was long cherished,[4] the 23rd of Iyar (April–May), when Simon entered it with waving of palm-branches, with harps and cymbals, with hymns and odes. According to one account he went so far in his indignation as not only to dismantle the fortress, but to level the very hill on which it stood, so that it should no longer overlook the Temple. It was agreed (so ran the story) in solemn assembly that the inanimate mountain should thus, as it were, be decapitated for its insolence, and, by working night and day for three years, the summit of the hill was cleared away, so as to reduce it from a towering peak to a level surface.[5]

But these military achievements are not the main grounds of Simon's fame. If Judas was the David of the Asmonean race, and Jonathan its Joab, Simon was its Solomon, the restorer of peace and liberty. In many forms this change is marked. From his accession a new era was dated, the first year of independence, when the nation ceased to pay the tribute which from the Persian kings downwards they had paid to each successive conquering dynasty. Henceforward the Jewish contracts were dated 'In the first year of Simon, the 'great High Priest, and General, and Leader of the Jews.'

Concurrently with this came the natural sign of nationality,

[1] 1 Macc. xiv. 33. [2] Derenbourg, 68.

[3] 1 Macc. xiii. 51.

[4] *Ibid.* xiii. 51. Derenbourg, 67.

[5] Jos. *Ant.* xiii. 6, 7. That this story of Josephus relates to the hill of the citadel of David, and not to 'the Lower 'Hill,' afterwards called Acra, is evident from the context. But it is difficult to reconcile the statement with the total silence of 1 Macc. xiii. 51–53, and also with the actual features of the ground. It is possible, however, that what was actually done was (as implied in the passage itself), not to change the relative altitudes of the citadel and the Temple, but to reduce the rock of the citadel so considerably as to deprive it of that insulting and menacing altitude which it once wore.

never before claimed, of striking coins for themselves. This privilege was formally granted by Antiochus VII., and, though there may be a few instances of such coinage before the actual permission was given, it is from this, the fourth, year of Simon's reign that the coins have unmistakably his name and superscription. The devices which appear on them are all indications of the peace[1] and plenty which he had ushered in—the cup, the vine, the palm-branches, the lily, the fruit-boughs of Palestine. The vine and the lily in sculptured emblem or in familiar phrase have since his time remained the heritage of his people. The prosaic historian of fifty years later warms almost into poetry as he describes how 'the land was at rest all the days of Simon;' how, following the wider views of his illustrious brother, and thus exemplifying the devices which he had carved on the family monument at Modin, he had turned Joppa into a port for the ships of the Mediterranean; how after the conquest of the three hated fortresses, the neglected agriculture and fruitage burst into new life; how 'the old men sat in the squares of the cities com-'muning of good things, and the young men put on their 'glorious apparel and their military mantles,'[2] the accoutrements in which they had won their country's freedom; how, as in the ancient days, 'each man sat under the vine' which overspread his own house, and 'the fig-tree' in his own garden; how all works of humanity and piety prospered under his hand—the provisioning and fortification of the towns, the study of the Law, the purification of the Temple. And it is not without a deep historical interest that we perceive the gradual intertwining of the destinies of the Jewish people, through this increase of fame and dominion, with the sway of that overweening power which Judas was the first to invoke, and which ultimately was to take the place of the foreign oppressors from whom they fancied that they had been for ever freed. Two messages came to Simon of unequal value. One, if so be, was from the shadow of the Spartan State, whose intercourse with Judæa is

Sovereignty of Simon. B.C. 141.

[1] Madden's *Jewish Coins*, 39-50.

[2] δόξας—στολάς, the usual phrases for military dress. See Grimm, on 1 Macc. xiv. 10.

so difficult to understand. But the other came from Rome, and to Rome once more ambassadors were sent with a golden shield full of gifts, and the treaty engraven on tablets of brass; and the Syrian king Demetrius, overawed by the spectacle of that great alliance, gave to the High Priesthood of Simon the ratification which was needed for the regularity of the succession, together with the title of 'the King's Friend.' His princely state, with his display of gold and silver plate, awed [1] the envoy even of the Kings of Syria. His own countrymen were convoked to ratify the decision of the Syrian Government. 'In the fore-court [2] of the people of God' (as it was solemnly called in the Hebrew tongue), on the 18th of the month of Elul (May), a document was drawn up and engraved on brazen tablets, and placed in the treasury of the Temple, commemorating the noble deeds of himself and his brother Jonathan, and recognising him as their prince and leader, and, in the splendid hyperbole of the ancient Psalm, granting to him his office, not merely as a transient personal honour, but to be hereditary in his own family, held as though it was 'a 'High Priesthood for ever.' And then, with a sudden consciousness of having, perhaps, been too bold, the historian adds the characteristic contradiction and reserve (not without a sense of the rude shock which Simon's elevation gave to the stricter notions of legitimate succession), 'until a faithful Prophet [3] 'should arise,' like Jeremiah or Elijah, who should read aright the secrets and the difficulties of their situation. It is the reserve and contradiction which in times of transition is the mark, not only of noble faith, but of homely common sense, and of far-sighted wisdom.

The close of Simon's life was hardly in keeping with his long and honourable career. He and his two younger sons were entrapped by his son-in-law into a drunken supper at the fortress of Dok, near Jericho, and there treacherously murdered.

B.C. 135.

Thus died the last of the five brothers. His aged wife was with him—a high-spirited woman, of whose early life strange

[1] 1 Macc. xv. 32. [2] *Ibid.* xiv. 28 (Ewald, v. 338). [3] *Ibid.* xiv. 41.

adventures were recounted in after days. When the most energetic of his sons, John, hastened to avenge the murder, the brutal assassin placed the venerable lady on the walls of the fortress and scourged her with rods before the eyes of her son to induce him to retire. She, with a courage worthy of the house into which she had married, entreated him to disregard her tortures. But he could not endure the sight, and raised the blockade. The delay threw the besiegers into the Sabbatical year. The murderer completed his crime by the execution of the mother and her two sons, and escaped to a friend, a Greek adventurer who had gained possession of the Trans-jordanic Philadelphia.

With the death of Simon the purest glory of the Maccabæan period ended. Yet it was not ended before he had finally established on the throne the only dynasty that has reigned over the undivided Jewish people, except the house of David. From that house the national expectations had in earlier days long hoped for a king. But when the Monarchy revived it was not in the house of Jesse, but of Asmon, not in the tribe of Judah, but of Levi.

John Hyrcanus. B.C. 135.

John, the survivor of the tragedy at Dok, was the one whom his father had long before appointed as commander of the Jewish forces at Gaza; and to him and his brother had been addressed those striking words which well express the feelings of the elder generation to that which is to take its place: 'I, and my[1] brethren, and my 'father's house, have ever, from our youth unto this day, 'fought against the enemies of Israel; and things have pros-'pered so well in our hands that we have delivered Israel often-'times. But now I am old, and ye, by God's mercy, are of 'a sufficient age; be ye instead of me and my brother, and go 'and fight for our nation, and the help from Heaven be with 'you!'

First of the Asmonean family, John bore a Gentile name, 'Hyrcanus,'—whether as the Greek[2] form corresponding to

[1] Macc. xvi. 2, 3.

[2] So Herzfel[1], arguing from the earlier John Hyrcanus.

Johanan, or from some[1] incident in his own life; and his reign was more like that of a Syrian than a Jewish prince. The records of it were preserved in the archives of the Priestly house, but are lost; and we are left to gather their contents from the brief narrative of Josephus. In Jerusalem he occupied and rebuilt the fortress[2] at the north-east corner of the Temple, once the site of the residence of the Persian, afterwards of the Roman, now of the Turkish, Governor. There, like the Regalia in the Tower, were deposited the pontifical robes which literally invested their possessor with the office.

Like his father and uncle, John was fortunate in finding a friend in the Syrian king, Antiochus Sidetes, to whom the Jews gave in consequence the name of Eusebius or the Pious, and from him received the full confirmation in his office. Two deadly enemies were crushed by his arms. The hated race of Esau were subdued and incorporated into the Jewish nation by circumcision. The Arab tribe of the Nabathæans, which had long been friendly to the Asmonean family and had occupied the ancient territory of the Edomites, doubtless assisted; and the proud Esau at last bowed his neck to the persevering Israel —only, however, to exercise once more a fresh and startling influence of another kind. Another cherished victory was that in which he razed to the ground the rival Temple on Mount Gerizim and totally destroyed the Greek city of Samaria, from which the Samaritans had migrated to Shechem in the time of Alexander.[3] It became henceforth known as 'the City of 'Graves.'[4]

For thirty-one years he carried on the vigour of his father's government, and combined with it a spark of that gift which was believed to have ceased with Malachi. He was, says Josephus, not only the Chief Ruler and the Chief Priest[5] but a Prophet. The intimations of his possessing this gift were, indeed, but slight, and exhibit almost the first example of the

[1] The killing of a Greek named Hyrcanus (5 Macc. xx. 1–3), or an expedition into Hyrcania (Eus. *Chron.* ii. p. 379). Sulpicius Sever. *H. E.* ii. 26 (Madden's *Jewish Coins*, 51).

[2] Jos. *Ant.* xviii. 4, 3.

[3] *Ibid.* xiii. 9, 1; 10, 2; *B. J.* i. 2, 6.

[4] Grätz, 60.

[5] Jos. *Ant.* xiii. 10, 7.

degradation of the word from its ancient high meaning to that of mere prediction. Once from the Holy of Holies he heard a voice announcing the victory of his sons over[1] the Samaritans on the day and hour that it occurred. Another time he[2] foresaw as if by divine intuition the fortunes of the three brothers who were to succeed him. It is useless to revive the narrative of the tissue of intrigues and crimes which convert the palace of the Royal Pontificate into the likeness of an Oriental Court. So completely had the Hellenising customs penetrated into the heart of the Asmonean family that the three sons of Hyrcanus, Judas,[3] Mattathias, and Jonathan, were respectively known as Aristobulus, Antigonus, and Alexander Jannæus. Of these the eldest, Aristobulus, had gained the character of 'the Philhellen,' or 'Lover of the Greeks,' and won the admiration of Gentile[4] writers by his moderation towards them, and by the energy with which, as his father had incorporated the Edomites on the south, so he conquered and absorbed the Ituræan borderers on the north. But that for which he was chiefly remembered was that he was the first of his family to assume the regal title and diadem. Once more there was a 'King[5] in Israel,' but bearing the name unknown before, and to acquire before long a solemn significance—'King 'of the Jews.' It was still, however, as High Priest that he reigned. And it was not till his brother[6] Jonathan mounted the throne under the name of Alexander that the coins alternately bear the names of Jonathan the High Priest (or, more rarely, the King) in Hebrew, and Alexander the King in Greek. In common parlance he was known by the two names combined, Alexander Jannæus. It is enough to indicate the general results of his long, troubled and adventurous reign. On the whole, in its external relations it carried on the successes of his predecessors. With the exception of Ptolemais, which remained Greek, he annexed all

Aristobulus. B.C. 107.

Alexander Jannæus. B.C. 106.

[1] Derenbourg, p. 74.
[2] Jos. *B. J.* i. 2, 8.
[3] Jos. *Ant.* xx. 10, 1.
[4] *Ibid.* xiii. 11, 3. Such was the opinion of Timagenes the Syrian, as quoted by Strabo.
[5] *Ibid.* xiii. 11, 1.
[6] Madden, 62, 68; Derenbourg, 95. These coins have been erroneously assigned to Jonathan, son of Mattathias, as those of Aristobulus to Judas.

the maritime or quasi-maritime towns [1] along the western coast from the Bay of Accho to Gaza. An anchor on his coins is, perhaps, the commemoration of this important accession. With the exception of Pella—the Macedonian settlement which, on refusing to adopt the Jewish rite, was destroyed—most of the Transjordanic settlements, whether Greek or Arab, followed the fate of Idumæa under his father, and of Ituræa under his brother.

In one of these obscure campaigns Alexander died, and to him succeeded—for the first time in Jewish history—a Queen, his widow Alexandra or Salome; possibly, the widow of his brother Aristobulus; the mother of two sons, the last independent Princes of the Asmonean dynasty.

Alexandra. B.C. 79.

It was one of the results of the peculiar warfare of the Asmonean Princes that Palestine gradually became studded with fortresses or castles apart from the main seats of their ancient history and civilisation, and commanding the passes in which they entrenched themselves against their enemies. Such had been Modin under Mattathias and Judas, and Masada [2] under Jonathan; such was Hyrcaneum under John Hyrcanus; such, under Alexander Jannæus, were Machærus [3] beyond the Dead Sea and Alexandreum on the mountains between Samaria and the Jordan valley, which subsequently became the recognised burial-place of the later Princes of the Asmonean family, as Modin had been of the first earlier. But Hyrcanus [4] and Alexander were interred, in regal or pontifical state, in tombs which long bore their names close to the walls of Jerusalem.[5]

This was the external course of the Royal Pontificate of Judæa—a period of nearly a century of mingled war and peace, but on the whole of independence and fame. It gave to the Roman writers their first idea of the Jewish State as of the union of the regal and priestly office, supposed by them, through a natural error, to be a long ancestral usage. Like the ancient

[1] Jos. *Ant.* xiii. 15, 4.
[2] Jos. *B. J.* vii. 8, 3.
[3] *Ibid.* vii. 6, 2.
[4] *Ibid.* vi. 2, 10.
[5] The precise sites of Hyrcaneum and Alexandreum are unknown; but they are possibly the 'Royal forts,' 'Tur Malka'—'Har Malcha' of later days. Grätz, 47, 127.

monarchy of David and Solomon, its success, at least under the reign of Simon, was sufficient to justify the deep impression which it left on the Gentile world of a more serious view of religion and a more sacred view of government, than elsewhere had come within their experience.[1] On the other hand, as in the earlier period, so now, the cynical or sagacious eye of Tacitus saw beneath this outward form the darker shades of 'revolutions,[2] banishments, massacres, murders—fratricidal, 'parricidal, conjugal.'

It will be the object of the remainder of this Lecture to penetrate into the interior of the Jewish life of this period, and bring out whatever instruction or interest it may yield of more than temporary value.

Literature of the period.

I. There are still heard in Palestine some echoes of the sacred voices of the past. Not only was the First Book of Maccabees, with all its stirring scenes, compiled immediately before or after the close of the reign of Hyrcanus, from the records kept in the Pontifical[3] registry, and about the same time the larger work of Jason of Cyrene, from which the Second Book of the Maccabees—probably half a century later—drew its materials; but the more hortatory and apocalyptic style, of which the Book of Daniel, whether in its narrative or its visions, is the great example, was continued, though in a less stately and impressive form, in the romantic tale of Judith and the prophecies of the Book of Enoch.

The Book of Judith.

The Book of Judith is so filled with chronological inconsistencies as to render it difficult to fix the date either of its authorship or of the events which it professes to record. But from its taking for the title of the enemy of Israel the name of a well-known Syrian general Holophernes[4] or Orrophernes, we may infer that it was composed under the Asmonean dynasty—whether in the time of Jonathan or of

[1] Justin, xxxvi. 2. 'Hic mos apud 'Judæos fuit, ut eosdem reges et sacerdotes 'haberent quorum justitia religione per- 'mixta incredibile quantum coaluere.' Similar remarks occur in Diod. Sic. xl. 1, though he was not aware that the title of King had been assumed.

[2] Tac. *Hist.* v. 8.

[3] 1 Macc. xvi. 24. Ewald, v. 463.

[4] A general of Demetrius I. Polyb. xxxiii. 12. Diod. *Eclog.* xxxi. Justin, xxxv.: Ælian, *Var. Hist.* ii. 41 (Ewald, v. 476).

Alexander Jannæus is immaterial. It is a tale intended to inspire the Israelite maidens with a sense of their duty in case of a new foreign invasion ; even as in our own days an imaginary battle in the hills of Surrey was intended to delineate in the possible future the needs of England under like circumstances. It is the story of Jael re-enacted in the midst of the pomp and luxury of Persia or of Syria, instead of the patriarchal simplicity of the Kenite and the Canaanite. The ancient battle-field of Esdraelon, with the approaches through the mountainous passes from the south, is fitly chosen as the scene, and if Bethulia itself cannot be identified, this is, perhaps, intended to stamp on the narrative its obviously fictitious character. It is the one book whose admission into the Canon was by Jerome [1] ascribed to the Council of Nicæa. This probably is an error. But it was unquestionably received amongst the sacred records of the ancient Church by Clement of Rome, and afterwards by Origen. In later times it inspired the splendid picture of Christopher Allori, and has the more questionable fame of having been said to have nerved the hand of Charlotte Corday [2] against Marat, and even in our own day to have been used in Roman pulpits to instigate the destruction of the King of Italy. It was the last direct expression of the fierce spirit of the older Judaism. It is the first unquestionable example of a religious romance.

More complex is the history of the Book of Enoch. A book of which the original language is unknown, which dropped out of the sight of the Jewish Church almost as soon as written, but which yet early attracted the notice of the Christian Church ; quoted as a sacred composition by the Apostolic writers, eagerly accepted by Tertullian, not refused by Irenæus, Clement, and Origen, placed in the Ethiopic Bible side by side with Job, [3] recovered after the obscurity of centuries by the energy of a British traveller—it forms an important link in that mixture of poetry, history, and prediction which marks the literature called apocalyptic. The latest researches place the appearance of its

[1] *Epist.* iii.

[2] Lamartine's *Girondins*, book xliv. c. 14.

[3] Laurence's *Preface to the Book of Enoch*, pp. vi. xiv. xv. xvi.

chief portion in the reign of John Hyrcanus during his wars with Syria.[1]

It is the 'Divina Commedia' of those troubled times, and disjointed, meagre, obscure as is its diction, the conception has a grandeur of its own. The hero of the vision is beyond the Captivity, beyond even the Idumæan Job, beyond Moses or Abraham; he is the mysterious solitary Saint of the antediluvian world, who 'walked with God 'and was not, for God took him,' who was already in Eastern legends regarded as the founder of astronomical[2] science. He it is who, for the sake of future generations of mankind, is called to hold converse with the angels.[3] The first vision at which he assists is no less than the fall of the Angels 'who kept 'not their first estate'—not the fall of Milton's 'Paradise Lost,' of which neither in the Hebrew nor the Christian Scriptures is there any trace, but the fall of Byron's 'Heaven and Earth,' which took place when the heavenly watchers descended on the snowclad top of Hermon—the highest height that an Israelite had ever seen—and intermixed with the daughters of men. Now for the first time we have the full array of the names both of the good and the evil hierarchy—some of which have struck root in Christian theology or poetry, such as Michael, Gabriel, Raphael, and Uriel; some of which have altogether passed away—Raguel, Surian, Urian, and Salakiel. Of the fallen spirits, the only name which coincides with the[4] Biblical imagery is Azazel.[4]

The Book of Enoch, B.C. 130. Its visions.

Thence Enoch moves on, the first of travellers, the patriarch of discoverers. Palestine is unrolled before him. He finds himself in 'the midst of the[5] earth,' according to the topography still perpetuated in the stone which in the Church of the Holy Sepulchre marks the centre of the globe. Every physical feature of the as yet unborn Jerusalem is touched with a true geographical instinct. He sees the holy mountain, with the mystic spring of Siloa flowing from

Its topography.

[1] Dillmann's *Preface to the Book of Enoch*, xliv.-xlvii.

[2] Alexander Polyhistor, in Eus. *Præp. Ev.* ix. 17. Fabricius, *Cod. Pseudep.* i. 315, 217.

[3] Enoch vi.

[4] Satan is only once mentioned incidentally, Enoch liii.

[5] Enoch xxvi.

beneath it; he sees the lower eminence in the west, parted from the Temple mount by the central depression of the city. He sees Mount Olivet, as yet unnamed, rising on the east, and 'deep, not broad,'[1] lies the dark glen through which flows its thread of water. Above and below he contemplates the steep precipices, with the olive trees clinging to their rocky sides, and he asks, as the sacred topographer might now ask: 'For 'what purpose is this accursed valley?' It is impossible not to be struck with awe, as thus in this primeval vision there is disclosed to us, not, indeed, the name (for no names could be admitted, from the nature of the work), but the theological significance of the locality which afterwards was to furnish forth the most terrible imagery that the world has ever known. It was the glen of the sons of Hinnom, the valley of Gehenna.

And then the scattered allusions of the ancient prophets are gathered into one point, and the angelic guide announces to Enoch that it is the vale reserved for those who are accursed for ever, where they who have blasphemed God shall be gathered together for punishment, where the Judgment shall be pronounced, and the just shall be severed from the bad. Until that Judgment, there is some deeper pit of fire, in which the fallen angels were to be imprisoned, reaching by subterranean channels down to the deep Dead Sea, from time to time, as it was believed, vomiting forth columns of sulphureous smoke.[2]

And thence the seer[3] wandered on towards those eastern hills which close the horizon beyond the Jordan valley, and looked into the wild woodlands and far-reaching desert of Arabia, and his view was lost in the mountains of myrrh and frankincense and trees of all manner of foliage in some blessed land far away, overhanging the Erythræan sea. The Judgment itself is described more clearly than ever before. The Ancient of Days, more especially in this book called

Its hopes.

[1] Enoch xxvi. xxvii. liv. xl. The valley described is not the valley commonly called the Valley of Hinnom, on the south of Jerusalem, but the glen, by Christians called the Valley of Jehoshaphat, by Mohammedans either the Valley of Hinnom or of Fire, and uniformly so called (sometimes in conjunction with the southern valley) in the Bible.

[2] Dillmann, 132. Probably Callirhoë. Enoch lxii.

[3] Enoch xxviii. xxix.

by the affecting name of 'the Lord of spirits,' convenes all the race of mankind before Him, and by His side is 'the 'Chosen,'[1] 'the Son of Man,' 'whose name was known to 'Him before the birth of the sun, or of the stars;' and with the severer images of Judgment are combined those figures of an inexhaustible goodness which are soon to receive an application that shall be immortal. 'There is near him a spring of 'righteousness which never fails, and round it are springs of 'wisdom; and all that are thirsty drink of these springs, and 'become full of wisdom and have their habitations with the 'righteous,[2] the chosen, and the holy.'

It is the first distinct intimation of a Deliverer who shall appear with the mingled attributes of gentleness and power, not, as in the older prophets, reigning over Israel, but as taking part in the universal judgment of mankind.[3]

From these and like figures was furnished forth the imagery from which four at least of the Books[4] of the Christian Scriptures have largely drawn; and one, the Epistle of St. Jude, by direct quotation of a splendid passage which is not unworthy of the impressive context to which it is transferred. Nor was there wanting a keen glance of historical insight. As in the vision of Milton's Adam, the Patriarch surveys, under the figure of a wandering[5] flock, the fortunes of the Chosen People, down to the last trials, thinly veiled, of the contemporary Asmonean princes.

Yet, perhaps, even more remarkable than these germs of the religious doctrine of the last age of Judaism and the first age of Christianity are the emphatic reiterated statements in which, as the Father of Science, Enoch is led through all the spheres of the universe and taught to observe the regularity, the uniformity[6] of the laws of nature which, indeed, had not altogether escaped the older Psalmists and

Its science.

[1] See note at the end of Lecture XLVIII.

[2] Enoch xlvi.-xlviii.

[3] There is a doubt whether the 'similitudes' which contain this representation are not of a later date (Colani, *Les Espérances Messianiques*, 334). But Ewald (v. 360) leaves them in this period, as well as the whole of the 3rd Sibylline book.

[4] 1 Pet. iii. 19, 20; 2 Pet. ii. 4, 5; Jude 14, 15; Rev. xx. 9-12.

[5] Enoch lxxxix.-xci.

[6] *Ibid.* i. xvii.-xxxvi. xli. lvii. lviii. lxv.-lxviii. lxxi.-lxxxi.

Prophets, but which had never before been set forth with an earnestness so exuberant and so impassioned. Had Western Christendom followed the example of the Ethiopic Church, and placed the Book of Enoch in its Canon, many a modern philosopher would have taken refuge under its authority from the attacks of ignorant alarmists, many an enlightened theologian would have drawn from its innocent speculations cogent arguments to reconcile religion and science. The physics may be childish, the conclusions erroneous. But not even in the Book of Job is the eager curiosity into all the secrets of nature more boldly encouraged, nor is there any ancient book, Gentile or Jewish, inspired by a more direct and conscious effort to resolve the whole system of the universe, moral, intellectual, and physical, into a unity of government, and idea, and development.

The rise of religious parties.

II. But there was a phenomenon more certainly connected with this epoch than these doubtful tales or predictions—a phenomenon of the most fatal importance for the history of Palestine, and also of the most universal significance for the history of the coming Church. It was the appearance of religious parties and of party-spirit under the name of Pharisee, Sadducee, and Essene, first appearing under Jonathan, developed under John Hyrcanus,[1] leading to fierce civil war under Alexander Jannæus, and playing the chief part in the tremendous drama which marks the consummation of this period. Of the origin of the first of these three famous names there can be no doubt. The idea which had never been altogether absent from the Jewish nation, and which its peculiar local situation had fortified and

The Pharisees.

justified, of 'a people[2] dwelling alone;' which had taken new force and fire under the stern reforms of Ezra and Nehemiah; which sprang into preternatural vigour in the Maccabæan struggle, had now reached that point at which lofty aspirations petrify into hard dogmatic form, at which patriots become partisans and saints are turned into fanatics, and the holiest names are perverted into bywords

[1] Jos. *Ant.* xiii. 5.

[2] Num. xxiii. 9.

and catchwords. There was one designation of this tendency which had preceded that of 'Pharisee,' in the time of Judas Maccabæus, and which already showed at once the strength and the weakness of the cause. It was that of the *Chasidim* or, as in the Greek translation, *Assideans*, 'the Pious.' It was they who furnished the nucleus of the insurgents under Mattathias; it was they whose obstinate foolhardiness vexed the great soul, whose narrow selfishness cost the life, of Judas. With him all notice of the party passes from sight, but to reappear under his descendants in the 'Pharisee' or 'Separatist'—the school or section of the nation, which sometimes seemed almost to absorb the nation itself, and which placed its whole pride and privilege in its isolation from intercourse with the Gentile world.[1] The name of Pharisee, which has acquired so sinister a sound to modern Christian ears, has been bandied to and fro by various parties to describe the characteristics of their opponents. Sometimes, as in the mouth of Milton, it has been applied 'to the scarlet Prelates, insolent to maintain traditions.' Sometimes, as with a playful critic amongst our modern poets, it has been applied to 'our British Dissenters.' In these contradictory comparisons there is a common element of truth in regard to the rigid separation from the outside world and the claims to superior sanctity, which have sometimes marked alike the pretensions of the hierarchy and of Puritanism. It may also be said that in their constant antagonism to the established priesthood and government of Palestine, the Pharisees, whilst 'Conformists' to every particular of the law, were 'Nonconformists' in their relation to the more moderate principles of the Asmonean dynasty.[2] But these imperfect analogies fail to exhaust their position. They were more than a sect. They were emphatically the popular party, which had the ear of the Jewish public, whose statements won an easier hearing than was granted to any words that came from the lips of King or Priest. 'They were the true children[3] of the age. They were 'the religious world.' It was a matter both of principle and policy to multiply the external signs by which they were

[1] See Lecture XLVIII. [2] Jos. *Ant.* xvii. 2, 4. [3] Ewald, v. 366.

distinguished from the Gentile world or from those of their own countrymen who approached towards it. They styled themselves [1] 'the sages' or 'the associates.' Tassels on their dress; scrolls and small leather boxes fastened on forehead, head, and neck, inscribed with texts of the law; long prayers offered as they stood in public places; rigorous abstinence; constant immersions; these were the sacramental badges by which they hedged themselves round. And in order to clothe these and all like peculiarities of practice and doctrine with a divine authority, there now entered into their teaching that strange fiction of which the first [2] appearance is in the reign of John Hyrcanus —that all such modern peculiarities as had either silently grown up or been adopted for the defence of their system were part of an oral tradition [3] which had been handed down from Moses to the Great Synagogue and thence to themselves. The maintenance of this hypothesis—entirely without foundation, but produced as the basis alike of usages the most trivial, such as the minute regulations for observing the Sabbath and the mode of killing their food, or doctrines the most sublime, though not taught in the Pentateuch, such as the immortality of the soul—would be almost unaccountable, were it not that analogous fables have been adopted in the Christian Church, with almost as little evidence. It is hardly more surprising than the belief that all the systems of Church government, Episcopates, Patriarchates, Presbyterian Synods, or Congregational Unions, were part of the original scheme of the Founder of Christianity, and handed down either by oral traditions or by obscure intimations, and then, as in the case of the Roman Patriarchate, embodied at a later period in official documents. The growths of the two fictions illustrate each other. Each has borne on its back a medley of truth and falsehood, institutions good and bad, which have been alternately a gain and a loss to the religious systems based upon it. In each case the best wisdom is to face the intrinsic value or worthlessness of the conclusions, and not to

The oral tradition.

[1] Kitto, iii. 696.

[2] Jos. *Ant.* xiii. 10, 5, 6.

[3] See Twisleton's article on the Sadducees in *Dictionary of the Bible.*

invest the heterogeneous mixture with an equal importance such as it could only have if the ground on which it rests were as true as it is in each case palpably false.

The name of the second section into which the Jewish community was now divided is wrapped in doubt. There is a tradition that the name of 'Sadducee' was derived from Zadok,[1] a disciple of Antigonus of Socho. But the statement is not earlier than the seventh century after the Christian era, and the person seems too obscure to have originated so widespread a title. It has been also ingeniously conjectured that the name,[2] as belonging to the whole priestly class, is derived from the famous High Priest of the time of Solomon. But of this there is no trace either in history or tradition. It is more probable that, as the Pharisees derived their name from the virtue of Isolation (*pharishah*) from the Gentile world on which they most prided themselves, so the Sadducees derived theirs from their own especial virtue of Righteousness (*zadikah*),[3] that is, the fulfilment of the law, with which, as its guardians and representatives of the law, they were specially concerned. The Sadducees—whatever be the derivation of the word—were less of a sect than of a class.[4] It is probable that, if the Pharisees represented or were represented by the Scribes or Rabbis, the Sadducees were the official leaders of the nation, and that their strength was in the Priests, whose chief during this period had so often been the head of the State. They were satisfied with the Law, as it appeared in the written code, without adopting the oral tradition on which the Pharisees laid so much stress. They were contented with the reputation of being 'just' (as their name implied)—that is to say, of fulfilling the necessary requirements of the law,[5] without aspiring to the reputation of 'sanctity;'

Sadducees.

[1] See Ginsburg, in Kitto's *Cyclopædia*, iii. 781, 782.

[2] See Geiger's *Urschrift*; Twisleton, in *Dictionary of Bible.*

[3] Löw (see Kitto, iii. 726); Derenbourg, 78. He meets the linguistic difficulty of their not being called *Zadikim* by supposing that *Zadukim* was adopted as more exactly corresponding to *Pharusim.*

[4] Jos. *Ant.* xiii. 16, 2; *B. J.* i. 5, 3; Acts iv. 1–6; v. 17.

[5] Comp. Luke i. 6, and the constant repetition of the word δίκαιος in the speech of John Hyrcanus on the occasion of his joining the Sadducees. Jos. *Ant.* xiii. 10, 5.

that is, of increasing the minute distinctions between themselves and their Gentile neighbours. Their view of human conduct was that it was within the control of a man's own will, and was not overruled by the mere decrees of fate. Their view of the future existence was that, as in the Mosaic law, a veil was drawn across it, and that, according to the saying of Antigonus of Socho, men were not to be influenced by the hope of future reward and punishment.

The name of the third sect has an edge somewhat less sharp than the two others, because its tendencies were less marked, and its part in the conflicts of the time less conspicuous. Yet here, as in the other two divisions, the most probable explanations of the word 'Essene' point not to any personal leader or founder, but to the moral and social characteristics of their school. It indicates either 'the watchful contemplation' or [1] 'the affectionate devotion' 'or the silent thoughtfulness' of those who retired from the strife of parties and nourished a higher spiritual life in communities of their own. Deep [2] in the recesses of the Jordan valley, where afterwards there arose the monasteries of Santa Saba and of Quarantania, or the hermits of Engedi, these early cœnobites took refuge. A corresponding Egyptian school in like manner were the precursors of the monks in the Thebaid. In their retirement from the outward ceremonial of the Temple, in their ascetic practices, in their community of property, in their simplicity of speech, in their meals, partly social and partly religious, we see the first beginning of those outward forms, and in some respects of those inward ideas, which before another century was passed were to be filled with a new spirit, and thus to attain an almost universal ascendency.

The Essenes.

It is in the reign of John Hyrcanus that these divisions start for the first time before our eyes. Under him, we trace the first appearance of those 'couples,' [3] of two leading sages who henceforth, in an unbroken succession, figure at the head of the Pharisaic school,

The couples, Joshua and Nittai.

[1] Ewald, v. 370; Professor Lightfoot on Colossians, 119.

[2] Jos. *Ant.* xiii. 5, 10; xvii. 1, 5; *B. J.* ii. 8, 2-4.

[3] Derenbourg, 93, 456.

perhaps [1] at the head of the national Council, and whose pithy aphorisms shine with a steady light through the darkness or the fantastic meteors of the Talmudic literature. Already this double aspect of truth had appeared in the two Josephs in the Maccabæan time—the son of Joazar insisting only on the value of learning, the son of John laying down rigid rules against exchanging even a word with women.[2] The same division is more strongly marked in Joshua, the son of Perachiah and Nittai of Arbela. 'Avoid a bad neighbour, choose not an 'impious friend, doubt not the judgment that shall fall on the 'wicked.' [3] So spoke the harder and more negative theology of Nittai. 'Get thyself a master and so secure a friend; 'throw thy judgment of everyone into the scale of his inno-'cence.' So spoke the more charitable and positive teaching of Joshua, the son of Perachiah. In a strange [4] legend of later times he is represented as having lived onwards to the final struggle of the Pharisaic school, and confronted its great adversary, and repelled Him by a harsh reproof. Rather, we may say, he has, by this one sentence, received by anticipation that Teacher's blessing; nor is it impossible that he had heard, in the exile to which he was afterwards driven in Alexandria, something of the true value of a teacher outside his own circle—something of Aristotle's doctrine of a disinterested friendship—something of that 'sweet reasonableness' which the Greek language expresses in one forcible word and which this fine old Hebrew maxim so well conveys in substance. To the teaching of which these two sayings are the highest expression, but which, doubtless, was mixed with the baser matter of the party, Hyrcanus devoted himself.

At last came a sudden crash. It was after the overthrow of the sanctuary of Gerizim and the city of Samaria that, at the close of his career, John Hyrcanus entertained at a splendid banquet the nobles and scholars of his court. With a characteristic combination of the present glories and the past

[1] The formation of the national Council at this time is so doubtful that it is not here discussed. (See Derenbourg, 90, 92.)

[2] Mishna, *Pirke Aboth*, i. 4, 5.

[3] *Ibid.* i. 6, 7.

[4] Derenbourg, 94.

sufferings of his dynasty, the tables were laden with the dainties of regal luxury, and the roots and herbs, such as those on which his ancestors had lived in the mountains.[1] On this solemn day, Hyrcanus, like Samuel of old, asked for an opinion on his administration[2] and his conduct. One guest took up the challenge. In him the growing jealousy of the fanatical party found a voice. It was Eleazar the Pharisee. For no moral delinquency, for no violence in war or peace, was the splendid Pontiff arraigned. It was the same religious scruple which allied 'the 'Pious' with Alcimus against Judas Maccabæus. It was the well-known perversity of theological animosity, which, under the cover of such scruples, allied itself with personal enmity, and, raking up the ashes of forgotten or invented scandals, insisted on questioning the validity of the Priestly descent of Hyrcanus on the allegation of an exploded calumny that his mother—the high-spirited wife of Simon—had once been a captive in the Syrian army, and thus shared the bed of Antiochus Epiphanes. The fiery spirit, the tender recollections of John were stirred up by this reflection on his mother's honour. At that moment another rose from the table. It was Jonathan the Sadducee. Now was come the time to reclaim the Prince from leaning to those whom the Priestly caste regarded as their rivals. In Eleazar he denounced the whole party, who, though with certain reserves, stood by their comrade. From that time John Hyrcanus broke away from the school which he had hitherto courted. From that time the feud between the two parties was alternately fostered and shunned by his descendants.

The rupture with the Pharisees. B.C. 109.

One dreadful interlude between these contests[3] introduces to us for a moment the third party, of which the real significance is reserved for the next generation. Aristobulus, the son of Hyrcanus, whose family affections were entirely absorbed in his brother Antigonus, had been brought back from his campaign in Ituræa by an illness, which confined him to the Palace

[1] Grätz. iii, 99, 453.

[2] Jos. *Ant.* xiii. 10, 5, 6; Derenbourg, 79, 80.

[3] Jos. *Ant.* xiii. 11, 2.

built by his father in the Temple precincts. Antigonus had gone in full military pomp, in splendid armour, and with his troops around him, to offer prayers in the Temple for his brother's recovery, choosing, as was the custom for all solemn occasions, the great festival of the Tabernacles. His enemies poisoned the mind of the King against him. He was invited to come and show his new suit of armour to the King, and, as he passed along the covered corridor from the Temple to the fortress, he was waylaid in a dark corner of the gallery and assassinated. The sudden shock of remorse brought on a violent fit of sickness in the unfortunate Aristobulus. The basin containing the blood which he had vomited was spilt on the pavement where his brother had fallen. The cry of horror which rang through the Palace gave a new shock to the King, who expired with his brother's name on his lips. Amidst these tragic scenes, it was remembered that a singular being, marked probably by his white dress, was standing in the Temple as Antigonus passed to the fatal gallery. 'Look,' he said, to his companions, 'I am 'a false prophet; for I predicted, and my words have never 'yet failed, that Antigonus would die this very day at Strato's 'Tower, and here he is on the evening of this day still alive.' He did not know that the dark corner where Antigonus was to fall was called by the same name as the seaside fortress; and that in a moment his prediction was to be fulfilled. This unerring prophet was Judas the Essene, first of that mysterious sect known to us by name, and one of the few who are ever discerned remaining amongst the haunts of men. But that solitary glimpse gives a foretaste of the effect to be produced by another Prophet who should appear in like manner, surrounded by disciples in the Temple court, also with dark forebodings, though on a grander scale, which would be verified by events in a still more startling catastrophe.

The Essenian prophet. B.C. 106.

This, however, was but a momentary flash from the secluded world in which the Essenes lived. In the succeeding reigns it is the contending factions of Sadducee and Pharisee that fill up the whole horizon. The hostility sown between the Pharisees and Hyrcanus continued through the reign of Alexander Jannæus. On one occasion they were not ashamed to revive the whole calumny against his grandmother, and at the Feast of Tabernacles the worshippers in the Temple, inspired by them, pelted the Royal Priest with citrons from the boughs[1] which they carried on that day, because the slight variation in his mode of performing the libation reminded them that[2] he neglected the Pharisaic usage. There long remained a remembrance of the insult in a hoarding of wood which he built round the altar to exclude the repetition of such outrages. But from this moment it seemed as if, in the mind of the Sadducean Prince, the passion of a tiger were enkindled by the mingled fury of revenge and of partisanship. On that occasion six thousand perished in a general massacre. On another, when the Pharisees, with the inherent vice of fanatics, sacrificing their patriotism to their partisanship, sided with the Syrians against[3] their King, he stormed the fortress where they had taken refuge, and then, at a banquet given to his harem on the walls of Jerusalem, ordered eight hundred of the leaders of the faction to be crucified. It was the first distinct appearance of the Cross on the hills of Palestine. It is not without significance that the ruling passion which led, whether to the eight hundred crucifixions under the High Priesthood of Alexander Jannæus, or the single crucifixion under the High Priesthood of Caiaphas, was religious party-spirit. The day on which[4] the remnant of the party escaped from these horrors to the slopes of Lebanon was observed, after their subsequent triumph, as a festival, and, with the usual Rabbinical exaggeration, the sea was at the hour of the execution said to have overwhelmed one-third of the habitable globe. The secret motives of the spirit of modern party are reflected in all their shapes in the closing scene of Alexander's life. He admitted on his deathbed that he had mistaken

Alexander Jannæus. B.C. 106.

B.C. 85.

[1] Jos. *Ant.* xiii. 13, 5. A like outrage was committed by the Jews of Babylonia against a Rabbi in the third century (Derenbourg, 99).

[2] Instead of pouring water on the altar, he poured it on the ground (Derenbourg 98).

[3] Jos. *Ant.* xiii. 14, 2.

[4] Derenbourg, 99.

his policy in alienating from him the Pharisaic influences, and advised his wife to conciliate them, in a speech which is a masterpiece of cynicism, and is the more remarkable as being recounted by a Pharisee. A most significant touch was added by the Rabbinical tradition[1] describing the hangers-on of a successful party as more dangerous than the partisans themselves: 'Fear not the Pharisees, and fear not those who are 'not Pharisees. But fear the hypocrites who pretend to be 'Pharisees—the varnished Pharisees—whose acts are the acts 'of Zimri, and who claim the reward of Phinehas.' Not less characteristic of such warfare is the sudden turn by which the King whom in life they had reviled as a usurper and a schismatic received from them the most sumptuous of funeral honours, and that the very Priest whose copy of the Law,[2] though written in letters of gold, they had forbidden to be used, came to be regarded as the second founder of their school.

Alexandra's adoption of this policy was rendered more easy by the circumstance that her brother was Simeon the son of Shetach. Under his auspices Pharisaism acquired an ascendency which it never lost. Already in[3] the reign of her fierce husband he had contrived to keep his place at court between the King and Queen, to bandy retorts with the King, to squeeze money from him for the needy Nazarites. After Alexander's death it was he who recalled his predecessors Joshua, the son of Perachiah, and Judah, the son of Tobai, who was recalled to Jerusalem from Alexandria, whither he had fled. 'Jerusalem the Great to 'Alexandria the Little. My husband, my beloved one, stays 'with you, whilst I remain desolate.'[4] The severe code of the Sadducean 'Justice' was abolished except when it suited the Pharisees to be severe,[5] 'for the discouragement of the Sad-'ducees.' The chiefs of that party were expelled from the Council. Like the less fanatical in all ages, the bond of cohesion between[6] them was more relaxed than in the hands of their

Alexandra. B.C. 79.

Simeon, the son of Shetach. B.C. 72.

[1] Derenbourg, 101.

[2] Jos. *Ant.* xiii. 16, 1. But see Derenbourg, 101.

[3] See the somewhat tedious story in Derenbourg, 96, 97, 98.

[4] Derenbourg, 94, 102.

[5] *Ibid.* 105, 106.

[6] Jos. *Ant.* xviii. 1, 4.

more determined and dogmatic opponents, and they were perforce compelled to bow to the public opinion, which sided with the Pharisaic [1] or popular party. The days of the 14th of Thammuz and the 28th of Tebet were in consequence celebrated as festivals. The libation of water in the Feast of Tabernacles, which Alexander Jannæus had neglected, though in itself wholly insignificant and without a shadow of warrant from the Law, was raised to the first magnitude, with illuminations, processions, and dances. 'He,' it was said, 'who has 'never seen this rejoicing knows not what [2] rejoicing is.' The whole congregation descended with the Priest to the Spring of Siloam—the water was brought back in a golden pitcher—with shouts of triumph, cymbals, and trumpets, which resounded louder and louder as the Priest stood on the altar. 'Lift up 'thy hand,' they said, as though the irreverent Pontiff was still before them, and the water was then solemnly poured to the west, and a cup of wine to the east, the song still continuing, 'Draw water with joy from the wells of salvation.' It is a striking example of a noble meaning infused into the celebration of a miserable party-triumph when, 'on the last great day of the 'Feast' of Tabernacles, a hundred years later, there stood in the Temple courts One whom the Pharisees hated with a hatred as deadly as that with which at times they pursued the memory of Alexander Jannæus, and cried 'with a loud voice'—piercing, it may be, through the clatter of chant and music—'If any man 'have thirst, let him come unto me [3] and drink.'

The description of these internecine feuds, to which the earlier history of the Jewish Church furnishes no exact parallel—not even in the angry factions [4] of the time of Jeremiah—shows how nearly we have approached to those modern elements which, as a great historian of our own day has well pointed out, are found in certain stages of every ancient nation.

They present the first appearance of that singular phenomenon of religious party, which, continuing down to the latest days of the Jewish commonwealth, reappears under other forms

[1] Jos. *Ant.*: Derenbourg, 104.
[2] Derenbourg, 103.
[3] John vii. 37 (see Godet).
[4] Lecture XL.

both in the early and in the later ages of the Christian Church —that is to say, divisions ostensibly on religious subjects, but carried on with the same motives and passions as those which animate divisions in the State. The true likenesses of the scenes we have just been considering are not, where Josephus looks for them, in the schools of Greek philosophy; but in the tumult of Grecian politics. The seditions and revolutions of Corcyra, with the profound[1] remarks of Thucydides, contain the picture of all such religious discords from the Pharisees and Sadducees downwards. The word by which in the later Greek of this epoch they are described, *hæresis*,[2] is the equivalent of the earlier word *stasis*—neither having any relation to the modern meaning of 'heresy,' both expressed by the English word 'faction.' The names of 'Pharisee' and 'Sadducee,' and perhaps 'Essene,' had, indeed, as we have seen, a moral or theological significance, but this meaning was often disavowed by the parties themselves and was constantly drifting into other directions. The appellations of 'the Isolated' and 'the Just,' and perhaps 'the Holy' or 'the Contemplative,' passed through the natural process to which all party names are liable ; first, an exclusive or exaggerated claim to some peculiar virtue, or else a taunt from some opposing quarter ; next, adopted or given, heedlessly or deliberately, by some class or school—then poisoned by personal rivalry, and turned into mere flags of discord and weapons of offence. Such in later times has been the fate of the names of 'Christian,' 'Catholic,' 'Puritan,' 'Orthodox,' 'Evangelical,' 'Apostolical,' 'Latitudinarian,' 'Rationalist,' 'Methodist,' 'Ritualist,' 'Reformed,' 'Moderate,' 'Free.' Whatever the words once meant, they in later times have often come to be mere badges by which contending masses are distinguished from each other.

In these, therefore, as in all parties, the inward and outwar, the formal and the real, divisions never exactly corresponded. There were Pharisaic opinions which should have belonged to those who were not 'Separatists,' and Sadducaic usages which

[1] Thucyd. iii. 84. See Keim, I. 322.

[2] Acts v 17, xv. 5, xxiv. 5, xxiv. 14, xxvi. 5, xxviii. 22, 1 Cor. xi. 19, Gal. v. 20, 2 Pet. ii. 1.

we should have expected to find amongst the Pharisees. The great doctrine of Immortality, which the Pharisees believed to have been derived from the oral tradition of Moses, was, if not derived, yet deeply coloured, from those Gentile philosophies and religions which they professed to abhor.[1] In the long and tedious list of ritual differences which parted the two sections, there are many minute particularities on which the Pharisees took the laxer, the Sadducees the stricter side.

Yet, further, though it might have seemed as if the whole nation were absorbed by these apparently exhaustive divisions, it is clear that there were higher spirits, who, though, perhaps, nominally belonging to one or other side, rose above the miserable littlenesses of each.

No loftier instruction is preserved from these times than that of two teachers who must at least be regarded as the precursors of the Sadducees. One is [2] Antigonus of Socho, whose doubt, if it were a doubt, on future retribution, is identical with that expressed in the vision of the noblest and holiest of Christian kings, to whom on the same shores of Palestine a stately form revealed herself as Religion, with a brazier in one hand to dry up the fountains of Paradise,[3] and a pitcher in the other to quench the fires of Hell, in order that men might love God for Himself alone. Another was Jesus the son of Sirach, whose solemn and emphatic reiterations of the power of the human will and the grandeur of human duty helped, even if ineffectually, to fill the void left by his total silence of a hope beyond the grave.[4]

Of the Pharisees we know that a hundred years later there was, as we shall see, a Hillel, a Gamaliel, and a Saul, who were to be the chosen instruments in preparing or in proclaiming the widest emancipation from ceremonial rites that the world had yet seen; whilst the doctrine of Immortality which it is the glory of the Pharisaic schools to have appropriated and consolidated, was, like an expiring torch, to be snatched from their hands, and kindled with a new light for all succeeding

[1] See Lectures XLVII., XLVIII.
[2] See Lecture XLVIII.
[3] Joinville's *Life of S. Louis*.
[4] Milman's *Hist. of Jews*, ii. 32.

generations. Of the seven classes into which the Pharisees were divided, whilst six were characterised even by themselves with epithets of biting scorn, one was acknowledged even by their enemies to be animated by the pure love of God.[1] Even in these first days of the fierce triumph of Pharisaism the Jewish Church at large owed much to the influence of Simeon the son of Shetach, who, during the reign of his sister Alexandra, ruled supreme in the Court and cloisters of Jerusalem. There were, indeed, stories handed down of him and his colleague which showed that the Pharisees could exercise as much severity in behalf of the Written Law as they were fond of alleging[2] against the Sadducees. Eighty witches were executed at Ascalon under Simeon's auspices, and he persisted, from a technical scruple, in the execution of his own son, though knowing that he was falsely accused. Nor can we avoid the thought that the advantages which he gave to the legal[3] position of women were suggested by the influence of his strong-minded Pharisaic sister, Queen Alexandra. But there are traces of a better and more enduring spirit in some of his words and works. That was an acute saying of his colleague, the son of Tobai: 'Judge, make not thyself an advocate; whilst the parties are before thee, regard them both as guilty; when they are gone, after the judgment, regard them both as having reason.'[4] That was a yet wiser saying of Simeon: 'Question well the witnesses; but be careful not by thy questions to teach them how to lie.' But his main glory was that he was the inaugurator of a complete system of education throughout the country. Under his influence, for the first time, schools were established in every large provincial town, and all boys from sixteen years and upwards were compelled to attend them. No less than eleven different names for places of instruction now came into vogue. 'Get to thyself a teacher,'[5] said Joshua, the son of Perachiah, 'and thou gettest to thyself a companion.' 'Our principal care,'[6] such

Simeon the son of Shetach.

[1] Munk's *Palestine*, 513.
[2] Derenbourg, 106, 107.
[3] *Ibid.* 108, 110.
[4] Mishna, *Pirke Aboth*, I. 8, 9.
[5] *Pirke Aboth*, i. 6.
[6] Jos. *c. Ap.* i. 12.

from this time was the boast of Josephus, 'is to educate our 'children.' 'The world,' such became the Talmudical[1] maxim, 'is preserved by the breath of the children in the 'schools.'

Compre-hensive-ness of the Jewish Church.

With nobler tendencies thus recognised on either side, we need not wonder, though we may stumble, at the startling fact that the Jewish Church and nation, even in its last extremities, was able to contain these three divergent parties without disruption. So strong was the common bond of country and of faith, that the Sadducee, who could find in the Ancient Law no ground for hope of a future existence, and who resolutely refused to accept the convenient fiction of an oral tradition, could worship—although varying on innumerable points, every one of which was a watchword of contention—with the Pharisee, to whom the Oral Law was greater than the written, whose belief in immortality was bound up with the heroic struggles of the Maccabees, and who was in a state of chronic antagonism to the hierarchical and aristocratic class of which the Sadducee was the guardian and representative; whilst even the Essenes, who withdrew from the strife of Jerusalem to their oasis by the Dead Sea, who took part in none of the ceremonial ordinances, unless it were that of ablution, were yet not counted as outcasts, but are described even by Pharisaic historians as amongst the purest and holiest of men; and when their seers wandered for a moment into the haunts of men, they were welcomed as prophets even by the fierce populace and politic leaders of the capital. So strange a latitude in the National Church of the Chosen People must have accustomed the first propagators of Christianity to a comprehension which to all their successors has seemed almost impracticable. When[2] Paul felt that the Corinthian Church could embrace both those who received and those who doubted the Resurrection of the Dead, he knew that it was no larger admission than had been made by the Jewish Church when it included both Pharisees and

[1] Dr. Ginsburg in Kitto, i. 728.

[2] 1 Cor. xv. 12.

Sadducees;[1] and when he entreated[2] the Roman Church to acknowledge as brothers both those who received and those who rejected the Jewish ordinances, it was in principle the same catholicity which had induced both Pharisee and Sadducee to recognise the idealising worship of the Essene.

And as particular individuals of each party were better than their party, as the Jewish Church itself was wider than the three parties, singly or collectively, so there were those who, from their commanding character and position, overlooked, and enable us to overlook, calmly the whole troubled sea of faction and intrigue. Such on the whole was the Asmonean dynasty, beginning with Mattathias, in his patriotic disregard of the superstitious veneration of his own adherents for the Sabbath; continuing throughout the great career of Judas Maccabæus, through the truly national policy of Simon and of his son John, through the keen if cynical insight of Alexander Jannæus.

Onias the charmer.

Such was the good Onias, perhaps an Essene,[3] 'that 'righteous man beloved of God.' He was renowned for the efficacy of his prayers. To the teeming fertility which had marked the reign of the Pharisaic Alexandra, there had succeeded an alarming drought. Onias, at the entreaty of his countrymen (so runs the tradition), stood within the magic circle which he had traced, and implored 'the Lord of the 'World' to send his gracious rain.[4] 'Thy children have asked 'me to pray, for I am as a son of Thy house before Thee. I 'swear by Thy great name that I will not move hence till 'Thou hast had pity upon them.' A few drops fell: 'I ask 'for more than this,' he said, 'for a rain which shall fill wells, 'cisterns, and caverns.' It fell in torrents. 'Not this,' continued he; 'I ask for a rain which shall show Thy goodness 'and Thy blessing.' It fell in regular descent until the people had to mount to the terraces of the Temple. 'Now,' they said,

[1] It is true that in the Seder Olam, c. 4 (p. 10), the Sadducees are condemned to everlasting punishment in Gehenna. But this later view brings out more forcibly the contrast with the time when the High Priests were all Sadducees.

[2] Rom. xiv. 1-6.

[3] Grätz, iii. 130, 133.

[4] The belief in the efficacy of the prayers of holy men for rain appears not only in the incidental allusions in 1 Kings xvii. 1, xviii. 41, James v. 17, but in the fixed belief of the Arab tribes that the monks of Mount Sinai have the power of producing it by opening or shutting their books. Robinson's *Researches*, i. 132.

'pray that the rain may cease.' 'Go,' he said, 'and see 'whether the "stone of the wanderers" is covered.' At this Simeon, the son of Shetach, the head of the Pharisees, contemptuously rebuked him and said: 'Thou deservest excom'munication. But what can I do? Thou playest before God 'like a spoilt child before its father who does all that it wishes.'[1] This was the innocent, infantine spell which Onias cast over the imagination of his people, as his memory remained in the Talmudic legends. But a more genuine glory attaches to his name as it appears in the sober history. In the fratricidal struggle which broke out between the two sons of Alexandra (it may be supposed, immediately after this drought), when the popular party of the Pharisees was ranged on the side of Hyrcanus, and the priestly party of the Sadducees on the side of Aristobulus, the old Onias was dragged from his seclusion to give to the besiegers the advantage of his irresistible prayers. He stood up in the midst of them and said: 'O God, the King of the whole world, since those that stand 'with me now are Thy people, and those that are besieged are 'Thy priests, I beseech thee that Thou wilt neither hearken to 'the prayers of those against these, nor of these against those.'[2]

B.C. 69.

That was the true protest[3] against party-spirit in every Church and in every age. With the insensibility to all superior excellence which this absorbing passion engenders, the fanatics amongst whom he stood stoned him to death. He died a martyr in a noble cause, a worthy precursor of Him who in a few short years was to condemn in the same breath the teaching common alike to Pharisee and Sadducee, 'which is 'hypocrisy'[4]—that is 'affectation,' acting a part; who was to denounce in the most unsparing terms that false[5] 'religious 'world' of which the murderers of Onias were the chief representatives—who was Himself to suffer, with His own first martyr, almost on the same spot, from the combination of the two parties, for both of whom Onias prayed, and for both of whom He and Stephen prayed also.[6]

[1] Derenbourg, 112.

[2] Jos. *Ant.* xiv. 2, 1.

[3] It is perhaps not quite certain that the Pharisees took the part of the people on this occasion, but we may be sure that the Sadducees were with the Priests.

[4] Matt. xv. 6.

[5] *Ibid.* xxiii. 1-39.

[6] Luke xxiii. 34; Acts vii. 59.

HEROD.

LECTURE L.

AUTHORITIES.

I. CONTEMPORARY.

1. Nicolas of Damascus, private secretary of Herod, 'Universal 'History,' in 144 books, quoted by Josephus (*Ant.* xiii. 12, 6; xiv. 1, 3; 4, 3; 6, 4; xvi. 7, 1; *C. Ap.* ii. 7).
2. Chronicles of Herod, quoted by Josephus (*Ant.* xv. 6, 3).

II. JOSEPHUS, *Ant.* xiv. 1; xviii. 8, 4; *B. J.* i. 6-23.

III. HEATHEN AUTHORITIES:

1. Dio Cassius, xxxvii. 8, 15-20.
2. Strabo, xvi.
3. Tacit. *Hist.* v. 4.
4. Plutarch, *de Superst.* 8; Lives of Pompey and Antony.
5. Cicero, *Pro Flacco*, § 28.
6. Appian, *de Bello Mithridat.*

IV. TALMUDICAL AUTHORITIES, as given in Derenbourg, c. vii. viii. ix. x. xi. and the Mishna.

LECTURE L.

HEROD

THE civil war between Hyrcanus and Aristobulus was interrupted by the appearance of a new actor on the scene. Fresh from his beneficent war against the pirates who infested the Mediterranean, from his more brilliant victory over the last of the mighty potentates of Asia, Mithridates, the marvellous king of Pontus—Pompey the Great, with all his fame in its first and yet untarnished splendour, moved towards Palestine. At Antioch he dissolved the last remnant of the Syrian monarchy, on the ground that it was an insufficient rampart against the inroads of the Armenians and Parthians from the far East. He then advanced to Damascus. It was a year memorable in Roman history for the consulship of Cicero, the conspiracy of Catiline, and the birth of Augustus. It was not less memorable for the meeting which, in the oldest of Syrian cities, took place between the illustrious Roman and the two aspirants for the Jewish Monarchy. The rivals were attracted by the enormous prestige of the man, who, having revived the terror of the Roman name in Africa, and crushed the most formidable insurrections in Spain and Italy, had now vanquished the kings of Asia. They were led yet more by his widespread fame for humanity and moderation which made him the arbiter of the contending princes of the East.[1] No personage of such renown and authority had been seen by any Israelite eyes since the meeting of Alexander and Jaddua. There was, indeed, something even in the outward appearance of the famous Roman which recalled the aspect of the famous Greek. The august expression, almost as of

Pompey the Great.

B.C. 63.

[1] Appian, *de Bell. Mith.* 251.

venerable age, which blended so gracefully with the bloom of his manly prime and his singularly engaging manners, the very mode in which his hair was smoothly turned back from his brow, the liquid glance of his eyes, resembled the traditional likeness of Alexander.[1] Modern travellers, as they stand before the colossal statues of Pompey, whether that gentler figure in the Villa Castellazzo, near Milan, or that commanding form in the Spada Palace at Rome, 'at whose base great Cæsar fell,' so wonderfully preserved through the vicissitudes of neglect, revolution, and siege, can frame some notion of the mingled awe and affection which he inspired and which the Jewish princes must have felt when they bowed before him. It was in such interviews that he must have shone conspicuously, of whom it was said that 'when he bestowed it was with delicacy, 'when he received it was with dignity; and though he knew 'not how to restrain the offences of those whom he employed, 'yet he gave so gracious a reception to those who came to com-'plain that they went away satisfied.'[2]

On one side was Aristobulus, the gallant King whose high spirit called forth at every turn the reluctant admiration of the cynical historian, and which displayed itself even in the very act of pleading his cause, blazing, like an Indian prince, with every conceivable mark of royalty, surrounded by his young nobles, conspicuous with their scarlet mantles, gay trappings, and profusion of clustering locks.[3] At the feet of the victorious general he laid a gift so magnificent that long afterwards it was regarded as one of the wonders of the Capitol—a golden vine, the emblem of his nation, growing out of a 'Pleasaunce'[4] and bearing the name of his father, Alexander. From all this barbaric pomp, which to the yet uncorrupted taste of the proud Roman citizen produced no other feeling than disgust, the conqueror turned to the other candidate. Hyrcanus was as insignificant as Aristobulus was commanding in character and appearance—then, as always, a tool in the

Aristobulus II.

[1] Plutarch, *Pompey*, c. 2. In his triumph he wore the actual 'chlamys,' or military cloak, of Alexander (Appian, *Bell. Mith.* 253).

[2] Plutarch, *Pompey*, c. 1.

[3] Jos. *B. J.* i. 6.

[4] τερπωλή. Strabo, in Jos. *Ant.* xiv. 3, 1.

hands of others. With him were the heads of the great party who, in their hostility to the Sadducaic and Pontifical elements represented by the rival brother, did not scruple to insinuate against him the charge that he was not a genuine friend of Rome. And with them, inspiring and guiding all, was the man destined to inaugurate for the Jewish nation the last phase of its existence. When John Hyrcanus subdued the Edomites, and incorporated them into the Jewish Church, he little dreamed that he was nourishing the evil genius that would be the ruin of his house. The son of the first native governor of the conquered Idumæa, who himself succeeded to his father's post, was Antipater or Antipas, father of Herod. With a craft more like that of the supplanter Jacob than the generosity of his own ancestor Esau, he perceived that his chance of retaining his position would be imperilled by the independent spirit of the younger brother, and might be secured by making himself the ally and master of the elder. To his persuasions the Roman general lent a willing ear, and Hyrcanus was preferred. Not without a struggle did Aristobulus surrender his hopes. From Damascus he retired to the family fortress, the Alexandreum, commanding the passes into southern Palestine. Thither Pompey followed, and after one or two futile parleys Aristobulus finally, in a fit of desperation, broke away from the stronghold, threw himself into Jerusalem, and there defied the conqueror of the East.

Hyrcanus II.

Antipater.

The crisis was at once precipitated. Every step of Pompey's advance is noted, like that of Sennacherib of old. But it was by a route which no previous invader had adopted. From the fortress of Alexandreum, instead of following the central thoroughfare by Shechem and Bethel, he plunged into the Jordan valley and encamped beside the ancient city where Joshua had gained his first victory over the Canaanites. It would almost seem as if it was the fame of Jericho which had occasioned this deviation. It was a spot, which, having sunk into deep obscurity, during this latter period revived with a glory peculiar to itself. There is a faint tradition that even as far back as the Persian[1] dominion it had

Pompey's march to Jericho.

[1] Solinus in *Polyhistor*, c. 38; see Hitzig, 308.

been raised to a rank rivalling, if not exceeding, that of Jerusalem, and this equality was henceforth never lost till the fall of both. Long afterwards in the homes of Roman soldiers was preserved the recollection of the magnificent spectacle which burst upon them, when for the first time they found themselves in the midst of the tropical vegetation which even now to some degree, but then transcendently, surrounded the city of Jericho. In the present day not one solitary relic remains of those graceful trees which once were the glory of Palestine. But then the plain was filled with a splendid forest of palms, 'the Palm-grove,'[1] as it was called, three miles broad and eight miles long, interspersed with gardens of balsam, traditionally sprung from the balsam-root that the Queen of Sheba brought to Solomon—so fragrant that the whole forest was scented with them, so valuable that a few years later no richer present could be made by Antony to Cleopatra. In this green oasis, beside the 'diamonds of the desert,' which still pour forth their clear streams in that sultry valley, but which then were used to feed the spacious reservoirs in which the youths of those days delighted to plunge and frolic in the long days of summer and autumn, the Roman army halted for one night.

It was a day eventful not only for Palestine. The shades of evening were falling over the encampment. Pompey was taking his usual ride after the march—careering round the soldiers as they were pitching their tents, when couriers were seen advancing from the north at full speed waving on the points of their lances branches of laurel, to indicate some joyful news. The troops gathered round their general, and entreated to hear the tidings. At their eager wishes he sprang down from his horse; they extemporised a tribune, hastily constructed of piles of earth and of the packsaddles which lay upon the ground, and he read aloud the despatch, which announced the crowning mercy of his Oriental victories—the death of his great enemy Mithridates.

Wild was the shout of joy which went up from the army.[2]

[1] 'Phœnicon' (Strabo, xvi. 2, 41; 4, 21).

[2] Plutarch (*Pompey*, 41) places this scene on his way to Petra. But, besides the positive statement of Josephus which fixes

It was as though ten thousand enemies had fallen. Throughout the camp arose the smoke of thankful sacrifice, and the festivity of banquets rang in every tent.

To Jerusalem.

Filled with this sense of triumphant success the army started at break of day for the interior of Judæa, after first occupying the fortresses which commanded that corner of the Jordan valley—those which were known by the name, perhaps, of the foreign mercenaries who manned them—as well as those which guarded the Dead Sea. Thus Pompey advanced in perfect security towards the mysterious and sacred city which possessed, no doubt, a special attraction for the curiosity of the inquiring Roman. From the north, from the south, from the west, the situation of Jerusalem produces but little effect on the spectator. But, seen from the east—seen from that ridge of Olivet whence Pompey alone, of its conquerors, first beheld it, rising like a magnificent apparition out of the depth and seclusion of its mountain valleys—it must have struck him with all its awe, and, had his generous heart forecast all the miseries of which his coming was the prelude, might have well inspired something of that compassion which the very same view, seen from the same spot ninety years later, awakened in One who burst into tears at the sight of Jerusalem, and mourned over her fatal blindness to the grandeur of her mission. From this point Pompey descended, and swept round the city, to encamp on the level ground on its western side.[1]

Once more Aristobulus ventured[2] into the conqueror's presence; but this time he was seized and loaded with chains. Then broke out within the walls one of those bitter internal conflicts of which Jerusalem has been so often the scene. The Temple was occupied by the patriots, who, even in this extremity, would not abandon their king and country. The Palace and the walls were seized by those who, in passionate devotion to their party, were willing to admit the foreigner.

it at Jericho, it is clear that the attack on Petra was left to Scaurus. And the localities of Jericho are far more suitable for it than the neighbourhood of Petra.

[1] Jos. *B. J.* v. 12, 2. But see Jos. *Ant.* xiv. 4, 2.

[2] The variations in the different accounts as to the time of this capture are not essential.

The bridge between the Palace and the Temple was broken down ; the houses round the Temple mount were occupied. Thus for three months the siege was continued. As if to bring out in the strongest relief the Jewish character in this singular crisis, the Sabbath, which, during the last two centuries had played so conspicuous a part in the history of the nation, was turned to account by the Romans in preparing their military engines and approaches, which, even in spite of the example of the first Asmonean, were held by the besieged not to be sufficient cause for a breach of the sacred rest. It may be that it was one of the instances in which the strict adherence of the Sadducees to the letter of the Law outran the zeal of their Pharisaic opponents. However occasioned, the Jewish and the Gentile historians concur in representing this enforced inactivity as the cause of the capture of the city. It was the greatest sacrifice that the Sabbatarian principle ever exacted or received. At last the assault was made.[1] So big with fate did the event appear that the names of the officers who stormed the breach were all remembered. The first was Cornelius Faustus, son of the dictator Sylla ; and, immediately following, the centurions Furius and Fabius. A general massacre ensued, in which it is said that 12,000 perished. So deep was the horror and despair that many sprang over the precipitous cliffs. Others died in the flames of the houses, which, like the Russians at Moscow, they themselves set on fire. But the most memorable scene was that which the Temple itself presented. On that solemn festival, which the enemy had chosen for their attack, the Priests were all engaged in their sacred duties. With a dignity as unshaken as that which the Roman senators showed when they confronted in their curule chairs the Gaulish invaders, three centuries before, did the sacerdotal order of Jerusalem await their doom. They

The capture of the city. B.C. 63.

[1] It is doubtful whether 'the Fast' spoken of in all the accounts was the Great Fast of the Day of Atonement, in autumn, or the smaller fast on the 20th of the winter month. On the one hand, 'the 'Fast' was the usual name for the vigil of the Tabernacles. Compare Plutarch, *Quæst. Conviv.* vi. 12 ; Acts xxvii. 9. On the other hand, the mention of the third month by Josephus, unless it means the third month of the siege, points to the month Chisleu (see Ussher's *Annals*, 545). Reimar, on Dio Cass. xxxvii. 16

were robed in black sackcloth, which on days of lamentation superseded their white garments, and sat immovable in their seats round the Temple court, 'as if they were caught in a net,' till they fell under the hands[1] of their assailants. And now came the final outrage. That which in Nebuchadnezzar's siege had been prevented by the general conflagration—that which Alexander forbore—that from which Ptolemy the Fourth had been, as it was supposed, deterred by a preternatural visitation—that on which even Antiochus Epiphanes had only partially ventured—was now to be accomplished by the gentlest and the most virtuous soldier of the Western world. He was irresistibly drawn on by the same 'grand curiosity' which had always mingled with his love of fame and conquest, which inspired him with the passion for seeing with his own eyes the shores of the most distant[2] seas, the Atlantic, the Caspian, and the Indian Ocean, which Lucan has in part placed in the mouth of his rival in ascribing to him for his last great ambition the discovery of the sources of the Nile.

Entrance into the Holy of Holies.

He passed into the nave (so to speak) of the Temple, where none but Priests might enter. There he saw the golden table, the sacred candlestick, which Judas Maccabæus had restored, the censers, and the piles of incense, the accumulated offerings of gold from all the Jewish settlements; but, with a moderation so rare in those days that Cicero[3] at the time, and Josephus in the next century, alike commended it as an act of almost superhuman virtue, he touched and took nothing. He arrived at the vast curtain which hung across the Holy of Holies, into which none but the High Priest could enter, and but on one day in the year, that one day, if so be, the very day on which Pompey found himself there. He had, doubtless, often wondered what that dark cavernous recess could contain. Who or what was the God of the Jews was a question commonly discussed at philosophical entertainments both before and afterwards.[4] When the quarrel between the two Jewish rivals came to the ears of the Greeks and Romans, the question

[1] Plutarch, *De Superst.* c. 8.
[2] *Ibid. Pompey*, c. 38.
[3] Cicero, *Pro Flacco*, c. 28.
[4] Plutarch, *Quæst.* v. 6, 1.

immediately arose as to the Divinity that these Princes both worshipped.[1] Sometimes a rumour reached them that it was an ass's head; sometimes the venerable lawgiver wrapped in his long beard and wild hair; sometimes, perhaps, the sacred emblems which once were there, but had been lost in the Babylonian invasion; sometimes some god or goddess in human form like those who sat enthroned behind the altars of the Parthenon or the Capitol. He drew the veil aside. Nothing more forcibly shows the immense superiority of the Jewish worship to any which then existed on the earth than the shock of surprise occasioned by this one glimpse of the exterior world into that unknown and mysterious chamber. 'There was no-'thing.' Instead of all the fabled figures of which he had heard or read, he found only a shrine, as it seemed to him, without a God, because a sanctuary without an image.[2] Doubtless the Grecian philosophers had at times conceived an idea of the Divinity as spiritual; doubtless the Etruscan priests[3] had established a ritual as stately; but what neither philosopher nor priest had conceived before was the idea of a worship—national, intense, elaborate—of which the very essence was that the Deity receiving it was invisible. Often, even in Christian times, has Pompey's surprise been repeated: often it has been said that without a localising, a dramatising, a materialising representation of the Unseen, all worship would be impossible. The reply which he must, at least for the moment, have made to himself was that, contrary to all expectation, he had there found it possible.

It was natural that so rude a shock to the scruples of the Jews as Pompey's entrance of the Holy of Holies should be long resented, that when the deadly strife began between the two foremost men of the Roman world they should join Cæsar with all his vices against Pompey with all his virtues. It was natural, though less excusable, that even Christian writers

[1] Dio Cass. xxxvii. 15.

[2] οὐδὲν ἐκεῖτο, Jos. *B. J.* v. 5, 5. 'Vacuam 'sedem, inania arcana,' Tac. *Hist.* v. 4. ἄρρητιν καὶ ἀειδή, Dio Cass. xxxvii. 16.

[3] See Cicero's contempt for the Jewish as compared with the Roman ritual. 'Istorum religio sacrorum a splendore 'hujus Imperii, gravitate nominis nostri. 'majorum institutis abhorrebat' (*Pro Flacco*, c. 28).

should represent the calamities which afterwards overtook the hero of the East as a Divine vengeance for this intrusion. Yet, surely, if ever in those times such intrusion were deemed admissible, it was to be forgiven in one whose clean hands[1] and pure heart, compared with most of the contemporary chiefs, David would have regarded as no disqualification for a dweller on God's Holy Hill—in one, through whose deep and serious insight, even if only for a moment, into the significance of that vacant shrine, the Gentile world received a thrill of sacred awe which it never lost, and the Christian world may receive a lesson which it has often sorely needed.

On the next day, with the same highbred courtesy that marked all his dealings, like that which distinguished even the Pilate and the Felix of a later day, he gave orders to purify the Temple from the contamination which he knew that his presence there must have occasioned, and invested with the Pontificate the unfortunate Hyrcanus, 'destined' (if we may here thus apply the description of another claimant of a shadowy sceptre) 'to 'thirty years of exile and wandering, of vain projects, of honours 'more galling than insults, and of hopes such as make the heart 'sick.'[2]

Conquest of Palestine.

With the rule of a master he took command of the whole country. The chiefs of the insurgents were beheaded. The Jewish race was once more confined within the narrow limits of Judah, which henceforth takes the name of Judæa. Gadara[3] was made over to its townsman, Pompey's favourite freedman, Demetrius. To all the outlying towns on the coast and beyond the Jordan, which Simon had subdued, he restored their independence. The ancient capital

[1] Modern historians have not been favourable to Pompey. But on the general character at least of his earlier years Arnold's verdict (Life of Cæsar, *Encyc. Metrop.* ii. p. 243) has on the whole not been reversed; and Macaulay (*Life*, i. p. 458), after speaking of Cato's splendid eulogy in Lucan's *Pharsalia* 'as a pure gem of 'rhetoric without one flaw,' adds, 'and in 'my opinion not very far from historical 'truth.'

[2] Macaulay's *Hist. of England*, ii. 363.

[3] There must have been two towns called Gadara. One, the fortress beyond the Jordan (Jos. *Ant.* xiii. 14, 4; *B. J.* i. 4, 2; 20, 3; ii. 18, 1; xv. 7, 3); the other, on the sea coast between Joppa and Ashdod (Strabo, xvi. 29). This is probably the birthplace of Demetrius, and intended in Jos. *B. J.* i. 7, 7; *Ant.* xii. 7, 4; xiv. 4, 1; xvii 2, 4, and perhaps the same as Gezer.

of Samaria, which John Hyrcanus had destroyed, was rebuilt by Gabinius, and bore his name until it took from a far greater Roman the title, which through all its subsequent changes it has never lost, in Greek 'Sebaste,' in Latin 'Augusta,' 'the city 'of Augustus.' The unity of government was broken into five separate councils, which were to sit with equal power at Jerusalem, Gadara, Amathus, Jericho, and Sepphoris. And thus, says Josephus, one might suppose with bitter irony, 'they passed 'from a monarchy to an aristocracy.'[1]

Meanwhile the Roman citizens witnessed the spectacle of Pompey's triumph—his third and greatest—the grandest that Rome had ever seen. First[2] came the huge placards, with the enumeration of the thousand castles and nine hundred cities conquered, the eight hundred galleys taken from the pirates, the thirty-nine cities refounded. Then followed the splendid spoils, and amongst them the golden vine of Palestine; then the mass of prisoners, who added a peculiar interest to the procession, by appearing not as slaves in chains, but each in his national costume. Immediately in front of the Conqueror himself, in his jewelled car, surrounded by the pictures of his exploits, came the 362 captive Princes of the East, and amongst them the King of Judæa. Even at the time the countrymen of Pompey selected from the vast variety of objects the trophies of the strange city and people of whom they had heard so much—and bestowed upon him as his especial title 'our hero of Jerusalem.'[3]

Triumph of Pompey.

It was the rare exception, the result of the rare humanity of the conqueror, that on reaching the fatal turn in the Sacred Way, whence the triumphal procession ascended the Capitoline Hill, the prisoners were not led to execution, but either sent back to their homes or remained in Rome for whatever fortunes might await them.

Amongst the train of the inferior captives who were thus left after the triumph, and who, on recovering their liberty, had either not the means or the inclination to return to their distant

[1] Jos. *Ant.* xiv. 5, 3, 4.
[2] Appian, *De Bell. Mithrid.* 253; Plutarch, *Pompey.*
[3] Cicero, *Ep. ad Att.* ii. 9.

country, was the large band of Jewish exiles, to whom was assigned a district on the right bank of the Tiber, convenient for the landing of merchandise to a people whose commercial tendencies were now developing. This singular settlement, receiving constant accessions from the East, became the wonder of the Imperial city, with its separate burial-places copied from the rock-hewn tombs of Palestine, with its ostentatious observance, even in the heart of the great metropolis, of the day of rest—with the basket and bundle of hay which marked the Jewish peasant wherever [1] he was found; with its mysterious power of fascinating the proud Roman nobles by the glimpses which it gave of a better world. By establishing this community Pompey was, although he knew it not, the founder of the Roman Church.

Foundation of the Church of Rome.

Amongst the more illustrious hostages were Aristobulus, his uncle Absalom, and his children. It will be our endeavour briefly to follow the fates of these last remnants of the Maccabæan race, whose spirit still showed itself in their unquenchable patriotism and their headlong resistance against the most overwhelming odds. Alexander, the eldest of the sons of Aristobulus—who had married a daughter of Hyrcanus, and thus might seem to represent both branches of the family—had escaped on the journey to Rome, and for a time defended himself in the family fortress of Alexandreum, against Gabinius and the reckless chief whose military capacity was first revealed on this excursion, Antony. It was taken, and the mountain fastnesses which had been erected by the Asmonean [2] Princes—'the haunts of the robbers'—'the strongholds of the tyrants,' as they are called by the Roman writers—were all dismantled. In a few months, however,[3] Aristobulus himself, with his son Antigonus, effected his flight from Rome, and fled, as if by instinct, to those same castles, which, even in their ruined state, were as the nests of that hunted race. The conflict revived in the famous

Remnants of the Asmoneans.

B.C. 57.

[1] Philo, *Legatio ad Caium*, § 23; Hor. *Sat.* I. ix. 71, 72; Juvenal, *Sat.* III. 14, VI. 542; Renan's *S. Paul*, 101–107; Grätz, iii. 124.

[2] Strabo, xvi. 37, 40.

[3] Jos. *Ant.* xiv. 6, 1.

scenes of Central Palestine. The Roman army, which had entrenched itself in the world-old sanctuary[1] of Gerizim, under the shelter of the friendly Samaritans, broke out and finally overpowered the insurgents on the slopes of Tabor, the field of so many victories and defeats from Barak downwards to Napoleon.

For a moment, by joining the cause of Cæsar, under whose standard some of their countrymen fought at Pharsalia, there seemed a chance for the Jewish Princes to retrieve their fortunes. But amidst their obscure entanglement in the struggle between the two mighty combatants for the empire of the world, Aristobulus by poison, Alexander by decapitation, were removed from the scene. There now remained Antigonus and his sister Alexandra, and the two children of Alexander, Aristobulus and Miriam or Mary—better known by the more lengthened Grecian form of Mariamne. Round these princes and princesses revolves the tragedy in which the Asmonean dynasty finally disappeared. But in order to catch the thread of that intricate plot we must introduce the new character who appears on the scene. Throughout the struggles which we have traversed it is easy to discern the tortuous and ambitious policy of the crafty Idumæan Antipater, who had made himself indispensable alike to the feeble Priest Hyrcanus and to the powerful chiefs of the Roman Republic. But Antipater himself now makes way for a name far more renowned in history, far more interesting in itself—his son Herod, whether by accident or design, surnamed the Great.[2] In the darker traditions of the Talmud, he was known only as 'the slave[3] of King Jannæus;' and the inferiority of his lineage was a constant byword of reproach amongst the members of the Asmonean family, in whose eyes his sisters were fit for nothing but sempstresses, his brothers[4] nothing but

B.C. 49.

Herod.

[1] Jos. *Ant.* xiv. 6, 2, 3.

[2] Derenbourg, 146, 151. According to the story of Christian writers (Eus. *H. E.* i. 6, 7; Justin, *Trypho.* p. 272, especially Epip. *Hær.* i. 20), Herod's grandfather, himself Herod, was a slave in the temple of Ascalon, too poor to ransom his son Antipater when carried off by Idumæan robbers. The story receives some confirmation from Herod's attentions to Ascalon (Jos. *B. J.* i. 21, 11), but is incompatible with the general account of the family given by Josephus (*Ant.* xiv. 1, 3; *B. J.* i. 6, 2).

[3] Jos. *B. J.* i. 16, 4; i. 24, 3.

[4] Comp. Jos. *Ant.* xiv. 8, 1; xx. 8, 7.

village schoolmasters. In the next generation, when his power on one side, and his crimes on the other, had drawn a halo or a cloud round his head, the descent of Herod was alternately glorified or debased. In the annals of his secretary, Nicolas of Damascus, he was represented as a scion, not of the despised and hated Edomites, but of a noble Judæan family amongst the Babylonian exiles. Nor was this closer kinship altogether disclaimed by the Jews themselves. 'Thou 'art our brother,' they condescended to say to one of the sons of Herod, who wept over his alien origin. But it is not necessary to go beyond the historical facts. Whether by race or education, he belonged to that Edomite tribe, which, with singular tenacity, had retained the characteristics of its first father Esau through the long years which had elapsed since, in the patriarchal traditions, the two brothers had parted at the cave of Machpelah. In their wild nomadic customs, in their mountain warfare—clinging like eagles to their caverned fastnesses, unless when they descended for a foray on their more civilised neighbours—they were hardly distinguishable from a Bedouin tribe; yet, with that sense of injured kinship which breeds the deadliest animosities, they maintained a defiant claim to hang on the outskirts and force themselves on the notice of the people of Israel; sheltering the revolted princes of Judah in their secluded glens; hounding on the enemies of Jerusalem in the hour of her sorest need; claiming complete possession of the whole country for their own, as if by the elder brother's right, which the supplanter had stolen from them. If for a moment they had bowed beneath the sway of the first Hyrcanus, and consented to reunite themselves with the common stock of Abraham by the rite of circumcision, it was that 'they might 'once again have dominion and break their brother's yoke from 'off their necks.'

His origin.

The first Antipater secured for himself the place of a vassal prince under Alexander Jannæus; the second, as we have seen, became the master of the Phantom Priest Hyrcanus, and, alternately siding with each of the two parties which divided the Roman world, mounted, through the favour

B.C. 47. His rise.

first of Pompey and then of Cæsar, to the high office of the Roman Procurator of Judæa. And now his son inherits the traditions of his house and nation, and the threats of that subtle influence by which Rome henceforth assumed the control of Judæa. Herod was hardly more than a boy—but fifteen [1] years of age—when he was brought forward by his father into public life. Already when he was a child going to school, his future greatness [2] had been predicted by an ascetic seer, from the Essenian settlement, who called him 'King of the Jews.' The child thought that Menahem was in jest; but the prophet smacked the little boy on the back, and charged him to remember these blows, as signal that he had foretold to him his future [3] destiny—what he might be, and what, unfortunately, he became. Like a true descendant of Esau, he was 'a man of the field, a 'mighty hunter.' He was renowned for his horsemanship. On one day of successful sport he was known to have killed no less than forty of the game of those parts—bears, stags, and wild asses. In the Arab exercises of the *jerreed*, or throwing the lance, in the archery of the ancient Edomites, he was the wonder of his generation. He had a splendid presence. His fine black hair, on which he prided himself, and which when it turned grey was dyed,[4] to keep up the appearance of youth, was magnificently dressed. On one occasion, when he sprang out of a bath where assassins had surprised him, even his naked figure was so majestic [5] that they fled before him. Nor was he destitute of noble qualities, however much obscured by the violence of the age, and by the furious, almost frenzied, cruelty which despotic power breeds in Eastern potentates. There was a greatness of soul which might have raised him above the petty intriguers by whom he was surrounded. His family affections were deep and strong. In that time of general dissolution of domestic ties it is refreshing to witness the almost extravagant tenderness with which, on the plain of Sharon, he founded, in

[1] It has been conjectured to read 25 for 15. But the remark of Josephus, twice repeated (*Ant.* xiv. 9, 2; *B. J.* i. 10, 4), that he was exceedingly young (νέῳ παντάπασιν ὄντι—κομιδῇ νέον) shows that he meant 15.

[2] *B. J.* i. 20, 4.

[3] Jos. *Ant.* xv. 10, 5.

[4] *Ant.* xvi. 8, 1; *B. J.* i. 24, 7; *Ant.* xiv. 9, 4.

[5] *Ant.* xiv. 15, 13.

the fervour of his filial love, the city of 'Antipatris;' to the citadel above Jericho[1] he gave the name of his Arabian mother Cypros; to one of the towers of Jerusalem, and to a fortress, in the valley which still retains the name, looking down to the Jordan, he left the privilege of commemorating his beloved and devoted[2] brother Phasael. In the lucid intervals of the darker days which beset the close of his career nothing can be more pathetic than his remorse for his domestic crimes, nothing more genuine than his tears of affection for his grandchildren.

His cultivation.

Nor were there wanting signs of a higher culture than any Judæan Prince had shown since the time of Solomon. He had an absolute passion for philosophy and history, and used to say that there could be nothing more useful or politic for a king than the investigation of the great events of the past. He engaged for his private secretary Nicolas of Damascus, one of the most accomplished scholars[3] of the age, and author of a universal history in 144 books; and on his long voyages to and from Rome, he loved to while away the hours by conversations on these subjects with Nicolas, whom for this purpose he took with him on board of the same ship. One example of his own philosophic sentiment is preserved in the speech which Josephus ascribes to him, endeavouring to dispel the superstitious panic[4] occasioned by an earthquake. How completely, too, he entered into the glories of Greek and Roman art will appear as we proceed, from the monuments which place him in the first rank of the masters of architecture in that great age of building. His contemporaries recognised in him one of those rare princely characters, who take a delight in beneficence, and in its largest possible scope. Not only in Palestine itself, but in all the cities of Asia and of Greece, which needed generous assistance, he freely gave it. At Antioch he left his mark in the polished[5] marble pavement of the public

[1] Jos. *B. J.* i. 21, 9; *Ant.* xiv. 7, 3.

[2] For the devotion of Herod to Phasael, see Jos. *Ant.* x. 16, 5, 2; of Phasael to Herod, *ibid.* xiv. 13, 10; *B. J.* i. 10, 5.

[3] Jos. *Ant.* xiii. 12, 6; xiv. 1, 3; 4, 3; 6, 4; xvi.; x. 7, 1; xiii. 8, 2; *c. Ap.* ii. 7 (see Ewald, v. 417); *Fragments of Valesius*, quoted in Clinton's *Fasti Hellenici*, A.D. 16.

[4] Jos. *B. J.* i. 29, 4.

[5] *Ibid.* i. xxi. 11, 12.

square, and in the cloister which surrounded it. In many of the cities of Syria and Asia Minor he founded places for athletic exercises, aqueducts, baths, fountains, and (in the modern fashion of philanthropy) annexed to them parks and gardens for public recreation. With a toleration which seems beyond his time, but which kindles an admiration even in the Jewish historian, he repaired the Temple of Apollo at Rhodes, and settled a permanent endowment on the games of Olympia, the chief surviving relic of Grecian grandeur, which he had visited on his way to Rome.

This was the man who now stepped into the foremost place of the Jewish history. It might have seemed as if the cry of Esau were to be again repeated : 'Hast thou but one blessing? 'Bless me, even me also, O my father.'

A chief of such largeness of mind, such generosity of disposition, such power of command, was well suited to take the lead in this distracted nation. Viewed as we now view him, through the blood-stained atmosphere of his later life, even the dubious eulogies of Josephus are difficult to understand. But viewed in the light of the nobleness of his early youth, and through the magnificence of his public works, it was natural that—as in the case of our own Henry VIII.—the judgment of his contemporaries should have differed from that of posterity, that he should have been invested with something of a sacred character, as a dreamer of prophetic dreams, a special favourite of Divine Providence,[1] and that a large party in the community should have borne his name as their most cherished badge, and regarded him as the nearest likeness which that age afforded to the Anointed Prince[2] or Priest of the house of David, who had been expected by the earlier Prophets.

The first scene on which Herod appears is full of instruction. Boy as he was, his father had appointed him to take charge of Galilee; which, partly from its 'border' character, whence it derived its name, partly from the physical peculiarities of its deeply-sunken lake, wild glens, and

His exploits in Galilee.

[1] Jos. *Ant.* xiv. 15, 12, 13.

[2] See the quotations in Professor Westcott on the Herodians, *Dict. of Bible*, i. p. 796.

cavernous hills, had become the refuge of the high-spirited insurgents, who in semi-civilised countries insensibly acquire both the reputation and the character of bandits—the Highlands, the Asturias, the Abruzzi of Palestine. The young 'Lord of 'the Marches,' fired with the same spirit, whether politic or philanthropic, which had conferred such glory on Pompey and Augustus in their repression of the pirates of the Mediterranean and the brigands of Italy, determined to crush those lawless robbers of his own country.

In Syria his fame rose to the highest pitch. In villages on the Lebanon his name was the burden of popular ballads, as their Heaven-sent deliverer from the incursions of the Galilean highlanders. But in Judæa these acts of summary justice wore another aspect. The chief of the robber band, Hezekiah, was, probably, in the eyes of the residents at Jerusalem—perhaps was in reality—the patriot, the Tell of his time, as he certainly was the father of a gallant family of sons, who were to play a like part hereafter.

B.C. 47. His trial.

Jerusalem was filled with the echoes of these Galilean exploits. On the one hand the messengers of Herod's victories vied with each other in[1] their reports, and in awakening the public apprehension of his possible designs on the monarchy. On the other hand, the mothers of the victims of his zeal hurried up to the capital, and every time that the Priest-King Hyrcanus appeared in the Temple Court beset him with entreaties not to allow the murder of their children untried and unconvicted to pass unchallenged. Reluctantly the feeble Prince summoned the son of his patron to appear before the Council of the Sanhedrin,[2] which now for the first time appears in Jewish history. It sat, probably, now, as afterwards, in the Hall of Gazith, or Squares, so called from the hewn, square stones of its pavement.[3] The royal Pontiff was present, and the chief teachers of the period. The legendary account of the scene, although disguised under wrong names and dates, is one of the very few notices which the Talmudic[4]

[1] Jos. *B. J.* i. 10, 6.
[2] See Lecture XLVIII.
[3] Mishna, *Yoma*, 25; *Sanhedrin*, 19.
[4] Derenbourg, 147. The king in this story is made Jannæus, and the fearless judge Simon the son of Shetach.

traditions take of the eventful course of Herod's life. 'The 'slave of the King of Judah,' said the Rabbinical tale, 'had 'committed a murder.' The Sanhedrin summoned the King to answer for the crimes of his slave. 'If the ox gore any one,'[1] said the interpreters of the law to the King, 'the owner of the 'ox shall be responsible for the ox.' The King seated himself before them. 'Rise,' said the Judge. 'Thou standest[2] not 'before us, but before Him who commanded and the world was 'created.' The King appealed from the Judge to his colleagues. The Judge turned to the right hand and to the left, and his colleagues were silent. Then said the Judge: 'You are sunk 'in your own thoughts. God who knows your thoughts will 'punish you for your timidity.' The Angel Gabriel smote them and they died.

It is instructive to turn to the actual scene of which this is the distorted version. It was indeed a splendid apparition, but not of the Angel Gabriel, that struck the wise Councillors dumb. When Herod was summoned before them for the murder of the Galileans, instead of a solitary suppliant, clothed in black, with his hair combed down,[3] and his manner submissive, such as they expected to see, there came a superb youth, in royal purple, his curls dressed out in the very height of aristocratic fashion, surrounded by a guard of soldiers, and holding in his hand the commendatory letters of Sextus Cæsar, the Governor of Syria, the cousin of the great Julius. The two chiefs of the Sanhedrin at that juncture were Abtalion[4] and Shemaiah. It was Abtalion, doubtless, who counselled silence. His maxim had always been: 'Be circumspect in your words.' But Shemaiah rose in his place and warned them that to overlook such a defiance of the law would be to ensure their own ruin. For a moment they wavered. But, warned by Hyrcanus, Herod escaped, and years afterwards lived to prove the truth of Shemaiah's warning, lived to sweep away the vacillating Council, though at the same time rewarding the prudence of Abtalion, if not the courage of Shemaiah.

[1] Ex. xxi. 28.

[2] Deut. xix. 17.

[3] Jos. *Ant.* xiv. 9, 3-5. This scene is represented at the entrance of the town hall of Basle.

[4] Derenbourg, 117, 148.

The story well illustrates the waning of the independence of the nation before the rise of the new dynasty, backed as it was by all the power of Rome. It was to Herod that the sceptre was destined to pass.

Antipater, his father, indeed, long held Hyrcanus in his grasp. But he at last fell a victim to the struggles of his puppet to escape from him, and the two brothers, Phasael and Herod, were left to maintain their own cause. At once Herod endeavoured to spring into his father's place by a stroke, which, but for the jealousies of his own household, would have probably been crowned with complete success.

Death of Antipater. B.C 43.

Contest with Antigonus. B.C. 42.

He had already in his early years married an Idumæan wife, Doris, by whom he had a son, whom he named after his father Antipater—a child now, but destined to grow up into the evil genius of his house. He now determined on a higher alliance. The beautiful and high-spirited Mariamne united in herself the [1] claims of both the rival Asmonean princes. She was the grand-daughter alike of Hyrcanus and of Aristobulus.

From this time Hyrcanus became the fast friend of Herod, crowned with garlands whenever he appeared, pleading [2] his cause before the Roman Triumvir. Aristobulus, however, had left behind him not only Mariamne, but a passionate and ambitious son, Antigonus, who could not see without a struggle the kingdom pass away even to his niece's husband. There was one foreign ally and one only whom he could invoke against the great Republic of the West. It was the rising kingdom of the East—the Parthian monarchy, which offered to play the same part for Judæa against Rome that Egypt had formerly played against Assyria. A natural brotherhood of misfortune and of joy seemed to have arisen from the fresh recollection of the campaign of Crassus. Jerusalem still suffered under the loss of its accumulated treasures, which the rapacious Roman, in spite of the most solemn adjurations, had carried off from [3] its Temple. Parthia still rejoiced in the

Crassus. B.C. 54.

[1] Jos. *Ant.* xiv. 12, 2. [2] *Ibid. Ant.* xiv. 12, 2; 13, 1.
[3] *Ibid. Ant.* xiv. 7, 1, 2; *B. J.* i. 8, 8.

triumph which its armies had won over his scattered host on the plains of Haran, the ancient cradle of the Jewish race. By force and by fraud, Hyrcanus and Phasael were induced to give themselves into the hands of the Parthian general, and were hurried away into the far East. Phasael died, partly by his own desperate act, when he saw that he was doomed, partly by the treachery of Antigonus, but not without a glow of delight on hearing that his beloved brother had escaped. The fate of Hyrcanus was singularly instructive. To take the life of so insignificant a creature was not within the range of the ambition of Antigonus. All that was needed was to debar him from the Priesthood. For this the slightest bodily defect or malformation was a sufficient disqualification. The nephew sprang upon the uncle, and with his own[1] teeth gnawed off the ears of the harmless Pontiff, and left him in that mutilated condition in the Parthian court. This strange physical deposition from a spiritual office in part succeeded, in part failed of its purpose.

The Parthians. B.C. 40.

In those remote regions, the prestige of one who had once been chief of the Jewish nation was not easily broken. Hyrcanus, after receiving every courtesy from the Parthian king, was allowed to move to the vast colony of his countrymen who still inhabited Babylon.[2] By them he was hailed at once as High Priest and King, and loaded with honours, which he gratefully accepted. What his fate was to be in Jerusalem we shall presently see.

Meanwhile the plot in Palestine had deeply thickened. On the day that Hyrcanus and Phasael had been carried off to Parthia, Herod escaped, with all the members of his family that he could collect, and hurried into his native hills in the south of Judæa. 'It would have 'moved the hardest of hearts,' says the historian, 'to have seen 'that flight'—his aged mother—his youngest brother—his clever sister—his betrothed bride, with her still more sagacious mother—the small children of his earlier marriage. Never was that high spirit so nearly broken. It was a march which he

B.C. 40. Escape from Antigonus.

[1] Jos. *B. J.* i. 13, 9. [2] *Ibid. Ant.* xv. 2, 2.

never forgot. Years afterwards he built for himself and his dynasty a fortress and burial-place bearing his name, and corresponding to those of which the Asmonean princes had set the example—the *Herodium*—on the square summit of the commanding height at the foot of which he had gained the success over his pursuers which secured his safety.[1] From thence he took refuge in the almost inaccessible stronghold of the ancient kings of Judah, afterwards destined to be the last fastness of the expiring people—Masada, by the Dead Sea. But even Masada—even Petra to which he next fled—was not secure. Regardless of the blandishments of Cleopatra at Alexandria, regardless of the storms in the Mediterranean, he halted not till he reached Rome and laid his grievances before his first patron Antony.

It was the fatal turning-point of his life. The prize of the Jewish monarchy was now unquestionably and for the first time offered to him by Antony and Octavianus Cæsar. He entered the Senate as the rightful advocate of the young Prince Aristobulus. He left it, walking between the two Triumvirs, as 'King of the Jews.' It was still after many vicissitudes and hair-breadth escapes that, with the assistance of the Roman troops, commanded by Sosius, he stormed Jerusalem. It was the twenty-fifth anniversary of the day on which Pompey had entered the Temple, and it only partially escaped the horrors of the same desperate resistance and the same ruthless massacre which has been the peculiar fate of almost every capture of Jerusalem, from Nebuchadnezzar down to Godfrey. But the noblest parts of Herod's finer nature were called forth. With a spirit worthy of Henry the Fourth of France, he exclaimed: 'The dominion of the whole civilised world would not compensate to me for the destruction of my subjects;'[2] and he actually bought off the rapacious Roman soldiers out of his own personal munificence.

He obtains the kingdom.

Capture of Jerusalem.

B.C. 37.

These brighter traits were now rapidly merged in the darkening shadows of his later career. The followers of Antigonus

[1] Jos. *Ant.* xiv. 13, 8.

[2] *Ibid. Ant.* xiv. 16, 3; *B. J.* i. 17, 18.

—including, according to the Jewish tradition, the whole teaching body of the nation—Herod pursued to death with a vindictiveness which he had learned only too well in the school of his friends the Roman triumvirs. Of the whole of that Council which had sat in judgment on his youthful excesses in Galilee, three only are said to have escaped—the prudent Abtalion, the courageous Shemaiah, and the son of Babas,[2] not, however, without the loss of his eyesight. Even the coffins of the dead were searched[3] to see that no living enemy might escape the vigilant persecutor. The proud spirit of Antigonus gave way under this overwhelming disaster. He came down from his lofty tower, and fell at the feet of Sosius in an agony of tears. The hard-hearted Roman, not touched by the disastrous misery of the gallant Prince, burst into roars[4] of brutal laughter, called him in ridicule by the name of the Grecian maiden *Antigone*, and hurried him off in chains to Antony at Antioch. Antigonus was in the hands of those who knew neither justice nor mercy. A bribe from Herod to Antony extinguished the last spark of compassion. So strong was felt to be the attachment of the Jewish nation to the Maccabæan race, whilst any remained bearing the royal name, that regardless of the scruple which had hitherto withheld even the fiercest of the Roman generals from thus trampling on a fallen king, the unfortunate Antigonus was lashed to a stake like a convicted criminal, scourged by the rods of the relentless lictors, and ruthlessly beheaded by the axe of their fasces.[5] With a Mattathais the Asmonean dynasty began, with a Mattathias it ended. Coins[6] still exist bearing the Hebrew name for his office of High Priest, and the Greek name of his royal dignity; whilst on medals struck by Sosius at Zacynthus to commemorate his victory, for the first time appears the well-known melancholy figure of Judæa[7] captive, with her head resting on her hands, and besides her crouches the form of her last

[1] Jos. *Ant.* xv. 1, 1 (Pollio).
[2] Derenbourg, 152.
[3] Comp. Dio Cass. xlix. 22; Plut. *Ant.*
[4] *B. J.* i. 18, 2.
[5] Jos. *Ant.* xv. 1, 2 (quoting Strabo).
[6] Madden's *Jewish Coins*, pp. 77–79.
[7] In the British Museum.

native king, stripped and bound in preparation for his miserable end.

Yet the Maccabæan family was not extinct. There still remained Hyrcanus, the original friend of Herod and Herod's father, and Aristobulus and Mariamne, the two grandchildren of Aristobulus the king. We will trace each of these to their end. Whether from policy or old affection, Herod, now seated on the throne of Judæa, invited Hyrcanus from his honourable retreat in Babylonia to the troubled scene at Jerusalem. Hyrcanus was to share the regal dignity with him, to take precedence of him—was called 'his father'—enjoyed every outward privilege which was his before, except only the High Priesthood, from which he was excluded by the extreme punctiliousness that, amidst all the scandalous vices of the time, still shrank from nominating a pontiff with the almost imperceptible blemish inflicted by the teeth of Antigonus. For this high office, Herod summoned a Jewish exile, an ancient friend of his own, of unquestionably priestly descent—Hananel, from Babylon. But this at once provoked a new feud. However much the royal dignity might be lost to the Asmonean house, yet there was no reason why the Priesthood, for which Hyrcanus was thus incapacitated, should not be continued in their line; and there was at hand for this purpose Aristobulus, the maternal grandson of Hyrcanus and brother of Mariamne, whom Herod had, shortly before his final success, married at Samaria, the city which the Romans had founded anew, and which was henceforth one of Herod's chief resorts. It was as if the majestic beauty which had distinguished the Maccabæan family from Judas downwards reached its climax in this brother and sister. And their mother Alexandra exhibited not less the courage and the craft which had been so conspicuous in Jonathan and the first Hyrcanus. She was 'the wisest woman,' so Herod thought, in his whole court, the one to whose opinion he most deferred. Both she and her daughter were indignant that the charming boy, who was now the sole representative of their house in coming years, should be kept out of the Priesthood by

B.C. 36. Priesthood of Hananel.

Priesthood of Aristobulus III. B.C. 35.

a stranger ; and, partly by remonstrances, partly by intrigues, they succeeded in inducing Herod, by the same authority that Solomon and the Syrian kings had exercised before him, to supersede Hananel, and appoint Aristobulus in his place. His mother's heart misgave her, and she had planned, with her friend, in some respects a kindred spirit, Cleopatra, a flight for herself and for him into Egypt. But the plan was discovered, and the fate which she had feared for her son was precipitated by the very object which she had striven to obtain for him. It was, as so often on other occasions in the Jewish history, amidst the peculiar festivities and solemnities of the Feast [1] of Tabernacles that he was to assume his office. He was but just seventeen ; his commanding stature, beyond his age, his transcendent beauty, his noble bearing, set off by the High Priest's gorgeous attire, at once riveted the attention of the vast assembly, and when he ascended the steps of the altar for the sacrifice it recalled so vividly the image of his grandfather, Aristobulus, so passionately loved and so bitterly lamented, that, as in the well-known scene in a great modern romance, the recognition flew from mouth to mouth ; the old popular enthusiasm was revived, which, it became evident, would be satisfied with nothing short of restoring to him the lost crown of his family.

The suspicions of Herod were excited. The joyous Feast was over, and the youthful High Priest, fresh from his brilliant display, was invited to his mother's palace amongst the groves of Jericho—the fashionable watering-place, as it had become, of Palestine. Herod received the boy with his usual sportiveness and gaiety. It was one of the warm autumnal days of Syria, and the heat was yet more overpowering in that tropical valley. In the sultry noon the High Priest and his young companions stood cooling themselves beside the large tanks which surrounded the open court of the Palace, and watching the gambols and exercises of the guests or slaves, as, one after another, they plunged into these crystal swimming-baths. Amongst these was the band of Gaulish guards,[2] whom Augustus had transferred from Cleopatra to Herod, and whom

Murder of Aristobulus.

[1] See Lecture XLIII.

[2] *B. J.* i. 22, 2.

Herod employed as his most unscrupulous instruments. Lured on by these perfidious playmates, the princely boy joined in the sport, and then, as at sunset the sudden darkness fell over the gay scene, the wild band dipped and dived with him under the deep water; and in that fatal 'baptism'[1] life was extinguished. When the body was laid out in the Palace the passionate lamentations of the Princesses knew no bounds. The news flew through the town, and every house felt as if it had lost a child. The mother suspected, but dared not reveal her suspicions, and in the agony of self-imposed restraint, and in the compression of her determined will, trembled on the brink of self-destruction. Even Herod, when he looked at the dead face and form, retaining all the bloom of youthful beauty, was moved to tears—so genuine, that they almost served as a veil for his complicity in the murder. And it was not more than was expected from the effusion of his natural grief that the funeral was ordered on so costly and splendid a scale as to give consolation[2] even to the bereaved mother and sister.

That mother, however, still plotted, and now with increased restlessness, against the author of her misery. That sister still felt secure in the passionate affection of her husband, on whose nobler qualities she relied when others doubted. But now the tragedy spread and deepened, and intertwined itself as it grew with the great struggle waging on the larger theatre of history. In the court of Herod there were ranged on one side the two Princesses of the Asmonean family, on the other the mother and the sister of Herod himself, Cypros and Salome, who resented the contempt with which the royal ladies of the Maccabæan house looked down on the upstart Idumæan family. In Egypt was Cleopatra, ambitious of annexing Palestine, now endeavouring to inveigle Herod himself by her arts, now poisoning the mind of Antony against him. In Rome were Antony and Augustus Cæsar contending for the mastery of the world, and Herod alternately pleading his cause before the one

[1] βαπτίζοντες, Jos. *Ant.* xv. 3, 3. The word, especially in that locality, whence in the next generation it acquired a new celebrity, arrests the attention, and, as used here, shows clearly its true meaning.

[2] Jos. *Ant.* xv 3, 4.

and the other—before his ancient friend Antony, and then, after the battle of Actium, before the new ruler, who had the magnanimity to be touched by the frankness with which

B.C. 30.

Herod urged his fidelity to Antony as the plea for the confidence of Augustus.[1] Meanwhile, like a hunted animal turned to bay, his own passions grew fiercer, his own methods more desperate. Aristobulus, the young, the beautiful, had perished. But there remained the aged Pontiff Hyrcanus.

Death of Hyrcanus. B.C. 30.

Insignificant, humiliated, mutilated as he was, there was still the chance that the same veneration which had encircled him in Chaldæa might gather round him in Palestine, and that even the Roman policy might convert him into a rival King. In a fatal moment listening to the counsels of his restless daughter, Hyrcanus gave to Herod the pretext needed for an accusation, and (so carefully were preserved the forms of the Jewish State) a trial and a judgment; and at the age of eighty the long and troubled life of the Asmonean Pontiff was cut off.

The intestine quarrels in the Herodian court now became so violent that the Princesses of the rival factions could not be allowed to meet. The mother and the sister of Herod were lodged in the fastness which was more peculiarly his own—Masada, by the Dead Sea. His wife and her mother remained in the castle dear to them as the ancient residence and burial-place [2] of their family—Alexandreum.

There is something magnificent in the attitude of Mariamne at this crisis of her history—never for one moment lowering herself to any of the base intrigues of man or woman that surrounded her, but never disguising from her husband her sense of the wrongs he had inflicted on her house.

Murder of Mariamne. B.C. 29.

When he flew back from his interview with Augustus, inspired by the passionate affection of his first love, to announce to her his success in winning the favour of the conqueror of Actium, she turned away and reproached him with the murders of her brother and her grandfather.

Now was the moment when Salome saw her opportunity.

[1] See Hausrath, *Zeit Christi*, 237.

[2] Jos. *Ant.* xvii. 8, 6.

She played on every chord of the King's suspicious temper, till it was irritated past endurance. Mariamne was arrested, tried, and condemned. Even in these last moments, she rose superior to all around her. Unlike her mother, she had never shared in mean plots and counterplots to advance the interests, or secure the safety of the Asmonean house. If she spoke in behalf of her kindred, it was boldly and frankly to a husband, on whose affections and generosity, if he was left to himself, she knew that she could rely. Unlike that ambitious princess, now in her extreme adversity she maintained a serenity in which her mother failed. It is the characteristic difference of the two natures that the restless woman who had employed every miserable art in order to protect her family, now that the noblest of her race, for whom she had hazarded all, was on the point of destruction, lost all courage, and endeavoured to clear herself by cowardly reproaches of her daughter in justification of the King. Mariamne, however, answered not a word. 'She 'smiled a dutiful though scornful smile.'[1] Her look for a moment showed how deeply she felt for the shame of a mother; but she went on to her execution with unmoved countenance, with unchanged colour, and died, as she had lived, a true Maccabee. Perhaps the most affecting and convincing testimony to her great character was Herod's passionate remorse. In a frenzy of grief he invoked her name, he burst into wild lamentations, and then, as if to distract himself from his own thoughts, he plunged into society; he had recourse to all his favourite pursuits; he gathered intellectual society round him; he drank freely with his friends; he went to the chase. And then, again, he gave orders that his servants should keep up the illusion of addressing her as though she could still hear them; he shut himself up in Samaria, the scene of their first wedded life, and there, for a long time, attacked by a devouring fever, hovered on the verge of life and death. Of the three stately towers which he afterwards added to the walls of Jerusalem, one was named after his friend Hippias, the second after his favourite brother, Phasael, but the third, most costly

[1] *Mariamne, the Fair Queen of Jewry*, act v. scene I.

and most richly worked of all, was the monument of his beloved Mariamne.[1]

It is[2] not necessary to pursue in detail the entanglements by which the successive members of the Herodian family fell victims to the sanguinary passion which now took possession of the soul of Herod. Alexandra was the first to fall. There remained the two sons of Mariamne, Alexander and Aristobulus, in whom their father delighted to see an image of their lost and lamented mother. He sent them to be educated at Rome in the household of Pollio, the friend of Virgil; and when they returned to Palestine, with all the graces of a Roman education and with the royal bearing, apparently inextinguishable in the Asmonean house, it seemed, from the popular enthusiasm which they excited, that they might yet carry on that great name; and their father, by the high marriages which he prepared for them—for Alexander with the daughter of the King of Cappadocia, for Aristobulus with his cousin the daughter of Salome—hoped to have consolidated their fortunes and reconciled the feuds of the two rival families. But all was in vain. They inherited with their mother's beauty, her haughty and disdainful spirit. They cherished her in an undying memory. Her name[3] was always on their lips, and in their lamentations for her were mingled curses on her destroyer; when they saw her royal dresses bestowed on the ignoble wives of their father's second marriage, they threatened him to his face that they would soon make those fine ladies wear hair-cloth instead; and to their companions they ridiculed the vanity with which in his declining years he insisted on the recognition of his youthful splendour, his skill as a sportsman, and even his superior stature. And now there was a new element of mischief—his eldest son Antipater, who watched

Death of Alexandra. B.C. 28.

End of the sons of Mariamne. B.C. 16–6.

[1] *B. J.* v. 4, 3.

[2] According to the Rabbinical traditions, compressing into one scene this series of crimes and sorrows, 'the slave of the 'Asmoneans' destroyed all the family except one young maiden, whom he proposed to marry. She, to escape, sprang from the housetop, and destroyed herself. He kept her body for seven years embalmed in honey (Derenbourg, 115).

[3] *B. J.* i. 24, 3; *Ant.* xvi. 8, 4.

every opportunity of destroying his father's interest in these aspiring youths—the very demon of the Herodian house.

B.C. 6. He and the she-wolf Salome at last accomplished their object, and the two young Princes were tortured, tried, and at last executed at Sebaste, the scene of their mother's marriage, and interred in the ancestral burial-place of the Alexandreum.[1] They were, if not in lineage yet in character, the last of their race. Their children, in whose behalf the better feelings of Herod broke out when, with tears and passionate kisses of affection which no one doubted to be sincere, he[2] endeavoured to make plans for their prosperous settlement, were gradually absorbed into the Herodian family; and although two of them, Herod Agrippa and Herodias, played a conspicuous part even in the sacred history which follows, they lost the associations of the Maccabæan name, and never kindled the popular enthusiasm in their behalf.

The death of Mariamne and her sons represents in the fall of the Asmonean dynasty the close of the last brilliant page of Jewish history. So long as there was a chance of a Prince from that august and beautiful race the visions of a Son of David retired into the background. It was only when the last descendant of those royal Pontiffs passed away that wider visions again filled the public mind, and prepared the way for One who, whatever might be His outward descent, in His spiritual character represented the best aspect of the Son of Jesse. And even then the famous apostolic names of the coming history were inherited from the enduring interest in the Maccabæan family—John, and Judas, and Simon, and Matthias or Mattathias. Above all, the name so sweet to Christian and to European ears, '*Mary*,' owes, no doubt, its constant repetition in the narratives alike of the Evangelists and of Josephus, not to Miriam the sister of Moses, but to her later namesake, the high-souled and lamented princess Mariamne.

And now came the end of Herod himself. The palace was

[1] *B. J.* i. 28, 6; *Ant.* xvi. 4, 7. [2] *B. J.* i. 28.

haunted by the memories of the Asmonean Queen. 'The 'ghosts of the two murdered Princes,'[1] writes the Jewish historian, rising from his prosaic style almost to the tone of the Æschylean Trilogy, 'wandered through every 'chamber of the palace, and became the inqui- 'sitors and informers to drag out the hidden horrors of the 'Court.' The villain of the family, Antipater, had paid at last the forfeit of his tissue of crimes. But his father was already in his last agonies in the Palace of Jericho—the scene of such splendid luxury, and such fearful crime. As a remedy for the loathsome disorder of which he was the prey, he was carried across the Jordan to one of the loveliest spots in Palestine—the hot[2] sulphur springs which burst from the base of the basaltic columns in the deep ravine on the eastern shore of the Dead Sea; issuing, according to popular belief, from the bottomless pit. There, in 'the Beautiful Stream,'[3] as the Greeks called it, the unhappy King tried to burn and wash away his foul distempers. It was all in vain. Full[4] in his face, as he lay tossing in those sulphurous baths, rose above the western hills the fortress which he had called by his name, and fixed for his burial. And now thitherward he must go. Back to Jericho the dying King was borne. The hideous command which in his last ravings he gave to cause a universal mourning through the country by the slaughter of the chief men of the State, whom he had imprisoned for that purpose in the hippodrome of Jericho, was happily disobeyed. His sister Salome, who had already so much on her conscience, spared herself this latest guilt; and when the body of Herod was carried to its last resting-place, it was attended with unusual pomp, but not with unusual crime. For seven long days the procession ascended the precipitous passes from Jericho to the mountains of Judæa. With crown and sceptre and under a purple pall the corpse of the dead King lay. Round it were the numerous sons of that

Death of Herod. B.C. 4.

[1] Jos. *B. J.* i. 30, 7.

[2] The legend is that they were discovered by a servant of Solomon, who was by his deafness proof against the incantation of the Evil One, from whose pit those boiling fountains gushed forth (Canon Tristram's *Land of Moab*, 237-250—the first full description of this interesting spot).

[3] Callirrhoë. (Jos. *Ant.* xvii. 6; Plin. v. 7.)

[4] Tristram, 240.

divided household. Then followed his guards, and the three trusty bands of Thracian, German, and Celtic soldiers, who had so long been, as it were, the Janissaries of his court.[1] Then through those arid hills defiled the army, and then five hundred slaves with spices for the burial. According to the fashion of those days, when each dynasty or branch of a dynasty had its sepulchral vault in its own special fortress, the remains of the dead king were carried up to that huge [2] square-shaped hill which commands the pass to Hebron, on the summit of which Herod, in memory of his escape on that spot thirty-six years before, had built a vast palace and called it by his name, Herodium.

Such, disengaged from its labyrinthine intricacy, is the story of the last potentate of commanding force and world-wide renown that reigned over Judæa. It is a character which, had it been in the Biblical records, would have ranked in thrilling and instructive interest beside that of the ancient Kings of Israel or Judah. The momentary glimpses which we gain of him in the New Testament, through the story of his conversation with the Magi and his slaughter of the children of Bethlehem, are quite in keeping with the jealous, irritable, unscrupulous temper of the last 'days of Herod [3] the King,' as we read them in the pages of Josephus. But this is but a small portion of his complex career. The plots bred in the atmosphere of polygamy, the 'foul and midnight murders,' the thirst for cruelty growing with its gratification, are features of Oriental and of despotic life only too familiar to us in the history even of David. There is something in the penitence of Herod which reminds us of that of Uriah's murderer, though it has never in Psalm or prayer been enshrined for the admiration of posterity. Besides the intrinsic interest of the story is the pathos which it possesses as the central element in the drama which closed the Asmonean history. He is the Jewish Othello,

His character.

[1] Jos. *Ant.* xvii. 8, 4.

[2] The conspicuous hill near Bethlehem called the 'Frank Mountain,' or Jebel Fureidis, was first identified with the Herodium by Robinson, *B.R.* iv. 173. It is described at length by Josephus, *Ant.* xvii. 8, 3; *B. J.* i. 21, 10; 33, 9.

[3] Matt. ii. 1. See Hausrath, *Zeit Christi*, 281.

but with more than a Desdemona for his victim. When the Moor of Venice, in his closing speech, casts about for someone to whom he may compare himself, it was long thought by the commentators that there was none so suitable as Herod, 'the 'base[1] Judæan, who threw a pearl away richer than all his 'tribe.' Whether this were so or not, a dramatic piece on the subject had already been constructed by a gifted English lady, with a knowledge of the Herodian age surprising for the seventeenth century.[2] When Voltaire apologised to the French public for having chosen Mariamne for the subject of one of his poetical plays, he rose to its grandeur with an enthusiasm unlike himself. 'A king to whom has been given the name of 'Great, enamoured of the loveliest woman in the world; the 'fierce passion of this king so famous for his virtues and for his 'crimes—his ever-recurring and rapid transition from love to 'hatred, and from hatred to love—the ambition of his sister—'the intrigues of his concubines—the cruel situation of a 'princess whose virtue and beauty are still world-renowned, 'who had seen her kinsmen slain by her husband, and who, as 'the climax of grief, found herself loved by their murderer—'what a field for imagination is this! What a career for some 'other[3] genius than mine!' And when at last another genius[4] arose, who had, as Goethe observed, a special aptitude for apprehending the ancient Biblical characters, there are few of his poems at once more pathetic in themselves and more true to history, than that which represents the unhappy king wandering through the galleries of his palace and still invoking his murdered wife—

> Oh, Mariamne! now for thee
> The heart for which thou bled'st is bleeding;
> Revenge is lost in agony,
> And wild remorse to rage succeeding.

[1] *Othello*, act v. sc. 2. So the older commentators and the first folio edition. The second folio and the later commentators read 'Indian.'

[2] 'The Tragedie of Mariam, the Faire 'Queen of Jewry, written by that learned 'virtuous, and truly noble ladie E. C.' (Lady Elizabeth Carew) 1613. One spirited chorus, on the forgiveness of injuries, deserves to rescue it from oblivion.

[3] Quoted by Salvador, i. 304.

[4] Byron's *Hebrew Melodies*.

Oh Mariamne! where art thou
Thou canst not hear my bitter pleading:
Ah! couldst thou—thou wouldst pardon now,
Though Heaven were to my prayer unheeding.

She's gone, who shared my diadem;
She sank, with her my joys entombing;
I swept that flower from Judah's stem,
Whose leaves for me alone were blooming;
And mine's the guilt, and mine the hell,
This bosom's desolation dooming;
And I have earned those tortures well,
Which unconsumed are still consuming!

But the importance of Herod's life does not end with his personal history. He created in great part that Palestine which he left behind him as the platform on which the closing scenes of the Jewish, the opening scenes of the Christian Church were to be enacted.

Few men have ever lived who, within so short a time, so transformed the outward face of a country. That Grecian, Roman, Western colouring which Antiochus Epiphanes had vainly tried to throw over the gray hills and rough towns of Judæa was fully wrought out by Herod the Great. It would seem as if, to manifest his gratitude for his gracious reception by Augustus Cæsar, and for the Emperor's visit to Palestine, he was determined to plant monuments of him throughout his dominions. At the extreme north, on the craggy hill which overhangs the rushing source of Jordan, rose a white marble temple dedicated to his patron, which for many years superseded alike the Israelite name of Dan and the Grecian name of Paneas by *Cæsarea*. In the centre of Palestine, on the beautiful hill of the ancient Samaria, laid waste by Hyrcanus I., the scene of his marriage with Mariamne, he built a noble city, of which the colonnades still in part remain, to which he gave the name *Sebaste*—the Greek version of *Augusta*.[1] On the coast, beside a desert spot hitherto only marked by the[2] Tower of

His public works in Palestine.

Cæsarea Philippi.

Sebaste. B.C. 25.

[1] Jos. *Ant.* xv. 8, 1.

[2] *Ibid. Ant.* xv. 9, 6; *B. J.* i. 21, 7.

Strato, with a village at its foot, he constructed a vast haven which was to rival the Piræus. Around and within it were splendid breakwaters and piers. Abutting on it a city was erected, so magnificent with an array of public and private edifices, that it ultimately became the capital of Palestine, throwing Jerusalem itself into a place altogether secondary. Houses of shining marble stood round the harbour; on a rising ground in the centre, as in a modern 'crescent,' rose the Temple of Augustus, which gave again the name of *Cæsarea* to the town—out of which looked on the Mediterranean two colossal statues;[1] one of Augustus, equal in proportions to that of the Olympian Jupiter, one of the city of Rome, equal to that of the Argive Juno. Further down the coast he rebuilt the ruined Grecian city of Anthedon, and gave to it, in commemoration of the visit of his friend the able minister of Augustus, the name of *Agrippeum*;[2] and, as over the portico of the Pantheon at Rome, so over the gate of this Syrian city, was deeply graven the name of *Agrippa*. In all these maritime towns, as far north as the Syrian Tripolis, and, not least, in that Hellenised city of Ascalon, to which Christian tradition assigned the origin of his ancestors, he established the luxurious and wholesome institutions of baths, fountains, and colonnades, and added in the inland cities, in the romantic Jericho, and even in the holy Jerusalem, the more questionable entertainments of Greek theatres, hippodromes, and gymnasia, which in the time of the Maccabees had caused so much scandal; and the splendid, but to the humane[3] and reverential spirit of the Jewish nation still more distasteful, spectacles of the Roman amphitheatre.

Cæsarea Stratonis. B.C. 10.

But the great monument of himself which he left was the restored, or, to speak more exactly, the rebuilt Temple at Jerusalem. A Jewish tradition connected this prodigious feat with the miserable crimes of his later years. It was said that he consulted a famous Rabbi, Babas the son of Bouta—the only one who, as it was believed, had survived the massacre of the Teachers of the Law, and who

The Temple of Jerusalem. B.C. 17.

[1] Jos. *Ant.* xv. 9, 6; *B. J.* i. 21, 7. [2] *B. J.* i. 21, 8. [3] Jos. *Ant.* xv. 8, 1.

himself had his eyes[1] put out—how he should appease the remorse which he now felt, and that the Rabbi answered: 'As 'thou hast extinguished the light of the world, the interpreters 'of the law, work for the light of the world by[2] restoring the 'splendour of the Temple.' If this be so, the Temple, in its greatest magnificence, was, like many a modern Cathedral—Milan, Norwich, Gloucester—a monument of penitence. It might, indeed, have been urged that this elaborate restoration was but the fulfilment of the idea of an enlarged Temple, on a grander scale, which, from the visions of Ezekiel down to those of the Book of Enoch,[3] had floated before the mind of the Jewish seers. But the sacredness of the building, and the mistrust of Herod, created difficulties which it required all his vigour and all his craft to overcome. So serious had they seemed that his prudent patron at Rome was supposed to have dissuaded the undertaking altogether. 'If the old building is 'not destroyed,' said Augustus, 'do not destroy it; if it is 'destroyed, do not rebuild it;[4] if you both destroy and rebuild 'it, you are a foolish servant.' The scruple against demolishing even a synagogue before a new one was built was urged with double force now that the Temple itself was menaced. It was met by the casuistry of the same wise old counsellor who had suggested the restoration to Herod. 'I see,' said Babas, 'a breach in the old building which makes 'its repair[5] necessary.' Not for the last time in ecclesiastical history has a small rift in an ancient institution been made the laudable pretext for its entire reparation. Herod himself fully appreciated the delicacy of the task. By a transparent fiction the existing Temple was supposed to be continued into the new building. The worship was never interrupted; and, although actually the Temple of Herod, it was still regarded as identical with that of Zerubbabel.[6] Amongst the thousand

The rebuilding.

[1] Derenbourg, 152. Comp. Jos. *Ant.* xv. 7, 10, where it is said that the sons of Babas, who had been faithful adherents of Antigonus, had been concealed after Herod's victory, by Costobarus, the husband of Salome; and that, being afterwards betrayed by her, they were put to death.

[2] Salvador, i. 320

[3] Enoch xc. 29.

[4] Talmud, in Salvador, i. 320.

[5] Derenbourg, 153.

[6] The forty-six years mentioned in John ii. 20 may be reckoned from B.C. 17, when the temple of Herod was begun,

waggons laden with stones, and ten thousand skilled artisans, there were a thousand priests [1] trained for the purpose as masons and carpenters, who carried on their task, dressed not in workmen's clothes, but disguised in their sacerdotal vestments. And so completely did this idea of the sanctity of the undertaking take possession of the national mind, that it was supposed to have been accompanied by a preternatural intervention which had not been vouchsafed either to Solomon or Zerubbabel. During the whole time (so it was said) rain fell only in the night; each morning the wind blew, the clouds dispersed, the sun [2] shone, and the work proceeded.

The more sacred part of the interior sanctuary was finished in eighteen months. The vast surroundings took eight years, and, though additions continued to be made for at least eighty years longer, it was sufficiently completed to be dedicated by Herod with the ancient pomp. Three hundred oxen were sacrificed by the king himself, and many more by others. As usual, a day was chosen which should blend with an already existing solemnity, but on this occasion it was not the Feast of Tabernacles, but the anniversary of Herod's inauguration. The pride felt in it was as great as if it had been the work not of the hated Idumæan, but of a genuine Israelite. 'He who has 'not seen the building of Herod has never seen a beautiful 'thing.' [3]

Let us look at this edifice, so characteristic of the time and temper of Herod, and so closely interwined with the fall of the Old and the resurrection of the New Religion.

The great area was now, if not for the first time, yet more distinctly than before, divided into three courts.

till A.D. 28, when the words in question were spoken. But as the actual building of Herod only took ten years, and its completion by Herod Agrippa was long afterwards, there is some ground for the interpretation of Surenhusius (*Mishna*, v. 316) —that the forty-six years relates to the period of the building of Zerubbabel's Temple, from B.C. 536 to 459, with the intermissions of the work, on the theory that Herod's Temple was not to be recognised.

[1] Jos. *Ant.* xv. 11, 3; Ewald, v. 433.

[2] Talmud, in Derenbourg, p. 153. Jos. *Ant.* xv. 11, 7.

[3] Derenbourg, 154. Comp. John ii. 20 · Mark xiii. 2.

The first or outer court, which enclosed all the rest, was divided by balustrades, on which was the double[1] inscription in the two great Western languages, forbidding the near approach of Gentiles. It was entered from the east through a cloister, which, from containing fragments of the first Temple, cherished like the shafts of the old Temple of Minerva in the walls of the Athenian Acropolis, was called the cloister of Solomon.[2] Besides those relics of the antique past, the face of the surrounding cloisters also exhibited the more fantastic accumulations of the successive wars of the Jewish Princes—the shields, and swords, and trappings of conquered tribes, down to the last trophies carried off by Herod from the Arabs of Petra.[3] Amongst these figured conspicuously—as a symbol, not of conquest, but of allegiance—the golden eagle of Rome, the erection of which[4] was Herod's latest public act. The great entrance into the temple from the east was the gate of Susa—preserved, probably, in whole or in part, from the time of the Persian dominion.

The outer court.

The court itself must have been completely transformed. Its pavement was variegated as if with mosaics. Its walls were of white marble. Along its northern and southern[5] sides was added 'the Royal Cloister,' a magnificent colonnade of Corinthian pillars, longer by one hundred feet than the longest English Cathedral, and as broad as York Minster. At the north-west corner was the old Asmonean fortress, founded by John Hyrcanus, but strengthened and embellished by Herod, and, in his manner, called Antonia, after his friend Antony. In this secure custody were always kept—with the exception of a few years in the reign of the Emperor Tiberius—the robes and

[1] One of these inscriptions was discovered lately by M. Ganneau (Palestine Exploration Fund).

[2] Jos. *B. J.* v. 5, 1. This apparently had been left untouched by Herod, and it was afterwards proposed to Herod Agrippa to restore it. But he also shrank from so serious an undertaking (Jos. *Ant.* xx. 9, 7).

[3] Jos. *Ant.* xv. 11, 3. It would seem that these took the place of the shields which adorned the porch of Solomon's Temple and the tower of his palace. See Lectures XX. and XXVII. Whether 1 Macc. iv. 57 refers to the inner or outer front is not clear.

[4] Jos. *B. J.* i. 23, 2.

[5] In general style, though not in detail, they resembled the contemporary columns of Baalbec or Palmyra, as may be seen by the remnants still preserved in the vaults of the Mosque.

paraphernalia of the High Priest, without which he could not assume or discharge the duties of his office, and the retention of which in that fortress marked in the most public and unmistakable form his subjection to the civil governor—Asmonean, Herodean,[1] or Roman—who for the time controlled Jerusalem. Beneath the shade of this fortress, in the broad area of the court corresponding to the Forum or the Agora, were held all the public meetings at which [2] the Priests addressed the people. It was surrounded by a low enclosure, over which the Priest could look towards the Mount of Olives.

Within this Outer Court rose the huge castellated wall which enclosed the Temple. It had nine gateways, with towers fifty feet high. One of these, on the north, was, like Boabdil's gate at Granada, called after Jechoniah,[3] as that through which the last king of the house of David had passed out to the Babylonian exile.

The inner court.

Through this formidable barrier, the great entrance was by the Eastern gate—sometimes called 'Beautiful,' sometimes, from the Syrian general or devotee of the Maccabæan age, Nicanor's [4] gate. The other gates were sheeted with gold or silver; [5] the bronze of this one shone almost with an equal splendour.

Every evening it was carefully closed; twenty men were needed to roll its heavy doors, and drive down into the rock its iron bolts and bars. It was regarded as the portcullis of the Divine Castle.

On penetrating through this sacred entrance, a platform was entered, called 'of the Women.' At the sides of this were the Treasuries. Thirteen receptacles of money were placed there like inverted trumpets. The women sat round in galleries as still in Jewish synagogues, and as of old in the Christian Church of St. Sophia. It was here that on the Feast of Tabernacles

[1] Jos. *Ant.* xv. 11, 4.

[2] *B. J.* ii. 17, 2; Middoth, i. 3; iii. 4.

[3] Middoth, ii. 6.

[4] Either from the suspension of his hand, or from the miraculous preservation of the gate at sea (see Lecture XLVIII.; Middoth, ii. 3, 6; Lightfoot's Works, ii. 1099). That there were only two great Eastern gates appears from the Mishna (*Taanith*, ii. 6).

[5] *B. J.* v. 5, 3.

took place the torchlight dance, and the brilliant illumination of the night.[1] It was a tradition that in this court none were allowed to sit except Priests or descendants of David.

The Court of the Priests.

From this platform, by fifteen steps, the worshipper ascended into the Court of the Priests. In the first part of it was the standing-place for the [2] people to look at the sacrifices, divided by a rail from the rest. The chambers round this court were occupied by the Priestly guard, and contained the shambles for the slaughter of the victims. In the centre was the altar, probably unchanged since the time of Judas Maccabæus. In the south-east corner was the Gazith or 'Chamber 'of the Squares,' where sat the Great Council, with a door opening on the one side into the outer court, on the other into this inner precinct.

Immediately beyond the altar was the Temple itself. This, sacred as it was, received various additions, either from the mighty Restorer or his immediate Asmonean predecessors. On the building itself a higher storey was erected. It was encased with white marble studded with golden spikes.[3] The Porch had now two vast wings, and was, in dimensions and proportions, about the same size as the façade of Lincoln Cathedral.[4]

The Porch.

In the Porch hung the colossal golden vine, the emblem of the Maccabæan period, resting on cedar beams, and spreading its branches under the cornices of the porch, to which every pilgrim added a grape or a cluster in gold,[5] till it almost broke down under its own weight. Later was added here the golden lamp presented by Helena, Queen of Adiabene.

Across the Porch, as also across the innermost sanctuary, hung a curtain [6] of Babylonian texture, blue, scarlet, white, and purple, embroidered with the constellations of the heavens (always excepting [7] the forbidden representations of the animals

[1] Mishna, *Suca*, v. 2, 4.
[2] Salvador, iii. 130.
[3] Jos. *B. J.* v. 5.
[4] See Fergusson on the Temple in the *Dictionary of the Bible*.
[5] Mishna, *Middoth*, iii. 8; Jos. *B. J.* v. 5, 4; *Ant.* xv. 11, 3; Tac. *Hist.* v. 4.
[6] There was a whole stock of curtains laid up in the Temple, which were regarded as amongst its special treasures (Jos. *Ant.* xiv. 7, 1).
[7] *B. J.* v. 5, 4, 5.

of the Zodiac.) Within the Temple was the table of Judas Maccabæus, but the seven-branched candlestick which replaced his iron substitute remained there till it was carried away by the Roman conqueror, to be for ever engraven on the arch of Titus in the Forum. Within the dark recess of the Holy of Holies, as disclosed by Pompey's visit,[1] there was nothing but the stone on which the High Priest laid his censer.

The Sanctuary.

Striking indeed must have been the appearance of this triple precinct; the lower court standing on its magnificent terraces, the inner court, surrounded by its embattled towers and gateways; within this, again, the Temple itself with its snow-white walls and glittering pinnacles of gold rising out of this singular group and crowning the view—and the whole scene soaring out of the deep and dark abyss of the precipitous glen which lay beneath it. It must, as the most competent authority of our time has said, have formed one of the most splendid architectural combinations to be found in the ancient world.[2]

This was the new sanctuary of the Jewish religion at the time of the greatest events that were ever to be transacted within its pale. By the side of Nicanor's gate sat the divers butchers, poulterers, and money-changers, who sold their cattle and sheep to the wealthier, their doves and pigeons to the poorer worshippers, and exchanged Gentile for[3] Jewish coinage, in order to preserve the treasury from the pollution of Greek emblems, until the day came when One, who cared more for inward reverence than for outward ritual, dashed the tables to the floor, and drove out the traffickers. In that antique cloister of Solomon, on the anniversary of the festival of the Maccabæan deliverance, walked to and fro the Master and his disciples, for shelter from the winter cold.[4] Into those inverted trumpets in the inner court the rich were casting[5] their superfluities, and the widow was casting in the small coin which was her all,

[1] Mishna, *Yoma*, v. 2.
[2] Fergusson, *Dictionary of the Bible*, iii. 1464.
[3] John ii. 14.
[4] *Ibid.* x. 23; Acts v. 12.
[5] Matt. xii. 41.

when that Countenance, so stern in its frown against the mere mechanism of public worship, smiled so graciously on genuine self-denial. The embroidered curtain, whether the inner or the outer, was that which was believed[1] to have been rent asunder from top to bottom, as a sign that the time for needless partitions between man and man, between Church and Church, between God and man, had ceased. Those prodigious towers, those piles of marble, were the 'buildings' and 'stones' to[2] which a little group of fishermen called the attention of Him who foretold their total overthrow—an overthrow which was the doom of all exclusively local sanctity all over the world for ever.

From the tragic story of the court of Herod, from the outward memorials of his energy in country and city, it is a strange transition to the inner life both of Jerusalem and Palestine, so far as we can discover it through the slight glimpses afforded.

Of all the exciting and brilliant scenes which we have hitherto recorded, the native traditions as preserved in the Talmud tell us, with the exception of three incidents in strangely-distorted forms, absolutely nothing. Of the factions of the rival priests and princes, of the invasion of Pompey, of the sacrilege of Crassus, of the triumphs of Herod, of Actium and Pharsalia, the same Rabbinical tradition is entirely silent.[3] It is a silence which corresponds to the brief, but pregnant statement of the historian,[4] that the large mass of the nation, at the time of the first appearance of Hyrcanus and Aristobulus before Pompey, were neutral in the strife of the two contending parties. But hardly less remarkable than this general indifference of Jewish tradition to the events which fill the pages of Josephus is the silence with which Josephus himself passes over the condition of the interior thought and sentiment of his countrymen ; big as it was with events and characters which he will also pass over in like manner, but which are now the chief motives for the interest of the civilised world in those external movements which alone he has thought fit to describe.

[1] Matt. xxvii. 51.
[2] Mark xiii. 1, 2.
[3] Derenbourg, 116.
[4] Jos. *Ant.* xiv. 3, 2.

We turn first to the Capital and to the Temple. On that splendid theatre it was still the ancient actors that seemed to walk. It is true that the succession of the High Priesthood, which the Asmonean family had broken, was never repaired. The obscure Hananel from Babylon, the still obscurer Jesus or Joshua the son of Phabi, and finally the two sons of Boethus [1] from Alexandria, were the nominees of Herod for the vacant office. But the sacred functions went on undisturbed through the revolutions which had overturned the order of those who performed them. Every morning before the break of day the captain or chief officer [2] of the Temple guard opened the door of the court, where the priests 'in residence' for the week had slept for the night, and the procession of ten passed round the court in white robes and bare feet to kill the morning sacrifice. As the first rays of the rising sun struck upon the golden lamp above the porch, the trumpets sounded; and those of the priests who had drawn the lot entered the Temple for the offering of incense. That was the moment, if any, for any preternatural visitation to the priests. Then they came out, and, having slain the lamb on the altar, they pronounced the benediction, the only relic of the sacerdotal office which has continued in the Jewish Church to our own time. On greater days the solemnities were increased, but the general plan was the same; and it was this worship, with its sacrificial shambles and its minute mechanism, that furnished the chief material for the theological discussions and ecclesiastical regulations of the Jewish Church of that period. The High Priest was still to be kept from falling asleep [3] on the eve of the great fast, by pinching him and by reading to him what were thought the most appropriate parts of the Bible—Job, Ezra, the Chronicles, and Daniel.[4] Five times over in the course of that day had he to take off and put on [5] his eight articles of pontifical dress, and on each occasion, behind a curtain put up for that purpose between him and the people, he

The priesthood.

[1] Derenbourg, 154, 155.

[2] *Middoth*, i. 2; John xviii. 12; Acts iv. 1, v. 24.

[3] Mishna, *Yoma*, 6, 7.

[4] *Ibid. Yoma*, 1, 6.

[5] *Ibid. Yoma*, viii. 5, vi. 7.

plunged into the great swimming-bath or pool, which, if he was old or infirm, was heated for him. He then dressed himself in his gilded garments—goat's-hair gilt—to penetrate into the innermost sanctuary and sprinkle the blood, like holy water, round the pavement, eight times, checking his movements, like the officer who laid on stripes on an offender, by numbering them.[1] When he came out he was thrice to utter the benediction, when all were hushed in deep stillness to catch the awful Name—which then only in each year of an Israelite's life could be heard—pronounced in that silence so distinctly that, in the exaggerated Rabbinical traditions, its sound was believed to reach as far as Jericho. On the night of that same day the young maidens, dressed in white, went out and danced in the vineyards near the city, and the young men came and chose their brides. On all the nights of the ensuing festival the trained devotees, like the dervishes of Constantinople, whirled round the Temple court in their mystic dance, brandishing their torches, whilst the Levites and priests stood on the fifteen steps singing the Psalms of Degrees, and blowing with all their might the sacred horns.[2] It was this, combined with the festoons and bowers erected throughout the courts, which gave to the Greeks the impression that the Jews,[3] like themselves, had a Dionysiac festival.

The day of Atonement.

The ceremony of the scapegoat[4] still continued, though it had all the appearance of a ritual in its last stage of decadence. The terrified creature was conveyed from the Temple to Olivet on a raised bridge, to avoid the jeers of the irreverent pilgrims of Alexandria—who used to pluck the poor animal's long flakes of hair with the rude cries of 'Get along and away with you!' Then he was handed on from keeper to keeper by short stages over hill and valley. At each hut where he rested, an obsequious guide said to him, 'Here is your food, here is your drink.' The last in this strange succession led him to a precipice above the

[1] Mishna, *Taanith*, iv. 8.
[2] *Ibid. Suca*, v. 4.
[3] Plut. *Quæst. Conviv.* iv. 6.
[4] It is used as an illustration in the Epistle of Barnabas, but never in the New Testament.

fortress of Dok,[1] and hurled him down,[2] and the signal was sent back [3] to Jerusalem that the deed was accomplished, by the waving of handkerchiefs all along the rocky road.

Beside the priesthood, ever since the time of Ezra, there had been insensibly growing a body of scholars, who by the time of Herod had risen to a distinct function of the State. Already under John Hyrcanus there was a judicial body known as the House [4] of Judgment (Beth-Din). To this was given the Macedonian title of *Synedrion*, transformed into the barbarous Hebrew word *Sanhedrim* or *Sanhedrin*. But it was not as members of a legislative or judicial assembly that the Scribes exercised their main influence. It was by the intrinsic, individual eminence which gave to each of them the Chaldæan name, now first appearing, of *Rab*, 'the 'Great'—*Rabbi*, *Rabboni*, 'my great one,' 'Master,' 'my 'master.'[5] By a succession increasing in importance we trace the 'pairs' or 'couples' of the distinguished teachers round whom the dividing tendencies of the schools grouped themselves. In the time of the first Maccabees were Josè the son of Joazar, and Josè the son of John; in the time of Hyrcanus, Joshua the son of Perachiah, and Nittai of Arbela. In the time of Alexander Jannæus there were Simeon the son of Shetach and Judah the son of Tobai. But it is in the trial of Herod, when the Sanhedrin is first distinctly mentioned, that the two chiefs of the order come into full prominence. Their names in a corrupted form, as Sameas and Pollio, appear even in the reticent record of Josephus. Shemaiah and Abtalion [6] were proselytes, and supposed to be descended from the Assyrian Sennacherib by an Israelite mother. 'The High Priest' (say the Talmudic traditions—we know not whether they speak of Hyrcanus, Aristobulus, or Antigonus) 'passed out of the Temple on the 'Day of Atonement, followed by the multitude. But the

The Sanhedrin.

The Rabbis.

Shemaiah and Abtalion.

[1] 'Zok' in the Mishna must surely be the same as 'Dok' in 1 Macc. xvi. 15?

[2] Mishna, *Yoma*, vi. 4, 5, 7.

[3] *Ibid. Tamid*, 8.

[4] Derenbourg, 86.

[5] The first unquestioned appearance of the word is in the New Testament. The first official use of it was for Gamaliel, the grandson of Hillel.—Lightfoot on Matt. xxiii., vol. ii. 273.

[6] Prideaux, ii. 572; see Herzfeld, iii. 253-257.

'moment they saw Shemaiah and Abtalion they deserted the 'High Priest to follow the chiefs of the Sanhedrin. The two 'doctors made their salutations to the High Priest. "Peace,"[1] 'said the Pontiff in parting from them, "to the men of the 'people." "Yes," replied they, "peace to the men of the 'people[2] who accomplish the work of Aaron, and no peace 'to the sons of Aaron who are not like Aaron."'

It is a striking illustration of the homage paid even in that ceremonial age to the Teacher above the Priest. It is a noble protest, worthy of the days of Isaiah, in behalf of the claims of moral and intellectual over official eminence. And when, in the trial of Herod for his lawless violence, the High Priest grovelled before him, it was Shemaiah who rebuked the cowardice of his colleagues; it was Abtalion who by his habitual caution conciliated them. Each spoke in exact accordance with the peculiar spirit enshrined in their traditional sayings. We see the sturdy independence of the maxim of Shemaiah, 'Love work, hate domination, and have no relations 'with those in authority;' the worldly prudence of the maxim of Abtalion, 'Measure well your words, else you will be banished 'to the stagnant[3] waters of bad doctrines.'

B.C. 47.

It was, perhaps, still in accordance with the tone of Abtalion's teaching that in the siege, when the High Priest Antigonus defended Jerusalem against Herod, they both agreed in counselling submission, and were both spared by the conqueror.[4]

It would seem that the chief places in the college of teachers were next occupied by an obscure family, 'the sons of Bether.' They were discussing one of the trivial ceremonial questions which then, as on later occasions, both in the Jewish and Christian Church, preoccupied the main interest of theological schools. It was the grave problem (as it seemed to them) whether the Paschal lamb might be killed on the

The sons of Bether.

[1] Derenbourg, 117.

[2] Or 'men of the Gentiles,' in allusion to their foreign descent (Raphall, ii. 284).

[3] The meaning of these words is much disputed. Derenbourg (p. 148) interprets them as above. But a somewhat subtler sense is given to them by Maimonides (*ibid.*): 'Use no ambiguous expressions; 'otherwise you will be accused of heresy.'

[4] Jos. *Ant.* xv. 1, 1.

Sabbath. They had heard of a famous[1] Babylonian teacher. His name was Hillel. He answered in the affirmative, with reasons from analogy, from the text, and from the context. They refused his decision, until he said, 'I am content to be punished if my decision has not been given 'to me by Shemaiah and Abtalion.' They had before regarded him as a stranger from Babylon; they now welcomed him as their chief. 'Whose fault was it,' he said, 'that you had recourse to a Babylonian?—you had not paid due attention to 'Shemaiah and Abtalion, the two great men of the age, who 'were with you all the time.' It was again a triumph of intrinsic over official authority, and the submission of the sons of Bether was long remembered as an example of admirable modesty.[2]

Hillel. B.C. 36.

This is the first public appearance of unquestionably the most eminent teacher of the generation of Judaism immediately preceding the Christian era.

Like Ezra, to whom his countrymen often compared him, Hillel belonged to the vast Babylonian settlement. Unlike Ezra, he was not of the Priestly class; but, like One who was shortly to come after him, descended from the house of David;[3] and, like Him, a humble workman, drawn to Jerusalem only by the thirst 'for hearing and asking questions.' He came with his brother Shebna, and worked for the scanty remuneration of half a denarius—the coin known in Latin as 'victoriatus,' in Greek as 'tropaïcon,' from the figure of the goddess Victory upon it. This he divided between the pay for his lodgings and the pay to the doorkeeper of the school where Shemaiah and Abtalion taught. On a certain occasion, when he failed in his work, the churlish doorkeeper would not let him enter. It was the eve of the Sabbath, there were no lights stirring, and he took advantage of the darkness to climb to the window-sill to listen. It was a winter night, and the listening youth was first benumbed and then buried three cubits deep under a heavy

[1] It is possible that the sons of Bether themselves were from Babylonia. See Jos. *Ant.* xviii. 2, 2; Ewald, *Jahrbücher der Bibl. Wissenschaft*, x. 67.

[2] Derenbourg, 179, 180.

[3] *i.e.* from Abigail, David's wife. Ewald (*Jahrbücher*, 66), who well points out the illustration it affords of the Gospel history.

snow-fall. As the day dawned, Shemaiah turned to his colleague, and said: 'Dear brother Abtalion, why is our school so dark 'this morning?' They turned to the window, and found it darkened by a motionless human form, enveloped in the snow-flakes. They brought him down, bathed, rubbed him with oil, placed him before the fire,—in short, broke, for his sake, their Sabbatical repose, saying: 'Surely he must be worth a violation 'of the Sabbath.'[1] He was,[2] in regard to the traditionary law, what Ezra was supposed to have been in regard to the written law. He it was who collected and codified the floating maxims which guided the schools. He rose to the highest place in the Sanhedrin; he was honoured[3] by Herod; he himself honoured what there was in Herod worthy of honour. He, with Shammai, was excused from the oath exacted by Herod from all his other subjects.[4] He became not merely the founder of a school, but the ancestor of a family, all of whom were imbued with his teaching—Simon, Gamaliel, and a second Hillel. In his lifetime he was overshadowed by his rival Shammai, the rigid advocate of the strictest literalism. At first sight, as we turn the dreary pages of the Mishna, there seems to be little to choose between them.[5] The disputes between himself and Shammai turn for the most part on points so infinitely little that the small controversies of ritual and dogma which have vexed the soul of Christendom seem great in comparison. They are worth recording only as accounting for the obscurity into which they have fallen, and also because Churches of all ages and creeds may be instructed by the reflection that questions of the modes of eating and cooking, and walking and sitting seemed as important to the teachers of Israel—on the eve of their nation's destruction, and of the greatest religious revolution that the world has seen—as the questions of dress or

B.C. 30.

[1] The story has often been given, but at the greatest length in Delitzsch's *Jesus and Hillel*, pp. 10, 11. See also Jost. i. 248-257. Deutsch's *Remains*, 30, 31.

[2] See Kitto, *Bibl. Cyclop.* iii. 167.

[3] 'Herodes senem Hillel in magno 'honore habuit: namque hi homines regem 'illum esse non ægrè ferebant' (Lightfoot, *Harm. Ev.* 470, quoted in *Dictionary of the Bible*, i. 796).

[4] Jos. *Ant.* xv. 10, 4; Derenbourg, 191, 464.

[5] See Keim, *Jesus of Nazara*, i. 345.

posture, or modes of appointment, or verbal distinctions, have seemed to contending schools of Christian theology.[1]

The net of casuistry spread itself over every department of human life, and the energies of the Rabbis were spent (to use the metaphor[2] adopted by them and thence transferred to other systems) in 'tying' and 'untying,' in 'binding' and 'loosing' the knots which they either found or made in this complicated web. In this occupation their resort was not to any original or profound principles of action, but to maxims of authority handed down, like legal precedents, from former Rabbis. 'The 'Doctors have thus spoken'—'It has been said by them of old 'time'—'I have never heard of such a maxim or practice before' —were the solutions then, as often since, offered for every difficulty. Memory thus became the one indispensable gift of an accomplished teacher—'a pit that lets not out a drop of 'water.'[3] The variety and the triviality of these decisions—shortly to be contrasted with the unchanging force of the inspired intuitions and simple convictions of a few unlettered peasants—are well summed up in a single chapter of the Mishna. There was a weighty question, which had run down through all the 'pairs' of teachers, on the point whether there was or was not to be an imposition of hands in the ordination of victims for sacrifice. Joseph, the son of Joazar, said, 'There shall be 'no hands imposed;' Joseph, the son of John, said, 'There shall 'be hands imposed.' Joshua, the son of Perachiah, said, 'There 'shall no hands be imposed;' Nittai, of Arbela, said, 'There 'shall be hands imposed.' Judah, the son of Tobai, said, 'There shall be no hands imposed;' Simeon, the son of Shetach, said, 'There shall be hands imposed.' Shemaiah

[1] *De Benedictionibus*, viii. 1–7. *De Septimo Anno*, iv. viii. *De Promissis*, i. *De Vasis*, ix. 2, xviii. 1, xx. 2, xxii. 4, xxvi. 6, xxix. 8. *De Decimis*, iii. v. *De Tectoriis*, ii. 3, v. 3, 11, xi. 1, 4-6, xiii. 1, xv. 8, xviii. 1, 8. *De Puritatibus*, ix. 6, 7, x. 4. *De Lavacris*, i. 5, iv. 1, x. *De Fluxu*, i. 1, ii. 6, v. 9, x. 1. *De Liquidis*, i. 3, 4, iv. 5. *De Fructus petiolis*, iii. 6. *De Sacrificiis*, iv. 1. *De Profanis*, i. 2, viii. 1. *De Primogenitis*, v. 2. *De Pœnis Excidii*, i. 6. *De Votis*, i. 1–9, ii. 2, 7. *De Principio Anni*, i. 1. *De Sacris Solemn.* i. 1–3, ii. 2–4. *De Sabbato*, i. 5, 6, xxi. 2, 3. *De Term. Sabbat.* i. 1. *De Paschate*, viii. 8. *De Tabernaculis*, i. 1, 7, iii. 5.

[2] Matt. xvi. 19; xviii. 18. For the overwhelming proof of the Jewish use of this metaphor, see Lightfoot (ii. 216).

[3] Hausrath, *Zeit Christi*, 82, 89; Jos. *Vit. c.* 2.

said, 'There shall be no hands imposed ;' Abtalion said, 'There 'shall be hands imposed.' Hillel and Menahem do not contradict each other ; but Menahem went out, and Shammai came in. Shammai said, 'There shall be no hands imposed ;' Hillel said, 'There shall be hands imposed.'[1] Such was the alternate 'binding' and 'loosing' which occupied the ecclesiastical authorities of the Jewish Church for two hundred years. There is a profound pathos, and at the same time a universal warning, in the story recorded in the Mishna of the deputation from the Sanhedrin which came to the High Priest on the eve of the Day of Atonement, with the urgent appeal : 'O my lord 'the High Priest, we are the representatives of the great 'Sanhedrin, and thou art our representative. We adjure thee 'by Him whose name dwells in this Temple that thou wilt not 'change any of all the things which we have said unto thee.'[2] He went away and wept to think that they should suspect him of heresy, and they went away and wept to think that they did suspect him of heresy. And what was the heresy for which those tears were shed, and for which this solemn adjuration was made? It was that the Sadducee High Priest had 'in that 'most difficult question of taking the proper handful of the 'grains of incense' preferred to put them into the censer outside the veil, instead of adopting the Pharisaic interpretation of reserving the fumigation till the veil was passed. How many tears of grief and rage have been shed, how many tests and adjurations have been imposed, for questions of a like character, though, it may be, of more intrinsic importance !

Yet still, as in the dim shadows of Alexandrian Judaism there were the clear streaks as of the coming day in the ethical treatises of Philo—as in our own scholastic ages there were the harbingers of a future Reformation in Scotus Erigena, Anselm, Roger Bacon, and Wycliffe—so in the yet deeper darkness of the Rabbinical schools of Palestine, Hillel was, as it were, the morning star of the bright dawn that was rising in the hills of Galilee. It has been reserved for modern times to recognise his extraordinary merit. The teacher over whom both Josephus

[1] '*Chagijah,*' ii. 2, in Surenhusius's *Mishna*, i. 417, 418. [2] *Ibid. Yoma*. i 5.

and Eusebius pass without a word, saw further than any other man of his generation into the heart and essence of religion. In him the freedom, the elevation, the latitude which had breathed through the poetic imagery and grand idealism of the Psalmists and Prophets in the days of the higher inspirations of Judaism, now expressed themselves for the first time in the direct, practical maxims of what we may call the modern thought of the Herodian, the Augustan age. Even amidst the trivial casuistry and ceremonial etiquettes which furnish the materials for the larger part of Hillel's decisions, they lean, not indeed invariably, but as a general rule, to the more liberal and spiritual side, and they foster the rights of the congregation and the nation as against the claims of a grasping [1] sacerdotal caste. And even where he appeared to submit, he introduced, if he did not create, a logical process by which, under a peculiar name [2] acquired in his hands, he contrived to 'minimise' the stringent effects not only of the tradition, but of the Law itself. But there are sayings which tower not only far above those questions of tithe, anise, and cummin, but above the merely prudential aphorisms of the earlier Rabbis, and which must have created around them an atmosphere, not only in which they themselves could live and be appreciated, but which must have rendered more possible both the origination and the acceptance of any other sayings of a kindred nature in that or the coming age. 'Be gentle as Hillel,[3] and not harsh as 'Shammai,' was the proverb which marked the final estimate of the latitudinarian compared with the rigorist teacher, when the spirit of partisanship had cooled before the calmer judgment of posterity. Two practical sayings alone have survived of the sterile teaching of Shammai. 'Let 'thy repetition[4] of the Law be at a fixed hour,' was the hard and fast line by which his disciples were to be bound down, as by an inexorable necessity, to the punctual reading of the Sacred Book, as of a breviary, at hours never to be lost sight of.

Teaching of Shammai.

[1] See Derenbourg, 180–190.
[2] 'Prosbol.' See Derenbourg, 188.
[3] Ewald, *Jahrbücher*, x. 69.
[4] Mishna, *Pirke Aboth*, i. 15, and Derenbourg, 191.

'Speak little and do much, but do what thou hast to do with a 'cheerful countenance.' That voice has a touching accent, as though he felt that the frequent professions and austere demeanour which were congenial to his natural disposition might perchance prove a stumbling-block to the cause which was dear to him.

But when from these 'scrannel pipes' of Shammai we turn to his less popular but more deeply beloved rival, we find ourselves listening to strains of a far higher mood.

Teaching of Hillel.

'Be of Aaron's disciples, who loved peace, pursued peace, 'loved all creatures, and attracted them towards[1] the 'Law.' Although not a priest himself, and by his position thrown into antagonism to the order, he yet had the rare merit of seeing in an ancient institution the better side of its traditions and its capabilities, and of commending it to his countrymen.

'He who makes his own name famous, and does not in'crease in wisdom, shall perish. He who learns nothing is as 'though he had done something worthy of death. He who 'makes a profit of the crowning glory of a teacher's place, away 'with him!'[2] This represents first the religious passion for mental improvement—secondly, the sacred duty of diligence, which carries within it the stimulus of all modern science—thirdly, the true ideal of 'the scholar.' It shows also the Socratic[3] disinterestedness in imparting knowledge transplanted into a sphere where it will give birth to one of the most striking characteristics of a future apostle.

'If I am not mine own, who is mine? yet, if I am mine 'own, what am I? And if not now, when?' It is one of those enigmas in which, from the time of Solomon downwards, the Jewish sages delighted, yet full of deep meaning.[4] It expresses

[1] Ewald, v. 73, 74. *Pirke Aboth*, i. 12 (Surenhusius, iv. 416, 417), where are given the traditional stories of Aaron, which justify the characteristics here ascribed to him. Compare Mal. ii. 5.

[2] *Pirke Aboth*, i. 13 (Surenhusius, iv. 417). Ewald (v. 74) interprets the first part differently: 'He who disguises the 'sacred name of God shall perish.' Derenbourg interprets the third differently (133).

[3] See Lecture XLVI. and 1 Cor. ix. 1–27.

[4] *Pirke Aboth*, i. 14 (Surenhusius, iv. 418).

the threefold mission placed before the human soul—the call to absolute independence, the worthlessness of selfish isolation, the necessity of immediate exertion to fortify the one and to correct the other. 'Had Hillel,' says Ewald, 'left us but this 'single saying, we should be for ever grateful to him, for scarce 'anything can be said more briefly,[1] more profoundly, or more 'earnestly.'

A heathen came to Shammai, and begged to be taught the whole Law whilst he stood on one foot. Shammai, indignant at the thought that the Law could be taught so simply and so shortly, drove him forth with the staff which he held in his hand. The Gentile went to Hillel, who accepted him, and said: 'What thou wouldest not thyself, do not to thy neighbour. 'This is the whole Law, and its application is, "Go and do 'this."'[2] We start as we read the familiar rule, but even Hillel was not the first who uttered it. Already it had dropped from the lips of Isocrates in Greece,[3] and Confucius in China, yet not the less original was it in the mouth of each; and most of all was it original in the mouth of Him who, in the nex generation, made it not the maxim of a sage, but 'the golden 'rule'[4] of a world.

'"Wish not to be better than the whole community, nor 'be confident of thyself till the day of thy death." This, Ewald remarks, 'is a strange truth for a Pharisee to have 'uttered; one which, had the Pharisees followed, no Pharisee 'would have ever arisen. Yet,' he adds, with true appreciation of the elevation of the best spirits above their party, 'it 'is not the only example of a distinguished teacher protesting 'against the fundamental error of his own peculiar tendencies.'

'Think not of anything that it will not be heard, for heard 'at last it surely will be; think not that thou canst calculate on 'the time when thou shalt have anything, for how easily will it 'come to pass that thou shalt never have it at all.'[5] 'The more 'meat at his banquets a man hath, so much the more is the

[1] Ewald, v. 73.
[2] *Ibid.* v. 70, 71.
[3] Isocrates to Nicocles, and see Lecture XLV.
[4] Matt. vii. 12. Hillel himself repeated the maxim in another form: 'Judge not 'thy neighbour till thou hast put thyself 'in his place.' Ewald, *Jahrbücher*, x. 75.
[5] *Ibid.*

'food for worms; the more wealth he hath, so much the more 'care; the more wives, so much the more opening for superstition; the more maidservants, so much the more temptation to 'license; the more slaves, so much the more room for plunder. 'But the more of Law, so much the more of life; the more of 'schools, so much the more of wisdom; the more of counsel, 'so much the more of insight; the more of righteousness, so 'much the more of peace. If a man gains a good name, he 'gains it for himself alone; if he gains a knowledge of the Law, 'it is for eternal life.' These are maxims which are more than philosophical; they are almost apostolical.

It is not needed to multiply these stories, or to recite the legendary portents which hovered round the name of Hillel. What has been said is enough to show that, as in modern times there have been those who, amongst heretics and sectarians, yet were catholic—amongst the rigidly orthodox, were yet full of the freedom which belongs to scepticism or heterodoxy—so among the Pharisees was at least one man in whom was foreshadowed the spirit of the coming age, in the life of whose maxims was the death of his sect, in the breadth of whose character was the pledge that he or his disciples should at last inherit the earth, and be the teachers in that Jerusalem which, being above, is free. In the schools of his native land he founded a dynasty of scholars: Simeon, Gamaliel, and the second Hillel—his son, his grandson, and his great-grandson. 'Ah! the tender-hearted, the pious, the 'disciple of Ezra,' was the lament over his grave.[1] In the same grave he and his rival Shammai rest side by side at Meiron,[2] amidst the Rabbis who were drawn thither from Safed, the holy city of a later age. But his fame soon perished; it is only now, after an obscurity of many centuries that he has been recognised to be of all the teachers of Judæa at that time the one who most nearly approached to the Light that was to lighten the heathen nations, and to be the glory of the people of Israel.

Death of Hillel. A.D. 6.

Yet, strange as it may seem, we must look for this realisa-

[1] Jost. i. 263.

[2] Robinson's *Researches*, vol. iii. 334; *Later Res.* 37.

tion, even for this preparation, not to the schools of Jerusalem, but to classes in which Hillel hardly ventured to expect it. 'No uneducated man,' he said, 'easily avoids sin; no man of 'the people can be pious. Where there are no men, study to 'show thyself a man.' The first part of the saying partakes of the contraction of the Pharisaic circle in which he moved; the last part shows how he rose above it. On the one hand he believed that, except in the schools of the learned, no real excellence could be found; on the other hand he felt that, even where all seems blank and void of interest, it is never too late to hope that a true man may discover himself. How far he was wrong in the first of these sayings, how far he was right in the second, we shall see as we proceed.

From the small casuistry and occasional flashes of inspiration in the schools of Jerusalem we pass to the different world or worlds, which even within the narrow limits of Palestine, were to be found, containing elements of life as unlike those which prevailed in the cloisters of the Temple as if they had belonged to another country.

The Essenes.

We first turn to the neighbourhood of the capital. It is one of the peculiarities of the Herodian age that the valley of the Jordan then leaped into vast prominence. The palaces, the baths, the racecourses, of the forests and gardens of Jericho became the resort of the fashionable world of that time. But side by side with these sprang up, as in gipsy encampments, a host of ascetics. In those wild jungles, or in the maze of verdure which clings to the spring of Engedi,[1] and clusters on the little platform by the shores of the Dead Sea, screened from the upper world behind the rocky barrier of the crags which overhang that mysterious lake, swarmed the Essenian hermits. It is true that in every town in Palestine[2] some of them were to be found. They were not entirely separated from the movement of the capital. There was a gate[3] in the city which bore their name as if from their frequenting it. More than once we hear of their appearances in the Temple

[1] Plin. *H. N.* v. 15.

[2] *B. J.* ii. 8, 4; Philo, *Fragm.* 632.

[3] *B. J.* vi. 4, 2.

Menahem, the Essene, in his playful manner, had foretold Herod's greatness when yet an innocent child, and, remaining faithful to him in his later years, was raised by him[1] to the second place in the Sanhedrin, in the room of Shammai, next to the illustrious Hillel. But, as in Egypt their chief haunt was by the shores of the Lake Mareotis, so in Judæa their main home was the insulated oasis beneath the haunts of the wild goats. Their form of religion, in many respects, was merely Pharisaism in excess. Their chief rites were Pharisaic ordinances raised to a higher level. The common meals, which the Pharisees established in imitation of the solemn banquets[2] of the Priests after the Temple sacrifices, were elevated by the Essenians to be an essential part of their worship. But, whereas the Pharisees, though not Priests, yet often frequented the Temple ceremonies, the Essenians, in their isolation, were constrained to invent a ritual for themselves—a ritual so simple that it almost escaped observation at the time, yet so expressive that its near likeness has, in altered forms, not only survived the magnificent worship of Jerusalem, but become the centre of ceremonials yet more gorgeous. For the first time, the common meal without a sacrifice, became a religious ordinance, in which the loaves[3] of bread were arranged by the baker, and the blessing asked and the repast transacted[4] with such solemnity that their little dining-halls seemed for the moment to be transformed into the appearance of a consecrated enclosure.

'The Pharisees,' said their Sadducaic rivals, 'want to clean 'the face of the sun.' And so to the Essenes cleanliness was not only next to godliness, but, as regards worship, we may almost say that it was godliness.[5] The badges of initiation were the apron or towel for wiping themselves after the bath,

[1] See Lightfoot, ii. 200, on Matt. xvii.

[2] Derenbourg, 142 162.

[3] The Essenes are described in Jos. *Ant.* xiii. 5, 9; xviii. 1, 5; *B. J.* ii. 8, 2–13; Plin. *Ep.* v. 15, 17; Philo, ii. 457, 471, 632. For ample discussions, which supersede any need for further detail here, see Dr. Ginsburg's article on the Essenes, in Kitto's *Cyclopædia*, Keim's *Jesus of Nazara*, i. 358–368, and the exhaustive essays of Bishop Lightfoot on Epistle to the Colossians, 83-94, 115–178.

[4] *B. J.* ii. 8, 5. The mention of the cook seems to imply something else than bread -probably fish.

[5] Jos. *B. J.* ii. 8, 5, 7; Bishop Lightfoot on Colossians, 120; Kuenen, iii. 128, 129, 131, 133.

the hatchet for digging holes to put away filth. Some Churches in later days have insisted on the absolute necessity of immersion once in a life. But not only did the Essenes go through the bath on their first admission, but day by day the same cleansing process was undergone ; day by day it was held unlawful even to name the name of God without the preliminary baptism ; day by day fresh white clothes were put on ; day by day, after the slightest occasion,[1] they bathed again. Down to the minutest points cleanliness was the one sacramental sign. The primitive Christians had their daily Communion ; the Essenes had their daily Baptism.[2] In the deep bed of the neighbouring Jordan, in the warm springs and the crystal streams of Engedi, in the rivulets and the tanks of Jericho, they had ample opportunities for this purification which in the dry hills and streets of Jerusalem they would have lacked.

When from these outward signs of the society we descend to its inner life, the difficulty of tracing its affinities is increased. In this respect 'the Essene[3] is the great enigma of Hebrew 'history.' On the one hand, it is no wonder that the solution of the enigma should have been sought in the conclusion that the early Christians[4] concerning whom the Jewish historian is strangely silent, and the Essenes concerning whom the Evangelists are no less strangely silent, were one and the same. The community of property, the abstinence from oaths, the repugnance to sacrificial ordinances, the purity of life, which enkindled the admiration alike of the prosaic Josephus and the poetic Philo, have one, and one only counterpart, in the coming generation. On the other hand, their rigid Sabbatarianism, their monastic celibacy, their seclusion from social life, their worship[5] of the rising sun, point to influences wholly unlike those which guided the first growth of the Christian society. But thus much seems clear. A community whose observances, if exaggerated, were so simple, and whose moral standard, if

[1] Derenbourg, 170.

[2] This was the case, even without identifying them with the ἡμεροβαπτισταί, daily or morning bathers. See Bishop Lightfoot, 132, 162 ; Derenbourg, 165.

[3] Bishop Lightfoot, 82.

[4] See the ingenious essays of De Quincey, vi. 270, ix. 253.

[5] Bishop Lightfoot, 88.

eccentric, was so elevated, must have drawn to the outskirts of their body individuals, even classes of men that would not have been numbered amongst them. Sometimes it will be a Hermit[1] who attaches to his side for three years the future historian and soldier of the age; dressed in a matting of palm leaves or the like, eating whatever fruits he picked up in the woods; like them a constant bather both by night and day. At another time it will be a young Priest, who shall look like one possessed by a ghost or a demon,[2] who from his boyhood has lived in these wild thickets, seated in his hut or amidst the waving canes of the Jordan;[3] with his shaggy locks loose-flowing round his head (if his[4] Nazarite vow had been duly performed); like the dervishes[5] of modern days, clothed only in a rough blanket of camel's hair fastened round his bare limbs with a girdle of skin; who shall undertake to be the universal Bather or Baptizer of the district; who shall catch for that purifying plunge[6] the tax collectors from Jericho, and the learned Scribes or Levites travelling thither from Jerusalem, or the soldiers marching down the Jordan valley, as once with Pompey before, to some skirmish with the Nabathæan Arabs. In the spots chosen for his haunts, in his scanty fare, in his frequent abstinence, in his long-sustained ejaculations of prayer, in his insistance on personal ablution, Johanan, or John, the son of Zechariah, is closely allied with the Essenian fraternity. Yet, on the other hand, his career breathed the spirit not of the Essenian seers, but of the prophetic force of older days, which seemed to show that Elijah had started again into life, or that Jeremiah, who had visited Judas Maccabæus in his dreams, was once more on the soil of his beloved Palestine, or that the voice which announced the return of the Exiles was once more sounding in the solitudes of the Jordan. The grandeur of his mission lay in the keen discernment with which he seized hold of the one ordinance which had, as it were, been engendered by the full-

Banus.

The Baptist.

John the Baptist.

[1] See the description of Banus, the preceptor of Josephus, *Vita*, c. 2.

[2] John i. 21; Matt. xi. 18.

[3] Justin adv. Tryph. c. 51; Matt. xi. 7, 9.

[4] Luke i. 15.

[5] Light's *Travels*, 135.

[6] Luke iii. 3–15.

flowing stream of the 'Descending river,' to bring before his countrymen the truth, ever old, yet ever new, that the cleanness, the whiteness of the human heart is the only fitting preparation for the Divine presence. He took advantage of that leap into the river or the reservoir to call upon one and all to spring into a new life, to wash off the stains upon their honour and their consciences, which choked up the pores of their moral texture and impeded the influx of the new truths with which the air around them was shortly to be impregnated.[1] He proclaimed the one indispensable condition of all spiritual religion, that the regeneration of the human spirit[2] was to be accomplished, not by ceremonies or opinions, not by succession or descent, but by moral uprightness. The substitution of the wholesome, invigorating, simple process of the bath, in which the head and body and limbs should be submerged in the rushing river, for the sanguinary, costly gifts of the sacrificial slaughter-house, was a living representation in a single act of the whole prophetic teaching of the supremacy of Duty. This startling note of the universal need for the creation of a new morality, for a 'transformation of the mind,' struck a chord which had not vibrated clearly since the days of Malachi. And of this the nearest contemporary likeness was in the Essenian maxim, 'The approach to Duty is as a battlefield,' and in the three Essenian virtues, 'Love of God, love of goodness, and 'love of man.'[3] Wherever any souls were penetrated with the sense of this truth, as the paramount definition of their religious calling, there a vast stride was made beyond the actual religions of the ancient world, and towards the ideal of all of them.

But there was yet a wider area to be winnowed by the spirit of the coming time than either the schools of the Temple or the shores of the Dead Sea. And even the Essenian teaching at its highest point was but as the flame[4] of a blazing torch that would pale and fade away before the steady sunshine of the coming day.

The Synagogues.

[1] Matt. iii. 1, 4, 11, 12; Luke v. 33.

[2] μετανοια is, in the New Testament, and the early fathers, the same as παλιγγενεσία—not merely 'penitence' or 'repentance,' but a 'regeneration or revolution of mind,' 'a second birth of the moral nature.' Matt. iii. 11; Luke iii. 3.

[3] Jos. *Ant.* xviii. 1, 5. Philo, *Vit. Contemp.* 877.

[4] John v. 35 (Godet).

Throughout the country, in town and village, increasing since the time of Ezra, had sprung up a whole system of worship, which to the Pentateuch and the Prophets and the early Psalmists was unknown. The main religious instruction and devotion of the nation was now carried on, not in the Temple, but in the synagogues.[1] Wherever there were as many as ten who desired it such a meeting-house for prayer was established —the 'ten men of leisure,' as they were called, who were capable of forming a congregation or filling the public offices. In Jerusalem it is said that there were no less than 480. In the smaller towns of the north they were stately marble edifices, with massive pillars and cornices richly sculptured,[2] which probably answered the purpose of the Town-hall as well as the church of the district. Each synagogue accordingly had its own small municipal jurisdiction, with the power of excommunication or exclusion, and extending to the right of inflicting lashes on the bare back and breast of the offender. A distinguished teacher of his time[3] was obliged, in the short space of a few years, to submit to this ignominious infliction no less than five times. Each of these little municipalities consisted of the chief official with his two associates, the three almoners, the leader of the public worship, the interpreter, and the beadle. These formed a little hierarchy in themselves, but having no relation to that of the sacerdotal caste, or to the order of Scribes. No office of teaching corresponding to that either of the Jewish Priesthood or Christian clergy existed in this body. The instruction was given by any scholar with any pretensions who presented himself for the occasion. The practice of[4] combining the office of teachers with some manual trade was a constant safeguard against their sinking into a merely sacerdotal or a merely literary class.

It is obvious how important a link this institution estab-

[1] See Ginsburg on the Synagogue. Kitto, iii. 902–905.

[2] See the description of the ruins at Tell Hum, Irbid, Kefr Birim, Meiron, and Kedesh Naphtali, in Robinson's *Later Biblical Researches*, 70, 74, 368; also Wilson, in *Recovery of Jerusalem*, 342, *et seq.*

[3] 2 Cor. xi. 24; Schöttgen, *Hor. Heb.* 714.

[4] Mishna, *Pirke Aboth*, ii. 2; Munk's *Palestine*, 521; Deutsch, 25.

lished between the Jewish settlements throughout the world. At Alexandria, at Rome, at Babylon there was no Temple. But in every one of those cities, and by many a tank or riverside in Egypt, Greece, or Italy, there was the same familiar building, the same independent organisation, the same house for the mingled worship and business of every Jewish community. And thus, inasmuch as the synagogue existed where the Temple was unknown, and remained when the Temple fell, it followed that from its order and worship, and not from that of the Temple, were copied, if not in all their details, yet in their general features, the government, the institutions, and the devotions of those Christian communities which, springing directly from the Jewish, were in the first instance known as 'synagogues,' or 'meeting-houses,'[1] and afterwards, by the adoption of an almost identical word, 'Ecclesia,' 'assembly-house.'

It is obvious further that in these synagogues of Palestine was the safety-valve, the open sphere, the golden opportunity for any fresh teaching to arise. Without convulsion, or revolution, or disorder, the development of a new idea, the expansion of an old idea, could be unfolded within the existing framework by some new-comer, and the shock would fly from synagogue to synagogue throughout the country, and, it may be, throughout the Empire. In those brief discourses which were there delivered we have the origin of the 'Homily,' 'the Sermon'—that is, the serious 'conversation'—which has now struck so deep a root in the Jewish, the Mussulman, and the Christian communities that we can hardly imagine them to have existed without it. It began, doubtless, as we have seen, in the expositions of Ezra, but it was in this later age of Judaism that it assumed its predominance. One example of such is preserved to us in the stirring appeal, partly philosophic, partly patriotic, founded on the story of the Seven Martyrs under Antiochus, and now known as the Fourth Book of Maccabees. Others are discernible in some of the treatises of the Alexandrian Philo. It thus became possible that some heaven-sent

[1] James ii. 2. Epiph. (xxx. 18). Bishop Lightfoot on the Epistle to the Philippians, 150.

Teacher might, by a first discourse, thus draw upon himself 'the hate of hate, the scorn of scorn, the love of love,' by which he should be afterwards followed even to the end, or that some 'word of exhortation' from a wandering stranger might drop a spark which should enkindle a slumbering flame that could never be extinguished.[1]

This leads us to the consideration of the religious condition and capabilities of the general population of Palestine, and of the materials on which any new influence would have to work, and in the midst of which it must grow up.

Nothing is more difficult than to detect the popular sentiment of a nation apart from its higher culture and its public events. Yet in this case it is not impossible. For the first time we are now entering on a period where 'the people of the land,'[2] the peasants of Palestine, found a voice in the literature, and took a part in the struggles, of the nation. In the provincial towns the system of schools had kept alive the knowledge of the sacred books, though often of another class than those studied in the capital. The parables and riddles with which, even in the grave colleges, the teachers[3] were wont to startle their drowsy hearers into attention were yet more congenial amongst the rural villagers. Instead of the tedious controversies of legal casuistry[4] which agitated the theologians at Jerusalem, the Prophets, with their bright predictions, were studied or read in the synagogues. Instead of the *Halacha*,[5] or 'the authoritative rule' for legal action, the rustic or provincial teachers threw themselves on the *Hagada*, 'the legendary,' or the poetical branch of the Scriptures. The Talmudical writers never mention the Hagadists, the Hagadists rarely mention the Talmudists; but not the less truly did they exist side by side.

The Peasants.

Almost for the first time since the death of Zerubbabel the expectations not merely of a Messenger, of a Prophet, but of a Personal Deliverer—of a son of the long-lost house of David—

[1] Luke iv. 21; Acts xiii. 14.

[2] Ginsburg on 'the Midrash' and on 'Education' in Kitto's *Cyclopædia*, i. 167, 731.

[3] Deutsch, *Remains*, 44.

[4] Derenbourg, 161.

[5] *Ibid.* 350. See Milman's *Hist. of Jews*, iii 42.

took possession of the popular mind. New prayers[1] were added to the Jewish ritual, for the re-establishment of the royal dynasty, and for the restoration of the national jurisdiction. Even the Romans had heard of an expectation that some conquering king would rise at this time out of Judæa.[2] It was natural that these aspirations should breed a fiercer spirit, and burn with more intense ardour, in particular localities. The district where they can be most distinctly traced even through the dry narrative of Josephus is Galilee. Not more clearly than the High Priests on the one side and the Scribes on the other dominate in Jerusalem, or the monastic Essenes in the basin of the Dead Sea, do 'the 'Zealots,' or the patriots, of the coming generation, prevail on that border-land of Jew and Gentile, where the hardy and secluded habits of the peasants and foresters kept them pure from the influence of the controversies and corruptions of the capital, where the precipitous and cavernous glens furnished inaccessible retreats, where the crowded population of artisans and fishermen along the shores of the Lake of Gennesareth teemed with concentrated energy. There were born and bred Hezekiah[3] and his gallant band whom Herod treated as robbers, but whose mothers, like the Rachel of Bethlehem, cried for vengeance against him for the shedding of the innocent blood of their sons, whom the stern Shemaiah took under his protection in the Jewish Sanhedrin. There was nurtured his son Judas, of Galilee, whether from the eastern or western side of the Lake, who, in the same cause, 'calling none master save 'God alone,' died a death of torture, and was believed to be enrolled amongst 'the just men made perfect.'[4] There were, still continuing the same heroic cause, his sons, James and Simon, who suffered for their revolt[5] on the cross. In the craggy sides of the romantic dell of Arbela, as it descends on the plain of Gennesareth, took refuge the band, whom Herod extirpated[6] by letting down his soldiers in baskets over the

Galilee.

[1] See Ginsburg on the Synagogues, Kitto, iii. 906, 907.
[2] Tacit. *Hist.* v. 13; Suet. *Vesp.* 4.
[3] Jos. *Ant.* xv. 10, 1; Derenbourg, 261.
[4] Jos. *Ant.* xviii. 1, 6.
[5] *Ibid. Ant.* xx. 5, 2.
[6] Robinson's *Researches*, iii. 288-292; Jos. *Ant.* xiv. 15, 4, 5; *B. J.* 16, 2-5.

cliff-side and kindling fires at the entrance of the caverns. Robbers, it may be, but, like the Maccabæan[1] patriots who had occupied the same hiding-places before, and the troops of insurgents[2] later, they numbered amongst them that fine old man[3] who, like the mother of the Maccabæan martyrs, stood at the mouth of the cave, and, as the suffocating smoke rolled in, rather than submit to Herod, whom he reproached with his Idumæan descent, slew one by one his seven sons and their mother, and then flung himself over the precipice, to the horror and compassion of his pursuers. Of this same[4] impassioned and devoted race were those multitudes of Galilee—men, women, and children—who adhered to their leader Josephus with a devotion and gratitude vainly sought amongst the dwellers in the capital and its neighbourhood. In this population, so simple in its creed, so uncorrupted in its manners, so fiery in its zeal—in those borders of the ancient Zebulon and Naphtali that had once 'jeoparded their lives unto the death' against the host of Sisera—in that country lying on the dim twilight of Judaism and heathenism, whence the Scribes and Pharisees were confident that no prophet could arise—where alone, as into the Bœotia of Palestine, the schools of Simeon the son of Shetach had not penetrated[5]—it was not altogether beyond expectation that a new cause should be proclaimed, and that, if it did, there would be found among those Galilean peasants a Simon,[6] perchance (like his namesake the son of Judas the Gaulanite) 'a Zealot' for his country's independence, or another Simon, rugged as a 'Rock'[7] of his own Lake, or another James counted 'Just,'[8] like the founder of these aspiring patriots, or yet another whose fiery spirit made[9] him like 'a Child of Thunder.'[10]

There is one more aspect of the life of Palestine which must not be omitted, though it includes a wider scope than

[1] Jos. *Ant.* xii. 11, 1; 1 Macc. ix. 2, where the caves are called *Messaloth*, the steps as of a ladder.

[2] Joseph. *Vita*, 37.

[3] *B. J.* i. 16, 4.

[4] Jos. *Vita*, 42, 43, 50. Deutsch, 140.

[6] Luke vi. 15; Jos. *Ant.* xx. 5, 2.

[7] John i. 42

[8] Eus. *H. E.* ii. 23; Jos. *Ant.* xx. 5, 2.

[9] Mark iii. 17.

[10] For Galilee at this time see Neubauer's *Géographie des Thalmuds*, 183.

any yet mentioned. From the time that the envoys of Judas Maccabæus signed the treaty in the Senate House, still more from the time that Pompey entered the Holy of Holies, the Roman power continued to make its presence more and more felt through every corner of Syria. The Lake of Gennesareth became studded with Italian towns and villas, like the Lake of Como. The hills of Herodium and Machærus were crested with Italian towers and walls and aqueducts, as if from the heart of the Apennines. The collectors of the imperial taxes and customs were at watch in every provincial town. Herod was regarded both by Augustus and by Agrippa as the second man in the Empire, each placing him next to the other.[1] The visible marks of foreign dominion, more deeply than ever before impressed on the face of the Holy Land, expressed the significant fact, that Palestine and its inhabitants had insensibly become merged in a vaster, deeper system. No doubt, the rapacity of the Roman officials was often pushed to intolerable extremities. No doubt, the zealots of Galilee, and even of Jerusalem, contended repeatedly against the influx of the Western Empire. The golden Eagle,[2] whose overshadowing wings Herod had placed over the portal of the Temple, was indignantly torn down by the band of gallant youths, whose leaders expiated their heroism at the burning stake. But the sense of the beneficent influence of the Roman sway had sunk too profoundly into the national feeling to render this extreme repulsion the general sentiment; and, although Josephus cannot be taken as a type of his countrymen, yet there must have been a wide-spread loyalty to the majesty of the Roman State which could have made it possible for Vespasian to claim, or for Josephus to concede to him,[3] the character of the Anointed Deliverer. The great[4] name of 'Cæsar' was, on the whole, a symbol, not of persecution or tyranny, but of protection and freedom. The Roman soldiers[5] were, in the eyes of the Galilean peasants, models of generosity and justice. The Greek language,[6] adopted by the Romans as

The Roman Govern-ment.

[1] Jos. *B. J.* i. 20, 4; *Ant.* xv. 10, 3.
[2] *Ibid. Ant.* xvii. 6, 2.
[3] *Ibid. B. J.* i. 6, 5, 1.
[4] Matt. xxii. 21; Acts xxv. 11.
[5] Luke vii. 2, 4, 9; xxiii. 47.
[6] Deutsch, 141.

their means of communication with the natives, received a new impulse in Palestine, and, whilst still leaving the native Aramaic in possession of the hearts of the people, became henceforth the chief vehicle[1] of general culture. It was the language which was compulsory in the schools, and in which the histories of the time were written. Even its drama penetrated into Jerusalem. The story of Susanna was turned into a tragedy by Nicolas of Damascus, and probably acted in the splendid theatre[2] decorated with the trophies of Augustus. The Roman or Grecian customs and postures, at social meals, superseded, even in the humblest ranks, the time-honoured usages of the East.

These were the elements from which a new nation, a new Church, a new Empire, might possibly be built up whenever a new leader should appear. And will it be possible for such a leader to appear? We have witnessed the shining ideal of a mighty future depicted by the Prophet of the Captivity.[3] We have seen the narrowing of that ideal in the rigid system[4] of Ezra and of the scribes. We have seen the partial opening of the Eastern horizon through the contact with Babylon and Persia, and of the Western horizon in the influence[5] of Alexander and the Alexandrian civilisation. We have seen the reanimation of the heroic and loyal spirit of the nation under the Maccabees.[6] We have seen the revival of religious and secular magnificence, first in the Royal Pontificate of the Asmoneans,[7] and then in the union of Western and Oriental splendour on the throne of Herod. We have heard the faint accents of a generous and universal theology from the lips of Hillel, the aspirations after a lofty purity and a simpler worship from the Essenes, the cry of the individual conscience and national independence in Galilee. We have watched the increasing intercommunion between the country-

The expectation of the future.

[1] See the case argued on one side by Professor Roberts in his *Discussions on the Gospels*, and on the other side by Professor Böhl, *Forschungen nach einer Volksbibel zur Zeit Jesu.* For the joint use of the two languages, see Merivale, *History of the Romans*, iii. 375.

[2] Deutsch, 141; Hausrath, 248, 249; Jos. *Ant.* xv. 8, 2.

[3] Lectures XL., XLII., XLIII.

[4] Lecture XLIV.

[5] Lectures XLV., XLVI., XLVII.

[6] Lecture XLVIII.

[7] Lecture XLIX.

men of David and those of Cicero. Shall there arise One in whom this long history, at times so strangely vacant, at times so densely crowded with incidents, shall be consummated—who shall be above all these jarring elements, because he shall have an affinity with each and a subjection to none—who shall give to the discords of his own age, and to the traditions of the past, and to the hopes of the future a note of heavenly harmony, a magic touch of universal significance, an upward tendency of eternal progress?

Full of instruction as the previous stages of that history may have been, they can never equal the interest of the events that shall fill its next seventy years. And those events are not the less attractive because they are overlooked alike by the Jewish and the Gentile historians, and are contained only in the impressive simplicity of fragmentary records which the authorities of the Jewish Church and of the Roman Empire disdain to mention. We do not venture to anticipate the coming time. But no account of the reign of Herod can be complete which does not tell that the next generation delighted to recount how, within sight of his palace and sepulchre on the high, rocky platform of the Herodium, in the very year when his blood-stained career was drawing to an end, was silently born (to use no other terms than those which almost all, of every creed and nation, would acknowledge) the Last and Greatest Prophet of the Jewish Church, the First and Greatest Prophet of the races of the future.

The Rise of Christianity.

The Roman [1] statesmen, the Grecian philosophers, the Jewish rabbis looked for nothing beyond the immediate horizon; but the Sibylline mystics at Alexandria, the poets at Rome, the peasants in Syria, were wound up to the expectation of 'some beginning of a new order of the ages,' some hero 'who from Palestine should govern the habitable 'world,' some cause in which 'the East should once more wax 'strong.' [2]

Such an epoch was at hand, but unlike anything that either

[1] Merivale, *History of the Romans*, ii. 538.

[2] Virgil, *Eclog.* iv.; Tac. *Hist.* v. 13; Suet. *Vesp.* 4; Jos. *B. J.* vi. 5, 1.

Greek or Jew of that time had conceived; a new hero, but unlike any character that in that age either Jew or Greek expected.

What was that new birth of time? What was to be the remedy for the superstition, infidelity, casuistry, ambition, impurity, misery of the age? Not a conqueror—not a philosopher—not a Pharisee—not a Sadducee—not a mere wonder-working magician—not an ascetic—not a vast hierarchical organisation—not a philosophical system or elaborate creed—but an innocent Child, an humble and inquiring Boy, a Man, 'who knew 'what was in man;' full of sorrows yet full also of enjoyment; gracious to the weak, stern to the insincere; 'who went about 'doing good,' and 'who spake as never man spake'—a homely, social, yet solitary Being, in whose transcendent goodness and truthfulness there was revealed a new image of the Divine nature, a new idea of human destiny—a Teacher, apart from the generation from which he sprang, yet specially suited to the needs of that generation—a fulfilment of a longing expectation, yet a fulfilment in a sense the reverse of that which was expected—Israelite, Oriental by race, but Greek in the wide penetration of His sympathy, Roman in the majesty of His authority.

The world was, as it were, taken by surprise. All His teaching abounded in surprises. But His own coming, His own self, was the greatest surprise of all; and yet, when we reflect upon it, we feel as if we ought not to have looked for anything else.

It was the arrival of an event which was but imperfectly understood at the time, which has been but imperfectly understood since; which was therefore not exhausted then, and is not exhausted now. The factious disputings of Pharisee and Sadducee, the wild fanaticism of the Zealots, the eccentricities of the Essenes, the worldliness of the Priests, the formalities of the Scribes, the cruelty, the profligacy, the domineering, hard-hearted ambition of the Roman world, the effete rhetoric of the Greek world, found their proper level in the presence of an influence which ran counter to them all. Not immediately, but gradually, at least in the forms then worn, all these things died away—surviving, indeed, for ages, but surviving as things long ago doomed—doomed not by direct attack or contradictious denial, but by the entrance of a larger affection, of a fresh object, of a grander spirit. The various pre-existing elements of good, even if for the moment they received a shock from the apparition of this new power, even if some graces died to revive no more, yet, on the whole, took courage, were reanimated and enriched. The ancient world, although sitting in the cold shade of death, was instinct at that time with a latent heat and light, which admitted a spiritual revolution, such as, either earlier or later, would have been, humanly speaking, impossible. In the Jewish Church the scattered sayings of the better Sadducees and the better Pharisees were waiting to be rescued from their obscurity and vivified by a new purpose. In the Gentile world the philosophy of Socrates and Plato—diluted, indeed, and distorted, but rendered popular through the East by the Schools of Alexandria—was reaching forward to some higher manifestation of truth. The researches of Grecian science, the influence of Roman law, though the coming religion long refused to admit them, and was by them long disdained, were ready to be received into it, and at length in a large measure were assimilated by it. The unexampled peace under Augustus Cæsar, the unity of the civilised world under his sceptre, gave a framework into which a new faith could spread without hindrance and without violence. The strong and growing belief in immortality, the intense apprehension of the burden of evil, needed only a new spirit to quicken them into a higher and deeper life. If ever there was a religion which maintained a continuity with ancient materials or parallel phenomena, it was that which avowedly came not to destroy, but to fulfil, the glories of Judaism; not to exclude, but to comprehend, the aspirations of all the races of mankind.

In the Book of Daniel,—which has, as it were, been the companion of this whole period,—succeeding to the wild shapes of winged lion, and ravenous bear, and flying leopard, and furious monster, followed the serene and peaceful vision of a figure, not clothed with fluttering pinions, or armed with clenching paws, and iron teeth, but only with the gentle, reasonable, upward human countenance—wrapped in a veil of cloud, and receiving the pledge of an empire which should be indestructible, because it would be inward and moral, not external or physical. 'I saw in the night visions, and, behold, 'one like a son of man came with the clouds of heaven, and 'came to the Ancient of days, and they brought him near 'before him. And there was given to him dominion and glory, 'and a kingdom, that all peoples, nations, and languages should 'serve him: his dominion is an everlasting dominion, which 'shall not pass away, and his kingdom that which shall not be 'destroyed.'[1] The scene conveys the same moral as that in the vision[2] of Elijah at Horeb. The Eternal was not in the wind, the earthquake, or the fire, but in the still small voice of the solitary conscience. The Eternal was not with the lion, the bear, and the leopard, but with the moral qualities by which, amidst all his manifold weaknesses, the man is raised above the most striking manifestations of the fierceness and strength of the brute creation. That vision, as it first appeared, was, not without ground, supposed to signify[3] the lofty yet gentle character of the Maccabæan hero who, as the representative of the Holy People, overbore with his scanty and imperfect resources the efforts of the Syrian oppressor. But in the interval between Antiochus and Herod it had taken a wider range. The same expressions had been used in the Book of Enoch to represent the Chosen Deliverer, who should judge the whole human race, and, in the times to which we are approaching, there was One who certainly applied them to himself; and whose empire over the intellect and affections of mankind has not passed away.

This in prospect is the epoch to which the course of this history was now hastening. There have been many retrospects of it. Perhaps, some new conviction may be awakened, some old objection cleared away, if we conclude with a passage, but

[1] Dan. vii. 13, 14 (Heb.)
[2] See Lecture XXX.
[3] See Lecture XLVIII. So Ephrem Syrus on Dan. vii. 13.

little known, from a famous writer of the last century, who saw with a clearness of insight which, if perverted at times by violent and unworthy passions, was never distorted by ecclesiastical prejudice. It is the close of a parable or dream, in which an anxious wanderer has passed through the various forms of ancient religion [1]

'The inquirer, perplexed by the troubles and superstitions 'around him, suddenly heard a voice from the sky uttering 'distinctly these words: "Behold the Son of Man: let the 'heavens be silent before him; let the earth hear his voice.' 'Then lifting up his eyes, he beheld on the altar, around which 'the idol-worshippers were assembled, a Figure, whose aspect, 'at once impressive and sweet, struck him with astonishment 'and awe. His dress was homely and like that of an artizan; 'but his expression was heavenly; his demeanour modest, and 'grave without austerity. There was a simplicity in it that 'amounted to grandeur; and it was impossible to look at him 'without feeling penetrated by a lively and a delightful emotion, 'such as has its source in no sentiment known amongst men. '"O my children!" he said, in a tone of tenderness which 'reached the bottom of the soul, "I come to expiate and to 'heal your errors. Love Him who loves you, and know Him 'who is for ever." At the same moment, seizing the idol, he 'overthrew it without effort, and mounting the vacant pedestal 'without agitation he seemed rather to take his own place 'than to usurp that of another. The people were seized with 'enthusiasm, the priests were irritated almost to madness. 'Champion of a Divine morality, he drew the world after him; 'he had but to speak the word and his enemies were no more. 'But he, who came to destroy intolerance, refrained from 'imitating it. He used only the means which accorded with 'the lessons which he had to teach and the functions which he 'had to perform; and the people, all whose passions are but 'forms of madness, became less zealous and cared not to

[1] 'Morceau Allégorique sur la Révéla'tion' (*Œuvres et Correspondances Inédites de J.-J. Rousseau*, first published from the manuscripts of M. Moultou in 1861 by his descendant M. Stockeisen Moultou, 183-185).

'defend him when they saw that he would not attack. He 'continued to speak still as sweetly as before; he portrayed 'the love of man and all the virtues with traits so touching, 'and in colours so attractive, that, with the exception of the 'ministers of the Temple, no one listened to him without being 'moved and without loving better his own duties and the good 'of others. His speech was simple and gracious, and yet 'profound and sublime; without stunning the ear he nourished 'the soul; it was milk for children and bread for men. He 'attacked the strong and consoled the weak, and the most 'variously and unequally gifted amongst his audience found 'something always at their own level. He spoke not in a 'pompous tone, but his discourses, familiar as they were, 'sparkled with the most entrancing eloquence, and his instruc- 'tions consisted of apologues and of conversations full of justice 'and of depth. Nothing embarrassed him; the most captious 'questions met instantly with the wisest solutions. It was 'needed only to hear him once in order to be persuaded; it 'was felt that the language of truth cost him nothing, because 'he had the source of truth in himself.'

What Rousseau, and others not less gifted than he, have seen by the intuition of genius, humbler students can learn by the sincere endeavour to penetrate beneath the surface of the events and beneath the letter of the records which cover this momentous period. There may be much that is dark and fragmentary; much that needs explanation or that defies analysis; but there is enough to enable us to discern, amidst the shadows of the remote past, and athwart the misunderstandings of later times, the sayings and doings of Him who is still, for all mankind, 'the Way, the Truth, and the Life.'

APPENDICES

GENEALOGY OF THE ASMONEANS.

GENEALOGY OF THE HIGH PRIESTS.

CHRONOLOGICAL TABLE.

GENEALOGY OF THE ASMONEANS.

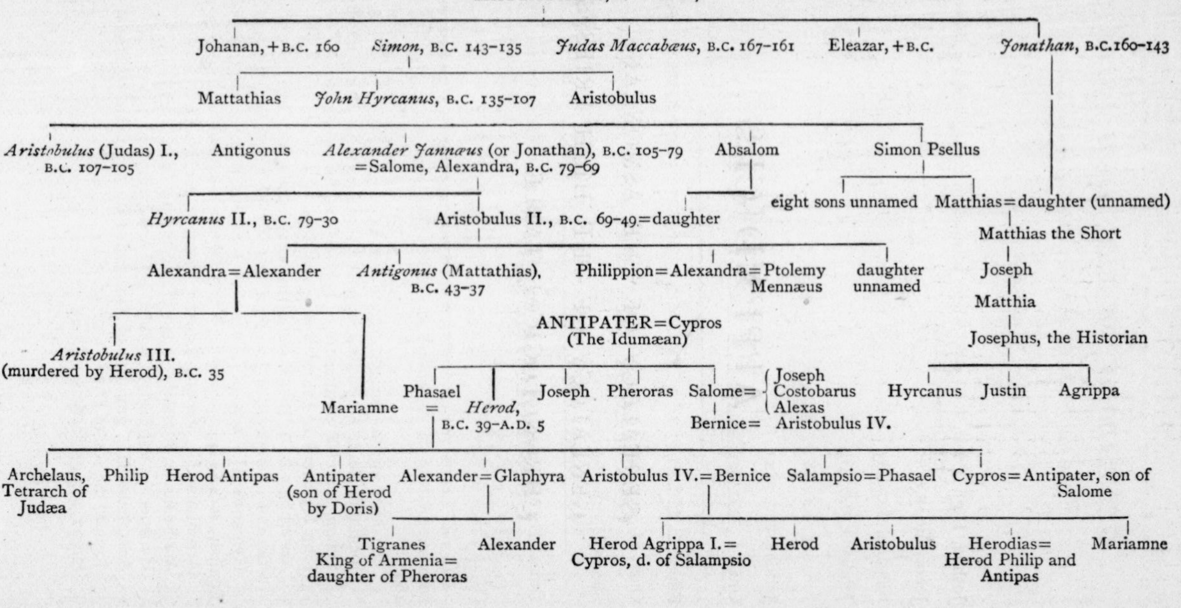

GENEALOGY OF THE HIGH PRIESTS.

(*See the lists in the Histories of Herzfeld and Hitzig.*)

Joshua, High Priest, B.C. 536, when permission was given for the return of Israel from Captivity
|
Jehoiakim, B.C. 499
|
Eliashib, B.C. 463
|
Jehoiada, B.C. 419
|
Johanan, B.C. 383
|
Jaddua, B.C. 351
|
Onias I., B.C. 321

Simon I., B.C. 310	Eleazar, B.C. 291	Manasseh, B.C. 276

Simon I., B.C. 310
|
Onias II., B.C. 250
|
Simon II., the Just, 219 B.C.

Onias III., B.C. 199	Jason, or Jesus (Joshua), B.C. 175	Menelaus (put to death at Berea), B.C. 172

Onias III., B.C. 199
|
Onias IV., B.C. 160 (High Priest in Egypt)

In 162, Lysias, the governor for Antiochus, appointed *Alcimus* High Priest, so passing out of the direct line of descent (Jos. *Ant.* xii. 9, 7). He died B.C. 160.

The office vacant from B.C. 160 to B.C. 153.

Jonathan, son of Mattathias, appointed by Alexander Balas, B.C. 153.

Simon, son of Mattathias, B.C. 143—elected by the people.

John Hyrcanus I., son of Simon, B.C. 135.

Aristobulus I., or Judas, son of John Hyrcanus, B.C. 107.

Alexander Jannæus, or Jonathan, son of John Hyrcanus, B.C. 105.

Hyrcanus II., son of Alexander Jannæus, B.C. 79–69; appointed by Pompey, B.C. 63–43.

Aristobulus II., son of Alexander Jannæus, B.C. 69–65.

Antigonus, or Mattathias, son of Aristobulus II. B.C. 43.

Hananeel of Babylon, appointed by Herod, B.C. 37.

Aristobulus III., grandson of Aristobulus II., appointed by Herod, B.C. 35.

Joshua, the son of Phabi, B.C. 35.

Simon, son of Boethus, B.C. 23.

CHRONOLOGICAL TABLE.

EVENTS IN THE WEST (EGYPT, GREECE, ROME), PALESTINE, AND ASIA.

B.C.	Events in Egypt, Greece, and Rome	B.C.	Events of Palestine	B.C.	Events in Asia
		606	Captivity of Jehoiakim		
600	Foundation of Marseilles by the Phocæans				
599	Thales the Milesian				
		598	Captivity of Jeconiah		
594	Legislation of Solon	594	Ezekiel called to prophesy		
		588	Nebuchadnezzar captures Jerusalen		
		584	Carries away remainder of Jews and Israelites		
578	Servius Tullius and institution of Comitia Centuriata				
570	*Amasis, King of Egypt*	570	Book of Ezekiel		
				562	Death of Nebuchadnezzar
				561	Evil Merodach
560	Pisistratus at Athens			560	Cyrus the Persian, King of Media
				559	Neriglissar (?)
				555	Laborosoarchod (?) Nabunid (?) Belshazzar (?)
		553	'Daniel's vision of the ram and he-goat,' Dan. viii. 1–27. The Evangelical Prophet, Isa. xl.–lxvi.		
546	Lydian monarchy overthrown by Cyrus				

EVENTS IN THE WEST, PALESTINE, AND ASIA—*cont.*

Events in Egypt, Greece, and Rome		Events of Palestine		Events in Asia	
B.C.		B.C.		B.C.	
				538	Babylon taken by Cyrus
536	Xenophanes of Elea	536	Cyrus restores the Jews. Jeshua, High Priest. ZERUBBABEL. Consecration of the Altar	536	Cyrus conqueror of Babylon
		535	Jews commence rebuilding the Temple		
532	Pythagoras				
				529	Cambyses (Achashverosh)
525	*Psammenitus, King of Egypt, overthrown by Cambyses*				
				522	Smerdis the Magian
		521	HAGGAI. ZECHARIAH		
		520	Building of Temple, interrupted by Samaritans, is resumed		
		516	Completion of the Temple	516	Darius I. captures Babylon (after usurpation of Smerdis)
510	The Regifuge at Rome				
500	The Ionic revolt				
494	First secession of Plebs to Mons Sacer	494	Jehoiakim, High Priest		
490	Battle of Marathon				
486	*Revolt of Egypt from Persians; reconquered* 484				
		485	Xerxes confirms the Jews in their privileges. Story of Esther	485	Xerxes (Achashverosh)
480	Thermopylæ: Artemisium, Salamis				
479	Platæa and Mycale				
				477	[Death of Confucius]
				475	[Death of Buddha]
472	Æschylus flourishes				

Events in the West, Palestine, and Asia—*cont.*

B.C.	Events in Egypt, Greece, and Rome	B.C.	Events of Palestine	B.C.	Events in Asia
466	Victory of Cimon at Eurymedon				
				465	Artaxerxes I. (Artashasht)
		463	Eliashib, High Priest		
462-405	*Revolt of Inarus in Egypt; Inarus is crucified,* B.C. 448. *Egyptians make Amyrtæus king,* 413				
461	Pericles				
		460	Artaxerxes		
		459	Ezra		
458	Cincinnatus				
456	Battle of Œnophyta. Herodotus				
451	Decemviri. Laws of the XII. Tables				
		445	Nehemiah		
441	Euripides				
431	Beginning of Peloponnesian war				
427	Aristophanes				
				424	Artaxerxes II. (Sogdianus), Darius II. (Nothus)
		419	Jehoiada, High Priest. Manasseh withdraws to Samaria		
404	Close of Peloponnesian war. *Saite dynasty in Egypt*			404	Artaxerxes III. (Mnemon)
401	Death of Socrates. Retreat of the Ten Thousand	401	MALACHI (?)		
398	*Mendesian dynasty in Egypt*				
396	Camillus takes Veii				
390	Rome taken by the Gauls				
387	Peace of Antalcidas				

Events in the West, Palestine, and Asia—*cont.*

Events in Egypt, Greece, and Rome		Events of Palestine		Events in Asia	
B.C.		B.C.		B.C.	
384	Birth of Aristotle				
		383	Murder of Johanan, the High Priest		
377–344	*Sebennyte Dynasty in Egypt*				
376	Licinian Rogations				
371	Battle of Leuctra				
362	Mantinea. Death of Epaminondas				
				359	Artaxerxes IV. (Ochus)
354	Demosthenes				
		351	Jaddua, High Priest		
350	*Egypt again a Persian province*				
347	Death of Plato, æt. 82				
338	Battle of Chæronea. Philip master of Greece			338	Arses
				336	Darius III. (Codomanus)
334	Expedition of Alexander. Battles of Granicus, Issus, and Arbela				
				331	Battle of Arbela
323	Death of Alexander. *Ptolemy, Viceroy of Egypt*			323	Death of Alexander
		321	Onias I., High Priest		
				312	Seleucus I. (Nicator) begins dynasty of Seleucidæ at Babylon
		310	Simon, High Priest		
301	Battle of Ipsus				
292	Romans subdue Samnites				
		291	Eliezer, High Priest		
285	*Ptolemy II.* (*Philadelphus*). The Septuagint begun				

Events in the West, Palestine, and Asia—*cont.*

B.C.	Events in Egypt, Greece, and Rome	B.C.	Events of Palestine	B.C.	Events in Asia
280	Achæan League			280	Antiochus I. (Soter)
		276	Manasseh, High Priest		
275	Pyrrhus defeated				
264	First Punic War				
				261	Antiochus II. (Theos)
				256	Foundation of the Parthian empire by Arsaces I.
250	Regulus	250	Onias II., High Priest		
247	*Ptolemy III. (Euergetes)*				
				246	Seleucus II. (Callinicus)
241	Agis, King of Sparta				
				226	Seleucus III. (Ceraunus)
				224	Antiochus III. (the Great). Battle of Magnesia
222	Ptolemy IV., Philopator				
219	Second Punic War. Hannibal	219	Antiochus the Great conquers Palestine. Simon II., the Just, High Priest		
		217	PtolemyPhilopator comes to Jerusalem		
208	Philopœmen, general of Achæan League				
207	Battle of Metaurus				
205	*Ptolemy V. (Epiphanes)*				
202	Battle of Zama				
		199	Onias III., the son of Sirach, High Priest Antigonus of Socho		
197	Battle of Cynoscephalæ				
190	Battle of Magnesia				
				187	Seleucus IV. (Philopator Heliodorus)
181	*Ptolemy VII. (Philometor), and Ptolemy*				

EVENTS IN THE WEST, PALESTINE, AND ASIA—*cont.*

EVENTS IN EGYPT, GREECE, AND ROME		EVENTS OF PALESTINE		EVENTS IN ASIA	
B.C.		B.C.		B.C.	
	Euergetes II. (*Physcon*). Aristobulus the Teacher				
		175	Jason buys High Priesthood of Antiochus Epiphanes. 'Prince of Judæa.'	175	Antiochus IV. (Epiphanes)
		172	Menelaus, High Priest. Antiochus devastates Jerusalem		
168	Battle of Pydna	168	Antiochus persecutes Jews. Fortress built on Mt. Acra. Probable date of the Book of Daniel. Probable date of the Psalter of Solomon		
		167	MATTATHIAS the ASMONEAN		
		166	JUDAS MACCABÆUS. Battles of Beth-horon and Emmaus		
165	Third Sibylline Book (?)	165	Battle of Bethzur. He recovers Jerusalem. Restoration of daily worship in Temple. Feast of Dedication instituted. Bethzur fortified		
		164	He conquers Edomites and Ammonites, slays Timotheus, and relieves the Jews of Gilead	164	Death of Antiochus Lysias and Antiochus V. (Eupator)
		163	Jo-é son of Jazer, and José son of Johanan		
		162	Alcimus, High Priest	162	Demetrius I. (Soter)
		162	Demetrius sends Bacchides, then Nicanor, against the Jews. Jewish alliance with Parthia (?) and Rome		
		101	Battle of Beth-horon. Judas defeats and kills Nicanor; Battle of Eleasa and death of Judas		
160	*Onias IV., High Priest in Egypt*	160	Jonathan, brother of Judas, is elected captain by Jews. Alcimus dies; Bacchides leaves the Jews in peace for two years		

EVENTS IN THE WEST, PALESTINE, AND ASIA—*cont.*

B.C.	Events in Egypt, Greece, and Rome	B.C.	Events of Palestine	B.C.	Events in Asia
		158	Bacchides returns to Judæa. Jonathan and Simon defeat him at siege of Bethbasi. Bacchides makes peace and returns		
		153	Jonathan, High Priest	153	Alexander Balas (usurper)
				148	Demetrius II. (Nicator) lands in Cilicia to recover the kingdom of his father, Demetrius I.
146	Destruction of Carthage and Corinth				
145	*Ptolemy Physcon*	145	He unsuccessfully besieges the fortress at Jerusalem	145	Tryphon opposes Demetrius, and brings forward Antiochus, son of Balas
		144	Demetrius and Tryphon quarrel; Jonathan supports Tryphon, and defeats generals of Demetrius; but is treacherously murdered by Tryphon		
		143	Simon Maccabæus, High Priest. He declares against Tryphon, the usurper of Syria. Demetrius makes him 'Prince of Judæa.' He sends an embassy to Rome		
		142	Simon takes the fortress of Acra	142	Tryphon usurps throne of Syria (Babylon)
		141	His sovereignty confirmed by the Jews		
				138	Antiochus Sidêtes, brother of Demetrius II.
		135	Murder of Simon. JOHN HYRCANUS. Book of Enoch (?)		
133-121	The Gracchi	133	Peace made with Syria		

EVENTS IN THE WEST, PALESTINE, AND ASIA—*cont.*

B.C.	Events in Egypt, Greece, and Rome	B.C.	Events of Palestine	B.C.	Events in Asia
				132–129	Campaigns of Sidêtes and Hyrcanus against Parthia; Sidêtes slain
		130	John Hyrcanus makes himself independent of Syria; destroys the temple on Mt. Gerizim		
		129	He conquers the Edomites		
		128	Renews the league with Rome	128	Return of Demetrius II. (Nicator)
				126	Alexander Zebina, an impostor, set up by Ptolemy Physcon
				125	Antiochus Grypus, son of Demetrius, vanquishes Zebina
116	*Cleopatra and Ptolemy Lathurus*	116	Joshua, son of Perachiah; Nittai of Arbela		
				114	Antiochus Cyzicenus, son of Sidêtes, makes himself master of Syria
		110	Aristobulus and Antigonus, sons of John Hyrcanus, attack Samaria, and defeat Cyzicenus, who comes to its relief		
		109	John Hyrcanus master of Judæa, Samaria, Galilee. First mention of Pharisees and Sadducees		
		107	Death of John Hyrcanus. ARISTOBULUS, who calls himself King of Judæa		
		106	Aristobulus conquers Ituræa. Murder of Antigonus and death of Aristobulus. ALEXANDER JANNÆUS. First mention of the Essenes		
102	Marius defeats Teutones at Aquæ Sextiæ				
		97	Jannæus captures Gaza		

EVENTS IN THE WEST, PALESTINE, AND ASIA—*cont.*

B.C.	EVENTS IN EGYPT, GREECE, AND ROME	B.C.	EVENTS OF PALESTINE	B.C.	EVENTS IN ASIA
				96	Antiochus Eusebes
		95	Jews mutiny against Jannæus		
		94	Jannæus subdues Moab and Gilead	94	Demetrius Eucerus
		92	Jannæus is defeated by Obodas, a king of Arabia; Jews take the opportunity to revolt		
90	Social war in Italy				
86	Death of Marius	86	Jannæus, having shut the rebels up in Bethome, crucifies 800 of them, and ends the revolt after six years	86	Antiochus Dionysius
84	Peace between Sulla and Mithridates	84	Enlarges his kingdom		
				83	Tigranes the Armenian, monarch of Syria till 69
82	Sulla, Dictator	82	His triumph at Jerusalem		
81	*Various Ptolemies; Ptolemy Auletes*				
		79	Death of Jannæus. His wife ALEXANDRA succeeds. She makes her eldest son HYRCANUS High Priest, and supports the party of the Pharisees		
78	Death of Sulla				
		75	Birth of Hillel		
74	Lucullus goes to Asia			73	Lucullus in Asia
72	Death of Sertorius	72	Simeon the son of Shetach, and Judah the son of Tobai. Birth of Herod the Great		
71	Spartacus defeated and slain by Crassus				
70	Consulship of Pompey and Crassus	70	Establishment of national education	70	War between Lucullus and Tigranes. Lucullus takes Tigranocerta

EVENTS IN THE WEST, PALESTINE, AND ASIA—*cont.*

B.C.	Events in Egypt, Greece, and Rome	B.C.	Events of Palestine	B.C.	Events in Asia
		69	ARISTOBULUS, younger brother of Hyrcanus, seizes the crown; Hyrcanus opposes Death of Onias 'the Charmer'		
				66	Pompey supersedes Lucullus, allies himself with Phraates of Parthia, and forces Tigranes to peace
63	Cicero, Consul; conspiracy of Catiline	63	Their claims are referred to Pompey, who confirms Hyrcanus on the throne. Pompey takes Jerusalem. Judæa confined to its narrowest limits		
60	First Triumvirate				
58	Cæsar begins the subjugation of Gaul				
		57	Aristobulus and his son Alexander escape from the Romans and create troubles in Judæa. They are put down by the Proconsul, A. Gabinius. Judæa divided into five parts		
56	Meeting of Triumvirate; break-up of Senatorial party				
		54	Crassus plunders the Temple		
				53	Orodes I., King of Parthia. Pacorus. Disastrous expedition of Crassus into Parthia; capture of the Roman standards
52	Pompey sole Consul			52	Cassius, quæstor of Crassus defeats Parthians who invade Syria

EVENTS IN THE WEST, PALESTINE, AND ASIA—*cont.*

EVENTS IN EGYPT, GREECE, AND ROME		EVENTS OF PALESTINE		EVENTS IN ASIA	
B.C.		B.C.		B.C.	
51	*The last Cleopatra, Queen of Egypt* The Wisdom of Solomon (?)				
				50	Parthians besiege Proconsul Bibulus in Antioch
49	Cæsar crosses the Rubicon	49	Death of Aristobulus and Alexander		
48	Battle of Pharsalia. *Alexandrine war of Cæsar; he makes Cleopatra Queen of Egypt in* 47				
		47	Antipater, father of Herod the Great, is made Procurator of Judæa. He makes Herod Governor of Galilee. Trial of Herod before the Sanhedrim, now first mentioned. Shemaiah and Abtalion		
46	Battle of Thapsus				
44	Assassination of Cæsar				
43	Second Triumvirate	43	Antipater poisoned by Melichus; his sons Phasael and Herod avenge him		
42	Battle of Philippi	42	Herod vanquishes ANTIGONUS, son of Aristobulus II.		
		40	Parthians masters of Lesser Asia; they take Jerusalem, slay Phasael, make Hyrcanus prisoner, and settle ANTIGONUS on the throne of Jerusalem. HEROD flees to Rome, where he is made King of Judæa.		
39	Horace, Virgil, Varius			39	Ventidius drives the Parthians out of Syria

EVENTS IN THE WEST, PALESTINE, AND ASIA—*cont.*

B.C.	EVENTS IN EGYPT, GREECE, AND ROME	B.C.	EVENTS OF PALESTINE	B.C.	EVENTS IN ASIA
		38	Herod marries Mariamne, and presses the siege of Jerusalem, aided by Sosius, Governor of Syria		
37	Agrippa crosses Rhine	37	Herod captures Jerusalem and establishes himself as King of Judæa. Death of Antigonus		
		36	Arrival of Hillel at Jerusalem	36	Death of Orodes of Parthia. Phraates, his son, succeeds. Unsuccessful expedition of Antony against Parthia
		35	Herod makes ARISTOBULUS III., brother of Mariamne, High Priest. and afterwards murders him		
		34	Hillel and Shammai		
		32	Herod, by order of Antony, makes war on Malchus, king of Arabia Petræa; brings him to terms the following year		
31	Battle of Actium				
30	*Death of Cleopatra*	30	Herod makes peace with Octavian		
29	Temple of Janus closed	29	Execution of Mariamne		
		28	Execution of Alexandra		
		25	Herod rebuilds Samaria and calls it Sebaste. Relieves the pressure of a famine in Judæa		
24	Virgil writes the Æneid. Horace publishes the first three books of the Odes				
				23	Phraates is expelled by the Parthians; but is restored by the Scythians and gains the friendship of Augustus

Events in the West, Palestine and Asia—*cont.*

B.C.	Events in Egypt, Greece, and Rome	B.C.	Events of Palestine	B.C.	Events in Asia
		22	Herod begins to build Cæsarea. Receives from Augustus Trachonitis, Auranitis, and Batanæa		
				20	Parthians restore the Roman standards
19	Death of Virgil				
		17	Herod, having spent two years in collecting materials, pulls down the old temple at Jerusalem and begins a new one		
		16	He marries his sons by Mariamne, Alexander to Glaphyra of Cappadocia, Aristobulus to Salome's daughter, Berenice		
		14	Obtains from Agrippa a confirmation of the privileges granted to the Jews.		
		13	Breach between Herod and the sons of Mariamne		
11	Drusus on the Rhine; Tiberius on the Danube	11	He accuses them before Augustus, who brings about a reconciliation. Herod names Antipater as his heir		
		10	Herod completes the building of Cæsarea. Builds the tower of Phasael at Jerusalem		
		9	Fresh quarrel between Herod and sons of Mariamne		
8	Augustus accepts the Empire a third time				
		6	Herod, having leave from Augustus to proceed against the sons of Mariamne, has them strangled		
		5	Birth of JESUS CHRIST		
		4	Death of Herod		
		A.D. 6	Death of Hillel		

INDEX.

Date Due